NORTH

Peter Pan Man; The Black and White Minstrels; Gynt!; You Are My Heart's Delight; To Be A Farmer's Boy; Bring Me Sunshine, Bring Me Smiles.

'Because no detail of human existence was too small for his attention, so no theme proved too large. C. P. Taylor was that rare and most happy breed of animal, simultaneously an artist of his region and of the world.'

(Peter Mortimer)

C. P. TAYLOR died aged 52 in 1981, leaving a monumental legacy of more than 70 plays written in little more than 20 years. Taylor was a unique author, equally at ease writing for the RSC or West End, working with mentally-handicapped children, penning a memorable string of plays for the Newcastle-based community company, Live Theatre Co., or creating a nativity play for his tiny Northumbrian village. Based in the North-East for most of his writing life, Taylor's work in many ways acted as a focal point for the community-based renaissance in that region during the 1970s. The six previously unpublished but successfully staged plays included here give some idea of C. P. Taylor's tremendous range and vision.

C. P. TAYLOR was born in Glasgow in 1929 but lived in Northumberland for the last twenty years of his life. He wrote over fifty plays for the theatre and television, many of them first performed at the Traverse Theatre, Edinburgh. These include *Bread and Butter* (1966), *The Black and White Minstrels* (1972; subsequently at Hampstead Theatre), *You Are My Heart's Delight* (Soho Poly, London, 1973), *Schippel* (1974; subsequently at the Open Space, London; then retitled *The Plumber's Progress* and starring Harry Secombe, at the Prince of Wales, 1975), *Walter*, *Some Enchanted Evening* and *Peter Pan Man* (all 1977). *Bandits* was staged by the Royal Shakespeare Company at the Warehouse, London, in 1977. He was closely associated with a community theatre group in Newcastle, The Live Theatre Company, for which he wrote, among others, *And A Nightingale Sang . . .* (1977) which was subsequently seen at the Queen's Theatre, London (1979) and on tour. He wrote a great deal for children and young people in the North-East, with plays such as *Operation Elvis* (1978), *The Magic Island* (1979), *Bring Me Sunshine, Bring Me Smiles* and *Saints* (Live Theatre, 1980) and *Happy Lies* (1981). *Good* was first performed at the RSC Warehouse, London in September 1981. Cecil Taylor died in December 1981.

The front cover illustration is of the Tyne Bridge, Newcastle upon Tyne (Picture: Photo Source)

NORTH

Six plays by
C. P. TAYLOR

with a preface by Peter Mortimer

Peter Pan Man
The Black and White Minstrels
Gynt!
You Are My Heart's Delight
To Be A Farmer's Boy
Bring Me Sunshine, Bring Me Smiles

A METHUEN PAPERBACK
in association with IRON Press

A METHUEN NEW THEATRESCRIPT

First published in 1987 as a paperback original
by Methuen London Ltd, 11 New Fetter Lane, London EC4P 4EE,
in association with IRON Press, 5 Marden Terrace, Cullercoats, North Shields, Tyne & Wear NE30
4PD.
Published in the United States of America
by Methuen Inc, 29 West 35th Street, New York, NY 10001

IRON Press gratefully acknowledges the assistance of Northern Arts

Copyright © 1987 by the Estate of the late C. P. Taylor

British Library Cataloguing in Publication Data

Taylor, C. P.
    North: six plays. –
    (A Methuen new theatrescript).
    I. Title
    822'.914   PR6070.A89

    ISBN 0–413–16470–5

Typeset by True North
Printed in Great Britain
by Redwood Burn Ltd, Trowbridge, Wiltshire

CAUTION
All rights whatsoever in these plays are strictly reserved and application for performance etc. should
be made to Michael Imison Playwrights Ltd, 28 Almeida Street, London N1; Abbe Levin, 105 West
70th Street, No. IR, New York, NY 10023; or Virginia Ferguson, 98–106 Kippax Street, Surry Hills,
Sydney N.S.W. 2010.

CONTENTS

PREFACE

When C. P. Taylor died in December 1981, we fellow writers in the North East were stunned. Sometimes I think we've become more stunned over the years that have followed. Cecil wasn't only the most prolific and talented playwright in the region, he was also the unofficial 'mentor' for many other authors, established or unknown.

He didn't write a word before he was thirty; in the twenty years that followed he wrote more than seventy plays. He wrote for community theatre and the Royal Shakespeare Company. He wrote for the West End and the handicapped. He wrote for television and for his local village. He wrote for radio and for specific schools.

The output was prodigious, and more remarkable for its quality. Cecil once told me he'd feel OK if six of his plays were remembered (come to think of it, how many dramatists can claim that?). There are six published here, but they may not be the ones he meant. He was never a hack simply churning it out. Many of his North-East regional plays, without ever resorting to that cosy 'Geordie' introspection, touched a chord in the area's consciousness. A Glaswegian by birth, he had long since adopted the North East as his home, and would, I believe, never have left (he was 52 at his death).

Cecil's relationship with the Newcastle-based Live Theatre Company was unique at the time and has remained so. From it sprang such plays as *And A Nightingale Sang*, *Operation Elvis*, *The Saints Go Marching In* (published here under its second title *Bring Me Sunshine, Bring Me Smiles*), *The Magic Island*, the *Rainbow Coloured Disco Dancer*, *Some Enchanted Evening* . . . the list goes on.

Wearing my reviewer's hat, I saw – and wrote about – almost all of these, usually in small community halls with audiences whose visits to Shaftesbury Avenue wouldn't be over common. Wearing my friend's hat, I visited Cecil and Liz often at their unpretentious cottage in the small Northumberland village of Longhorsley. The visits always charged you up, both as friend, and as writer, and I've since learnt just how many other people were 'charged up' by them; the long country walks, chicken and chips, tea from the Thermos flask (all the teapots were used for flowers), and that sing-song voice, whose humour often belied the relevance of what it was saying. In between writing seventy plays in twenty years, Cecil was an enormous help to a great number of people. I can't even imagine how many scripts he received, read and commented upon. For so many writers it seemed the natural thing – send your script to C.P.

Iron Press published two of his plays in the '70s, *Bandits!* and *The Killingworth Play*, and another three were reprinted with a fourth as a joint publication with Methuen, *Live Theatre* (1981). Methuen also published *And A Nightingale Sang* and *Good* in the Modern Plays series. This present book brings the total up to more than a dozen. Cecil's son Avram first mooted the idea of a 'bumper'-size collection and he also pointed me towards some of the plays which I hadn't previously seen or read but which he – and later myself – thought well worth putting into print.

I hope these six give some idea of the author's range, both in style and subject matter. *Peter Pan Man*, though first performed by Live Theatre in 1977 (then titled *Peter Pan and Emily*) is, I think, one of the best potential youth theatre plays to come from this region, zappy, satirical, and reworking a classic tale in a way that both celebrates the original, but isn't afraid of highlighting its smug and cosy nature.

The Black and White Minstrels, a much more 'wordy' play than usual, began life at the Traverse Theatre, Edinburgh in 1972, and symbolises many of the conflicts of political belief put alongside personal behaviour (if that sounds heavy, let me remind you it's a hugely funny play) as the beleaguered left-winger attempts to come to terms with the Nigerian lodger blocking his creativity.

Gynt! is included to show the man's talent at reworking theatrical classics (it was first peformed by Tynewear Theatre Company in 1973). Cecil also jumped into the ring with

Sophocles, Brecht, Rostand, and Sternheim at different times. *You Are My Heart's Delight* is a modest play with fairly limited boundaries, but it is beautifully observed and economical (it began life at Soho Poly in 1973 and was later adapted for BBC radio).

To Be A Farmer's Boy was also adapted for radio. The play was commissioned by the one-time Live Theatre director Paul Chamberlain, for the Devon-based Orchard Theatre Company. Live Theatre Company later picked it up under director Teddy Kiendl, who transferred the setting from rural west country to rural North East. Following the fortunes of the farming family, it's a sort of radical *The Archers*. I always thought many of Cecil's Tyneside-based plays compare in some ways to *Coronation Street*, though encompassing as many issues and concerns into two hours as the soaps languorously allowed to drift over several years. And of course, created by one man, not a team.

Bring Me Sunshine, Bring Me Smiles, premièred by Live Theatre Company as *Saints* in 1980, typifies that fruitful relationship between company and author, and is, I believe, perhaps the best of his North-East 'domestic' plays. Again, the play is constantly funny, but also moving, and with a strong relevance for its native North-East audience (a relevance incidentally which I don't feel made the work at all parochial; as in all art, capturing the particular is the first step to embracing the universal).

I recall one scene in particular, when the six protagonists are gathered in the kitchen; suddenly all the different concerns and strands of the play are aired, the crises and conflicts of the characters, all come tumbling out in rapid succession. The dialogue whizzes round the stage like pinballs bouncing off their electric mushrooms, yet never once do we lose track of who is screwed up about what, or why. Only later do you realise the creative achievement here, balancing the issues like revolving plates; vigorous, funny, and perfectly-controlled writing.

Cecil Taylor's first play was in 1962, *The Blaydon Races*, which he believed would cause his audience to rush out, storm the barricades, and begin the revolution. As he later understood more of the complexities of human beings, his attitudes changed. 'I now write plays,' he said 'as a novelist writes novels, or as a poet writes poetry, to communicate my narrow odd vision of the world as I see it at the time of writing. Always in the hope that my hang-ups, flaws, insecurities and fears will at times cross those of my audience and they might feel a bit less on their own in this big world, as I do when I read a real book or see a real play.'

Which isn't to deny his political nature (there was an early joke about C.P. standing for Communist Party). Cecil was a lifetime socialist; with him it was more a faith than a political belief. He believed in socialism with a deep, biding belief, yet also knew there were no easy answers, and that artists shouldn't try to offer them. His deep commitment was to humanity which I think he saw ultimately as inseparable from his socialism.

There's no 'best' time to die, but with Cecil the timing was particularly cruel. His work was entering a whole new dimension, one which I think first stirred in *Bandits!* a play centred on the murky waters of the North-East clubland of the '60s and premièred by the student group On the Side, Newcastle, in 1976, with a cast including the present Live Theatre Director Max Roberts, and took real shape in his final play *Good* (performed by the RSC) where an honest, decent man finds himself slowly sucked into the Nazi machine until he becomes an Auschwitz functionary.

In both these plays, the work became both broader, but also sharper-edged. Cecil's humanity at times brought a weakness in his work, a reluctance to show mankind's darker side, a desire always to pull his characters back from the black abyss. It is a fine instinct but sometimes a playwright needs to offset good feeling and compassion with something else, and it was this 'something else' which I believe was beginning to emerge. I would dearly have loved to have seen his play on Stalin (incomplete at his death). Who knows what he would have produced by now? Who knows what would have been his continuing effect on theatre in the North East (which in an age of contraction, timidity and lack of imagination, desperately needs someone of his vision)?

One of his dreams was for Live Theatre Company to have their own theatre base, as well as their tours of one-night stands (which he believed too fragile a foundation on which to build). He died too soon to see their present Newcastle Quayside premises and theatre (the auditorium is named after him) just as he died too soon to see the great invigorating output of regional plays from the North East in the '70s squeezed to a trickle by short-sighted policies from various sources. On the credit side, Northern Arts and Northern Playwrights Society have managed to establish a C. P. Taylor Bursary, enabling the region's dramatists to work with the region's theatre companies, to produce plays from the same sort of community area in which Cecil operated so imaginatively. So far Tom Hadaway and Steve Chambers have been recipients, and the bursary's future, in the short term at least, looks healthy.

This volume of plays is planned as a forerunner to a C. P. Taylor season in and around Tyneside, with, I hope, several of the book's pieces given live performance. Since C. P. Taylor's death, his reputation has grown, his work has continued to be performed world-wide, yet no one has so far mounted such a season. It is fitting that this should be in the North East, just as it is fitting that this, the largest collection of his work yet published, should have a North-East connection.

Nor should such a season be a nostalgic indulgence, more a reminder of what has been possible in the past, a stimulus to what we can achieve in the future.

Four of his words above all stay in my mind, a piece of advice about writing, after we'd been talking about a clever, avant-garde, but ultimately vacuous piece of theatre. He tilted his head to one side in that distinctive manner, the eyes seemed to roll slightly, and he said 'start with something *real*'.

Whatever their differing styles, subject matters or devices, all these plays start with 'something real'. Cecil's huge concern with the human condition, his instinct through his art to create some kind of sense from the absurdities and cruelties, plus the total lack of transparency evident in his work, make him a very special kind of playwright. Because no detail of human existence was too small for his attention, so no theme proved too large. He was that rare and most happy breed of animal, simultaneously an artist of his region and of the world. His early death was a great blow, compensated only by the ever-growing realisation of what his life achieved.

Peter Mortimer
Editor – IRON Press
Tyneside. November 1987

Peter Pan Man

Characters

THE CHILDREN
PETER PAN
WENDY
JOHN
MICHAEL
GEORGE
JACK
PETER
SINDY
BARBI
ACTION MAN
INDIANS
PIRATES
SOLDIERS
EMILY
EMILY'S BROTHERS AND SISTERS
THE BOY

THE ADULTS
J.M. BARRIE
HIS MOTHER
HIS FATHER
MINISTER
TEACHER
GOD
MARY BARRIE
SYLVIA DAVIES
GILBERT CANNAN
CAPTAIN HOOK
SMEE
CHIEF RISING SUN
GENERAL BULL
GENERAL PORNILOV
GENERAL MAO
SHEIK MOHAMMED HASSAN
THE REGISTRAR OF BIRTHS, DEATHS AND MARRIAGES

ANIMAL
THE CROCODILE

ACT ONE

Scene One

The CURTAIN COMES UP on a stage divided into two areas. There are two back-projection screens. On one, representing the present time, a coloured slide of a multi-storey flat is projected: on the other, representing 1904, is a sepia photograph of J.M. BARRIE.

The boy is trying to study this photograph but is imprisoned in a human chain — his father and mother, brothers and sisters, teachers, ad men, etc.

EMILY: *(banging at door)* Let us in! Let us in! Ma! he won't let us in!

MOTHER: What the hell are you doing in there? You've been stuck in that bloody toilet for hours!

EMILY: Ma – he's not doing anything. He's just sitting there. Writing again.

MOTHER: Emily! Get away from that door, will you! What do you think you're doing, peeping at your brother on the toilet!

EMILY: He's not doing anything, Ma. He's just sitting there writing!

FATHER: Now, nobody can say I am not a tolerant man. I've been too bloody tolerant with this family. That's the whole trouble!

SISTER: *(with a Barbi Doll, pulling at the cord of the doll and making the doll speak to the BOY)* I have a date tonight. Which new dress shall I wear? What's showing at the Cinema?

FATHER: This morning, when I left for work, there were two tins of sausages and beans in the cupboard.

MOTHER: Emily's wetting her pants. Will you get out of there! For God's sake, boy!

EMILY: I need something more, Ma.

FATHER: Now everybody is out for school dinners. We had sausage rolls for tea. A full and nourishing meal. Where did that tin of saugages and beans go to? *(knocking at the door)* Boy, did you knock off a tin of sausages and beans? and half the Thin sliced's gone! You're not going to tell me your Mother's scoffed half a thin-sliced for her dinner!

MOTHER: *(to FATHER)* He's writing in the toilet again.

FATHER: Boy. Are you writing in the toilet again? Answer me, boy. What have I told you about monopolising the toilet?

MOTHER: If you don't come out this instant and Emily dirties her knickers *you* can bloody wash them!

(The BOY gives up and moves away, putting on a jacket. But the chain follows him. He moves to a bus stop, still surrounded by a chain ... A MAN is waiting by the stop, reading a newspaper)

AD MAN: America is the country where tomorrow happens today – like soft, Blue Band Margarine.

TEACHER: Boy ... If the North Pole is one magnet repels the North Pole of another magnet ... and the same happens with the South Poles and if the South Pole of one magnet attracts the North Pole of the other, what law do you deduce from these findings?

AD MAN: No other powder can soak away biological stains. For a whiter white – biological Radiant!

Scene 1a

The BOY is trying to move nearer the portrait of Barrie. The MAN watches him.

MAN:	Problems?
BOY:	Trying to get this thing out ... For school. Kind of a play.
MAN:	Oh ... a play, now. You writing a play?
BOY:	Just a con. To try and get us to do the Teacher's job ... You know? Want us to learn about this writer, Barrie ... So they get us to do a kind of play about him ...
MAN:	Barrie! Oh, yearh. Barrie. *(not a clue who BARRIE is)*
BOY:	The man that wrote "Peter Pan". I'm stuck, you see. Can't be bothered with it ...
MAN:	That was by Walt Disney, wasn't it? Peter Pan. Easy enough to make a play about Peter Pan ... Just get hold of the book, wouldn't you?
BOY:	Not about Peter Pan. About Barrie. The man who wrote it. James Barrie.
MAN:	Walt Disney.
BOY:	Walt Disney did the picture. Barrie wrote the play.
MAN:	Still easy enough. Just get hold of his life story ... And put it all down. I could give you a few ideas for a play. Some of the stuff they put on the Telly ... could do as good as that rubbish any day. And better!
BOY:	Got hold of a book about him. He was escaping from life. This character, Barrie ... You know? Running away from life ...
MAN:	You get sick of life Definitely!
BOY:	What do you do when you get sick?
MAN:	Get sick of work. Work in a Power Station, don't I? Watching the clocks. Meters. You get sick of that.
BOY:	What do you do then, when you get sick?
MAN:	Can't do anything, can you? I play with the kids. I wrestle with them. How many kids had this Barrie bloke?
BOY:	Didn't have any. He couldn't have any.
MAN:	Oh ... One of them, was he? *(the BOY doesn't see the joke. The MAN shrugs his shoulders)* Oh, well. *(holds up an annual and tries to pass it to the BOY)* Just bought them this. Captain Scarlet ... Go mad about Captain Scarlet, the kids! *(the BOY is trying to reach out for the book between the gaps of the cage)* Captain Scarlet's indestructible. That's a real story ... You need something special about the characters ... Like him being indestructible. Or your Peter Pan ... Not growing up ... My youngest – he says to me: *(the BOY at last has managed to grip the book. He draws it into the cage)* My youngest – he says to me:

Me mam's Colonel White.
Me Da's a mysteron.
I'm Captain Scarlet.
I'm going to kill you, Mysteron!
You going to kill yer Da? I says to him.
No ... I'm going to kill the Mysteron.

(Laughing. Waits for the BOY to share in the joke. The BOY has now opened the book and is studying the pages)

MAN: *(in case the BOY has missed the point)* You going to kill yer Da? No, I'm going to kill the Mysteron! *(laughing)*

(The book has worked some magic on the cage and the BOY. The people forming it recede, leaving the BOY free to move about the stage. There is the sound of someone crying. The BOY searches for the source as the LIGHTS SLOWLY COME UP, first on the portrait of BARRIE ... and on BARRIE himself, imprisoned in his cage)

BOY: *(to BARRIE)* Why are you crying? Why are you crying?

(The BOY squats on the stage, his eyes on the portrait of BARRIE, as the play moves back to 1904 and the next scene)

Scene Two

BARRIE is locked in a similar cage to the BOY. Circling round him in their order of importance are − his MOTHER, his TEACHER, a MINISTER of the Free Church, his SISTERS, his BROTHERS ... and his FATHER, and above all of them − GOD.

MOTHER: We are two of a kind, Jamie, are we not? You and me. I had the same fear as you, son. Of growing up and having to give up all my games ...

MINISTER: *(pointing out GOD)* There He is, James. Clearly. For all to see.

TEACHER: You are writing with your *left* hand again, Barrie! Use your right, boy. Use your right! Your right, Boy!

MINISTER: From His position on high, James. He can see the activities of every soul in every part of the Universe. There is no hiding from Him. His Eye is upon every human creature, everywhere, for all Eternity.

MOTHER: I used to cry myself asleep at night, Jamie ... To think of growing up and never being able to play like a child again!

TEACHER: Your right, Boy. Use your right!

MOTHER: A mother and son, Jamie. That is the most wonderful thing God has made in this world. It is a wee taste of the love God has for his creation.

FATHER: Character, Jamie. Character.

MOTHER: You don't bother your head, son, about these horrible things these sinful boys were telling you. These private things between a husband and wife, Jamie.

FATHER: If you cut your finger, Jamie is that worse than losing your cap?

MOTHER: You're right, Jamie, turning your head from them, son. They're necessary. The world would come to a stop without them.

FATHER: No. Your finger would heal, Jamie, in God's time. But you would never grow a new cap!

TEACHER: A Gold Star for the father of that boy!

MOTHER: Every coin has its good side and its bad, Jamie. A wife just has to submit to her husband. It says so in the Bible, son.

MINISTER:	We pray for our country and for its dominions and dependencies that Thou would'st inspire them with Godly fear and establish them in righteousness and truth.
MOTHER:	Don't you worry your head about these things, Jamie ...
MINISTER:	For our Sovereign Lord King Edward, Alexander, The Queen, George, Prince of Wales and all the Royal House. Grant them Thy Blessings and keep them in Thy Way. Direct and rule all who exercise authority throughout the Empire that we, under them, may lead quiet and peaceable lives in Godliness and honesty, to the Glory of Thy Name. *(the cage responds with "Amen")*
MOTHER:	A mother and son, Jamie. That's a wee taste of the love God has for His creation ...
	(Breaking through all these demands on BARRIE the voice of WENDY grows louder and louder, repeating ... "why are you crying?" ... till BARRIE, in his obsession to trace the source of the voice breaks through the cage into the Darling's Nursery ... and the first scene of "Peter Pan" ... He stands watching the scene unfold as he creates it in his mind ... The cage recedes ... and while he is watching and creating, the BOY is watching him ... and creating in his own way, or beginning to create)

Scene Two A

WENDY:	*(courteously)* Boy, why are you crying?
	(PETER PAN jumps up and, crossing to the front of the bed, bows to her in a fairy way. WENDY, impressed, bows back)
PETER:	What is your name?
WENDY:	*(well satisfied with it)* Wendy Moira Angela Darling. What is yours?
PETER:	*(finding it lamentably brief)* Peter Pan.
WENDY:	Is that all?
PETER:	*(biting his lip)* Yes.
WENDY:	I'm so sorry.
PETER:	It doesn't matter.
WENDY:	Where do you live?
PETER:	Second to the right and straight on till the morning.
WENDY:	What a funny address.
PETER:	No, it isn't.
WENDY:	Is that what they put on letters?
PETER:	Don't get any letters.
WENDY:	But your mother gets letters.
PETER:	Don't have a mother.
WENDY:	Peter!
	(She leaps out of bed to put her arm round him, but he draws back. He does not know why. But he knows he must draw back)

PETER:	You mustn't touch me.
WENDY:	Why?
PETER:	I don't know. *(he is never touched by anyone in the play)*
WENDY:	No wonder you are crying.
PETER:	I wasn't crying. But I can't get my shadow to stick on.
WENDY:	It has come off. How awful. *(looking at the spot where he has lain)* Peter, you have been trying to stick it on with soap.
PETER:	*(snappily)* Well, then.
WENDY:	It must be sewn on.
PETER:	What is "sewn"?
WENDY:	You are dreadfully ignorant.
PETER:	No, I'm not.
WENDY:	I will sew it on for you. Sit here. I dare say it will hurt a little.
PETER:	*(a recent remark rankling)* I never cry. *(she seems to attach the shadow. He tests the combination)* It isn't quite itself yet.
WENDY:	Perhaps I should have ironed it.
	(The shadow awakes and is glad to be back with Peter as he is to have it. He and his shadow dance together. He is showing off. He crows like a cock. He would fly in order to impress WENDY further if he knew there was anything unusual in that)
PETER:	Wendy, look! Oh, look! The cleverness of me!
	(The BOY moves nearer the nursery and calls to PETER)
BOY:	Peter! Peter Pan! Peter Pan!
	(PETER PAN turns to the BOY)
PETER:	*(to the BOY)* What do you want? Do you know anyone who can help me with my spring cleaning …?
BOY:	My sister, Peter Pan. There she is. Over there.
	(And the LIGHTS COME UP ON 1971 and the next scene)

Scene Three

Elswick, Newcastle upon Tyne. 1971. Emily's House. The Kitchen.

Total chaos. EMILY is feeding her baby with a bottle while nursing another. CHILDREN litter the room. Crowd round her. EMILY throws instructions at all angles.

EMILY:	Empty your pottie into the toilet, Johnny. Betty, put your nightie on. You can put it on yourself. Sammy, take your bloody dirty fingers out of the treacle! *(and into this chaos, steps PETER PAN)*
PETER:	Hullo, I've come for the Spring Cleaning.
EMILY:	If you want me Mum, she doesn't do any cleaning no more. She got into trouble with the Social Security for doing cleaning and lifting money from them.
PETER:	You're supposed to ask my name first.

EMILY:	If yer mam's out at Bingo like ours, and you're needing looking after, go somewhere else, son. I've got enough on my hands here.
PETER:	Do ask my name.
CHILD:	Ask his name, Em. Go on ...
EMILY:	*(to PETER)* Reach us that Gripe Mixture on the shelf up there, while you're here.
	(PETER flies to get it)
CHILD:	Look! He can fly!
EMILY:	Don't be daft, Jackie. *(not seeing)* Nobody flies ...
PETER:	I do. I do. I can fly!
EMILY:	It's no skin off my nose, son if ye can fly or ye can't.
PETER:	I do wish you'd ask me my name, Wendy. We're getting everything wrong!
EMILY:	If ye're talkin' about getting everything wrong, son, let's start with you. I'm *Emily*, not Wendy.
PETER:	You're Wendy Darling. Definitely.
CHILD:	She's Emily. What's *your* name?
PETER:	Where's Wendy?
EMILY:	Who the hell's Wendy?
PETER:	Wendy's house did look much nicer than this. It has a nicer smell.
EMILY:	You go back to Wendy, then!
PETER:	This is Kensington, isn't it? Wendy lives here ... I'm quite sure of it. She had a lovely pink cot. And a rocking horse over there. And Michael's bed was at that wall ... and John's over there ... And a lovely, soft, silky carpet on the floor. I wish you'd ask my name ... I can't do anything till Wendy asks my name.
EMILY:	Well, you've got a problem there, son. There's no Wendy to ask it.
PETER:	I suppose you'll have to do, then. It's quite a nice name, Emily. It grows on one, doesn't it. Go on – Say: "What is your name"!
EMILY:	Don't bother us, will you! I've to put all these bloody kids to bed!
PETER:	You said a naughty word!
CHILD:	Ask him, Em. See what happens.
PETER:	Please, Emily.
EMILY:	Right! What's your bloody name, then?
PETER:	Oh ... Not like that, Emily.
EMILY:	How, like? You're holding me back. Pass us that nappy, while you're standing around.
PETER:	Ask me nice. Please!
EMILY:	What's your name?
PETER:	All right, then. Since you want to know ... Peter Pan!
EMILY:	You're sitting on the safety pins.
PETER:	Now ask me where I live.

EMILY:	Me Mam showed us how to do it with one pin ... See ... You make a triangle.
PETER:	Please ask me where I live, Emily.
EMILY:	Where do you live?
PETER:	Second to the right and straight on to the morning. *(he waits for the effect. There is absolutely none)*
CHILD:	Are you a Mysteron?
PETER:	I've come to take you to your secret island, Emily. Where you've always longed to go. With the green waves lapping on the warm, white sand. And the crystal, blue lagoon —
A VOICE:	She hasn't got an island.
PETER:	*(looking round for the source of the voice)* I beg your pardon.
CHILD:	She says she hasn't got an island. Em hasn't.
PETER:	Who said it?
CHILD:	Sindy doll said it.
PETER:	Of course she has an island. With the green waves lapping on the warm sand. And the sun shining every day.

(SINDY DOLL has climbed out of her toy box. She is dressed in Sindy's 'Lounging' outfit)

EMILY:	*(with a cough bottle)* John, take your Linctus, now.
SINDY:	You're wasting your time, trying to get Em to take a trip, Peter Pan.
CHILD:	That's Sindy Doll. We got her for Xmas.
SINDY:	I *came* for Xmas.
CHILD:	She doesn't like thinking anybody bought her.
SINDY:	Only kids have islands and Never-Never lands, son.
CHILD:	She's got a boy-friend called Paul, and a girl-friend called Tressy. We're getting Paul for next Xmas.
SINDY:	All these kids talk about is what they're going to buy! *(as she is talking, BARBI, who is inseparable from SINDY, climbs out to see what is happening)*
BARBI:	I have a date tonight.
CHILD:	That's her friend, Barbi.
SINDY:	What you on about, kid! That walking gramohone record a mate of mine!
BARBI:	How shall I wear my hair?
PETER:	*(a little off his balance)* You're very big for dolls.
EMILY:	Who's he talking to now? I think you're off your nut, son. You're a right head-case!
CHILD:	He's only talking to Sindy.
EMILY:	You'll have a great conversation talking to Sindy!
PETER:	I wish I was in Wendy's house, I really do. I'm not sure I like this place at all.
SINDY:	She can't hear me talk, see?

(SINDY stands in front of EMILY and makes rude faces at her. Shouts "Boo." EMILY carries on with her work, not hearing)

	You see. No grown-up people can see me when I start moving around.
PETER:	She's only ten. I know she's only ten because I wouldn't have come for her if she was older than eleven. Or twelve, anyway ...
	(EMILY has gone to the bread box and is counting the slices of bread)
BARBI:	*(throwing out a likely phrase)* Which new dress shall I wear?
PETER:	What's she doing now?
CHILD:	She's counting the bread. She's got to count the bread. We'd be in a pretty bad state if she didn't count the bread.
PETER:	Isn't she ten? She looks ten.
SINDY:	Don't know what her age is.
EMILY:	Got to make sure none of these thieving kids have knocked off a slice. I'm going to check the other groceries, too.
PETER:	Emily, what age are you?
EMILY:	*(counting)* Sixteen, seventeen.
SINDY:	The point is, she's grown up. That's the point.
CHILD:	*(to PETER)* Last week, Martin knocked off a tin of sausages and beans. He had a sausages and beans sandwich.
BARBI:	Which new dress shall I wear?
SINDY:	That's a question I never need to ask. All I've got is on my back.
CHILD:	She's a liar. She's got a nightie.
SINDY:	I can't walk about in my nightie during the day! *(to PETER)* There's a fabulous new trouser suit in the shops now.
PETER:	I think we should start again. Emily, ask my name.
SINDY:	It's no use, man. Emily's grown up.
CHILD:	Emily's older than me Mam.
CHILD:	Older than my Gran.
CHILD:	She's not. She's just the same age as our Granny.
SINDY:	Look in her pocket where she kept it, if you don't believe me.
PETER:	Emily — you must know what age you are.
EMILY:	How would I know what age I am. Me Mam lost my Birth Certificate years ago.
SINDY:	Look in her pocket, man!
	(PETER approaches EMILY)
EMILY:	What are you after now, son?
	(PETER looks into the pocket made by the lower lid of Emily's right eye)
EMILY:	*(struggling)* Get off! Get off! Watch it, now. I'll bash you, son! *(but he is able to see that SINDY is right. Her childhood is not there)*
PETER:	You've lost it, Emily. When did you lose it?
EMILY:	Just watch yourself, son!
PETER:	Emily, do try and remember. When do you think you lost your childhood? Have you looked for it?
SINDY:	If she didn't know it had gone, how would she look for it?

PETER:	Oh, you're so clever. You're just too clever to live! I know! School. That's where most children lose it. There's thousands and thousands of cases of childrens' childhood dropping out during lessons in school. Do you think you dropped it at school, Emily?
EMILY:	What you on about now, son?
CHILD:	Em ... Can we have some cocoa?
SINDY:	We could have a world-wide search. That would be interesting. Having a world-wide search for Em's childhood!
PETER:	I don't see how we need a world-wide search. She hasn't been anywhere else but here, has she?
EMILY:	I've been all over the place, if you're interested. Blackpool. Bolton. Preston. Woolton ...
PETER:	But you haven't been to Africa or China ...
SINDY:	Watched it on the Telly. That would count.
PETER:	What's "the Telly"?
EMILY:	I wish you'd stop talking to yourself, son. It gives us the shivers.
SINDY:	If you haven't been around, man, since ... Queen Victoria ... you've got a lot of catching up to do.
PETER:	King Edward. I once went to the Palace, and watched him playing cards. He had a very jolly beard.
CHILD:	(switching on the telly) That's the Telly.
	(PETER entranced. Trying to grab the images on the screen)
CHILD:	It's just pictures. Like in a book.
PETER:	I say! Isn't this jolly exciting. Look! What's 'Jelly Tots'? They sound lovely.
THE TELLY:	Bags I Jelly Tots, etc. ...
CHILD:	They're great.
PETER:	What's 'Margarine'?
SINDY:	John. Switch it off. I can't hear myself talking. (JOHN switches it off)
PETER:	It's all gone away.
SINDY:	We're not going to have you stuck in front of the Telly all night. We've got to start this world-wide search for Em's childhood.
PETER:	Couldn't we start in an hour? After I've watched Jelly Tots a bit more?
CHILD:	There's no more Jelly Tots on. That's all there'll be tonight. The next'll probably be about Soap Powder or Windolene or something stupid like that.
PETER:	(to SINDY) Emily will have to come with us, if we're going to search for her childhood. Emily – will you come with us?
CHILD:	If you promise to buy her a Fish Supper and bread and butter and tea, she'll come.
SINDY:	(going to the toy box) I'll get Elmer. We're definitely going to need him. (calling) Elmer, Elmer, honey! (Elmer comes out of the box. He is an Action Man) Elmer, we've a fantastic job for you!
ELMER:	(Eyeing PETER with great suspicion as he pulls out a cigarette and lights up) yeah ... Who's the doll?

SINDY:	Oh ... It's just a Character. Peter Pan!
ELMER:	*(going into his box and bringing out his radio)* gonna get a clearance on her from Washington.
SINDY:	It's a *Him*, Elmer.
ELMER:	Him or Her ... Don't dig ... got a Russkie look about him ...
CHILD:	That's Action Man. *(ELMER sits down at his radio)*
SINDY:	If we're going to have a world-wide search for Em's childhood, we need Elmer with us. Elmer has access to all the files of the Central Intelligene Agency.
ELMER:	For Christ's sake, man! What you shouting to the rooftops classified info. like that for! What's the briefing? Em's had her childhood stolen and sold to the Russkies? Or the chinos? I want a clearance from Washington and a Licence to kill on this trip.
PETER:	*(quite lost at all this jargon)* Emily, if we have a Fish Supper and bread and butter and tea on the way, will you come with us to look for your childhood?
EMILY:	You taking us out for a Fish Supper? Serious? You'll have to take all of us. I can't leave the kids on their own.
PETER:	Of course. I'm taking everybody.
EMILY:	Show's your money.
PETER:	*(lost)* If you draw me what you mean – I'll wish it real.
CHILD:	Draw him a Pound.
ELMER:	He's giving us a false name. No Peter Pan on file at Washington.
EMILY:	Let's see. There's six of us ...
SINDY:	*(to ELMER)* He's all right. I'm telling you. He's a friend of mine.
EMILY:	Bread and butter and tea. Chocolate biscuits. We'll need more than a Pound.
ELMER:	Probably need a helicopter on this mission.
CHILD:	*(to PETER)* You can get them in the shops, now. Helicopters for him.
EMILY:	Can we have double helpings?
PETER:	Anything you want.
EMILY:	Right! *(drawing)* There's Five Pounds. That should be enough with plenty to spare.
	(PETER takes the paper and wishes it into a real five pound note)
SINDY:	First thing to do is see the Birth Man. To make sure Em is really a child. that would be a great scene – us having this world-wide search for her childhood and she's really a grown-up!
	(ELMER has heaved his radio on his back, slung his machine gun over his shoulder and other tactical weapons)
ELMER:	Company! Form ranks! Attention!
SINDY:	Elmer, man! This is a *Secret* Mission. We can't go about like soldiers!
ELMER:	Yeah ... Right ... Check. You just shoot me the real briefing. That's all. Just shoot me the real briefing, man. Right. Check. All forces go! You're looking great, man ... Great!

(They go out to the Fish and Chip Shop. The BOY moves over to 1971)

Scene 4

The Nursery of the Davies' Home in Kensington Park Gardens.
BARRIE is marching the CHILDREN round the room.

JOHN:	Left, right, left, right, left, right, left, right. Halt! About turn. At ease ...
GEORGE:	I say. That's just how the *real* Guards do it in Buckingham Palace!
PETER:	Are you a real Guard? Have you come to teach us how to be real Guards for the King?
BARRIE:	Silence in the ranks, if you please, Company! No one allowed to speak until they are formally dismissed.
WENDY:	I don't want to be a Guard. I want to be a Lady-in-Waiting.
BARRIE:	Company! Attention!
GEORGE:	I say, what is your name?
BARRIE:	Dis – miss! Now, you may ask me my name.
WENDY:	What is your name?
BARRIE:	James Barrie.
PETER:	Is that all?
BARRIE:	There's a Matthew in the middle, if you like. Would that be better?
JOHN:	It's not very much.
WENDY:	It's not *too* bad. James Matthew Barrie. *(trying it)* It lasts about half a breath.
JOHN:	Where do you live?
BARRIE:	Second to the right and straight on till the morning.
PETER:	Now you're being patronising.
BARRIE:	No ... I do. Really ... In a way. I do live somewhere there ...
WENDY:	And have you come all that way, just to see *us*?
BARRIE:	You ... and your toys ... and dolls. And of course your Mother. And your Father. I was very kindly invited by your Mother and Father to tea.
WENDY:	Can't go to tea till we've dusted everybody's head.
PETER:	*(explaining to BARRIE)* Nannie says we have to dust away all the silly thoughts in our heads.
JOHN:	Do you have silly thoughts?
WENDY:	*(with a huge rag doll, fixing a feather duster to its hand and assuming a Nanny's voice)* Children! Dusting time, if you please ...
	(The CHILDREN line up and the RAG DOLL stops opposite each CHILD in turn)
GEORGE:	*(confessing his latest silly thought)* Peter Pan?
RAG DOLL:	*(dusting the untidy thoughts out of his head)* How old is he?
GEORGE:	Twelve. He's always twelve. He stays twelve for ever and ever ... *(RAG DOLL dusts away furiously)* I *think* he's twelve ... *(RAG DOLL at PETER)*
PETER:	Not much, really. I just dropped in to see how the Pirates were keeping ... And Captain Hook asked me to join his band.

RAG DOLL:	*(dusting)* This is Kensington Park Gardens. Miles and miles from the sea. And piracy is quite illegal nowadays.
PETER:	Yes, Nanny.
RAG DOLL:	*(at WENDY)* Jack shot one of my lagoons flying over a flamingo.
GEORGE:	The Pirates threw a stone at one of your flamingos flying over the lagoon, idiot!
RAG DOLL:	*(at BARRIE)* Bend down, please. I can't reach you.
BARRIE:	*(to RAG DOLL)* If I may be excused the feather dusting, Nanny. I am given to understand that I am quite real. So my friends assure me.
PETER:	*(to RAG DOLL)* His name is James Matthew Barrie, Nanny.
RAG DOLL:	*(as WENDY throws her on the floor on the entrance of her mother, Sylvia Davies)* Delighted, I'm sure.
SYLVIA:	*(going towards BARRIE)* Mr. Barrie! How very nice of you to come.
BARRIE:	*(taking her hand with no attempt to disguise his admiration for her)* Mrs. Davies. How very nice of you to ask me. Mrs. Barrie is detained in the country and sends her apologies. *(still holding her hand)* Mrs. Davies ... Shall I make a confession to you?
SYLVIA:	*(escaping, to the CHILDREN)* George. Jack. Wendy. Have you any idea who this gentleman is?
BARRIE:	*(pursuing her)* Since that evening when we first met, Mrs. Davies. Mrs. Davies, do you find that there are some people one recognises even at the first meeting as kindred souls?
SYLVIA:	*(smiling politely as some kind of answer to this)* Children, this is James Barrie! The famous playwright, who writes all these clever books and marvellous plays! Arthur and I were at CRICHTON again, the other evening. For the fifth time. More exciting and amusing than ever, Mr. Barrie!
BARRIE:	Since last Thursday evening, Mrs. Davies, when we first met ... *(taking her hand again)* I have been a mass of vibrations ... *Longing* to see you again ...
SYLVIA:	Children. Do come and shake hands with Mr. Barrie. *(the CHILDREN come forward and are introduced formally to BARRIE) (to BARRIE)* – George, Peter ... And Wendy.
BARRIE:	*(taking up teddy)* And this is Teddy. He wishes to tell me some secret.
WENDY:	He's always telling people secrets. *(BARRIE makes the teddy whisper in his ear)* Teddy! It's very rude to whisper. I'm always telling you that!
SYLVIA:	Mrs. Barrie is quite well, Mr. Barrie?
BARRIE:	*(pausing in his secret conversation with the teddy to turn to SYLVIA)* Exceedingly, Mrs. Davies ... Never better. *(turning back to the teddy's secret again, listening to teddy)* Teddy says he is being treated with great unkindness in this house. He says you make him eat nasty, horrible porridge for breakfast ... and bone broth for lunch.
WENDY:	Oh, don't you believe him. He's just a spoiled Teddy Bear.
PETER:	*(bringing BARRIE a toy soldier)* Sergeant Brown wants to tell you something, too.

BARRIE:	*(listening to the SERGEANT)* I see ... Yes ... *(to the CHILDREN)* Sergeant Brown says he cannot recruit me into his Company as I am only five foot one inch. He does not accept recruits below five foot eight inches ...

(SYLVIA looks at BARRIE with a new awareness ... He catches her look and she smiles at him)

Such a fascinating smile, Mrs. Davies. Crooked. Sweet. Something quite unique. Perhaps the charming tilt on the nose ...

SYLVIA: Strange, Mr. Barrie. Until you mentioned your height just now ... I was quite unaware of it. I felt you ... *tall. (the tea bell is ringing)* Shall we go in to tea, Mr. Barrie ... That's the maid ringing now.

BARRIE: Alas, I am being held to ransom by this Teddy Bear and Sergeant Brown. They refuse to release me unless you agree immediately to their demands. They demand, instantly, a Sherry Trifle, a bar of Vanilla Chocolate, and a plate of Strawberry Ice.

GEORGE: Greedy gluttons!

SYLVIA: Shall we go in, Mr. Barrie?

BARRIE: Shall we capitulate and agree to their demands? Perhaps if we offered them just the Vanilla bars ...

PETER: I say ... Why can't we all band together. And attack the toys.

GEORGE: I was just about to give the command to attack. *I'm* the Captain.

BARRIE: Be quick, Captain. Teddy has heard your plans and is bringing out cannon against you.

(The teddy is placed behind a dangerous-looking cannon)

GEORGE: Company – Draw your swords ...

(The MAID rings the teabell again. This time clearly with impatience)

SYLVIA: *(smiling)* Mr. Barrie. I see I shall have to be as severe with you at tea time as I am with the other children. Margaret is growing impatient to serve tea, from the sound of her ringing. I shall have to pull you from your games. Really, you're quite as naughty as the children, getting lost in games at mealtimes.

BARRIE: *(delighted at this)* Do you see me as a boy, Mrs. Davies, now? Do you really? *(to the CHILDREN)* Company! *(leading the CHILDREN against the toys)* Charge!

(He leads the charge on the toys, sending them scattering. Another great victory.

The LIGHTS DIM on the Davies house and COME UP SLOWLY on the Darling's nursery, and in a corner of Barrie's house, showing BARRIE at a desk, writing.

PETER PAN is having problems, coping with WENDY. She is back in bed, with a sheet over her face. PETER moves towards the bed)

PETER: *(popping on the edge of the bed)* Wendy, don't withdraw. I can't help crowing when I'm pleased with myself. Wendy, one girl is worth more than twenty boys.

WENDY: *(peeping over the sheets)* You really think so, Peter?

PETER: Yes, I do.

WENDY:	I think it's perfectly sweet of you and I shall get up again. *(they sit together on the side of the bed)* I shall give you a kiss if you like?
PETER:	Thank you. *(he holds out his hand)*
WENDY:	*(aghast)* Don't you know what a kiss is?
PETER:	I shall know when you give me it. *(not to hurt his feeling she gives him a thimble)* Now I shall give you a kiss.
WENDY:	*(primly)* If you please. *(he pulls an acorn button off his person and bestows it on her)* I will wear it on this chain round my neck.
	(... The BOY approaches PETER with a bag of chips. He leads him from the bed to the Town Hall, handing him the bag of chips which PETER proceeds to attack ... As they move into 1971 again and the next scene)

Scene Five

Outside the Civic Centre. A Full Moon.

PETER and EMILY and the rest of their company enter with their bags of chips. ACTION MAN is receiving strong signals from his radio. He squats down to check his bearings.

ACTION MAN:	Hold it, everybody! Hold it! *(checking dials)* Read-out of our position just coming through. We are approaching the Civic Centre.
SINDY:	Elmer. This is the Civic Centre. Look. There it is.
ACTION MAN:	*(suddenly aware of the Civic Centre in front of him)* We are at the Civic Centre. That's what I'm telling you. Everybody. We have arrived at the Civic Centre.
EMILY:	It's all closed up. Look. Not a light anywhere.
PETER:	*(to ACTION MAN)* Elmer, it's closed. There's not a light anywhere.
ACTION MAN:	What do you expect, man, in this declining country. How do you think Britain got from top of the League to the bottom in less than half a century, man. They don't know how to work, man. Got no drive ... Soon as the sun goes down, they shut up shop and hit the sack ...
EMILY:	*(going, giving it up)* Come on. Anyway, the Fish and Chips were smashing, Peter.
SINDY:	We've got to find the Birth Man. Can't we find out where he lives and go to his house?
ACTION MAN:	I'm working on that now, Sindy, doll ... Checking with Washington.
PETER:	I know. We'll magic him back. Emily, we'll magic the Birth Man back to the Civic Centre.
ACTION MAN:	Yeah ... Sure ... Great idea, Pan! Magic him back! What do we do – suck him out of his house or something? *(sucks in his breath)*
PETER:	Like that. Only harder. And everybody has to do it. Everybody sit down. And suck in your breath. As hard as you can. *(They all sit in a line.)*
PETER:	Ready. Suck in as hard as you can. One ... Two ... Three ... *(Elmer hasn't quite got the idea)* Not like that, Elmer. Like this!
ACTION MAN:	Yeah ... man. Just tuning in, Pan.
PETER:	Ready ... One ... Two ... Three ...

(They all suck in their breath as hard as they can and the Registrar of Births, Deaths and Marriages is sucked from his bathroom in the act of powdering himself with only a bath towel round his waist)

REGISTRAR: Here! What are you doing in my bathroom?

PETER: It's not your bathroom, Sir. Look, it's the Civic Centre.

REGISTRAR: So it is. It's the Civic Centre. How did I get here? Must be this Talcum Powder.

PETER: This is Emily, Sir.

REGISTRAR: Hullo, Emily.

PETER: *(to EMILY)* You have to say to him. "Good evening, Registrar of Births, Deaths and Marriages."

EMILY: Good evening, Registrar of Births, Deaths and Marriages.

REGISTRAR: Good evening, Emily.

PETER: Do you remember writing out Emily, Sir, in your Birth Book?

REGISTRAR: *(searching his memory)* Emily – Emily – Emily ... Lots of Emilies ... Hundreds of them. Emily – Emily ... *(to PETER)* You'll have to help me, young man. *(PETER gives him kick in the behind)* Emily – Emily – *(kick)* Emily Darling. Emily Darling. Mother:- Janet Darling. Father:- Patrick Donovan.

EMILY: That's a lie.

REGISTRAR: Sex: Female. Born in the City of Liverpool. 3rd February, 1960.

PETER: *(trying to work this out)* 1960 ...

ACTION MAN: *(at radio)* I'll get a line to our computer. Third February, 1960 ...

SINDY: That's eleven years ... She's eleven years old.

ACTION MAN: That makes her ... eleven years old.

SINDY: She's still a child, Peter.

ACTION MAN: She's still a child.

PETER: *(jumping up and down with excitement)* Emily – you really are a child. You're eleven years old. *(to REGISTRAR)* Tell her, Sir, please. She's eleven years old!

REGISTRAR: You're eleven years old.

PETER: And she's still a child.

REGISTRAR: You're still a child.

EMILY: Great! Big deal! I'm still a kid.

REGISTRAR: It's getting chilly. Do you think someone might get me a taxi or some discreet conveyance home?

PETER: We'll blow you back, Sir. If you'll just kind of bend down ... *(showing him)* Like that ... We'll blow you all the way home again, Sir. *(to the others)* Everybody stand in a straight line.

ACTION MAN: Company! Form ranks! Attention!

PETER: Ready. Blow! *(they blow)*

REGISTRAR: *(looking round)* Am I still here?

PETER: Harder – Much, much harder.

(They all blow the BIRTH MAN home. But his towel is torn off in the process and flaps on to the stage)

EMILY: *(picks it up)* Good towel, that ...

PETER: Emily. You've really lost your childhood. I told you.

EMILY: I never lose anything. I don't lose things. Find things. *(holding up towel)*

ACTION MAN: *(at radio)* Red Alert coming through.

EMILY: Only thing I ever lost in my whole life was a pie. Half a pie.

ACTION MAN: Chinos converging on Speke Airport. Russkies parachuting into City Centre.

PETER: If you think hard, Emily. You must have dropped it somewhere.

ACTION MAN: Smoke signals coming from direction of Liverpool Docks. Indians moving into City Centre.

PETER: One minute you'd feel like a child, Emily ... And the next ... after you dropped it ...

SINDY: Ask her about the pie, Peter. Ask her what happened to the pie.

PETER: I'm not wasting time asking her about silly pies. I can't see what a pie could have to do with anything. I know. Let's all go back to that Fairy House ... and we can play with the apple machines.

CHILD: Fruit machines.

PETER: We can play with the fruit machines while Emily's trying to remember.

SINDY: Please yourself, son, but it could easily be the pie. Anything beautiful ... that's what we're looking for, isn't it? that's how you drop your childhood. When you stop getting turned on by beautiful things.

ACTION MAN: Quiet everybody. Secret cable coming in from Washington.

PETER: I wouldn't say a pie was beautiful, would you, Sindy?

EMILY: Anyway, I didn't lose it. It was knocked off. I was halfway through it. It was a smashing pie. I put it down on a bench in the park, to see to Betty. And some rotten gutsy thief knocked it off when my back was turned.

ACTION MAN: C.I.A. Report Russkie conspiracy to use lost childhood of child for political purposes. All Europe and Atlantic Seaboards on Orange Alert.

EMILY: Smashing pie, it was. Dead fresh from the shop. Still hot. Gravy dripping out of it ...

SINDY: *(to PETER)* See?

PETER: All right. We'll go and look for the pie. I just thought we'd go and watch that coloured Telly in the shop for a bit. It was ripping. But everybody's in such a hurry to find the pie ... We'll go and find it.

EMILY: It's eaten, man. You'll never find it now. It was knocked off ... Years ago ...

CHILD: In Elswick Park.

PETER: That's easy enough. We just go to Elswick Park and find it.

EMILY: I'm going home.

ACTION MAN: *(at radar screen)* Can't go anywhere, doll. We're ringed round all the way ... Can't break out even if we had a helicopter.

CHILD: You reckon all these people want Em's childhood. Elmer?

ACTION MAN:	You'd be surprised what these Russkies and Chinos want, son!
EMILY:	Mind ... If I could get the rest of the pie. Like it was ... *(her mouth watering)* I fancy it.
SINDY:	There you are. Told you.
PETER:	It's too easy. I don't believe it's as easy as that, finding Emily's childhood.
SINDY:	Isn't easy at all. We can't get through the enemy lines. We're surrounded.
PETER:	I suppose that's true. I know – we'll all go back to the Fairy House and play the apple machines till the morning. And they'll go away ...
SINDY:	Yes. And so will you.
PETER:	Yes. But I'll come back in the morning.
SINDY:	And so will they.
BARBI:	What's showing at the Cinema?
SINDY:	Oh, drop dead will you!
EMILY:	You going to get me the pie, or do I just go home, son?
ACTION MAN:	Cape Kennedy plotting a course to Elswick Park via the moon.
CHILD:	I fancy going to the moon.
ACTION MAN:	Hullo. Space Control. Request for emergency Moon Spacecraft.
CHILD:	If we had Captain Scarlet here. Bet you he'd wipe out everybody. He's indestructible.
ACTION MAN:	Is that an expression of no confidence in my Command, son? Course set; We go to the moon and bounce back on a carefully plotted trajectory right down to Elswick Park.
SINDY:	Swinging, Emily. That's going to really turn me on!
	(The INDIANS and the PIRATES and the RUSSIANS and CHINESE and VIET-CONG and EL FATAH are converging on the children and the Civic Centre.
	The crocodile can distinctly be heard ticking)
PETER:	That's Crocodile, now Hook can't be far away now. He loves confetti. If you throw it to him you can watch him eating. It's jolly interesting!
ACTION MAN:	Standing by now for reception of spacecraft. Request permission to use tactial nuclears ... Specifically grenades and mortars. Over ...
	(The CHILDREN feed the crocodile and the others watch. ACTION MAN patiently sits at his equipment waiting for the spacecraft)
	And the Play moves back to 1904.

Scene Six

The grounds of Mary's House at the Black Lake.

Chairs have been arranged on the lawn. BARRIE is seated, a manuscript on his lap. MARY BARRIE is beside him. She takes his hand.

MARY:	I do mean it, Jim. It is absolutely nothing to be worried about. Nor in the slightest degree to be the cause of any anxiety, love. It is very common. Countless men are affected by this.

BARRIE:	Mary, love. Believe me, I am perfectly happy as we are. Couldn't be happier.
MARY:	*(watching him. Lightly)* Jim. When you asked me to marry you dear, did you imagine our marriage would be something like this?
BARRIE:	Not like this, no ... Nothing as idyllically happy as this, dearest. Mary, there is not a married man on earth as happy as I. My love for you is so great ... and pure ... Mary ... I feel no need for these obligatory intimacies usual between man and wife. Believe me, Mary. I have no need for them. I feel we are the closer without them. Do you not feel this?
MARY:	Close, yes. Perhaps ... sometimes ... too close. *(he looks up, puzzled)* No ... very close, Jim.
BARRIE:	Such a tiny part of marriage, in any case, Mary my love. And unaesthetic, really. *(he turns to her, for confirmation of this)*
MARY:	Yes. I suppose it *could* be looked upon as unaesthetic.
BARRIE:	*(looking towards the house)* Jocelyn is on the telephone an unusually long time, Mary.
MARY:	Jim, love. You don't mind ... from time to time ... Us still trying? You do love children so much, dear.
BARRIE:	Yes. Quite, Mary ... Yes ...
MARY:	Not being at all anxious about what happens. But ... Just occasionally. Do you think we might try, Jim? *(as she is talking WINIFRED EMERY and her HUSBAND enter)*
BARRIE:	*(rising to meet them)* Mary. Winifred Emery is here.
MARY:	You wouldn't mind that terribly, would you, dear?
BARRIE:	*(going to WINIFRED)* Not at all, dear. Of course ... By all means.
	(BARRIE takes WINIFRED's hand, and guides her to a chair next to his)
BARRIE:	Miss Emery, how kind of you to come and beautify our garden! *(holding a chair for her)* You must sit here. Next to me.
JACK:	*(noticing the script on BARRIE's chair)* I say. You haven't started yet, have you, Mr. Barrie? Terribly sorry if we're late.
MARY:	Not at all, Mr. Emery. You are in very good time.
BARRIE:	*(taking Winifred's hand)* Miss Emery, I have been phrasing a confession. I have been wanting to make to you all week. May I make it? I shall! Without asking permission.
WINIFRED:	*(drawing BARRIE's attention to her HUSBAND)* You remember Jack, Mr. Barrie ... *(BARRIE looks blankly at JACK for a moment)* My husband.
BARRIE:	*(still not releasing Winifred's hand. With no great enthusiasm to JACK)* Yes ... Nice to see you again, Emery.
JACK:	We've been looking forward to the reading all week, Mr. Barrie. Winifred tells me it's all about a boy who never grew up, coming to Kensington.
BARRIE:	Kensington Gardens. Yes.
JACK:	Sounds fascinating.
BARRIE:	*(turning to WINIFRED. Quite dismissing JACK)* Your performance, Miss Emery. At the Opening Night! My wife – who is quite the most objective of authorities on the stage –

MARY:	I thought you were very, very good, Miss Emery. Quite delightful.
BARRIE:	*(not satisfied at this)* Miraculous, Mary. There is no other word to describe such a performance. You were Lady Babbie born! I kept saying to myself all evening – I absolutely adore that glorious girl!
JACK:	Very good of you to ask us, Mr. Barrie. It's a very great privilege indeed to be invited to a reading of a new play by J.M. Barrie.
MARY:	Shall we start, Jim?
BARRIE:	Jocelyn appears to be still on the telephone, Mary. *(turning to look into WINIFRED's eyes)* Such exquisite loveliness. The very essence of your sex.
JACK:	Glad you approve so highly of my wife's interpretation of your lines, Mr. Barrie.
BARRIE:	*(drawing WINIFRED's hand to him)* Sitting in the Theatre, Miss Emery. I will make a confession to you. I was not merely listening to your rendering of my words and drinking in your performance. I was quite making love to you!
JACK:	*(laughing it all off. About all he can do about it)* Clearly, I shall have to gaurd my wife from Mr. Barrie, Mrs. Barrie.
MARY:	*(with the merest hint of bitterness)* Yes, I understand Constables can be hired from Scotland Yard at so much the hour, Mr. Emery.
	(As she is speaking, SYLVIA DAVIES approaches, troubled)
BARRIE:	*(rising to greet her)* Ah ... Jocelyn ... It *was* Arthur, was it? He is on his way ... as I told you.
SYLVIA:	It was Arthur. But he is so disappointed, Jim. *(to MARY)* My husband sends his apologies to you, Mary. He was so looking forward to the reading, Jim! But his jaw is very painful this afternoon.
BARRIE:	I shall look in on him in the morning, Jocelyn. *(turning to introduce her to the EMERYS)* You know Winifred Emery and her husband? *(she smiles at them. They shake hands)* My very dearest of friends, Jocelyn Davies.
MARY:	*Sylvia*, Jim. You will confuse Mr. and Mrs. Emery.
BARRIE:	*(taking Sylvia's hand)* "Sylvia" to her husband and the world. But to me ... Jocelyn. Always Jocelyn. Most beautiful of mothers. *(to JACK)* There is some spiritual change, do you know, Emery? That is wrought on a woman who becomes a Mother. A certain softness of features. And sweetness. A look of understanding. One sees it on her face, now.
SYLVIA:	*(drawing her hand away)* Jim!
BARRIE:	Do you catch it, Emery? *(looking at SYLVIA)* Ah, at last I understand what this world is about!
JACK:	*(desperately trying to move the conversation into something safe)* I say! What a ripping lake. Have you a boat, Mr. Barrie? Can I volunteer to take the ladies on the lake, after the reading?
	(GILBERT CANNAN enters as he is speaking. Mary's manner changes immediately on his entrance. Her eyes glow. Her face softens. She goes to him, without thinking of the others watching her)
MARY:	Gilbert, you are very late. But we shall forgive you on this one occasion.

BARRIE:	*(taking Cannan's proffered hand)* Meant to drop you a line, Cannan, about the last play you were kind enough to let me see. Some very fine writing in it. Congratulations.
GILBERT:	*(his face lighting up)* I thought ... there were odd things in it. Thank you, Mr. Barrie.
MARY:	You know everyone here, don't you, Gilbert? Sylvia Davies. Mr. and Mrs. Emery.
GILBERT:	*(bowing to each in turn)* Yes. Of course.
WINIFRED:	You shall have to let me read some of your plays, Mr. Cannan.
BARRIE:	Now, Miss Emery. I warn you. I must have absolute faithfulness from my actresses!
GILBERT:	*(sitting beside MARY)* You need have no fear of my supplanting *you*, Mr. Barrie!
MARY:	Can we start then, Jim?
BARRIE:	*(taking up the script)* I thought I'd start with the scene in the Lagoon. *(taking up his script)* Hook is the Captain of the Pirate Band in Never-Never land. He is sitting on a rock with Smee, one of his band. I'll just read some random scenes from the play, to give some idea of the mood and the tone of the piece.
JACK:	I see. Splendid, Mr. Barrie.
BARRIE:	*(reading)* I want their Captain, Peter Pan. 'Twas he cut off my arm. I have waited long to shake his hand with this. *(flourishing his hook)* Pan flung my arm to a Crocodile that happened to be passing by. *(as BARRIE reads, SYLVIA moves back to her anxious expression)*

Scene Six A

SMEE:	I have often noticed your dread of Crocodiles.
HOOK:	Not Crocodiles. But of that one Crocodile. The brute liked my arm so much he has followed me ever since from sea to sea ... and from land to land. Licking his lips for the rest of me. Lucky chance he swallowed a clock, too. And it goes 'tick, 'tick' inside him. So before he can reach me, I can hear the tick and bolt. *(as he is speaking, a tick is clearly heard)*
HOOK	The Crocodile!
	(A huge Crocodile passes across the stage, ticking. The PIRATES run off in the opposite direction.
	BARRIE breaks off from his reading for a moment)
JACK:	I say. Did anyone hear a tick there?
GILBERT:	Thought I heard it, too. *(SYLVIA is growing more and more anxious)*
BARRIE:	Probably a Blackbird. Or a robin. Robins tend to make that kind of noise. *(there is a distinct 'tick' now. BARRIE leafs through his manuscript)* I thought I would go back now, to the Opening Scene.
SYLVIA:	*(rising)* Jim. I'm so enjoying the reading ... But you will have to excuse me. I'm uneasy about Arthur. I do think I should go back to him.

BARRIE: *(rising)* Yes. By all means, Jocelyn. Of course. I'll have the car brought round.

SYLVIA: The doctors are saying they may have to operate, Jim.

BARRIE: Jocelyn, dearest. He will be well again. I am sure of this.

SYLVIA: I'm so sorry, disturbing everyone like this.

MARY: Not at all, Sylvia. It's quite understandable.

SYLVIA: I'll just get my bag. I think I left it by the telephone.

MARY: I do hope Arthur will be well soon, Sylvia.

BARRIE: I'd better drive up with her, Mary. You will excuse me, Miss Emery ...

MARY: *(going after him)* Jim, dear. Before you go. I thought you'd like to know that Gilbert has very kindly offered to join me on holiday with the Cuthbertsons in Normandy in your place.

BARRIE: Very decent of him.

MARY: I realise it would be unfair to take you away from the Davies family at a time like this, Jim.

BARRIE: Very understanding of Gilbert. You're quite right. I would feel uneasy leaving them at such a time.

MARY: *(irritated, despite herself, at his tone)* We shan't be away more than three or four weeks. I'm sure you won't miss us, with your 'family', round you, Jim.

BARRIE: Mary, I have very strong reasons for not coming with you to Normandy.

MARY: *(watching him. Beginning to make the break from him)* I used to say, Jim, I loved you more than God. Do you remember?

BARRIE: Perhaps that is something one should never say.

MARY: But I *felt* it. What difference did it make saying it? God would know it was so, whether I said it or not. And I always used to thank Him ... For giving me you.

BARRIE: I think you should know, Mary, that Arthur is very seriously ill. Arthur has cancer.

GILBERT: *(approaching. Nervous)* Can I get the car for you, Mr. Barrie?

MARY: I thought he might have, Jim. That's dreadful luck.

BARRIE: If you could get Shields, thank you, Cannan.

             (GILBERT makes to go)

MARY: I'd better come with you. Our driver is one of these gentlemen who are impossible to find when they are needed!

             (They go off together; despite the need for discretion, their hands touch as they cross the lawn.

             BARRIE stands, looking into the trees, his mind travelling to Never-Never land where there is no cancer and no sexual responsibilities in marriage _ or in any activity in life)

BARRIE: *(to himself)* I did so want to catch a Mermaid ...

             (The thought is picked up by Peter Pan in Never-Never land as the LIGHTS FADE on the Garden and COME UP on the Lagoon and the next scene)

Scene Seven

The Mermaids' Lagoon.

WENDY and PETER are on a rock. WENDY crestfallen at her failure to catch a mermaid.

WENDY: I did so want to catch a Mermaid.

PETER: It is awfully difficult to catch a Mermaid. They are such cruel creatures, Wendy, that they try to pull boys and girls like you into the water and drown them.

            (BARRIE looks at PETER, scanning his face, as if there is some deeper meaning in this)

WENDY: How hateful!

            (A cold shiver comes over the water. The sun has gone. PETER knows that evil is creeping over the Lagoon, and a moment later the voice of HOOK is heard, calling SMEE and STARKEY, on a rock opposite PETER and WENDY)

HOOK: Boat ahoy!

SMEE: It is the Captain.

            (HOOK is swimming. They help him to scale the rock. He is in a gloomy mood)

HOOK: The game is up! The boys have found a Mother!

STARKEY: Oh, the evil day!

SMEE: What is a Mother?

WENDY: *(horrified)* He doesn't know!

HOOK: Dost not know, Smee? A Mother is –

            (he finds it more difficult to explain than he expected. He finds an illustration in a great bird which drifts past in a nest as large as the roomiest basin)

HOOK: There is a lesson in Mothers for you! The nest must have fallen in the water but would the bird desert her eggs?

            (HOOK ponders on this illustration for a moment ... The BOY gently approaches him and leads him into 1971 for an important international conference in the next scene)

BOY: Do you want to catch Peter Pan?

HOOK: *(flourishing his cutlass)* Pan! Where is he?

BOY: Then come down here!

            (HOOK leaves his Lagoon for Newcastle)

Scene Eight

The stage is blacked out, except for a SINGLE SPOT. An important conference of all the Commanders in the field is about to take place. As each GENERAL arrives, he announces himself in the SPOT.

GENERAL BULL:	Bull. United States Army.
HOOK:	Hook – Jolly Roger.
MOHAMMED HASSAN:	Mohammed Hassan – El Fatah.
HOOK:	Hook – Jolly Roger.
RISING SUN:	Rising Sun – Red Panthers.
MAO:	Mao – People's Republic of China.
HOOK:	Hook – Jolly Roger.
GENERAL PORNILOV:	Pornilov – Union of Soviet Socialist Republic.
ALL THE GENERALS:	*(to PORNILOV)* You're late.

(The LIGHTS COME UP and the Conference begins)

GENERAL
BULL: Gentlemen. We have called this truce to give us an opportunity of pooling all available information on the subversive activities of Pan to ensure and guarantee his ultimate defeat. I draw your attention to the Roman Catholic Cathedral behind us, and remind you that we have chosen this Holy ground as a suitable neutral Meeting Place for this Conference.

PORNILOV: We have intercepted messages from space, showing Pan is in a rocket with the child, Emily, on a reflectory trajectory which will bounce her off the moon and back to earth at a point called the Park of Elswick.

BULL: Check! Minor correction, General Pornilov, – Elswick Park.

PORNILOV: That is correct. The Park of Elswick, Newcastle-on-Tyne.

HOOK: The Jolly Roger can go anywhere in the world. There is not a sea in the world she can't sail. But she's not built to go to the moon.

RISING SUN: The plan, White Brothers, is simple. We move to the Park of Elswick and await the return of Pan and the child.

MAO: No, Comrade. The Americans are in possession of vital information – namely, why Pan has come to the child, Emily. They are consequently in a position of advantage over the rest of us. We have General Bull here. He is one. We are five. The tactic clearly is to extract the missing information from the respected General.

BULL: *(looking round for some means of escape)* General Mao ... Believe me. By my Army Bible. By that Cross on the Cathedral, General. I have no such information. I am acting only under the orders of the Central Intelligence Agency. The Central Intelligence Agency alone knows the reason for Pan's interest in the child, Emily.

MOHAMMED
HASSAN: *(drawing a rather nasty dagger)* But if you were, how shall I say, "persuaded", General, might you not find this valuable information is hidden deep in your heart, after all?

                         (The FIVE GENERALS advance on BULL)

BULL: Gentlemen! Gentlemen! We are all civilised soldiers! This is Holy, Consecrated ground, Gentlemen. I swear ... Only the C.I.A. have this information.

PORNILOV: And Pan.

HOOK: Listen to me, me hearties. While we're argy-bargying Pan is on his way back to the Earth.
                        (They all look up ... and in fact catch the sight of the rocket on its return journey to Elswick Park)

BULL: Pan is moving into earth orbit now.

HOOK: We all know Pan. If Pan is after Emily, he's after her for good reason. And that's good enough for me. I say – Forward me hearties, to Elswick Park ... and give him and his party hearty welcome when they land!

RISING SUN: *(expressing the strongest approval in his vocabularly)* Ugh!

HOOK: **Then, forward me hearties! And may the best man win!**

                        (The GENERALS break up and go to their respective radios to call their respective headquarters)

PORNILOV: Prince Igor here! Scramble! No evidence Americans have found lost childhood yet. Present flight, trial flight, to follow Pan's descent to Earth. Lost childhood in lost half of pie. Mission now almost certain success. Aim to capture pie and be first Nation to put Childhood on the Moon almost accomplished.

MAO: Li Tai Po ... Scramble! Russians plotting to be first country to put Child on Moon. Aim now clearly to punish Russians for their revisionist action in engaging in bourgeoise sporting competition with Fascist Yankees. Childhood to be captured and kept on the Earth.

MOHAMMED
HASSAN: Omar Khayam here. Scramble! Chinese attempting to spite Russians by preventing them from being first nation to land Childhood on Moon. Aim to assist Russians in return for one hundred MIG fighters and twenty-five ground-to-air missiles for war against Zionist Imperialism.

                        (The GENERALS go off to further their respective plots)

Scene Nine

The LIGHTS COME UP on Leazes Park ... and PETER PAN and EMILY.

Leazes Park. The Pond. PETER PAN and the CHILDREN have just splashed down. SINDY has had a slight accident and has been soaked climbing out of the space capsule. She is wringing out her dress, almost in tears. PETER PAN has gone off to look for Elswick Park.

SINDY: This'll never be the same again! Look at it! It's absolutely ruined!

ACTION MAN: *(setting up his equipment)* A splash-down's a splash-down, Sindy.

SINDY:	Don't speak to me! Certainly *never* use my first name!
EMILY:	The whole thing was just a stupid waste of time.
CHILD:	We saw the Moon, Em.
CHILD:	I'm a bit dizzy ...
SINDY:	Look at my hair!
BARBI:	How shall I wear my hair?
SINDY:	*(stamping her feet)* Shut your stupid face!
EMILY:	Anybody knows there's no proper pond in Elswick Park. I mean ... Look ... Here we are ... Back to where we started.
ACTION MAN:	It was a natural mistake. I assumed every Park would have a pond. Nobody's saying anything about the fantastic achievement of manually steering the capsule from total devastation in Elswick Park to a safe splash down here!
EMILY:	If Peter Pan can just fly around looking for Elswick Park – why can't he just pick up the pie and bring it back here. Instead of all that stupid bother ...
CHILD:	Why couldn't he have, Elmer?
ACTION MAN:	Sorry. Can't answer that. Classified.
EMILY:	I wish you'd stop talking to these toys. It gets on my nerves.
SINDY:	Personally, I don't see what Peter sees in her. She's nothing but an extremely disagreeable, boring, dull, illiterate child!
ACTION MAN:	She's not a child, Si – *(SINDY warns him not to use her name with a savage look)* Miss ... That is the point of the exercise.
SINDY:	I did not address you.
ACTION MAN:	The point of this exercise is that Emily is eleven years of age and she is not a child.
SINDY:	I shudder to think what her I.Q. might be!
EMILY:	He'd no answer, had he, when I said to him we'd wasted our time going to the Moon.
SINDY:	*(to CHILD)* Tell the stupid bitch, will you. He needed some Moon-dust. To find her stupid childhood.
CHILD:	He needed the Moon-dust, Em, to find your childhood.
EMILY:	That was just made up. To kid everybody we hadn't been wasting our time. I didn't see him taking any Moon-dust.
CHILD:	I think I did, Em.
ACTION MAN:	Personally, I'm inclined to side with Emily on this point. I can't see any real scientific basis for –
SINDY:	You being too clever and knowing just about everything about everything there is to know!
ACTION MAN:	It's only the bottom of your dress.
SINDY:	And my nylons – and my shoes – and my hair ...
BARBI:	How shall I wear my hair?
SINDY:	Under your stupid knickers!
CHILD:	*(pointing)* Look! There's Peter now ... Over the trees ...

EMILY:	It's an owl.
CHILD:	It isn't … It's him – Peter! Peter!
ACTION MAN:	Order in the ranks! Complete silence during take-offs and landing … Pan … Pan … Control here. You're looking good. Forty-three point four feet height …
PETER:	*(coming down and ignoring Elmer's science)* I've found the right Park.
EMILY:	With swings and a green hut for the tennis and the bowling greens?
PETER:	And the House with pigeons and rabbits and a goat … The goat couldn't sleep …
ACTION MAN:	Map References, please …
SINDY:	Oh, shut up! Peter! Look at my dress.
PETER:	Oh, poor Sindy.
EMILY:	You found the pie?
PETER:	Yes, but I can't move it from the bench. Only you can move it, Emily. *(to SINDY)* I'll brush your dress with some Moon-dust, Sindy … *(he brushes some moon-dust on Sindy's dress)*
SINDY:	Oh, that's lovely. It's dry … and warm … and clean … and everything. Thank you, Peter. You're so … nice and considerate. Not like some people! *(looking at ELMER)*
PETER:	Come and I'll show you the pie, Emily. We'll climb right to the top of that high tower over there.
EMILY:	That block of offices.
PETER:	It's a Giant's Tower.
ACTION MAN:	How do we get up there, Pan? Jump? …. *(taking a running jump)*
PETER:	We just fly up. It's easy.
ACTION MAN:	Oh, yeah … Great! We fly … I should've thought of that myself … Yeah … We fly … Flap your wings everybody and fly!
PETER:	Everybody hold hands … Very tightly … Look straight in front of you … Close your eyes.
ACTION MAN:	How do you look straight in front of you with your eyes closed?
SINDY:	Oh, do shut up, Elmer!
PETER:	Ready …
ACTION MAN:	Count down … Ten … Nine … Eight …
PETER:	Four … Two … One …
EMILY:	We're not flying.
PETER:	That means somebody doesn't believe we can fly. Who is it? *(looking down the ranks)* One of us doesn't believe we can fly. *(ACTION MAN looks away, guiltily)* Elmer … Two paces forward. About turn.
	(PETER takes the others, holds hands … and they fly off … leaving the unbelieving ELMER on the ground)
ELMER:	Hey! Wait for me!

Scene Ten

HOOK is sitting on a rock with SMEE.

HOOK: I want their Captain, Peter Pan. 'Twas he cut off my arm. I have waited long to shake his hand with this. *(flourishing his hook)* Oh, I'll tear him! Pan flung my arm to a Crocodile that happened to be passing by ...

SMEE: I have often noticed your dread of Crocodiles.

HOOK: Not Crocodiles – but of that one Crocodile. The brute liked my arm so much, he has followed me ever since from sea to sea and from land to land. Licking his lips for the rest of me. Lucky chance he swallowed a clock, too. And it goes 'Tick', 'Tick', 'Tick', inside him. So before he can reach me, I can hear the tick and bolt ...

(As he is speaking a 'tick' is clearly heard and the LIGHTS COME UP on the Black Cottage ... Arthur's coffin is being carried out, watched by BARRIE and SYLVIA)

The Crocodile!

(A huge crocodile passes across the stage, ticking. The PIRATES run off in the opposite direction and the sound comes up on the Black Cottage and BARRIE and SYLVIA)

BARRIE: *(watching the coffin being carried out)* Forty-four, dearest Jocelyn ... In his prime!

SYLVIA: Before he went, Jim ... He said of you: "Of one thing I am certain, J.M. Barrie is the best friend in the world. He will always be ready to advise and help out of his great love for my dear family." His last words, Jim ...

BARRIE: I am signing the Lease for Camden Hill House in the morning. You are sure it is suitable and it pleases you, dearest?

SYLVIA: Jim, dear ... It is beautiful ... Such lovely, sunny rooms for the children.

BARRIE: Ah ... a Mother, dearest ... My mother would have admired you very, very much, Jocelyn.

SYLVIA: And I her, I am sure, Jim.

BARRIE: In times like these, how one longs for one's Mother. When you looked into my Mother's eyes, Jocelyn ... You knew, as if God had told you with His own voice, why He had sent her into the world ...

SYLVIA: Dear Jim. There are no words I can say to tell you how much I appreciate your taking this beautiful house for us. But to take on the entire financial responsibility for me and the children, Jim ...

BARRIE: Jocelyn, I tell you – I made £44,000 this year. And will make something like that the next ... and no doubt the next ... god sent my Mother, Jocelyn, to open the minds of all who looked to beautiful thoughts. Do you see my meaning, dearest? I still see those beautiful, loving eyes ...They have been my guide all my life. God grant they may remain my only earthly judge to the last, dearest.

SYLVIA: Arthur was so brave, Jim.

BARRIE: To the last, Jocelyn ... At the very beginning, when Roughton told him no further operation was possible, He said to me: "Whatever is in store for me, I hope I shall bear it as befits the son of a brave and wise man." And this hope he fulfilled. To very utmost! George, of course, will stay on at Eton.

SYLVIA:	Jim, if this was possible ...
BARRIE:	And Peter at Berkhampstead ... Jack, of course, will go on to Osborne.
SYLVIA:	Oh, I do hope he will get his Entrance, Jim.
BARRIE:	For the summer, dearest, I'm taking a Lodge in the highlands. Splendid fishing, I'm told.

(As he is speaking, HUNT, the Gardener, has approached and stands, respectfully, at a distance, waiting to attract BARRIE's attention. BARRIE at last sees him)

	Yes, Hunt?
HUNT:	If I might have a word with you, Sir, in private ...

(BARRIE moves aside to talk to HUNT. SYLVIA walks into the house)

	It's Mrs. Barrie, Sir. She's complaining about the way I prune the floribundae ... Grabbed the secateurs off me, Sir, and wouldn't let me get on with my work. As you know, Sir, that's why you took me on. I've specialised in roses. People all over the country come to me for hints on roses ...
BARRIE:	Hunt, this is *Mrs.* Barrie's province. You know this very well, Hunt. The garden is her province.
HUNT:	What I'm saying is, Sir, as if she's any room to talk, the way she's carrying on, if you'll excuse me, Sir ...
BARRIE:	Hunt! I don't follow your drift, man.
HUNT:	We kept back telling you about this, Sir ... Not wanting to make any trouble ... But I felt it my duty ... And Mrs. Hunt felt it her duty, Sir. Mrs. Hunt especially, Mr. Barrie. She's caught them at it time and time again ...

(BARRIE is still waiting for some articulate statement from HUNT)

	Mrs. Barrie and Mr. Cannan, Sir.
BARRIE:	Mrs. Barrie and Mr. Cannan, Hunt. Yes ...?
HUNT:	In the house and in the garden, Sir. Carrying on ... Embracing!
BARRIE:	Hunt, I beg your pardon!
HUNT:	Mrs. Barrie and Mr. Cannan, Sir ... Embracing and kissing and carrying on. Mrs. Hunt's caught them at it two or three times.
BARRIE:	*(trying to react correctly to this)* I see ... I see ... *(decides on the calm investigator)* I see, Hunt. Mrs. Barrie and Mr. Cannan ...
HUNT:	We didn't know what to do ... Not wanting to make any trouble ... At the same time, we thought it wasn't right. Keeping a thing like that from you, Sir ...
BARRIE:	*(calm. Lawyer now. In control)* Yes, Hunt. I quite see your position. Very good of you to tell me. Thank you. I appreciate your loyalty.
HUNT:	You've always been very good to us, Sir. We have nothing personal against Mrs. Barrie.
BARRIE:	Quite, Hunt ... Would you be so kind as to telephone the Station and enquire when the next train leaves for London.

(HUNT goes off. BARRIE is left on his own. He paces the garden. Struggling to make some order out of the chaos of his feelings. He looks round. Up at the trees)

How still the night is ...

(And as he speaks the LIGHTS COME UP on the Bridge of the Jolly Roger. HOOK simultaneously speaks the lines with BARRIE ... HOOK communing, as BARRIE will write in his script, with his ego)

Nothing sounds alive. Now is the hour when children in their homes are a-bed, their lips browned with the good night chocolate.

(BARRIE goes into the house ... The LIGHTS DIM in the Garden ... HOOK is left on his own)

And their tongues drowsily searching for belated crumbs housed insecurely on their shining cheeks.

Barrie has gone to his mahogany desk to write more lines for me, curse him! And he is cursed! His wife playing around with young Cannan. Saddled with the responsibility of a mother and five children. With no hope of any reward from life except chunks out of his Bank balance every year till they grow up. Good! Splendid! 'Tis my hour of triumph!

... and yet some dusky spirit compels me to make my dying speech, lest, when dying, there be no time for it. All mortals envy me, yet better perhaps for Hook to have less ambition! Oh, fame, oh, fame ... Thou glittering bauble ... Thou –

(But he breaks off immediately ... There is an ominous tick ... and HOOK has only just time to run for his life as the crocodile crosses the stage again in his unceasing quest for HOOK. The boy takes the curtains ... As soon as the stage is safe again and the crocodile out of sight, and pulls them close for the End of Act One)

ACT TWO

Scene Eleven

Elswick Park. The swing park.

PETER is stage-managing everybody for the Pie Scene ...

PETER: Everybody go on the swings. Emily – you sit on the bench where you lost your pie!

EMILY: *(going to bench)* Look! There it is, there! It's me pie!

ACTION MAN: I still maintain that was a highly inadvisable manoeuvre, Pan!

EMILY: What about the boy that knocked it off?

PETER: He'll be there ...

EMILY: *(eating the pie with lust)* Hey, it's great!

ACTION MAN: With the considerable ground forces employed against us it was a highly irresponsible action ... I will have no alternative –

SINDY: Will you drop dead, man!

                (EMILY continues enjoying her pie. The CHILDREN swing)

ELMER: I am sorry, Miss. It would be just as irresponsible on my part not to report this action to H.Q. There are certain subversive elements in Pan's actions that I am not entirely –

                (But we never find out what entirely ACTION MAN is saying as, while he is speaking, one of the children falls from his swing)

CHILD: Em! Em! Em!

                (Bawling. EMILY rushes to him. The pie is left on the seat. A BOY quickly runs up to take it, but this time PETER has his hand firmly on it. The boy retreats, foiled.

                EMILY returns to finish the pie)

SINDY: *(going up to her)* Well?

                (EMILY still can't hear her)

PETER: She's finished it ... and she still can't hear you.

SINDY: Can you hear me?

PETER: *(looking into her eye pocket)* Still not there ...

SINDY: Can you hear me, girl?

EMILY: Stop it, Betty! Dangling that stupid doll in front of me eyes!

SINDY: Really, man! Is she worth bothering about?

ACTION MAN: Your dress is fine, now Sindy ... I don't see why you should still be nasty to me ...

EMILY: Is it not there? Maybe it might take a bit of time ...

PETER: No ... It should work right away.

ACTION MAN: You and me, Sindy. We've always had this great scene together ... I mean ... All right ... Your dress got wet ...

SINDY: One of those things, son. You go off people ...

BARBI:	Shall I put a record on?
EMILY:	The pie was smashing. Smashing pie, Peter. *(trying to comfort him. And he needs it. He looks absolutely dejected at that moment ... but quite suddenly he brightens up)*
PETER:	It was Sindy's idea. *I* never said it was the pie, did I? I said it probably wasn't the pie ...
SINDY:	It was Em's idea, man. She kept going on and on about how marvellous and fantastic her stinking old pie was.
BARBI:	Shall I put a record on?
SINDY:	Yeah ... On your head!
ACTION MAN:	*(at radio)* Intercepted Russkie radio message. For Chrissake, man! The Russkies have developed a new electronic Childhood Detector ... Man! That's something even we haven't got yet! They're homing in on her Childhood right now ...
PETER:	Where?
ACTION MAN:	*(listening)* Scotswood Road. They're reporting positive signals from Scotswood Road.
PETER:	Emily – Have you ever been in Scotswood Road?
EMILY:	We go walks along Scotswood Road, down to the Tyne.
CHILD:	You can see the river, when you're walking along it.
PETER:	Quick. We must get to Scotswood Road.
EMILY:	How we going to get to Scotswood Road, man? It's miles away.
ACTION MAN:	Checked with Central Computer, Washington. Late night bus passing Leazes Park along Scotswood Road in three hours ... If we hurry ... We can just catch it ...
PETER:	*(taking Emily's hand, and pulling her)* Hurry up, everybody! We've got to catch a bus!
	(... as they run to catch it, a thought occurs to him ...)
	What's a bus?
	(The LIGHTS DIM on 1971 and COME UP on 1904 and the next scene)

Scene Twelve

Barrie's house in London.

A dramatic confrontation between BARRIE and his WIFE.

BARRIE:	I am not concerned with the sources of my information, Mary. My concern is whether these charges laid against you are true. This is my only concern, Mary.
MARY:	They are quite true, Jim. Absolutely true. *(BARRIE covers his face with his hands)* I'm sorry, Jim ... You see ... In my mind ... It seemed that you knew already about my feelings for Gilbert. And for reasons known to yourself ... chose not to notice them ...
BARRIE:	*(taking her hands ... which she allows him)* I love you, Mary. You are my wife. Before Man and God, Mary ... We are husband and wife!

MARY:	I see, now, Jim, this was an excuse to myself ... For lacking the courage to tell you openly, Jim ... Jim, you can see ... I'm so sorry ... I wish it had never happened ... like this ... I love Gilbert ... Gilbert loves me ...
BARRIE:	*(breaking down)* Mary ... I love you ...
MARY:	Jim, do try to be calm.
BARRIE:	Cannan's a boy, Mary. Twenty ... You are forty!
MARY:	We must have a Divorce, Jim. This is the easiest and least painful thing for all of us.
BARRIE:	Quite out of the question! *(dismissing it out of hand)*
MARY:	I am very sorry, Jim. I do blame myself entirely for what has happened.
BARRIE:	Rule this entirely out of you mind, Mary. A Divorce is absolutely out of the question. I will not have it!
MARY:	It's quite early, Jim. If we were to ring Lewis, now, we could both go over to his Office and the preliminaries could be started immediately ...
BARRIE:	Mary ... Do you know how much I need you. My whole life ... All my work ... It all rests on the foundation of you and I.
MARY:	Jim, you will have to accept this. It will spare you a great deal of pain, if you understand this. I am not to be turned from a Divorce. Gilbert and I wish to be married as soon as possible.
BARRIE:	Please, Mary ... Don't say that ... Please ... 'Gilbert and I'.
MARY:	I want this so much, Jim. I will force it on you.
BARRIE:	Mary. I promise you. I will close my eyes to everything that has happened in the past.
MARY:	One can only go loving in the wind so long, Jim ...
BARRIE:	Everything that has happened between you and Cannan. You understand me, Mary? I obliterate it. From this moment. From my mind, love.
MARY:	Nothing you can say, Jim, can turn me from a Divorce. If you accept this, Jim, it will be so much easier for you ...
BARRIE:	On your part, you must promise to obliterate all memories and thoughts of Cannan. In your heart of hearts, Mary ... I know ... We love each other ... Despite all our difficulties ... We have been together fifteen years, love ... Growing together ... Loving each other ... This Cannan thing. I understand. These things do happen ...
MARY:	Jim, if you are not going to be calm about this ...
BARRIE:	*(almost crying ... taking her hands)* Mary ... Don't leave me ... Please, Mary ... For God's sake ... Don't leave me, Mary ...
MARY:	I am sorry, Jim. I am very, very sorry, Jim ...
BARRIE:	It's not possible, Mary ... You cannot leave me ...
MARY:	I have been Gilbert's mistress, Jim. Do you not understand this. Many, many times. We are pledged to marry one another ...
BARRIE:	I tell you, obliterate this. Put it from your memory ... You know, Mary ... The depths of my love for you ... *(MARY is rising ... putting on her gloves to go)* I know, dearest ... In my heart ... *(he takes her hands. Pulling at her to stay)* You will never leave me. We are man and wife, Mary ... Before God ... We love each other ... I know this ...

MARY: *(gently slipping from his grasp)* Goodbye, dear Jim ...

BARRIE: *(crying now)* Mary ... Don't leave me ... I have this Academy Dinner, this evening. You know the trouble I have putting on all the Ceremonial Livery without your help ... Look at me ... I'm only half ready ... The tie, Mary ... *(but MARY has gone. There is the sound of great applause ... Shouts of 'Author', 'Author', 'Author' ...)*

Scene Twelve A

BARRIE: Ladies and Gentlemen, the Author, unfortunately, is not in the House. But I know he would be gratified and honoured at the reception you have accorded his latest work of genius. On behalf of Mr. Barrie, Ladies and Gentlemen, I thank you. Thank you very much ...

(BARRIE continues to dress for the Academy Dinner. As he puts on each item of clothes, so he takes on a role that will allow him to endure the disaster that has overtaken him)

Tonight is the Academy Dinner. You may conceive I have been hard at work inking my coat sleeves. I feel sure a philosopher could deduce all sorts of profundities from a study of an Academy Dinner. In all the world there cannot be a much more solemnly dull festivity. No one would like it so well if it were less dull. The day the President makes a joke or the Japanese Ambassador smiles, it will begin to go down in public estimation. It is the rigid etiquette we are so proud of. For the time being, we all feel ourselves as important as the red-coated footmen at the Carlton. Once a year we feel we have calves. That must be it!

(BARRIE is roused out of his dark thoughts by a shout from the boys. The LIGHTS COME UP to show BARRIE on board the Jolly Roger)

JACK: *(from the yardarm)* Pirates ahoy, Cap'n!

BARRIE: Look there?

JOHN: Hook leading the band, Cap'n!

GEORGE: Indians coming up in the rear, Cap'n!

(BARRIE sits for a moment, without speaking ... Overtaken by new images ... and he begins to create the last scene of Peter Pan. The LIGHTS COME UP in the Darlings' Nursery. JOHN and MICHAEL and WENDY climb through the window into the room. The youngest is in a daze but the other two are shining virtuously like holy people who are about to give two other people a treat)

Scene Thirteen

MICHAEL: *(looking about him)* I think I have been here before.

JOHN: It's your home, you stupid!

WENDY: There is your old bed, Michael.

MICHAEL: I had nearly forgotten.

WENDY:	Look! It's father!
MICHAEL:	Let me see Father. *(disappointed)* He is not as big as the Pirate I killed.
JOHN:	*(chilled)* It is very careless of Mother not to be here when we come back. *(the piano is heard)*
WENDY:	Hush! *(she goes to the door and peeps)* That is her playing. *(they all have a peep)*
MICHAEL:	Who is that lady?
JOHN:	Hush! It's mother. Let us creep in and put our hands over her eyes.
WENDY:	*(more considerate)* No. Let us break it to her gently.

(She slips between the sheets in her bed. The others follow. The music stops and MRS. DARLING enters. She sees the three bumps in the beds but she does not believe she sees them)

MRS. DARLING:	I see them in their beds so often in my dreams that I seem to see them when I am awake! I'll not look again. *(she sits down and turns her face away from the bumps)* So often their silver voices call me, my little children whom I'll see no more!
WENDY:	*(perhaps rather silvery)* Mother!
MRS. DARLING:	That is Wendy.
JOHN:	Mother!
MRS. DARLING:	Now it is John.
MICHAEL:	Mother!
MRS. DARLING:	Now, Michael ... and when they call I stretch out my arms to them, but they never come, they never come!

(This time, however they come and there is joy once more in the Darling household. She takes them all in her arms ... kissing them in turn ... kissing and kissing them ...

... And she is still kissing them and embracing them as the LIGHTS DIM and the scene moves to Newcastle and 1971)

Scene Fourteen

Two or three bus stops from Scotswood Road flats.

ACTION MAN enters, supported by PAN. Round his neck is a road-sign "Low Bridge" — "Low Headroom." He collapses on the ground.

ACTION MAN:	Pan ... I don't feel so good. I feel very bad. What happened, Pan?
PETER:	I was riding on the top of the bus.
ACTION MAN:	That's right ... You were riding on the roof of the bus ...
PETER:	And you came climbing up after me. Right up the side of the bus. That was jolly clever, Elmer.

ACTION MAN:	Suction pads, Pan. Easy ... I had to come after you. What do you think you were doing, Pan, jumping up and down on the roof of a bus, riding into a battle zone ...
PETER:	Then we came to that low bridge. *(ACTION MAN holds up the sign)* I jumped right over – and you ...
ACTION MAN:	I fell off. These British bridges, Pan. Small people – small bridges!
PETER:	I say, do you think you've broken any bones, Elmer? I could try and find a splint for you ...
ACTION MAN:	I don't feel so good, Pan. If you could sing something. Yeah ... The American National Anthem.
PETER:	I don't know it. I'm sorry.
ACTION MAN:	You don't know the American National Anthem?
	(He begins to hum it. Gradually the Anthem works its magic on him. He rises to his feet. He begins to march up and down. PETER joins in the tune and the march)
ACTION MAN:	Right ... You're looking great. You're looking great!! Left, Right. Left, Right ... *(but as they are marching, PETER becomes aware of a shadow on the road)*
PETER:	Elmer ... It's a shadow. With a Hook!
ACTION MAN:	*(studying)* Moving in an anti-clockwise direction round the building.
PETER:	It's Hook. *(moving stealthily after him)*
	(ACTION MAN consults his radio for the file on Hook. At last HOOK and PAN confront one another)
HOOK:	*(flourishing his hook)* Brimstone and gall! Pan!
PETER:	Hook!
HOOK:	Pan!
	(But ELMER has his file on HOOK, now. He steps between them and confronts HOOK)
ELMER:	Captain Frederick Cyril Hook of "The Jolly Roger"?
HOOK:	That is my name and rank and ship, Sir.
ACTION MAN:	Captain Frederick Cyril Hook, in the name of the people of the United States of America, I do solemnly arrest you on the charge of subversive activities in the Pacific Sea. Item: That you did openly persecute a band of Red Indians as part of a Communist plot to alienate the Asian and African blocs from the Free World. Item: That you did steal twenty-four crates of Coca-Cola from the U.S. Frigate, George Washington, while that ship was in service in the South Pacific Seas.
HOOK:	Insolent dog! The crates of these beverages were washed up on the beach ...Take back that charge instantly, or answer for it with your life ... I challenge you to a duel!
PETER:	I say ... It's not fair! He's mine. It's not fair! I've been chasing and chasing him ...
ACTION MAN:	In the name of the people of the United States of America I accept. Back to back ... Ten paces forward ... *(they go through the ritual of a duel)*
PETER:	*(jumping up and down in his fury)* It's not fair! It's not fair!

HOOK:	*(counting)* One ... Two ... Three ... etc.
PETER:	If you fight Action Man, Hook, I'll never speak to you again! I jolly well warn you!
HOOK:	Ready!
	(They turn to face each other and raise their right hand, realising at the same time they have no weapons)
PETER:	That's just stupid! You haven't got any real weapons to fight a proper duel anyway. I'm going off to find a sword or some weapon ... Then I'm coming back to really fight you, Hook ...
ACTION MAN:	*(desperately looking for some kind of action to show HOOK he knows exactly what he is doing)* Right ...
HOOK:	Right!
ACTION MAN:	Escalation!
HOOK:	Escalation!
ACTION MAN:	First thing Noives!
HOOK:	Noives? *(this is too much. What's he letting himself in for?)*
ACTION MAN:	Noives. Do you know what a 'noive' is?
HOOK:	Of course I know what a knoiv is ... It's a long, sharp instrument with a point at the end ...
ACTION MAN:	*(demonstrating with a poke in Hook's ribs)* That's a noive.
HOOK:	Oh, that kind of noive! Why didn't you say so in the first place. Right ...
ACTION MAN:	Right ... Me first ...
	(Taking a careful aim and poking him in the chest. HOOK staggers back crying in agony. The great battle continues for some time. Then ACTION MAN, feeling he might be losing at noives, breaks away)
ACTION MAN:	Right! Next stage in escalation.
HOOK:	Next stage in escalation.
ACTION MAN:	Jokes.
HOOK:	Jokes!
ACTION MAN:	*(throwing it at HOOK as if it was some missile)* What did one wall say to the other wall?
HOOK:	I don't know. What did one wall say to the other wall?
ACTION MAN:	Meet me at the corner!
	(HOOK staggers at the impact of this, as well he might, clutching his heart. ACTION MAN roars with laughter at his torment)
HOOK:	*(when he has recovered)* Right. My turn. Why does a Stork stand on one foot?
ACTION MAN:	I don't know. Why does a Stork stand on one foot?
HOOK:	Because if he lifted the other one he'd fall down.
	(ACTION MAN staggers. This is dynamite. He clutches his chest but with a great effort recovers)
ACTION MAN:	Right ... Right ... How do you make a Maltese Cross?
HOOK:	Stamp on his feet.
ACTION MAN:	That's not fair.

(The joke duel goes on for a few more jokes until HOOK comes out with his winner)

HOOK: Why did the one-armed man cross the road?

ACTION MAN: *(giving up)* I don't know. I don't know. Why did the one-armed man cross the road?

HOOK: *(hammering home this one)* To get to the second-hand shop!

(This is the coup de grâce. ACTION MAN staggers. Utterly defeated. He falls on to the ground. HOOK pounces on him ... lifting his hook for the final blow)

ACTION MAN: Finish it quick, man. And send my Crucifix home to my Mother.

(HOOK attempts once again to strike ACTION MAN with his hook and fails)

I'll close my eyes ...

HOOK: *(giving it up)* I can't do it! I can't do it! Brimstone and gall!

ACTION MAN: *(sitting up)* You can't kill me, Hook?

HOOK: *(a broken man)* I can't do it. I've never killed anybody in my life. I can't do it. I can't bring myself to make the first incision with my hook into your skin.

ACTION MAN: *(with genuine concern)* Hook, man ... You've gotta problem, baby ... You gotta big personality problem. Jesus, man!

HOOK: *(with hope)* Have you come across anything like this before?

ACTION MAN: You just lie down there, Hook. Relax ... I think I can help you.

HOOK: My career is in ashes! All my life I have prided myself in my inexhaustible fund of evil and violence. I have lain in bed at night, devising horrible ends for Pan and his companions.

ACTION MAN: *(clamping an electrode on to Hook's hook)* Relax, baby ... I'm linking you with the Psychiatric Computer in the Pentagon.

HOOK: Thank you very much. This is very kind of you. Very decent of you ...
(The computer flashes ... and bumps ... and bleeps ... HOOK goes into a trance. Suddenly ... He breaks into song in a Scots accent)
By yon bonnie banks and by yon bonnie braes,
Where the sun shines bright on Loch Lomond.
Where me and my true love will never meet again,
On the bonny, bonny, banks of Loch Lomond.
(ACTION MAN switches off the computer. Removes the electrode. Snaps his fingers at HOOK and brings him out of his trance)

ACTION MAN: All right, Hook. Relax ...

HOOK: *(sitting up)* Is there hope?

ACTION MAN: Yeah ... Simple case here ...

HOOK: I thought I heard a voice ... Singing.

ACTION MAN: You got a simple superimposed personality case, Hook. You got some early Twentieth Century puritanical Scottish personality with a strong subconscious streak of violence superimposed on you.

HOOK: Barrie! I knew the villain would be the death of me!

ACTION MAN: You don't want to kill Pan.

HOOK:	I don't want to kill Pan. I love Pan ...
ACTION MAN:	You don't want to kill little children.
HOOK:	I don't want to kill little children. I love children.
ACTION MAN:	You love children.
HOOK:	I love you. I love the world. This is a beautiful world. I love children. Suffer little children to come unto Me.
ACTION MAN:	Yeah ... Great scene!
HOOK:	Do you know how I see myself? I see myself with my comrades on the Jolly Roger ... Anchored in some pleasant haven ... Perhaps the Thames.
ACTION MAN:	The Thames!
HOOK:	Coloured lights in the riggings. A White Star in the Yardarm. Surrounded by happy, smiling children ...
ACTION MAN:	You want children all round you?
HOOK:	I love children. Suffer little children to come unto Me.
ACTION MAN:	I'll give you an introduction .. You don't want to bum around a sewer like the Thames. You know the Atlantic ...
HOOK:	Like the back of my hook!
ACTION MAN:	You go right across the Atlantic. Give this card to the President of the United States. You anchor in Long Island, New York. With an attraction like a Pirate Ship and a Pirate Captain ... and a crew of Pirate chicks ... you'll gross a billion dollars a year, Hook.
HOOK:	*(shaking ACTION MAN's hand)* Thank you, Colonel. I will return to my ship immediately and chart a course across the wine dark sea. *(But as he is going PAN returns with an iron railing. He rushes at HOOK)*
PETER:	Hook! I have you at last.
HOOK:	Forgive me, Pan, my boy. You see before you a liberated man. I have triumphed over the dastardly machinations of Barrie at last and found my true self.
PETER:	Hook ... I say ... You're not ill, are you?
HOOK:	*(going)* Farewell and God bless you, Pan!
PETER:	*(to ACTION MAN)* What have you done to him? It's not fair. He's a nasty, horrible wicked Pirate. He is ... isn't he wicked ...
ACTION MAN:	That's the scene, baby, today ... He's not bad ... He's not good ...
PETER:	He is! He's bad. He's horrible ...
ACTION MAN:	Today, baby ... No bad guys ... No good guys ... All just screwed up, twisted, bent bastards!
PETER:	*(stamping his feet)* It's not fair! It's not fair! I've nobody left to fight now!
ACTION MAN:	You've got the Russkies ... The chinos ... The V.C.'s ... The Black Panthers. The Vociferous Minority ... Man – you've got plenty to fight ... Let's go, man ... *(They go out ... The LIGHTS COME UP on Scotswood Road, and the next scene)*

Scene Fifteen

Scotswood Road.

The GENERALS have all taken up key positions surrounding a huge, forty-storey block. PORNILOV and MOHAMMED HASSAN are both preparing to blow up the block under which Emily's lost childhood is buried ... GENERAL BULL is on the radio to the President of the U.S. clearly, he is a broken man.

BULL: Yes, Sir. Immediately, Mr. President. We will prepare to withdraw all forces. Just as a point of information, Mr. President ... I would like to say, we were not beaten by Russian soldiers. But by Russian technocracy ... No, Sir, I am not making any criticism of the absolute superiority of American Technology, Sir ... Not at all, Sir . . . Yes, Mr. President . . . I am prepared to answer any charges directed at me at a Senate Investigations. All I am saying, Mr. President, is that the Russians have this device for detecting Childhood. Yes, Mr. President ... Only ... It does seem unfair to blame me for not possessing the advanced instrumentation Russian technocracy has given the Russian Army ... No, Sir ... I would not like that remark to be put on record. Very kind of you, Mr. President ... Yes, Sir. Right away, Mr. President. *(he turns to give the command to his troops)* All forces to withdraw and return to base. Immediately!

(PORNILOV interrupted by the 'bleep' of the radio in the middle of his countdown ... A broken man from the first sentence of the General Secretary on the radio to him)

PORNILOV: No, Comrade Secretary ... No step has been taken so far. I see, Comrade Secretary. Yes! Of course ... It is a complete error in my dialectical approach. I see this immediately, now you point it out, Comrade Secretary, that it was unfortunate that the Lost Childhood should have been built on ... in this manner ... I mean to say ... As a block of workers' houses ... rather than a block of Capitalist Offices ... I do see this ... clearly ... In sacrificing all these workers' lives for the sake of the Childhood of one child ... Absolutely, Comrade Secretary ... As you say ... Moving back to the cult of the individual. I am prepared to make a public statement in Moscow, yes, Comrade Secretary ... I admit I overlooked this important theoretical aspect ... At the same time, Comrade Secretary ... If only the child had dropped her childhood another five inches to the left ... All that would have been necessary would have been to take up the pavement and – Yes, Comrade Secretary ... Immediately ...

(He turns to give the command to his troops)

All forces to withdraw. Remove charges from flats. Return to base. A full dialectical analysis of the reasons for the withdrawal will be published in tomorrow's Pravda.

GENERAL
MAO: *(watching the retreat of the Russians and the Americans. Addressing the Troops)* Comrade soldiers, the Russians and the Americans have retreated in the face of real Commnist strategy. Terrified by our united solidarity and the indisputable rightness of our cause and dialectical analysis of the situation, they have run from our forces without even daring to lift a single rifle in our direction. Comrade soldiers, I congratulate you on your bearing and your courage in this great victory.

There has been some change of our plans. The aircraft which dropped us has returned to base and will not be returning. 'Since we are here, Chairman Mao asks you to understand the thought: Since we are here, this is the Communist thing to do. If a Communist is in Newcastle, he asks me to tell you, that is where he should be. And he further expounds:- Why would a Commnist be here! You are here to infiltrate into the lives of the people on the Tyne. How can you infiltrate into the lives of the people on the River Tyne? he further asks, and further expounds:— By dispersing, one by one, and setting up Chinese restaurants to steep the natives in the beauty of Chinese culture. Chairman Mao gives you the Slogan: "THE seeds of the flower of the Revolution will be planted in the stomach of the Tyne." Long live the Revolution.'

MOHAMMED
HASAN: *(directing the removal of the charges from the flats)* Brothers, just in time, I have uncovered a Jewish plot to besmirch the good name of the Arab people all over the world. We have been tricked into attempting to destroy this beautiful building housing over 600 Gentiles by the diabolical plot of the Jewish playwright, Cecil Philip Taylor, whose real name is Isidore Hyman Abraham Gerscovitch. A Press Conference will be held at the Station Hotel late today to expose Isidore Hyman Abraham Gerscovitch and all his black, evil, Jewish, Fascist, perfidy!

Brothers! Peace go with you!

(They retire, following the other forces so that when PETER and EMILY and the others finally arrive they find the flats deserted)

Scene Sixteen

Scotswood Road.
EMILY and the others are sitting, waiting for PETER PAN. ACTION MAN and PETER creep into the road on their bellies.

CHILD: There they are, Em. They're coming.

ACTION MAN: Hit the deck, everybody! This is the central battle zone. Hit the deck!

EMILY: *(to PETER)* Taken your time, haven't you? Told you to stop messing about on the bus.

ACTION MAN: For Chrissake, Pan! Tell her to get under cover ... This is central battle zone.

PETER: You're supposed to get under cover, Emily. It's the battle zone.

EMILY: Look, man. There's nobody here. What do you want us to do here, anyway?

PETER: There's nobody here, Elmer.

EMILY: It's just a block of flats. You're not going to find anything here.

ACTION MAN: Where is everybody? *(at radio)* Hi, Sindy ... Be with you in a minute ...

SINDY: Don't speak to me. *(trying to repair her face)* Just look at my face ...

ACTION MAN: Sindy, baby. You're more beautiful than ever. You get lovelier and lovelier.

SINDY: *(looking sweetly at PAN)* I was very worried about you, Peter ...

ACTION MAN:	*(listening to Washington)* Everybody's withdrawn. The Russkies, Chinos, Everybody ... You can all relax ... They're all gone ...
EMILY:	Peter! Where are you going now? *(PETER has suddenly flown up to the top of the flats)*
CHILD:	Look, Em. He's flying to the top. He's sitting at the very top.
PETER:	*(shouting from the top)* Hullo, everybody. You look very, very tiny.
EMILY:	Peter ... I'm going home. *(to the others)* Come on.
PETER:	*(flying down)* It's lovely up there, Emily. It sways back and forwards like a giant palm tree.
ACTION MAN:	*(still at radio)* Some unspecified reason for the change in plans. Bull's been recalled ... Reasons for Russkies running off unknown ... Ditto, Chinos.
	(EMILY has suddenly become aware of the chuch dwarfed by the multi-storeys round it)
EMILY:	Look ... That Church, Peter.
PETER:	Yes. Isn't it jolly. I love steeples. *(but EMILY doesn't hear him. She is staring at the church)*
EMILY:	It wasn't like that. It's all closed in now. By them big flats. It wasn't closed in, then. It was open.
CHILD:	It's like a cage, Em., isn't it ... It's caged in. Like a tiger.
EMILY:	Yes ... It was open. And big. It was fantastic. It had kind of clouds round the steeple, it was so big. It was going along here. The sun was going down. Big and red. And the steeple was black. Pointing up to the sun.
	(PETER is excited now. This might at last be the right track)
PETER:	What happened, Emily? You must tell me exactly. Every single thing that happened.
EMILY:	I was wheeling Dennis in his pram. And the sun was going down. All the sky was red. The whole sky ... Not just the sun. And I saw this big church in front of us. Like a kind of castle. In the red sky. This big steeple. Pointing away up to the sky. Like a big black pencil, touching the sun. *(looking round)* But it was all open; it wasn't closed in, with all them flats. And it was big. It was gigantic.
PETER:	You were walking up this road?
EMILY:	Not that one. That's a new one. The old one. The old one had cobbles. Gave you a funny feeling in your hands when you wheeled the pram along it. Like an electric shock. I saw this church. The clouds were shining. Like in the pictures when all the music comes up and everybody kisses. It was great. I just fancied sitting down and watching it for all the time it was there. If I could've flown up like we did before ... And kind of been in it ... I had this queer feeling.
PETER:	Sad?
EMILY:	I wanted to be kind of swimming in all the clouds. Touching them ... And then Dennis started moaning. And I remembered I had to give the kids their tea. It was me Mam's Bingo night. And I just had to go away from everything. I was dead mad. I was flaming, all night ... I went back the next night. But the sky was all black ... And grey ... And the church didn't look anything ...

PETER:	*(jumping up and down with excitement)* That's where it happened, Emily! We've found it! We've found it! Hooray! Hooray!
SINDY:	Where, Peter? I can't see anything.
EMILY:	It was really big ... that church. And it was all open. Not shut in, like now ... And there used to be trees round it. It was a kind of Park ...
	(PETER is sprinkling moon-dust all over the pavement, searching for the lost childhood)
ACTION MAN:	It would be great if they'd built that sky-scraper right over Emily's lost Childhood. Great scene, that!
SINDY:	Oh, you would think of a thing like that, wouldn't you?
ACTION MAN:	It could happen. We've gotta be prepared for all eventualities.
	(PETER has gone into the flats in his search)
EMILY:	*(to CHILD)* You reckon we're going to find it ... *(PETER returns wild with excitement)*
PETER:	I've FOUND it! I've FOUND it!
ALL:	*(jumping with excitement)* He's found it. He's found it!
PETER:	You should see the Moon-dust jumping up and down on the floor. It's just under these flats there ... Just in the middle ...
ACTION MAN:	*(jumping)* It's just under these flats! Where you say it was, Pan?
PETER:	Just in the kind of middle of that big flat there. *(he suddenly realises the significance of his discovery)* Don't worry, Emily, I'll get it ...
SINDY:	Peter, it isn't! It couldn't be!
PETER:	I've got the plan all made, Emily. I'm going to go round all the people living there and whisper dreams in their ear so that they all get out of the flat. Then I'm going to borrow some gunpowder from Hook and blow it all up ... That's very easy ...
EMILY:	*(giving it all up)* Come on ... Let's go home.
PETER:	Then ... All we need to do ... Is dig up the Childhood.
SINDY:	Hook would never give *you* gunpowder.
PETER:	I'd ask him very nicely, and promise to read one of his stories.
	(EMILY is leading the children home)
	Emily ... Come back! I'm making our plan.
EMILY:	You can't blow up hundreds of peoples' houses, man ... Even if you could do it ... which I doubt very much, son.
PETER:	It's only houses, Emily ... It's only things ...
EMILY:	I'm going home.
PETER:	But we've found it. Come inside and I'll show you the Moondust dancing on the floor, all over it. There's a ripping cage inside, too ... You go inside and press a button and you go shooting right up to the top ...
	(But EMILY has already moved away from the flats ... PETER follows her and the children)
	Don't you want to see the Moon-dust jumping, Emily?
	(She holds out her hand to him. He holds out his, in imitation.
	EMILY and PETER walk down the road, their right hands held out — as the play moves back to 1904)

Scene Seventeen

BARRIE is now nearing the final curtain of PETER PAN. MRS. DARLING — she is at the loveliest age for a woman, but too old to see PETER clearly, and is trying to hold PETER for WENDY and stop him flying away for ever.

MRS.
DARLING: Peter, where are you? Let me adopt you.

PETER: Would you send me to school?

MRS.
DARLING: *(obligingly)* Yes.

PETER: And then to an Office?

MRS.
DARLING: I suppose so.

PETER: Soon I should be a Man?

MRS.
DARLING: Very soon.

PETER: *(passionately)* I don't want to go to school and learn solemn things. No one is going to catch me, Lady, and make me a Man. I want always to be a little boy and have fun.

MRS.
DARLING: Where are you to live, Peter?

PETER: In the house we built for Wendy. The fairies put it high up among the tree tops where they sleep at night.

WENDY: *(rapturously)* To think of it! Mother, may I go?

MRS.
DARLING: *(gripping her for ever)* Certainly not. I have got you home again and I mean to keep you.

WENDY: But he does so need a Mother.

MRS.
DARLING: So do you, my love.

PETER: Oh, all right!

MRS.
DARLING: *(magnanimously)* But Peter, I shall let her go to you once a year for a week to do your Spring Cleaning.

      (WENDY revels in this but PETER, who has no notion what a Spring Cleaning is, waves a careless thanks)

MRS.
DARLING: Say 'good night', Wendy.

WENDY: Good night, Peter.

PETER: Good night, Wendy.

WENDY: You won't forget me, will you? Before Spring Cleaning time comes.

      (There is no answer for he is already soaring high. BARRIE is admiring this scene. Gazing in rapture and adoration at MRS. DARLING)

Scene Eighteen

MRS. DARLING herself pulls off her smock ... and the wig ... and shows herself as SYLVIA. She takes up a position on a deck chair and we see, now, we are in a Garden ... SYLVIA looks very ill ... BARRIE goes to her, adjusting her rugs ...

BARRIE: Are you comfortable, my dear?

SYLVIA: I am fine, Jim.

BARRIE: *(taking her hand)* Jocelyn, dearest ... I feel so very close to you ... Could we be any closer to one another than we are now?

SYLVIA: *(really too ill to respond except in words)* Impossible, Jim.

BARRIE: Some say a man can never really get to know a woman without this physical thing between them ... I know ... This is nonsense ... The physical thing ... I can only see as a barrier ...

SYLVIA: It can be ... Yes ...

BARRIE: to be with you ... To have you with me every day ... What more can a man wish for, dearest? We have reached such happiness together, have we not, Jocelyn ...? I cannot believe many men and women have achieved such heights ... *(there is a 'tick' of the distant crocodile — now recovered again? ... and a DOCTOR enters)*

BARRIE: Ah ... Here is Doctor Spicer, now, dear.

            (The DOCTOR gestures to BARRIE, taking him aside)

SPICER: Not, I fear, Mr. Barrie, happy news.

BARRIE: I see, Doctor ...

SPICER: Not operable, Mr. Barrie. The growth is far too near the heart to even look at it!

BARRIE: I feared something like this, Doctor ...

SPICER: *(to SYLVIA)* Just giving Mr. Barrie something to ease your pain, Mrs. Davies ... Look in the morning to see how it is helping ... *(taking BARRIE's hand)* Very, very sorry, Mr. Barrie ...

SYLVIA: *(calling)* Jim ... Jim ... Could you bring me my mirror please.

BARRIE: *(handing it to her, reluctantly)* Dearest ... I understand why you cannot wear my ring in front of the boys ... I would not want it otherwise, Jocelyn ... Just ... If you might wear it now and then, dearest ... When we are alone ...

SYLVIA: *(looking in the mirror and recoiling from what she sees there)* Jim, please ... Don't let the boys see me again! Please, Jim!

BARRIE: Dearest ... Believe me ... You are as beautiful as ever ...

SYLVIA: If you look in the drawer by my bed, Jim ... I've made a list. When you get down to Eton ... I'm so sorry that I have to burden you with all these things, Jim ... You will need to buy two dozen white collars for Peter ... And two dozen white ties ...

BARRIE: *(studying the list)* I see ... The same pattern as George wears. You have it down here.

SYLVIA: I'm afraid you can only buy them at Eton, Jim. At Lingwood's.

BARRIE: *(writing)* I'll make a note of it, dearest. *(showing her his writing)* Can you see how well I write with my left hand ...

SYLVIA: *(looking at his other hand)* Your poor swollen finger, Jim ...

BARRIE: My right withers ... But my left thrives ... Can you see, Jocelyn ... My writing is quite legible. Anyone can read it ... *(but SYLVIA dies in the act of reading his handwriting)*

(the crocodile passes across the back of the stage. BARRIE gently covers her face with the sheets)

BARRIE: Dear God, I know now why I have been punished by You like this. I have been punished because I dealt iniquitously with the gifts You blessed me with. I have made a fortune out of the theatre and untruths.

(BARRIE looks out into the distance ...)

It is early morning. I am out on a highland road. The myrtle is damp and sweet with the dew. It is the time before I knew anything of sorrow, pain or death. It is the morning of life ... of the world.

(And as he is speaking ... SYLVIA, his MOTHER, his FATHER, SISTERS ... TEACHERS ... all rise from the dead and wheel round him, throwing at him a montage of their demands)

Don't write with your left, Barrie.

Two dozen White Collars. A dozen White Ties.

Mother and son. Mother and son.
Character. Character.
No hiding from him.
More! More! More!

(But BARRIE pushes out of the cage ... He stands looking out into the future ... and from it come PETER, EMILY and the others ... and the next scene)

Scene Nineteen

EMILY leads the others back into the kitchen of her house.

PETER: I really did find it, though, Emily, didn't I? That was jolly clever of me, tracking it down like that, wasn't it?

CHILD: Can I have a piece of bread and jam, Em?

CHILD: Can I have some cocoa?

CHILD: Can *I* have some cocoa?

EMILY: Wait a minute! Let's get me coat off.

SINDY: I must say! Leading us a dance all through the night. Keeping people from their sleep. And all just to get back to exactly where we started!

ACTION MAN: That is not a fair evaluation of the night's work. I consider that to be –

SINDY: Oh, drop dead, son, will you! My feet!

PETER: I know what we could do, Emily ... If I brought all the lost boys back ... And we dug and dug in that flat ...

EMILY: It doesn't matter, Peter ... Honestly ... Don't worry about it.

PETER: I bet you we'd soon find it. I bet you we wouldn't have to dig more than a week ... A month at the most.

EMILY: I'm telling you, man, I don't want it. What do I want with my Childhood, now Peter? *(buttering a slice of bread)* Don't be daft.

CHILD: You mean, Em ... after all that bother. You don't want it?

PETER: If I said to Hook: 'I say, Captain Hook. Read me one of your lovely stories' ... I bet you he *would* give me some gunpowder.

EMILY: I couldn't be bothered with it, Peter. You not hear us! Childhood would be more bother to us than it was worth. If I started wanting to play again and acting like a kid ... In the middle of looking after that lot ... That would be me worse off than I am now ... wouldn't it?

SINDY: If there's one thing I detest, that's a child with attitudes beyond her years!

EMILY: Anyway ... The Church is caged in now, isn't it? I'll never see it again ... Like when I dropped my Childhood.

(PETER is gazing enviously at the bread and jam EMILY is handing out. She catches his look ... and makes him a jam sandwich.

BARRIE has now put on an academic gown and board. He is on a platform, making his rectorial speech at St. Andrew's)

BARRIE: There is much I conceal from other people, my friends. But today, I have resolved, because you have done me such great honour in electing me Rector of St. Andrew's, in some kind of poor return for this, I wish to expose every cranny of my mind ... My theme is courage. Courage as you should use it in the great fight that seems to be coming between youth and their betters. Youth has for far too long left exclusively in our hands the decisions in national matters that are more vital to them than us. Things about the next War, for instance, and why the last one ever had a beginning.

Your betters had no share in the immediate cause of the War, but for fifty years or so we heeded not the rumblings of the distant drum. And when War did come, we told Youth, who had to get us out of it, tall tales of what War is and the clover beds to which it leads. We were not meaning to deceive, but that does not acquit us of failings such as stupidity and jealousy, the two black spots in human nature.

PETER: *(moving to the telly)* I say. Can we turn on the Picture Box!

EMILY: Don't be daft, man. It's the middle of the night. There's nothing on just now.

(PETER switches the television on ... and twiddles the controls)

BARRIE: If you prefer to leave things as they are, we shall probably fail you again. Do not be too sure that we have learned our lesson and are not at this very moment doddering down some brimstone path ...

PETER: I know ... I'll change all the Television People's clocks. And make them start working now ... *(EMILY is busy undressing them ready for bed)* Will I, Emily?

EMILY: Please yourself.

(PETER concentrates very hard ... Suddenly a picture appears on the television)

CHILD: Look, Em! It's working!

PETER: I say ... Are there any picture stories about Cowboys and Red Indians?

CHILD: Tell you what's smashing, Peter. 'The Virginians' ... Get 'The Virginians' ...

            (Barrie is now at his desk. His last words come through again)

BARRIE: Do not be too sure we have learned our lesson and are not at this moment doddering down some brimstone path ...

            (PETER has succeeded in getting 'The Virginians')

CHILD: Look, Em ... He's got it ...

EMILY: *(dimly hearing BARRIE'S words)* You hear anything there?

            (BARRIE is now asleep, but his words continue to come through)

BARRIE: We shall probably fail you. Do not be too sure, we have learned ...

            (But his voice is drowned by the sounds of the seventy years between BARRIE and EMILY ... Hitler's voice ... The flight over Hiroshima ... General Gowon ... Planes screaming overhead in Vietnam ... and the theme of 'The Virginians')

BARRIE: And are not at this moment ...

EMILY: Kind of noises ...

PETER: *(now esconced in front of the telly, with great excitement)* I say! What a ripping tune!

BARRIE: Doddering down some brimstone path ...

            (But EMILY gives it all up. There is no catching the voice through the chaos of sounds ... She pulls on a pair of pyjamas on a child)

PETER: It really is ... It's the most exciting, jolly tune I've ever heard!

            (... The boy guides EMILY to link hands with the children, trying to reach out to the audience. He takes PETER and adds him to the human chain, then all the characters in the play, approaching nearer and nearer to the front row. They are now standing at the very edge of the stage. The boy goes to BARRIE and gently leads him down on to the floor of the auditorium. He puts Barrie's hand in Emily's ... The boy, by holding Barrie's hand, can now just reach the front row of the audience. He touches the hands of those in the audience within his reach ... 'The Virginians' swell up ... and across the back of the stage crawls the crocodile ...)

The Black and White Minstrels

Characters

CYRIL
GIL
HARRY
PAT
ATARA

ACT ONE

Scene One

Morning. Late Winter.

The living-room of the Jackson's semi-detached villa in King's Park, Glasgow. A corner of the room has been adapted as a "field kitchen". A camping stove has been set up. Surrounded by water containers, a canvas larder, and cooking utensils.

CYRIL is at the stove, wearing an old black overcoat, happily absorbed in cooking breakfast. A car is heard drawing up outside. Doors are opened and slammed. CYRIL leaves the stove to look out the window, through the curtains. Immediately, his mood changes. He becomes tense and on the defensive. He wraps his overcoat tighter round him. He goes to the doorway and calls.

CYRIL:	Gil! Gil ... It's bloody Harry!
GIL:	*(off)* Are you making any mushrooms, Cyril?
CYRIL:	Yes ... I said, it's bloody Harry. He's just drove up ... *(Returning to his stove)*
GIL:	(OFF) I'll come down in a minute ...

CYRIL bends over his stove. There is the sound of the front door being opened.

CYRIL steels himself against the invasion. HARRY, carrying a weekend bag, followed by PAT, enter. HARRY surveys the scene for a moment with open criticism.

HARRY:	What's all this fucking camping gear, Cyril?
PAT:	Did Atara push you out of the kitchen, pet?
HARRY:	Fucking camping in a fucking living room in fucking King's Park!
PAT:	Has Atara pushed you out of the kitchen at last, pet?
HARRY:	You're fucking besieged, Cyril, man! Do you know that? You're in a state of fucking siege!
PAT:	*(to CYRIL)* Do you want any help, sweetheart?
CYRIL:	*(looking at the weekend case)* You came to stay the night, like?
PAT:	Harry hasn't been able to sleep at nights all week, Cyril. He's soaked through two pair of pyjamas a night!
HARRY:	*(taking off his things and making himself at home)* I've been in a state of anxiety, Cyril. All fucking week!
CYRIL:	*(his eyes still on the weekend case)* It's Thursday. Not Friday ... You know it's Thursday.
PAT:	We talked about it upsetting your routine, honey ... But he's really worked himself into a terrible state, Cyril.
HARRY:	*(lifting a bread bin from the settee to allow himself to sit down)* I mean ... This isn't even bloody basic socialism, man! For Christ's sake! Alright ... A state of hostility exists between you and Black Power ...
CYRIL:	*(not listening ... To PAT)* How did he react when you talked about it upsetting my routine, you coming a day earlier, Pat?

PAT: You don't know what he's been like, Cyril. I've never seen him in a state like this before ...

HARRY: Hostilities exist between you and Black Power. Right. Fuck, then! Do it on an equitable basis, man! There's three of you – five every other weekend – and one of her. Push *her* out the bloody kitchen! Let *her* use the camping gear, man!

(CYRIL's only response is to wrap his coat tighter round him.)

PAT: Are you warm enough like that, pet?

CYRIL: I'm fine.

PAT: You look cold, pet ...

HARRY: Leave him alone. For Christ's sake, man! His mother'll buy him a dressing-gown for his birthday ...

CYRIL: Just now ... You're an irritant. I don't mean that in an offensive way, Harry.

(to PAT) Just him. Not you, Pat. I find your presence soothing ... You never jar on me. Monty's phoned just now. Looking for his car.

PAT: Oh ... Poor pet.

CYRIL: I didn't speak to him. Gil answered the 'phone. I've to phone him back. I was just working out some feasible story to tell him when Harry's bloody brakes drove everything out of my head.

HARRY: I don't feel guilty about this, Cyril. When I tell you what I've been working out.

PAT: Cyril, pet ... Did you mean that? When you said I didn't jar on you ...

CYRIL: I've got to phone back before ten ...

HARRY: *(to PAT)* I told you last night, Pat ... You and Cyril ... A fucking computer couldn't have organised a better match!

CYRIL: He says to Gil: where's the firm's car?

HARRY: He should have given you it, for fuck's sake. As a gift to the arts ... When you left.

CYRIL: Cyril is no longer working for the firm, is he? Cyril stopped working for Diamonds thirteen months ago.

HARRY: Either you're a fucking writer or you're a fucking record salesman ... You have this qualitative change ... You stop fucking selling records and you sit down at your fucking typewriter and become a professional writer.

CYRIL: I thought he'd given me the car ... as a present. Why should Monty give me a car, Pat? Do you think he's found out I've been using his car to sell records for Jerry?

PAT: I don't think so, pet. How could he? Anyway, I shouldn't let it worry you.

HARRY: Commitment. That's what we're on about. What you frightened of Monty for, for fuck's sake. Monty's not your fucking boss now.

PAT: He's driving Monty's car.

CYRIL: I love you, Harry. Definitely. I love you. But I don't want you about the house. Win or lose, this afternoon ... If the Rent Tribunal says Atara can stay or has to go ... I don't want *you* around, Harry ...

HARRY: For fuck's sake, Cyril –

CYRIL:	I was looking forward to two clear days to myself before you turned up at the weekend ... To get myself adjusted and orientated ...
HARRY:	Cyril ... That's what I'm here for. I've been sweating on this all week, man ... That's the fucking work ... Orientation ...
CYRIL:	Don't tell me, Harry. Do me a favour ... If you don't want to alienate yourself further from me, keep it to yourself.
HARRY:	Pat'll tell you, man! I haven't had a full night's sleep –
CYRIL:	Harry, the kind of things you have sleepless nights over! Trivia, son ... Arms to South Africa ... The Industrial Relations Bill ... The Revolution! ... I don't believe it, Harry ... It's not real ... Panicking about abstractions like that!
HARRY:	I'm talking about fucking Black Power, man! That a fucking abstraction! I was sweating over you and Black Power.
CYRIL:	'Don't Believe' maybe isn't quite accurate. What it is, your stupidity gets on my nerves, Harry ... You still believing you can do anything about anything in this world ... *(to PAT)* You know what I mean, Pat.
HARRY:	You gave Black Power a month's notice to quit. Black Power is contesting that at the Rent Tribunal 3 p.m. this afternoon, Mack! Black Power through the wall there. A real, concrete, black bird!
CYRIL:	When the tide rushes out from you, it carries everything with it ... Monty's shouting at me to get his car back ... STV pulling at me for my first draft of Walter Scott ... Maxie's going on at me, now ... I phoned Maxie, this morning ...
HARRY:	Tell Monty. Straight. I've got the car.
CYRIL:	Miriam answered. Maxie was at the synagogue. It's the anniversary of his father's death ... On the same day as the Tribunal. His father died forty years ago today ...
HARRY:	Tell him straight. Yes. I've got your car. You never asked for it back.
CYRIL:	You know what Maxie's like, Pat. He'll be crying all day about his father. Dead forty years ago ... I need his mind to be absolutely *focussed* on this Tribunal ... I can't afford emotional dissipation on ancestor worship ...
HARRY:	Cyril ... You're talking about Maxie! Super Jew!
PAT:	He's not dead all that long, is he, Cyril ...
HARRY:	Super Lawyer, Maxie, for fuck's sake!
CYRIL:	I don't know when he died.
HARRY:	You're talking about super lawyer, Maxie, for fuck's sake, Cyril! He's got this thing ... Once he gets into a court ... He gets switched on ... All forces go ... He can bend a whole fucking court to see exactly how he wants them to see ...
PAT:	It'll be alright, pet ... You know how you get all worked up about things ... And they turn out alright in the end ...
HARRY:	*(finding clue in crossword)* You bastard!
PAT:	Cyril, I know, pet ... I know nothing seems to be working out for you, these days. And all our ideals being smashed. Heath in Downing Street. The Russian Communists fighting the Chinese Communists ...
	The phone rings.

CYRIL: That's Monty again ...

HARRY: *(going to the phone)* Fuck, fucking Monty! I'll speak to the cunt! *(Into phone)* Harold Vine here ... I'm not sure if he's available ... *(To CYRIL)* You don't want to speak to that fat old cunt, do you, man?

CYRIL: *(taking the phone from him)* Hullo ... Mr Monty ... How are you keeping? I see ... yes, Mr. Monty ...

HARRY: Taking black birds to Fucking Rent Tribunals, Cyril. That's not our scene, man.

CYRIL: Yes ... I've got the car, Mr. Monty ...

PAT goes to the cooker ... and turns the bacon.

HARRY: I don't blame you, Cyril. These last few years have been a right fucking sod, politically.

CYRIL: What it was, Mr. Monty ... I just thought ... You not asking for it back ... I just took it for granted. You not having any other travellers in this area ... I'm trying to be clear, Mr. Monty ...

PAT: How many eggs would you like, Cyril?

CYRIL: I just thought ... you wanted me to, hold on to it ... till you needed one ... *(To PAT)* Just one, Pat, please. ... I mean ... Hold on to it ...

HARRY: For fuck's sake! Tell the cunt! You're a major fucking dramatist ... The Glasgow Herald said HOW DOES A KING DRINK TEA was the best thing the Avram Greenbaum Players had done since the fucking war.

CYRIL: No ... I didn't pay the tax and insurance, Mr. Monty ... I assumed you would be ... yes ...

HARRY: I know ... we're moving through a right sod of a period just now ... But some things we can do something about, Cyril ... Black Power we can do something about ...

PAT: Harry, let him concentrate on his boss ...

HARRY: We can start talking to her again ... We can initiate some kind of dialogue, again, Cyril ...

CYRIL: No ... I wouldn't say in very good condition, Mr. Monty.

HARRY: Without bringing all the fucking apparatus of the fucking state into it ... and calling in fucking Rent Tribunals as fucking referees to blow the fucking whistle between us.

CYRIL: About fifty thousand miles, Mr. Monty ... yes ...

HARRY: *(grabbing the phone from CYRIL and speaking into it)* Excuse me, friend ... But I wonder if you happen to know that Cyril Jackson is a highly talented playwright ... He was recently awarded a bursary by the Scottish Arts Council ...

CYRIL: *(getting the phone back)* No ... Just a friend, Mr. Monty ... Not at all ... Certainly not ... Not derogatory, Mr. Monty ... Just a point of information ... *(As he is talking, GIL enters)*

HARRY: *(taking her in his arms and kissing her and generally feeling her up)* Gil, honey? Look at her? You look fantastic, sweetheart. You've got a new nightie on!

CYRIL: *(to GIL)* Monty wants us to buy the car, GIL ...

HARRY:	For fuck's sake ... Buy it, man ... Offer him ... £250 ... We'll flog it for £350 ...
CYRIL:	Could I ring you back, Mr. Monty ... Definitely I will ... I just want to think it over ... Definitely before lunch, Mr. Monty. *(Putting down the phone)*
GIL:	*(breaking away from HARRY)* Atara's still sleeping. She mustn't be going to her classes, this morning.
HARRY:	*(admiring her)* I like that nightie. Don't think it would work with Pat, though ... Too big breasts for it ...

CYRIL *puts down* GIL's *breakfast in front of her.*

GIL:	*(studying the plate)* Did you not make an egg for us Cyril?
CYRIL:	*(going to cooker)* I'll put one on for you, Gil ... Gil ... If I have no car ... If I give it back to Monty ... How can I get to Greenock to see the kids??? I'm stuck here ... In bloody King's Park, Gil ... and my calls ...
GIL:	You get a train ... There's trains every hour to Greenock ...
HARRY:	Listening to you, just now, Cyril, on the phone *(A fantastic insight here)* I saw exactly what you were doing. How you got this fucking shit heap: Coitus interruptus. Intellectual, spiritual and physical coitus interruptus.
CYRIL:	Harry's come to lead us in peace talks with Atara. You're out of luck on four counts, Harry, son: (1) I've got big problems with Walter Scott. (2) I have to resolve the big car problem. (3) I'm running into bankruptcy (4) I've totally gone off Atara ... Probably all Nigerians. Probably all blacks.
PAT:	Cyril ... You can't give up like that, pet ...
CYRIL:	You can, Pat. It's easy. Gil gave up at thirteen.
GIL:	Fifteen ... I got bored with the Y.C.L. Didn't fancy anybody in it ...
CYRIL:	I can't stand her. She blocks my creativity. She totally blankets it out. Since she came here, I haven't finished one major piece of work ...
HARRY:	You see what we're on to now, Cyril ... Naked fucking racialism. We move further and further backwards ... I'm telling you, man. The road to Fascism is paved with fucking apathy.
CYRIL:	Not her skin, Harry ... I don't hate her skin, son. It's her guts. I hate her guts!
PAT:	Pet, you don't really ... *(Worried)* You're just a bit upset, and –
CYRIL:	I hate her. I turn white when I think about her. Look at me: I'm thinking about her now!
HARRY:	That's what I'm telling you. How this hatred developed, man. Intellectual, spiritual and physical coitus interruptus. *(Watching CYRIL cooking, his mouth watering)* You got a spare rasher of bacon ... or a sausage?
PAT:	You'll be starving, Harry. *(To the others)* He had no breakfast. Couldn't take a thing ... He was so worked up.
CYRIL:	I need absolute emotional security for my work. It's like painting the Forth Bridge, living with that woman. As soon as you've recovered from one emotional pogrom, she's starting another ...
HARRY:	I'm talking about this game of yours, Cyril, man ... Pushing it in and pulling it out before you've shot your load ... That's what's brought us to this Tribunal, this afternoon ...

CYRIL: If I lose the car ... The kids live miles away from the Greenock Station ... And how to go about selling records ... for Jerry ... Without a car?

HARRY: You've got to stop selling records, man ... That's what I'm on about. You stop fucking about flogging fucking records round the shops and get down to the serious business of making your contribution to the fucking Scottish theatre.

CYRIL: You fancy a bacon sandwich, Harry?

HARRY: It's all right, Pat'll cook us something when you're done ...

CYRIL: *(to GIL)* I could go to Decca, Gil ...

GIL: They'd give you a brand new car for nothing.

CYRIL: Fifteen hundred a year plus commission. I could get it ... They've already put out feelers.

PAT: Cyril, that's not what you want to do all your life. Go around selling records.

HARRY: Where is this fucking bacon, Cyril?

CYRIL: *(forcing the rasher on to HARRY)* Here. *You* cook it. After I've finished this egg.

HARRY: *(trying to give it back to CYRIL)* Cyril, man.

CYRIL: Go on. *You* can cook it, Harry.

HARRY: *(left with the bacon)* You know I can't cook, man. Especially on these fucking things.

CYRIL: I don't want to go around flogging records all my life.

GIL: *(noticing the weekend case)* It *is* Thursday, isn't it? Not Friday?

PAT: We just thought ... Seeing we were coming here, anyway. We might as well lock up the house ... and stay for the weekend. It's your house anyway, this week, Gil.

GIL: Is it? I lose track ...

HARRY: *(piqued)* Christ! You forget last weekend, Gil, honey!

CYRIL: Even if we get a car for a hundrd quid, Gil ... there's the tax and insurance.

HARRY: There you are, Last Saturday, Cyril! There's an example of what I'm on about. You fucking shoving it in and pulling it out again. We all go up for a bath ... except fucking you.

CYRIL: What's happened, son, is the whole world's collapsed around us ... It's a fact of life, Harry. Like a shell ... Harry. With no foundations ... It's just collapsing.

HARRY: Everybody goes up for a bath ... Except C.J.

CYRIL: I don't want to bath with you, son. Obviously I'm subsconsciously a raving queer. I can't endure physical contact with my own sex.

HARRY: I understand, Cyril ... All this tension ... It's bound to make you aggressive, this morning.

CYRIL: The whole world has collapsed round us, man! It's a fact of life. My relationship with the one black that came into contact with me has totally disintegrated in violence and hate ... The Revolution through the Tenant's Association collapsed as soon as we organised the Winston Churchill Multi-Storey's central heating.

HARRY: No ... No ... Not at all, Man ...

CYRIL: Their militancy evaporated with their increase of body temperature ...

GIL: Can I have some butter, please Cyril?

CYRIL: The whole of the Socialist world has exploded into a million bloody fragments ... Russian communists are marching alongside bloody American capitalists to destroy Chinese Capitalists ... Monty's screaming for his car back. My lawyer's stuck in the synagogue, crying over his dear father. I'm not interested in Walter Scott.

HARRY: Cyril, man ... You're winning ... You're winning, man ...

CYRIL: These are all facts of life, Harry ... The world is collapsing. It's sad ... But it's happening.

HARRY: Cyril, Man ... You're winning I'm telling you ... You've been winning for the last four years. Four years ago ... When I first saw you at that Vietnam meeting, Man ...

            Yes you were losing right, left and centre ... Couldn't even get a fucking story in the Jewish Echo ... A year later ... The Avram Greenbaum Players are packing them in with HOW DOES A KING DRINK TEA ... Rave fucking rave notices. You've got a fucking Arts Council bursary. A telly contract from STV ... You've got it up, Cyril, man ... Stiff and straight and right in, Cyril. For fuck's sake ... Don't fucking pull it out before you've shot your load.

            CYRIL hands him the frying pan.

PAT: *(taking the pan)* I'll do it for him, Cyril.

HARRY: Yes, Cyril, we're facing a major collapse of ideals, definitely. Yes.

            CYRIL is at the table, concentrating on his breakfast.

GIL: You've made my egg raw, again, Cyril ... You always make it raw ...

HARRY: I've been in a state of panic all week. Pat'll tell you ... I've been in a panic state.

PAT: He's been terrible, Gil.

CYRIL: If it was for the right thing. I'm happy for you Harry. It's healthy ... If you're facing up to the objective facts of life and you recognise your total impotence ... That's good.

HARRY: This Black Power problem, man, it's got me really fucked up Cyril!

CYRIL: Everything is transient, Harry ... She'll go away —

HARRY: That's the point, Cyril ... You're right ... Yes ... That's exactly what I said to myself. Everything is transient ... So what the hell are you doing, going through two pair of pyjamas a night over an issue like this ... And then it clicked, Cyril ... Pat'll tell you ...

CYRIL: *Intellectually*, Harry ... I accept concepts like us all having baths together ... But to actually carry it out in practise ...

HARRY: I'm not talking about fucking baths, man! I'm telling you about this major insight I got, last night ...

CYRIL: Same with lovemaking ... I see absolutely that to make love-making a secret act between two people is totally reactionary. Even the Catholic church has started changing their bread and wine into the body of Christ without curtains ...

HARRY: I'm telling you something, man ... Everything fell into place. A great feeling of peace came over me. Pat'll tell you. She felt it, too. It was like floating on the warm sea on a sunny day ... *(Looking to PAT for support)*

PAT: But it depends on Cyril and Gil, Harry ... Doesn't it? How they feel about it.

HARRY: Black Power is a focus, Cyril ... *(Waiting for the light of his insight to penetrate and illuminate CYRIL's mind. But CYRIL is chewing at his bacon ... Waiting for HARRY to tell him something.)*

I wasn't panicking about Black Power, Cyril ... What I'd been panicking about was *us* . The fuck between Black Power and you Cyril, has thrown a light on the breakdown of relationships between the quartet, Cyril ... between us, Cyril ... The quartet has reached a major crisis in its development.

CYRIL: The whole trouble is Atara's a Uoruba ... If she'd've been an Ibo, man, there'd've been no problem ...

HARRY: *(to GIL)* You see what I'm getting at, Gil ...

GIL: Harry ... How about this. You tell us your latest needs ... And it could be you mightn't need to bother manipulating us into answering them. They might be ours too.

PAT: Gil, honey ... Harry's not like that ... Honestly ...

HARRY: They are, Gil, man. They're everybody's needs ... That's it ...

CYRIL: What happened was Atara reacted to my historic role ... as a Jew ... She started treating me like a white Ibo the first day she moved in ...

HARRY: Christ, Cyril! You still on this fucking Jew kick. Your mother's a fucking Elim Hall bloody Baptist, man!

GIL: I'm trying to work this out, Harry. Atara's anti-social behavour ... Like putting sugar in Cyril's petrol tank ... and taking all my pans off the stove ... and putting pepper in the custard. What she's really doing, is reacting to the breakdown in communications between the four of us.

HARRY: That's it, Gil. She's got it! All that violence and hate against Black Power couldn't be generated just by her taking off an odd pan of yours off the cooker ... All that energy, man. Comes from a block. It's never having it off for a fucking year and it all piling up inside you, man!

CYRIL: It's an interesting concept, Harry ... I gave her notice to quit not because she kept bringing her friends in at all hours of the night ... Starting fights with them and having screaming matches. I said to her ... Do us a favour Atara ... My kids are coming from Greenock ... You know that ... I'd like to give them a nice happy, secure week with their father ... Go easy with your friends ... And we have a bloody pogrom the first night they're here ... the vet bashes my kids ...

HARRY: One kid, Cyril ... Let's not be fucking emotive ...

CYRIL: But I gave her notice to quit not because of all that ... But because I was sexually frustrated.

HARRY: There is a time for a revolution to stand still and consolidate ... And there is a time for a revolution to move forward ... It's time we were moving forward, Cyril ...

CYRIL: ... What's a revolution, Harry? What revolution? It doesn't do anything to me ...

HARRY:	*(looking round the table)* You not left a roll for me.
GIL:	Sorry, Harry ... I didn't think you'd want any ...
HARRY:	You know I like hot rolls, Gil, honey.
PAT:	Cyril, pet ... That's what you're *saying*. It is important what happens to Atara ... You know it is.
CYRIL:	You should try giving up fighting against the current, Pat ... And just let yourself drift ... It's lovely.
HARRY:	Cyril ... That's not your scene, man. That's not you. You're a fighter, Cyril ... You can't give up, like that.
	One move, Cyril ... One obvious move. On to the next stage ... *(He was going to say "of the revolution" but cuts himself short)* And we're completely out of the shit. No Black Power problems ... The Quartet moving again ... No Fucking Tribunal ...
CYRIL:	I could do without the Tribunal, this afternoon, Harry. Definitely ... That weighs on me ...
HARRY:	A minor but fundamental change that'll start us moving again ... Give the whole relationship a new lease of life ... And answer every single need of our present situation. You and Pat change over to having the weekdays together. *(Waits for reaction. There is none)* I told Pat, she had lift off ... She was up all night with me ... Singing about it.
PAT:	I think it would be a nice change ... If Cyril and you wanted it, Gil ...
	CYRIL has been completely shaken by this new concept thrown at him by HARRY ... This is something he can't cope with at all.
CYRIL:	*(playing for time)* Articulate this a bit clearer, Harry. I don't understand you ...
GIL:	Don't be stupid, Cyril! It's a simple change round. I spend the weekdays with Harry and the weekends with you.
HARRY:	That's it!
GIL:	It couldn't be any more boring than what we have just now.
CYRIL:	*(to HARRY)* I know, Harry ... I'm a slow thinker ... I mean ... This is the basis for the great dialogue between us? I go in and tell her: Harry's taking Gil and I'm taking Pat ... The relationship of the quartet is blasting off, again ...
HARRY:	Basically, the Black Power problem is you ... Will you get us a cup of tea, Pat?
CYRIL:	I don't accept your attitude seriously, Gil. This boredom kick ... Everything bores you. I don't believe you would go in for a change like this for trivial reasons such as it fits in with this bored personality you keep projecting ...
GIL:	Cyril, that's what I am ... It's not projecting ... I'm a trivial person ... That's me.
HARRY:	This is how it works out, Cyril ... You move into our house in the golf course with Pat during the week ... I move in here with Gil ...
	CYRIL turns away at this. Clearly the idea of living in the golf course tempts him. And partially compensates for losing another part of Gil.

The Black Power problem is basically you. *You* can't live with Black Power and Black Power's got her assegai out for *you*. *You're* the character she's taking to the Tribunal this afternoon.

CYRIL: If I took the car round the salesrooms ... See who'd offer the best price ... If I could get a car and three hundred. That would pay the tax and insurance for a year, Gil ...

HARRY: You and Pat in the Golf Course ... Cyril, is the ideal arrangement. You've got the summerhouse in the garden to work in ... No traffic about ... Trees all round you ... Pat doesn't need to leave her kitchen. We don't disrupt Clair at her nursery school with Gil staying here.

GIL: You must be in a right state, Harry love. Sacrificing your stone-built dream house for me!

HARRY: For all of us, Gil ...

CYRIL: You want this change round, too, do you, Pat?

PAT: You know how close Harry and I are, Honey. What Harry wants, I want.

CYRIL: You want it because Harry wants it.

PAT: Both of us, honey. That's how we are, Cyril, you know that.

CYRIL: No, Pat ... Basically ... No ... I don't understand you ... I don't get you, Pat ... Now we're on the subject. I don't understand you ... That's the big problem between us ... It disturbs me ... That I can't get you ...

GIL: I can't work out if Harry would be any better than Cyril for a five day stretch ...

CYRIL: From the beginning, Pat ... I've never been able to understand you ... I love you ... Definitely.

HARRY: Think about this change, Cyril ... It works on all counts. The relationship is crying out for a new stimulus ...

CYRIL: Right at the beginning ... Before we were all sleeping with each other, Pat ... Harry seducing Gil because he fancied her ... That I could get ... I could get that ... Yes. But Harry sleeping with Gil because *you* wanted him to sleep with her because *he* wanted to sleep with her ... He loves Gil, so you love Gil – I'll be honest with you, Pat ... That's been bothering me for the four years we've all been together ... I've never been able to get it ... It's too exalted for me, that kick ... It could be, Pat ... It could well be that's exactly how it is ... But it's beyond me ... That kind of thing is totally beyond me ... Pat.

PAT: Cyril, pet ... Honestly ... You do understand me ... I saw what Harry saw to love in Gil ... And I loved her, too ... We both love her ... You understand, Gil, don't you?

GIL: No. But it doesn't matter, Pat. It doesn't bother me. It's not important ...

HARRY: On simple erotic grounds, Cyril. With Gil as your mistress and Pat as mine, Cyril ... The whole erotic element will take on a new dimension.

PAT: *(still trying to make CYRIL understand)* I'm so close to Harry, love ... I understand absolutely how he wants this change ... And I want it, too.

HARRY: This is the next logical step in the revolution. See what I'm getting at, Gil?

GIL: I think if you'd've suggested bringing in another couple ... A bit kinky ... That would've been exciting. But this doesn't seem to be much better than what we have already. At least Cyril can cook ... and wash ... and look after kids ...

HARRY: I mean ... It's not a *major* emotional upheaval. The difference is between three and four. You have four nights with Pat instead of three ... and three nights with Gil instead of four.

CYRIL: Harry, son ... I know it's an obvious question. But if it makes no difference ... Why change round in the first place.

HARRY: Cyril, man. For Christ's sake ... Look at us! Objectively ... We're going the same way as Russia, Cuba, Israel ... Ideals collapsing all down the line ...

CYRIL: Harry. It doesn't worry me ... It doesn't do anything to me. That's it, Harry! It doesn't. *(Major insight)* I'm sitting here drinking my tea ... And I'm not bothered Harry ... About Apartheid ... or the collapse of Socialsim ... Nothing ... the collapse of God ... Marx ... Engels ... Freud. The revolution. That's a terrible situation to be in ... It worries me, Harry ... How can you not worry about big issues like these!

PAT: Cyril ... You do ... You do *really*.

HARRY: I'm happy for you, Cyril. You're a happy man. Nothing worries you.

CYRIL: Look at us, Harry. I'm not happy, Harry.

PAT: What are you worried about, pet?

GIL: He's told you. He's worried about not being worried ...

CYRIL: Yes. What am I worried about? What *is* getting me down just now, Pat? *(Working things out)* Yes ... Two things, I think ... One – I'm not a *failure* as a writer, am I, Harry?

HARRY: You're fantastic, man. I keep telling you.

CYRIL: That's what I want to hear.

GIL: He keeps waiting for the Nobel prize.

CYRIL: And two: You know what really gets me down. This infertility of Harry's ... Having to use condoms all the time with Pat ... That's completely turned love-making into a big responsibility. Like the big hurdle you've to clear every weekend.

PAT: Harry, honey ...

HARRY: Christ, Cyril! That's really fucking pathetic! Jesus, man! Give him a Nobel prize and let him fuck Pat without Durex and that's his new fucking Jerusalem! Jesus, Cyril!

CYRIL: You don't need to tell me, Harry ... I know.

PAT: Cyril, sweetheart ... I never realised it was as bad as that for you ... I know. Sometimes you used to go on about it being un-erotic, and not nice ...

HARRY: This is a focus, Cyril. You realise that. This is an obvious focus for deeper, *real* problems.

GIL: What for, Harry? For Racialism and the failure of the British Labour Party ...

HARRY: Cyril! That's being a right bastard, man. Keeping a thing like that from Pat! That's being absolutely withdrawn, Cyril! We established this form from the beginning. You were in absolute agreement with it. Pat's got big enough breasts as it is, without going on the fucking pill! It's nothing to do with thrombosis risks or anything else ... It's sheer fucking aesthetics!

GIL: Harry ... You're so emancipated and light years ahead in sexual ethics and everything else.

HARRY:	I'm not saying this. I'm not claiming this for a minute.
GIL:	Then why has Cyril to use anything? Why can't Pat just have a kid by Cyril?
	HARRY is completely shaken by this proposition ... He turns away, trying to rally himself ... PAT is obviously excited.
CYRIL:	*(he has been thinking on his own all this time)* There's nothing else ... That's all that really worries me.
HARRY:	*(to GIL)* This is the first time this question has come up, Gil. I'm prepared to discuss it calmly and objectively.
CYRIL:	And the Tribunal bothers me a bit. The Tribunal would rate as number three problem on my mind ... Monty's car a wee bit too: yes ...
HARRY:	Pat, honey ... Is this a big issue with you? Do you want a kid?
PAT:	If you wanted one, Harry ... It would be nice ... Yes ...
HARRY:	*(trying PAT again)* Pat ... You should be absolutely clear in your mind on this. Do you want a kid. Or do you just want to be pregnant and lie in a nice white nightie in the nursing home, with the baby in its cradle beside you ... And a bowl of grapes and boxes of chocolate liqueurs ...?
GIL:	What the hell is that, Harry – if it isn't wanting to have a kid?
PAT:	I'd like a baby, pet ... Of course I would. Everybody does, Harry ...
HARRY:	Fair enough, Pat. We've got that straightened out for the record.
PAT:	But only if you wanted one, Harry.
CYRIL:	What it is, Harry ... is it's an impotence complex. Basically, that's what it is ...
PAT:	Honey, if I'd've known it was a problem to you ... We could've used something else ... It's just. Never having used anything with Harry ... I mean ... I could've got fitted out with a diaphragm or something.
GIL:	Pat, sweetheart You don't need to do anything. Harry is aware of your need, now. You want to have a kid. That's all Harry wants. Objective facts about life.
HARRY:	If we'd've been one, living organic family, Gil. A real four-handed marriage, there'd be no problem. That way, the kids would've had two fathers and two mothers, but fucking Cyril refuses ...
CYRIL:	Harry, I don't blame you ... If I was in your position, I'd feel the same.
HARRY:	The Caravan moves as fast as its slowest camel.
CYRIL:	I don't blame you at all, Harry. I'd be exactly the same in your position. I'd have a major block in that area too ...
HARRY:	*(turning on him)* We're all different, Mack! Don't try and fucking analyse me in the terms of your twisted childhood and prolonged adolescence!
PAT:	Harry, love. Honestly ... I'm not obsessed with having a baby, honestly. If it's going to spoil anything between us, Harry ... in the least degree.
HARRY:	For fuck's sake, Pat! It's established now. You want a kid.
	The phone rings.
CYRIL:	God! Who's that?
HARRY:	It's like a flower, Pat ... Never fruiting ... And you want to throw it on me ... For blocking your fulfilment ...

CYRIL:	*(lifting the phone)* I don't want any more kids. I've enough kids. *(Into phone)* Hello.
GIL:	You're not having one. It'll be Pat's ...
CYRIL:	Cyril Jackson here ... Hullo ... Hullo ... *(to others)* He's hung up.
PAT:	If you don't want it, Harry ...
GIL:	But *you* want it, Pat.
	CYRIL is on some new track as he returns from the phone, obviously shaken.
CYRIL:	It was a Nigerian. "Mr. Jackson?" Then he hung up.
PAT:	You're the most important thing to me, Harry. The baby isn't even conceived, yet ...
CYRIL:	Listen to this ... this is a classic case of neurosis. It's paranoid. As soon as the phone rang, this image formed in my mind. I was disturbing deep psychic tribal forces. If I didn't make my peace with Atara, she'd organise some kind of Ju Ju on me ...
HARRY:	Fuck, man ... You're fucking mad.
CYRIL:	Harry ... I know ... This is paranoid. But remotely. As a remote possibility it could've been a witch doctor. Can you see Atara getting a witch doctor to work some kind of Ju Ju on me?
HARRY:	You're developing into a raving fucking racialist, man! Give yourself a fucking shake!
CYRIL:	Something happened to me, when I answered that phone. Definitely it could be. I did it to myself. On the other hand, that's maybe the way Ju Ju works.
GIL:	It's scientifically established. Ju Ju has a sound physiological and psychological basis.
HARRY:	Don't start encouraging him, for fuck's sake, girl!
CYRIL:	A witch doctor in Lagos can make a man ill in Rutherglen, thousands of miles away, Harry. There's definite case histories.
PAT:	*(to HARRY)* You understand, sweetheart, the most important thing for me is you. The baby isn't conceived yet ...
CYRIL:	*(to GIL)* On the other hand. It could be some kind of focus for guilt.
HARRY:	That's it, Cyril! You've got the message I'm telling you ... You've got lift off.
CYRIL:	I've definitely never talked about the things I wanted to talk to her about ... Yes ... I fancy that. That turns me on, Harry. Definitely.
HARRY:	That's what I'm saying man. You've got lift off!
CYRIL:	What I'd like to discuss with her is her husband in Lagos. Has Atara *got* a husband? Is that what she's really doing in Glasgow? Taking a commercial course so she can help her husband with his business ...
HARRY:	I'm telling you, Cyril ... There's a rich seam in Atara you haven't even tapped yet, man.
CYRIL:	*(to GIL)* That's the kind of things we should have talked about, Gil ... Basics ... Like how she could leave her kids and her husband for three

years ... Does she turn her statue of the Virgin Mary to face the wall every time she takes one of her friends to bed.

CYRIL getting up from the table. HARRY is now worried.

GIL: Does it matter, Cyril? You reckon it matters?

CYRIL: It gets me moving again ... Definitely. I get the feeling of missed opportunities that I can still grab if I shake myself ... It makes me want to talk to her again ... I mean ... She's never once said anything about me running away from my first wife ... I've never talked about my father to her. *(Going)*

HARRY: *(stopping him)* Where you going, man ... For Christ's sake!

CYRIL: I'm going to get dressed. I'm going in to Atara ...

HARRY: Jesus, Cyril ... You're not going to start a fucking fight about the conflict between her Sacred Heart and her promiscuity! For fuck's sake, Cyril!

CYRIL: To a Catholic, Harry ... Marriage is a Sacrament, man ...

HARRY: Cyril ... If that's your line of approach ... Leave her alone ... I'm telling you ... You're heading for a bigger ballsup.

CYRIL: That's all I want to discuss with her, Harry ... How she resolves this Catholicism/Adultery conflict ... It's fantastic!

GIL: Yes, it is. It's very interesting!

HARRY: Can you not fucking just go in and speak to her. Say ... Hullo or: Fucking good morning ... There's a fucking Black and White Curtain to break through Cyril ... You can't charge head on like a fucking great bull into it ...

CYRIL: Harry, you're right ... That's a valid point ...

GIL: I'm going to get dressed ...

CYRIL: The climate does not exist, Harry. You're right ... The climate does not exist to walk into her room and say: Atara ... What about the Marine Engineer and the Vet and the Accountant and the Pope? It's not there, Harry. You're absolutely right ... I'm going to get dressed.

HARRY: Tell you what, Cyril. Leave her to me. I'll speak to her first ... You get dressed.

CYRIL: Harry, that's better. That's an altogether better line of approach. If you can go into her and talk her out of this Tribunal, this afternoon.

HARRY: I might have to talk about the possibility of you moving to the golf course, Cyril.

CYRIL: The Tribunal wouldn't kill me, Harry, but it's definitely going to be painful. If it could be avoided ... Pain is not my scene.

HARRY: I'm talking about dropping a hint about you going to the golf course, Cyril.

CYRIL: Talk about the golf course, yes. But leave a dotted line for who goes with who over there ... You could be right, Harry ... The golf course could be exactly the environment I might need to achieve the kind of tranquillity to get out a major dramatic work ...

GIL: You going to the bathroom first – or am I, Cyril?

CYRIL: *(holding him back)* Harry ... If you get a chance ... Try and get her on to Ju Ju. See what kind of reaction you get ...

HARRY: *(going)* I'm going to talk about the real world man. Hard reality ... Not neurotic fantasies and wet fucking dreams.

CYRIL: *(going after him)* You could point out to her it's something the Pope is totally opposed to ... She's probably never looked at it from that angle, Harry ...

Scene Two

ATARA's room next door. A few seconds after the end of Scene One. ATARA is lying in bed enjoying the luxury of doing nothing. HARRY is knocking at the door.

HARRY: Atara ... Atara, doll. You up?

               ATARA lies still for a moment not answering.

HARRY: *(off)* Can I come in a minute, honey?

ATARA: *(getting up)* Who is that, please?

HARRY: *(off)* It's me, doll. Harry! I want to speak to you, honey.

ATARA: *(throwing a robe over her and going to the statue)* I'm just getting up, Harry. Wait a minute, please.

               ATARA makes the sign of the cross. Praying ...

               My God, I offer this day all I shall think or do or say, uniting it with what was done on earth by Jesus Christ, thy Son.

               She says this quickly, not like a prayer, but rather as some incantation to ward off whatever evil spirits might be threatening her. She takes a wig off its stand. Puts it on and adjusts it in front of the mirror. She is now ready to receive HARRY. She goes to the door and lets him in.

HARRY: Did I wake you up, doll? I thought I heard you moving about.

ATARA: I had to get up, anyway. I have a lot of things to do today.

HARRY: I've been trying to come over and have a session with you all week, doll. But I've got this bloody course at college *(Standing back to admire her)* That's nice, honey ... You in that robe.

ATARA: I was going to phone you, Harry ... and pick a bone with you. You got me bad bloody marks with your ideas about Shakespeare.

HARRY: Atara, hen ... I told you ... God forbid that anybody should listen to me!

ATARA: I wrote in this essay about Shakespeare, Harry. The best thing for Shakespeare and everybody else would be if they would bury his works.

HARRY: I didn't say that, doll. Look, I've just been talking to Cyril ...

ATARA: I got the worst bloody marks I've ever had for an essay *(Showing him the exercise book)* Look!

HARRY: I didn't say bury him, Atara.

ATARA: You bloody said, bury him ... To God, Harry! You said his plays should be buried for the betterment of the theatre.

HARRY: For a Sabbatical, doll. For seven years. Not for all bloody eternity. No, you see, Cyril is in a bit of a state ...

ATARA: See what Mr. Evans has written at the bottom of the page.

HARRY: I don't see that as valid comment, Atara.

ATARA: *(going over to her larder and bringing out a mouldy pineapple. She cuts a slice)* Ayo bought me some pineapple. You want some?

HARRY:	*(reading the notes in the exercise book)* Typical academic's reaction – 'Look up a complete bibliography of Shakespeare.'
	ATARA offers him a slice of pineapple.
	I'll maybe have a bit later, Atara. Cyril is very upset, Atara ...
ATARA:	I counted them. There are over 2000 books written about William Shakespeare, Harry.
HARRY:	Doll, what does that show? There's 2000 bastards so devoid of any original ideas they have to act as parasites on Shakespeare's. Fuck Shakespeare and these 2000 wets, doll.
ATARA:	If a man has 2000 books written about him, Harry, to God, he can't be not important. Can he? 2000 people haven't written about bloody Cyril, have they?
HARRY:	Early days, hen ... Give them time. They'll latch on to Cyril, too. That's what I'm on about, Atara ... You and Cyril ... I mean, for Christ's sake, Atara. You and Cyril ... I mean ... He loves you, man ... You love him ... Great mutes like you and Cyril, Atara ... Fucking hell, doll!
ATARA:	I pray about your language, Harry. To God, I pray every day about your bloody language!
HARRY:	*(moved)* Christ! You don't, do you, hen?
ATARA:	I read Hamlet in Lamb's stories of Shakespeare ... Then I read the play ...
HARRY:	What do you say, Atara? When you pray for us?
ATARA:	I think Hamlet is a great play ... You're wrong, Harry. Shakespeare is a great writer.
HARRY:	He could be, doll. I don't know ... Don't listen to me, honey.
ATARA:	*(confronting him. Getting down to basics)* I think you are a good friend to me, Harry ... I think so.
HARRY:	Christ, honey, you know that ... I love you, doll.
ATARA:	*(at her desk, flourishing a wad of notebooks)* I am not going into classes this morning, Harry ... I am getting ready all the notes for this trial, this afternoon.
HARRY:	Tribunal, doll. Yes, honey. That's what we've got to talk about.
ATARA:	To God! I am going to make sure I have everything written down on paper ... So that I can tell everybdy the whole truth in this trial!
HARRY:	Tribunal, hen, not trial.
ATARA:	If I haven't it all written down in front of me ... When I see all these people listening to me ... My tongue will be choked *(Breaking down a little)* To God, Harry! My heart is bursting! I have no bloody friends Harry. In this country, I am on my own ... I am treated everywhere as nothing ... In this house they treat me like I was poison!
HARRY:	*(comforting her)* Honey ... They love you. Cyril and Gil ... They admire you, doll ... the sacrifices you make for knowledge. Going away to a foreign country ...
ATARA:	*(breaking away)* To God! I tell you, Harry ... They treat me like bloody poison in the bloody house, man!
HARRY:	Cyril's a writer, honey. That's the basic problem. He's got this super-sensitivity ...

ATARA:	My husband is an important man in Lagos. He has twelve people working for him.
HARRY:	Atara, doll. You and Cyril, doll. You're both lovely beautiful people. I love you both ... That's why it's so fucking sad to see you apart like this.
ATARA:	The first time I come to this house, she treats me as a nothing. I said to her: the curtains are very thin. Can I not have better curtains. She says I'm sorry, we can't afford new curtains, just now. If the room doesn't suit you you know what to do about it.
HARRY:	I know, doll ... The way they've fitted out this room for you is fucking outrageous.
ATARA:	They didn't even give me a wardrobe ... I have to go upstairs to Clair's. I can't even keep my clothes in my own room.
HARRY:	I know, doll, I'm telling you ... A writer's life is a bugger, doll ...
ATARA:	Cyril would go out and buy me a cooker, tomorrow. If it was up to Cyril. But that bloody woman ...
HARRY:	Doll, now ... That's not true, doll. Gil's not blocking ...
ATARA:	To God, that bloody Gil even comes between me and Jesus! When I'm on my own in England, I say to my husband ... I will go every first Friday in the month to Communion ...
HARRY:	... This is Gil reacting to Cyril ... it knocks your nerves to hell ... Living with a writer seven days a week.
ATARA:	At home, I have the children ... And my husband to look after ...Always things to stop me ... Once, I managed to reach five ... Never nine ... Gil knows this ... She was a Catholic once herself. She stops me out of spite. I know this, Harry ...
HARRY:	*(lost)* Nine what, doll?
ATARA:	Communions, man! I'm talking about taking communion every first Friday of the month ... To God, I tell you this over and over again, Harry. Our Lord promised if you take communion nine first Fridays in the month running you won't die without receiving whatever you need for salvation.
HARRY:	Yes ... That's right ... I'm with you, now ...
ATARA:	The first Friday in the month is the special devotion of the Sacred Heart ...
HARRY:	I know ... I'm with you now, doll.
ATARA:	I've managed four First Fridays, Harry ... Tomorrow would have been five ...
HARRY:	It's Thursday, doll. You've still got plenty of time. You'll be alright.
ATARA:	Like this! To God! You think I can take Holy Communion when I'm shouting and hating Gil like poison! How can I take the Body of Our Lord like this! Tell me.

HARRY is totally lost.

Always she bloody does this, Harry. She gets me into a bad temper, the night before. Or even the same morning.

She goes over to the statue of Our Lady. HARRY stands for a moment wrestling with this new situation. At last the light of an insight glimmers in his eye. He grabs at it.

HARRY:	That's it, doll. That's the root of the problem!
	But ATARA has picked up Our Lady and is showing it to him.
ATARA:	I show you something, Harry. Look at this. *(She indicates a chip on the statue ...)*
HARRY:	You believe that Gil's deliberately getting at you.
ATARA:	You see, Harry?
HARRY:	Working you out of your state of grace or whatever you call it. To stop you getting in your nine First Sundays ... Fridays ...
ATARA:	To God, Harry ... I haven't come out of the bloody jungle yesterday like some people think! I'm showing you something man! Look ...
HARRY:	It's very nice, Atara.
ATARA:	To God, I swear I never do this. I come into my room one night and find a chip off Our Lady's nose.
HARRY:	*(examining it)* Yes ... it's fucking chipped right enough. Not deliberately, Atara ... That's what I'm talking about, doll. Think about it. Can you really see Gil deliberately damaging your statue, Atara, honey ... People just aren't like that ... People wouldn't go about knocking up your statues like that ...
	ATARA shuts up ... She turns away from him.
	Maybe she went into your room and had an accident with the statue ... Yes.
ATARA:	What's she doing in my room? She has no need to come near my room ... I asked her for a lock to my room. I've been asking her for months. It doesn't suit her to have my room locked up ... She can't come in and look at my letters and try on my clothes ...
HARRY:	Basically, the problem is from the beginning you've liked Cyril better than Gil. Yes ... Yes? ... Atara? Fuck! Atara!
ATARA:	I tell you how much I think of Cyril, Harry ... Remember that competition they have in TV Times, Harry ... about the guests you would like for a dinner party ...
HARRY:	Yes ... You have this fantastic admiration ...
ATARA:	I put Cyril's name down for the competition, Harry ... I had Elsie Tanner, Edward Woodward, Lulu, Englebert Humperdink ... And Cyril Jackson.
HARRY:	That's nice honey.
ATARA:	That's how much I think of Cyril!
HARRY:	That's what I'm talking about. You have this fantastic admiration for Cyril ... But he's a writer. He's a bugger to live with.
ATARA:	To God, Harry. Cyril is a good man. I know this. It's bloody Gil that turns him against ...
HARRY:	It's Jill, doll, not Gil ...
ATARA:	Gil is a bad woman, man. One night I come into the house and find her making love to Matthew. She was making love to him, Harry.
HARRY:	Making love? I mean ... really making love, doll? In your room?
ATARA:	She was kissing him. I'm sure she was kissing him. To God, they were doing something together. He had the smell of her on him all night.

HARRY: That's what I'm telling you, Atara, doll. She's overflowing with fucking love, Atara. Not this hate you keep on about. Gil's a focus, Atara. Think about it, doll.

ATARA: *(now raging)* To God, don't you try to tell me anything about bloody Gil! I know everything about that bloody woman! A woman who can go into family and take away the husband from his wife and the father from his children.

HARRY: Doll ... That's not a fruitful line ... That'll ...

ATARA: Listen, there is nothing to speak about that bloody woman! A woman who can lead a good man like Cyril into adultery and bloody sin! I don't want to talk about her, Harry!

HARRY: Doll ... For Christ's sake ... We've hit the root of the problem. We've got lift off, now ... Cyril and Gil *are* married – I'm not saying there's anything particularly great about that ... But obviously it worries you ... They're married, doll ... I was a witness ...

ATARA: Harry, I told you. I don't want to talk about these things with you.

HARRY: But if you've got this hang-up about them not being married, Atara – You think they're not married, doll.

ATARA: There's nothing to be gained talking about these things. Your married is not my married ... Cyril is married to the mother of his first children. This is his wife in front of God.

HARRY: Angela's in Greenock just now, for Christ sake, Atara. Going round with an insurance man.

ATARA: Some things are a waste of time talking between people.

HARRY: Doll ... Nothing is a waste of time, talking with you ...

ATARA: I know ... God put Cyril and his first wife together. He didn't put Cyril and Gil together. They put themselves together against God, bringing themselves together ... But you don't believe this the same as you believe in bloody anything. Why should we talk about these things, then. In a minute, we'll start shouting at each other again, like when we talk about the bloody Ibos ... Or you start laughing at me!

HARRY: Christ, honey, *I* can laugh at *you!* Doll ... I accept this ... what you say about Cyril and Gil ... I accept this as absolutely true ... Christ, honey. *I* can laugh at *you!*

ATARA: To God, Harry! What do you do? You turn Catholic!

HARRY: I'm talking about for *you.* It's true. The truth is what you believe in. If you believe in God, he exists. At the same time, honey ... Alright ... There could be this character God ... But think about it. If he's any cop as God, doll ... He's going to know every fucking thing that's been discovered and will be discovered ...

ATARA: To God, Harry! I will bloody pray for you ... You are bloody desperate for prayer!

HARRY: Cyril was a late maturer ... He took a long time to grow up. He still hasn't fucking grown up yet ... But Christ, Atara, how could he have wished a man with a potential like Cyril stuck all his life to that sick woman ... She's got deep personality defects ... Probably fucking brain damage ... And you say they should stick together. What for? Because fucking God wants it. If that's what he fucking wants, fuck him!

ATARA:	To God, Harry! You are a bloody ignorant man! You think that is what God wants? To torture people ... He sends His own Son to be crucified ... Because he wants to torture people!
HARRY:	From Vietnam ... and Buchenwald ... Doll ... and Biafra ... It could be ... yes ...
ATARA:	You don't understand anything about what God does, man! He gave Cyril this wife ... To make him grow bigger ... Like God sometimes makes other people ill ... You are ill ... And you get better ... Your faith grows stronger, and when your faith grows strong, you know the love of God has been poured into your heart by the Holy Spirit.
HARRY:	You've lost us, doll. What does that mean, honey.
	She turns away, giving up.
	No, Atara ... If I'm missing out on something ... tell me ... You're a good catholic, Atara ... it's your whole framework ... I believe you. It's the big thing for you — like socialism is for me and you're married, Atara ...
ATARA:	I think we would be better talking about getting a wash hand basin and a cooker into this room, Harry.
HARRY:	You're fucking married, doll. You've got a husband and four kids in Lagos.
ATARA:	What the hell you come here for, Harry? You come to talk about my family!
HARRY:	Your friends, Atara ... They're great. I like them. They're lovely, easy people ... I'm talking about your friends ...
ATARA:	*(switching off completely)* To God! You get to bloody hell out of here!
HARRY:	Atara, sweetheart ... I'm not condemming you in the slightest degree.
ATARA:	I have a good husband I thank God I have a good husband. What are you saying to me? I am no bloody use as a Catholic! You trying to tell me how to love my own religion!
HARRY:	*(trying to stem the flow)* Atara, honey ... I'm not ...
ATARA:	If I have sins Christ and my husband will take them from me. To God! You think I make love to any man who wants me ... Like a bloody prostitute ... I tell you, the first woman you should look at is your own wife ...
HARRY:	Atara, honey ... you're right. It's obviously something we can't talk about ...
ATARA:	I've seen your wife making eyes at Cyril. And put her hands on him. Cyril is a good man. But to God! It would serve Gil bloody right if Pat took her man away from her!
	This is the end clearly for HARRY. There is obviously no dialogue possible with ATARA on the changeover ... All he wants now is to get out as quick as he can ...
HARRY:	Atara ... I'd better see what's happened to Cyril, honey.
ATARA:	*(calming down ... returning to the business of keeping her room)* I am telling you, Harry, you keep a strong hand on your wife. I've seen her eyes on Cyril. I am telling you, Harry ... As a good friend to you.
HARRY:	*(going)* I'll try and get hold of Cyril, Atara ...

ATARA: *(brings out one of her Mail Order Catalogues)* Everything we need for this room, you can get in here, Harry ... If you tell Cyril ... If he buys from this catalogue, I could recommend him as a customer ... and I would give him the commission I get from the order to make it cheaper for him.

HARRY: *(escaping)* Yes ... That's a possibility, Atara ... The first thing is to get Cyril talking with you. That's the first step, doll.

ATARA: Tell Cyril ... even for five minutes, Harry to come and talk to me. I know he is a good friend. If Cyril wants me to stay and he can fix up my room properly ... I'll stay.

           HARRY escapes.

HARRY: I'll be right back, doll.

CURTAIN

Scene Three

The JACKSON's living room. A minute or so after the end of Scene Two.

PAT is tidying the room ... She finds GIRL's new nightie thrown on a chair ... holds it up, admiring it, tries it against herself looking at the effect on the wall mirror. She takes off her dress and tries it on over her slip, poses in it. Admires herself. CYRIL returns in the middle of this Narcissism. He is sweating, obviously in some kind of panic. He stands for a moment, not knowing how to cope with PAT on her own with him for the first time after all this talk about their relationships.

PAT catches him watching her.

PAT:	I just fancied trying it on. Do I look nice in it? *(She knows very well she does)*
CYRIL:	*(totally unsure how to handle the situation or her now)* Lovely ... yes ... You look nice in it ...
PAT:	*(going to him, innocently. He is obliged to take her in his arms to show nothing has changed)* Harry said I wouldn't ...
CYRIL:	Suits you even better ...
PAT:	I think it'll be lovely, the change round, Cyril. Honestly.
CYRIL:	Yes. It could be. Yes.
PAT:	*You'll* still have Gil, honey. And I'll have Harry.
CYRIL:	*(gently, with careful tact, easing away from her)* I went into my hut and put a sheet of paper in the typewriter ... Pat ... I'm bloody mad ... I'm a neurotic.
PAT:	*(taking his hand)* Could you not get down to your work, pet?
CYRIL:	Feel my shirt, Pat. After five mintues ... I was in a sweat.
PAT:	*(feeling his shirt)* It's soaking, love. You'd better take it off and get a dry one. Will I get one for you, pet?
CYRIL:	I said to myself: I'm sitting here, convincing myself Atara's worked some kind of African hypnotism. I won't call it 'Ju Ju' ... But by some psychological means ... She's blocked my writing ... That's stupid, Pat ... I don't believe that! Do I? How can I believe *that*!
PAT:	Why don't you, pet? Maybe she has ...
CYRIL:	I kept battering away at the typewriter. I couldn't string two bloody sentences together.
PAT:	She could have done something like that, couldn't she, Cyril? Do you think she could?
CYRIL:	I'm not having it! It's bloody pathetic! I'm going to break out of this bloody thing! Sitting there ... saying: maybe she'd done something to me. It's myself. I'm blocking myself! With this stupid bloody neurosis.
PAT:	Honey. Do you think you can always understand what's happening to you?
CYRIL:	I've given it up. I don't understand anything. It could be, of course, that's exactly how Ju Ju works. Who bloody knows?

Looking at PAT and aware of how attractive she is to him for a moment.

That's a nice slip. You look nice in it.

Holding her a minute and stroking her.

PAT: I like clothes. I get kicks out of wearing nice clothes. I like looking at myself in mirrors ... Is that Narcissism, Cyril?

CYRIL: If you get an orgasm, doing it.

PAT: No ... I don't get an orgasm, I sometimes feel sexy, but ...

CYRIL: Do you think Gil gets enough kicks out of life, Pat? I get enough. Definitely. Maybe that's what's wrong with me. I'm a happy man ... Christ, it could be!

PAT: I was watching you all morning, honey ... I love you more than ever, Cyril.

CYRIL: *(with no great conviction)* It's mutual. Definitely.

PAT: Harry wants this change very badly, Cyril. I was thinking before, it would be terrible if he went back to what he was like before we all came together.

CYRIL: *(not listening)* Yes. I was basically even reasonably happy with Angela. I could've probably stuck with Angela all my life. Do you think I could've stuck with Angela all my life, Pat? Christ. Maybe I could've!

PAT: If he didn't get this change, Cyril ... Do you think Harry might start sleeping around again?

CYRIL: Could be ... Yes ...

PAT: It's terrible for him, Cyril. It completely isolates him from me ... He's absolutely on his own ... And it's terrible for the budget ... Always having overdrafts and getting letters from the bank manager.

CYRIL: I couldn't be bothered. That's the big difference between us. All that work till you get a girl into bed ...

PAT: And it completely exhausts him. After a few months. Out all night. He looks terrible, Cyril.

CYRIL: The golf course attracts me, Pat. In the summer, being able to read in the garden in peace. Without bloody ice-cream vans clanging out Greensleeves all day. That would be an improvement ... Definitely.

As he is talking HARRY enters. He pauses tactfully in the doorway.

HARRY: Are you starting – or have you just finished? Not a snide remark. Point of information.

PAT: Neither, honey. *(Going for her dress)* I'm going to start lunch.

HARRY: I went to your hut, Cyril ... I wanted to have a talk with you. Just the two of us. Christ! You didn't graft very long, did you?

CYRIL: I don't think you're happy, are you, Harry? I am ...

HARRY: You didn't even finish the page, Cyril. You stopped in mid-sentence.

CYRIL is watching PAT at the cooker, now, she is slicing capiscums.

CYRIL: Gil wouldn't have thought of that ... Frying peppers with hamburgers.

HARRY: *(pimping for her)* I'm telling you, man! She's living poetry ... She's a fucking treasure ... Her whole life1 Think about it. The way she bloody moves. Cooking. Dressing. Undressing ... Fucking poetry, Cyril!

PAT: Harry, pet! Stop it!

HARRY: It is, Pat, honey. 't's a fact. *(To CYRIL)* You didn't tell us you were doing a play for kids, Cyril. I thought you were working on Walter Scott this morning.

CYRIL: **I'm going to phone STV this morning. We're completely off the track** with Walter Scott. *Burns* is the man. *Burns* definitely excites me, Harry.

HARRY: That sentence you stopped at, Cyril. About the King making a law, forcing everybody to eat Raspberry Jam? Why does he want everybody to eat raspberry jam?

CYRIL: I don't know.

HARRY: Christ ... You've got it down in fucking black and white, man ... You must know why he does it.

CYRIL: Mabe that's just what the hero thinks. That's his black and white picture of the world.

CYRIL is now trying to articulate this. The light of yet another new insight beginning to glow in his eyes.

If the King isn't a saint: he must be a devil.

HARRY: Whose fault is the law for Raspberry Jam, then Cyril?

CYRIL: That's it, Harry ... That's why I came to a bloody stop ... That's the whole lock!

PAT: Harry, feel Cyril's shirt ...

HARRY: I'll tell you something, Cyril ... You're absolutely right about Black Power ... Fascism, Cyril, man. That's all you can describe it as.

Black Power's our fault, Cyril. It's our fucking fault, man ... *We've* pushed her right back!

CYRIL: What is this Raspberry jam story, Harry? Obviously it's about the nature of democracy. The need for mutal responsibility in a democracy ...

PAT: Honey ... is that not a bit complicated ... for children, pet.

CYRIL: The play under the play, I'm talking about, Pat ...

HARRY: It's like fucking Hitler, Cyril ... Dictating terms. I want a wash hand basin, I want a cooker. A new wardrobe ... A settee. fridge ... A lock in my door. A fucking list of demands. I want Czechoslovakia ... Hungary ... Vietnam ... Biafra ...

He turns to CYRIL. But CYRIL has his notebook out and is making notes totally absorbed in following the new light. Seeing HARRY's eye on him he explains the development so far.

To God, she says, I want to choose my own stuff. I want to get it from my mail order catalogue. So that I can get the commission.

PAT: Harry, have you changed your mind about spending the weekdays with Gil, honey?

HARRY: Is that going to help Black Power? That's the point I am making, Cyril ... Giving in to her like that!

PAT: But her room's terrible, Harry ... You can't live in it. You said that yourself.

HARRY: Her image of the world, Pat, is totally twisted, just now. *(To CYRIL)* She went on and on about you sticking with Angela ... That was the only way you could achieve spiritual fulfilment – whatever the fuck that means ...

CYRIL: That's perceptive comment ... Yes ...

PAT: Cyril, pet, you're not taking a superficial comment like that seriously, are you?

CYRIL: You can't write it off ... that's what I'm saying.

HARRY: If you keep giving in to her demands, like that, Cyril ... Is that helping her to grow ...

CYRIL: That's obviously something I should talk to her about, Pat.

HARRY: You're absolutely right, Cyril! What's the point in letting her stay ...

PAT: Harry ... Cyril can't throw her out like that. Just now ... in the winter ... that's terrible. You said so yourself.

CYRIL: I'm not throwing her out, Pat ... I'm not going to give up trying to communicate with her.

HARRY: For Christ's sake, man! You can't fucking live with her! That's what's fucked up your writing this last year. She weighs on you. She choked the fucking life out of you.

CYRIL: I know Harry ... that's the problem ... she weighs on me ... yes ... but I've got to fight it ... I've got to find some way of living with her. I'm that kind of writer, Harry. I put myself into my work, man. If I lead a directionless, pointless existence, I turn out directionless, pointless writing.

PAT: You do, honey – that's why you do – you put all yourself into your writing.

HARRY: For fuck's sake, Pat, leave him alone a minute ... Don't encourage him. You don't know what he's talking about!

CYRIL: Walter Scott. It has no spring to it! No life-force bubbling out. No passion to change the world.

HARRY: If you fucking don't believe you can change the world, for Christ's sake, you can't fucking work yourself into a passion to change it! If Black Power makes you want to throw up, mack, you can't fucking put your arms round her and get it up stiff and hard for her, can you!

CYRIL: I'm out of apathy, Harry ... I'm working again ... I'm fighting ... I feel it ... The sap is rising.

           As he is talking, the phone rings.

           Who's that now? *(Into phone)* Hullo. Yes, Mr. Monty.

HARRY: Cyril, man. You can't believe in something because you think it's going to get you writing better plays, man.

CYRIL: Yes, I've been away from the firm about fourteen months, Mr. Monty. That's right.

HARRY: What kind of a fucking philosophy is that, Cyril? You're a socialist not because you believe in social justice for everybody but because it's the only way to keep your typewriter fucking hammering away!

CYRIL: I'm talking about directions, man, that's what's wrong with Walter Scott. *(into phone)* I'm not sure what was in my mind, Mr. Monty. I think maybe it was you kindly letting me use the car. To help me establish myself as a writer ... I think.

HARRY: You know what you're doing, man.

PAT: Harry ... I think the important thing we should be talking about just now is ... me having a baby. When I said, I wanted a baby, sweetheart ...

HARRY: Wait a minute. Pat!
(to CYRIL) You're turning socialism into fucking pot, man! turning Marx fucking upside down. Socialism is the pot of the intellectuals!

CYRIL: I don't know Mr. Monty ... Why should I think that ... Yes, it's fair ... That I should have at least paid the tax and insurance ... possibly the depreciation ... yes ... at the same time, Mr. Monty –

HARRY: Put that fucking phone down. Tell the cunt to go have a fuck to himself! MONTY! FUCK OFF!

CYRIL: I'm not in a position really to pay anything, just, now, Mr. Monty ... no.

PAT: *(to CYRIL) You* understand, Cyril, about me wanting to have a baby ... don't you?

HARRY: You need medical treatment, man. You're a totally unstable personality.

CYRIL: Yes, Mr. Monty ... It sounds interesting ... I see ... on a part-time basis ...

CYRIL: *(to HARRY)* He wants us to go back to flogging records for him. *(Into phone)* A new bargain label ... yes ... I heard you, Mr. Monty ...

HARRY: One minute you're lying down, waiting to die, the next, you've got your fucking rifle and you're marching out on to the fucking streets to take over the fucking City!

PAT: I'm not pushing it on Harry, am I Cyril? Saying I don't want a baby, if he doesn't want one ...

Onto this bursts ATARA, raging.

ATARA: To God! I see how you bloody come straight into me!

CYRIL: Hullo, Atara ... I want to speak to you. *(Into phone)* Yes, Mr. Monty ... I get you ... you give me a retainer ... *(to HARRY)* Jesus, Harry! God! *(To ATARA)* I want to have a long talk with you, Atara. It's Monty ... He's on the phone to us.

ATARA: To God! Listen to me!

She pulls the phone out of his hands.

You'd think I want to stay in this bloody house! Being treated like a bloody nothing!

CYRIL: *(trying to get phone off her)* Something urgent's turned up, Mr. Monty. I'll ring you back in a minute.

ATARA: The first time I come into this house, she treat me as a nothing. I said to her, the curtains are very thin, can I not have better curtains? She said, if the room doesn't suit you, you know what to do about it. You think I am so desperate for a room, I have to bow to bloody people like you! All I take you to this bloody trial for is to make sure I get justice in this country, and to tell people the bloody things people do to me in this bloody house!

She waves notebook at CYRIL
Phone rings again.
CYRIL answers it.

CYRIL: Hullo ... not at all, Mr. Monty ... I didn't cut you off ... no ... I said I'd ring you back ...

ATARA: *(waving her notebook like some secret weapon)* I tell you! I have every-
              thing down here! I tell them everything you people do to me in this bloody
              house! I bloody tell you!

              *She charges from the room ... CYRIL is still struggling to pacify MONTY.
              White and trembling.*

              *PAT keeps turning over her hamburgers. Only HARRY has the situation
              in hand.*

HARRY: Fucking black fascist bastard! FUCKING BLACK FASCIST BASTARD!

ACT TWO

Scene One

The JACKSON's living room. About ten-thirty. The same day. CYRIL is at the table, making notes. GIL sits cross-legged on the carpet, studying the fire. PAT is handing a cup of coffee to the latest crisis in the life of the quartet _ MAXIE.

CYRIL: Maxie. Don't think that I regret the happy evenings I've spent in your house. I enjoyed them. I hope they'll continue.

MAXIE looks at his watch.

GIL: Max, just go. He's just performing ... The whole thing ... Bringing you here ... Making you wait for Harry ... It's just a stupid performance ...

MAX: I'm not worried about the synagogue, Gil. If necessary, I can say the Prayer for the Departed *here*. In my head!

CYRIL: *Before* this thing emerged between you and Gil, Maxie ... Basically, I didn't like you ... Even while you were giving us big kosher, free range chicken dinners in Newton Mearns ... And appreciating my guitar playing, Maxie ... I didn't admit it to myself ... You understand? I had a strong desire to like you ...

PAT: *(to GIL)* Do you love each other?

GIL: *(looking at MAX)* I don't know ...

PAT: Gil, pet ... It's not a thing you play around with. Is it? Loving people.

MAX: At the same time, Cyril ... I think you might like me a bit more than you realise.

CYRIL: Christ! I admire you. That's a beautiful thing! Every anniversary of your father's death, to go to the synagogue and say The Prayer for The Departed. I was going to ask you ... Maxie. Do you think I should do that for *my* father?

PAT: Is it, Gil?

GIL: It's just another body. Don't start getting into a panic about it. If I take the Pill ... Why should I stop at some arbitary kind of boundary like holding hands ... or kissing ... if I fancy sleeping with somebody ...

CYRIL: It's Maxie that's the problem, Gil. You fancying *Maxie* ... *(to MAX)* the thing is Maxie. I'd have to say this prayer for my father in Hebrew, wouldn't I? If I went to the synagogue ...

MAX: It's written in the English script ... At the back of The Prayer Book.

PAT: I mean ... You keep having these things, Gil ... Don't you ...? Writing to Len Deighton ... and John Updike ...

MAX: At the back of the book. Yisgadal, Veyistabach, Sheme Rabbo ...

CYRIL: Listen to him! That's beautiful! Listen to him!

MAX: Cyril, man ...

CYRIL: I'm serious. It's beautiful, Maxie. Maxie ... *(Getting his coat)* I think you should go to the synagogue ...

PAT: You do ... don't you, Gil?

GIL: Yes ... I do ...

CYRIL:	Here's your scarf and hat, Maxie.
MAX:	It's too late, Cyril. I told you ... It's half past ten ...
CYRIL:	Would you like to go into the corner and say it?
	MAXIE waves away the suggestion.
PAT:	What would be really stupid, would be to upset, Harry ... over nothing ... There's nothing to tell him ... You haven't done anything to tell them *about*. Have you, Gil?
GIL:	It's nearly four months since I wrote to John Updike ... isn't it, Cyril ...
CYRIL:	Gil ... I'm grateful to him ... I am, Maxie ... At last I'm connected up ... Up till now. I have not really been connected up ... It's like you get a sudden emotional jar ... You see ... And you get connected up ... It's not sexual jealousy, you understand, Gil ... It's *Maxie* ... Look at him ...
MAX:	Cyril, you don't need to tell me ...
CYRIL:	If it was somebody about twenty, Gil; with long black hair ... And a firm beautiful body ...
GIL:	*(studying MAX)* That's just you being conformist about male beauty. That's all. Max is lovely to look at. Isn't he, Pat?
PAT:	I like him. I do. I like him very much. I always have, Max.
CYRIL:	I'm not knocking you and Maxie, Gil. I'm a happy, excited man! Look at me. At last, I've made contact with my subconscious ... I'm tapping my subconscious well. I've made a strike. Thoughts are gushing into the air!
	As he is speaking, a car draws up outside. MAX goes to the window, clearly anxious.
MAX:	I think Miriam accepted the anti-apartheid meeting story, Cyril. Do you?
CYRIL:	Why do you say that, Maxie? *(Joining him at the window)* You think Miriam's checking on you. It could be Miriam's car ... I can't see who it is, in this fog ...
GIL:	*(to PAT)* These crushes I get ... John Updike and Len Deighton, Pat ...
CYRIL:	It's not Black Power ... It's a car ... Not a taxi ...
GIL:	*(pointing to MAX)* That's a solid body ... isn't it ... They were just books ... Getting turned on by books ...
MAX:	*(at window, growing more and more anxious)*, It's not impossible. She could drop in, Cyril ... To offer help at the meeting ...
CYRIL:	*(leading him on)* Yes ... She could do, Maxie ... Couldn't she?
	As they are talking, HARRY enters.
	He is knocked off his balance by the presence of MAX but quickly adjusts his mask according to the new situation. He embraces MAX, CYRIL and affectionately feels up the women.
HARRY:	Victory, comrades! Total victory.
CYRIL:	Could be. We'll see.
HARRY:	Black Power out! Black Power out! *(Embracing MAXIE again)* Man! She's got to go, now, man! There's a fucking order to quit been issued. *(To MAXIE)* Maxie. A major talent! Watching your performance this afternoon, I kept thinking: Some people you can love ... Maxie ... I definitely love you. Definitely!

CYRIL: Harry, son ... Just relax for a minute ... Relax ... New dimension to Maxie's personality's emerged ...

HARRY: I'm talking about Maxie, Super Lawyer! *(To MAXIE)* For fuck's sake, Maxie! Don't blush! It's true ...

MAX: Harry ... Honestly ... There was no case ... You didn't need a lawyer ... Atara completely alienated the whole Tribunal.

CYRIL: Biccy, Harry? What I'm thinking of doing, Harry, is sibbing the lock and barring Black Power from the house when she gets back tonight. You reckon she'd accept it calmly ... Or do you think she might start a fit of hysterics and throw bricks at the windows, screaming rape?

HARRY: As long as we have Maxie, around ... No problem ... Jesus, Maxie ... Fantastic ... The way you handled her. Black Power screaming away at you: To God, this man is not fit to be in this trial because he is sleeping with Jackson's wife five afternoons a week.

CYRIL: This is the new dimension to the situation we want to talk to you about, Harry ... I checked with Maxie ...

MAX: *(nervously)* Harry ... I want you to know this ...

CYRIL: I asked him, Harry: Maxie, how long would you have played around with Gil, without coming into the open about it, if Black Power wouldn't have revealed all, this afternoon.

MAX: Cyril ... I think Harry should know this ... It's a mutual thing, Harry ... Isn't that right, Gil?

PAT: Harry, pet ... There's nothing to tell ... You're getting all worked up over nothing ...

MAX: It wasn't a case of me running after Gil, Harry ... We moved towards each other ... You know what I mean ...

PAT: *(desperately)* It's just Cyril, Harry ... You know how he goes on about nothing, at times ... It's nothing ... All it adds up to is a lunch now and then in Lewis's ... And once Max came over in the afternoon for a coffee ... But she had Clair with her.

MAX: But the big thing, Harry ... The important point is, I didn't know you had this beautiful scene going between the four of you ...

PAT: It's absolutely nothing, Harry ...

MAX: *(to HARRY)* This thing, the four of you have, Harry ... It's beautiful ... It's living revolution ... I envy you ... It's fantastic ...

           HARRY is at the fridge bringing out a bottle of wine. Pouring himself a glass. Generally giving himself time to work out his tactics for this new situation.

CYRIL: See, Maxie ... It has no future. On a simple, mathematic basis alone. It's a dead end. Even if we fancied sleeping with Miriam ... Work it out for yourself. If the four of us started bringing in boyfriends and girlfriends ... and the boyfriends and the girlfriends started bringing in boyfriends and girlfriends ... Before we know it, we're going to need the City Hall for sexual congress!

HARRY: *(his tactics established. Now looking at MAX)* He's a sexy bastard, Gil. No fucking doubt about it!

GIL: I know he is. He's lovely.

HARRY:	Partly your clothes, Maxie ... The way you wear them ... That's part of the attraction ...
MAX:	You know how these things happen, Harry ...
HARRY:	I know, Maxie ... You don't need to tell me ...
MAX:	You're not aware of what's happening to you ... You cross the boundary ... Without noticing it ...
CYRIL:	Boundary ... Of love ... Maxie?
MAX:	*(not sure, quite)* Yes ...
CYRIL:	You cross into the boundary of love.
PAT:	It's no reflection on you and Gil, Harry. It's just ... You know this hard, logical mind she has ... Isn't it, Gil?
GIL:	I don't know what it's a reflection on ... You could at least pour me out a glass too, while you're bloody drinking!
HARRY:	*(pouring and handing a glass to her)* Maxie ... I don't blame you. To know her – is to love her. *(Taking off his tie)* You know me, Maxie ... I'm going to start having fucking property hang-ups over my women? *(Sits down and takes off his shoes)* Fuck Gil, Maxie ... Fuck Pat, if you fancy her ... *(Putting the shoes carefully away)* It's their fucking bodies, for fuck's sake! Relax, Maxie, take your clothes off.
MAX:	Oh Harry, come on now ...
GIL:	We're having the big strip, are we?
HARRY:	You know yourself. This fucking great value placed on fucking's a hangover from the age of property. *(Off with sweater)* Take your clothes off, Maxie ... Relax ... What's everybody got their clothes on for, for fuck's sake ... We love each other ... We're trying to touch each other ... Maxie ... Relax ... Take your clothes off ... *(Off with his shirt)*
MAX:	I'm fine, thanks Harry ... I'm fine the way I am ...
	GIL *takes* HARRY's *discarded sweater and puts it on.*
GIL:	Save us going upstairs and getting one ...
HARRY:	Gil ... Pat ... for fuck's sake ... Let's see you ...
PAT:	Harry, pet *(Anxious)* It's not warm enough to go about like that ... I'll get you a dressing gown ... *(His trousers coming off now)*.
HARRY:	They've got fucking central heating, Pat ... Cyril's fucking crucifying himself paying for it ... What's the fucking point fucking crucifying yourself paying for central heating if you have to go about with fucking clothes on ... Yes, Maxie?
CYRIL:	What about your pants, Harry?
HARRY:	Gil, sweetheart ... For fuck's sake ...
GIL:	When I'm really sure of you, Maxie ... I'll let you see my stretch marks ...
CYRIL:	You forgot to take your underpants off, son. You frightened of getting a chill in your gear ...
HARRY:	How can you move together ... Close, Maxie ... With all these layers between people ...? Body to body ... Naked skin to naked skin ... Fucking flesh ... That's the only way you can get moving.
PAT:	*(taking off her dress)* I'll just keep on my slip ... Harry ... Till the room warms up.

MAX:	There's two kinds of people ... Isn't there?
CYRIL:	You not going to show Maxie your gear, Harry?
HARRY:	I'm stripping for comfort and real communication ... Maxie know that ... Maxie ... If I took off my pants ... I'm not taking them off for sexual competition ... You understand that ...
MAX:	There's people ... you see ... who get turned on by naked bodies ...
CYRIL:	True, Maxie ... Christ! True!
MAX:	And other people ... get turned on by clothed bodies ... Like clothes making bodies more erotic to them ...
GIL:	Like Cyril and Atara's knickers, Maxie ... Harry ... What was Cyril doing with Atara's knickers? Maxie was saying something to Cyril about it ... but they shut up as soon as we came in ...
HARRY:	He's got this unclassified deviation, Gil ... A secret collection of knickers of all the tribes of Africa ...
MAX:	You see, Harry ... It's what you're used to.
HARRY:	Maxie ... If you don't feel like stripping off, man ... For fuck's sake! I still love you ... Your position, I can understand absolutely ... You're right, man ... You're not used to it ... But fucking Cyril, here!
PAT:	I'll try and blaze up the fire, will I, Gil?
HARRY:	What I am saying, Maxie ... And what you will have to be absolutely clear about ... and on guard against ... is we are dealing with a very insecure character in our friend here ... In all the years we've been together, I have never once seen his fucking prick ...
CYRIL:	Other people's penises do nothing to me ... how do they work with you, Maxie? ... Put me off ...
HARRY:	Not that I would get any fucking kick out of seeing it ... but out of togetherness ...
GIL:	That would be interesting – The two of you crossing penises ... nice ...
HARRY:	I mean ... Bringing you here tonight, Maxie. What for? What for, Cyril?
CYRIL:	Harry, son ... I am not being malicious or aggressive ... But I am not interested in anything you have to say. Don't get emotional about it, Harry ...
HARRY:	What for, Cyril? To have a great confrontation with me?
	Gil is sitting very close to MAX now ... Taking his hand MAX tries to act as if everything is normal ... but is clearly embarrassed.
CYRIL:	It's just a flat statement of fact, Harry ...
HARRY:	Why have a confrontation between Maxie and me, Cyril? She's your fucking wife. (*Annoyed at the closeness of GIL and MAXIE*) I'm fucking speaking to Cyril and Maxie. Gil! Can you not fucking leave him alone for one minute.
CYRIL:	I just am not interested, Harry, in anything you have to say to me ... You can give me nothing, now, Harry ... I've moved on ... I'm light years beyond you now, Harry!
GIL:	(*to PAT*) Is it just *me* ... Pat? You not fancy him?
PAT:	He's nice. I've always liked him ... I've always enjoyed your company, Max ...

MAX:	*(absolutely lost. Trying to shake himself into some kind of reality)* Do you ever say to yourself: What am I doing here?
HARRY:	*(blue with cold)* Pat ... Give the fucking fire a fucking poke, will you!
MAX:	You see yourself, like looking down from the ceiling. And you sitting there.
HARRY:	Why bring Maxie to me, Cyril? What do you want us to do ... Kick him in the teeth for fucking your wife.
CYRIL:	I could be wrong, Harry ... It would be nice if I was wrong. But basically, we don't have a thing further to say to each other, son. That's it ...
MAX:	What I mean ... It's not real ... I'm not *real* ... I know I *am*. But I don't feel real. Obviously, there's something seriously wrong with my personality.
	HARRY goes out the room a minute, slams the door.
CYRIL:	What it is, Pat ... Is Harry is not connected up ... That's the basic trouble.
MAX:	Take a mirror, now, Gil ... A mirror I find very bad ... I get embarrassed looking at myself in a mirror ...
CYRIL:	That I can understand, Maxie ... You looking in a mirror and being embarrassed ...
	HARRY returns with an electric fire.
	What you going to do with that, Harry?
HARRY:	What the fuck do you think I'm going to do with it?
MAX:	I wasn't talking physically, Cyril ... That goes without saying ... I get no pleasure looking at myself in a mirror ...
CYRIL:	You're not going to plug that in ... We've got a fire ... We've got central heating ... That eats money, Harry ... For Christ's sake ...
PAT:	Cyril ... You don't really mean that about Harry ...
CYRIL:	He's not connected up ... That's the basic problem. I'm not being superior, Harry. You're just not connected up ...
HARRY:	Look, Mack ... If anybody made any fucking connections ...
CYRIL:	You've got two bars on, Harry ... Double bars ...
GIL:	If you're cold, Harry ... Why don't you put some clothes on ...
HARRY:	*(giving CYRIL money)* Here you are, son ... That'll last a couple of hours ... Give us a shout when you need some more ...
CYRIL:	Harry ... I can't take your money like that ...
HARRY:	I'm telling you, man ... If anybody made any fucking connections this afternoon it was fucking me, Mack ...
CYRIL:	You've got twice as much coming in as me ... haven't you, Harry. *(Pocketing the money)* and only two mouths to feed.
HARRY:	Sitting there, listening to Black Power throwing at you every fucking perversion in the book and out of it!
MAX:	I'm talking about myself as a whole, Cyril. Looking in a mirror ... You see yourself and what you add up to ... You know everything there is to know about the character you're looking at ... It's painful, Cyril ... You understand ...
HARRY:	Alright you didn't rape her back in front. Or feel her up ... Or wave your prick to her ... Or bring wee girls into the house ... Or pose for fucking

porn films ... But some fucking fraction of the truth there must have been in that recital, Mack!

As he is speaking a car draws up outside ... CYRIL goes to the window.

HARRY:	For fuck's sake, Cyril. I'm not asking what your kink is, man.
CYRIL:	Christ, Gil, it's Black Power, in a taxi.
HARRY:	I love you, Cyril. It doesn't make any difference to me if you wear a fucking skin diving suit or a corset or knickers or fucking nothing, man.
CYRIL:	She looks very low, her hair's soaking.
HARRY:	It's not important, Cyril.
PAT:	I'd like it, if it was lingerie or something ...
MAX:	Transvestism is more common than you realise ... I've defended at least three cases in the last nine months ... one man kept going into Marks and Spencers —
PAT:	I'd like that ... I'd enjoy it ... Buying him knickers and things like that ...
CYRIL:	*(still at the window)* She's coming in, now ...
GIL:	You going to snib the bolt ... and lock her out, Cyril?
CYRIL:	*(still at the window)* Two months ago ... I was buying her tights ... I made her cocoa ...
HARRY:	What I'm talking about, Cyril, is an entirely new idea, an emotional sabbatical. I can cope with Maxie. I love Maxie. I can cope. *(To MAXIE)* You and Pat. And me Gil, Maxie. No problem.
CYRIL:	*(shaking himself: in the grip of a blinding insight)* Maxie, you're right, Christ. You're right, Maxie ... It's not real ... Standing here, Maxie ... It's not real.
GIL:	I don't think I fancy you in bra and knickers, Cyril ... I mean ... if you *had* to do it ...
HARRY:	It's Gil's body, Maxie ... What's a fuck between mates for fuck's sake! The pattern's Absolutely clear, Cyril. We have this sabbatical ... *You* stay all week with Pat ... I stay all week with Gil.
CYRIL:	Atara comes home ... Soaking wet, miserable. Hitting the ground and we're sitting here ... talking about barring her from the house!
HARRY:	I'm talking to you about this sabbatical, man ...
PAT:	*(in a panic)* Harry, honey ... is that what you want us to do? Break up ... like that ...
HARRY:	I'm not talking about breaking up, Pat ... We're talking about growing closer and closer together. *(His arms round GIL)* Moving to greater and greater fulfilment.
CYRIL:	That tribunal this afternoon, Maxie ... That wasn't *real* was it? Did you feel it was *real*, Maxie?
MAX:	I know what you're talking about, Cyril, yes ...
PAT:	But we'd see each other at times, wouldn't we, Harry? We wouldn't completely separate? You don't want that, sweetheart?
CYRIL:	I mean ... You playing the defence, Maxie ... Atara throwing fantasies all over the place ...
PAT:	Would you, Harry?

HARRY: Pat, sweetheart ... I love you ... I'd have to keep seeing you ... But no interfucking, of course, Pat. Total sexual insulation between couples for the sabbatical.

PAT is shattered at this.

GIL: *(to CYRIL)* You'd be happy with Pat ... wouldn't you, Cyril?

CYRIL: I'm a happy man ... Pat's a happy woman, Gil ...

PAT: What it is, Harry ... Is it you don't want us any longer?

CYRIL: I mean, Me. Maxie ... Playing the honourable, compassionate, injured man. For Christ's sake, Maxie!

GIL: I mean ... you had this great scene going with Angela, didn't you ... You were even happy with Angela ... Cyril ... bathing the kids ... and making their meals ... and scrubbing the floors ...

HARRY: I love you, Pat, for fuck's sake. This is just a purely temporary arrangement.

MAX: Harry ... I wouldn't like to be the cause of this beautiful thing the four of you have –

CYRIL: It's exactly the same process as Buchenwald and Dachau and the Nazis, Maxie. Pushing Atara into something less than a human being.

HARRY: What you fucking on about now, Cyril ... She's beaten you up, morally, spiritually, physically ... She fucking hates you.

CYRIL: Exactly like the Nazis, Maxie ... Anybody you can't cope with ... you push him into something less than a human being.

ATARA enters, storms through the room and through the kitchen to the bathroom.

(Listening) She's going up to the bathroom.

HARRY: If she could fucking get away with it, Mack, she'd stick fucking assegais into every fucking part of your body ... She'd fucking fry your fucking balls, man, and eat them on fucking toast!

CYRIL: As soon as you look at the Jews as something less than human, you can shove them in the gas chambers ... Or the Vietnamese ... You can drop napalm on them.

MAX: Cyril ... I see this ... It's a beautiful concept.

CYRIL: This is exactly what we're doing, Gil. On a small scale. Atara's something less than human. So throw her out in the middle of winter. Reject any chance of communicating with her.

HARRY: Cyril, man, everything's fucking resolved, now you stupid cunt! She's got a month's notice we're ready to move on to the next stage. Don't start fucking it up with ...

CYRIL: I'm connected up, now, Harry ... Look ...
            (Touching chair) I can touch that chair ... I'm touching things now.
            (Listening) She's coming down, now.

MAX: It's just sometimes so hard, at times, Cyril. Isn't it ... getting back to reality ... you've got to watch yourself all the time.

HARRY: That fucking order, giving her a month to quit, for fuck's sake ... That's not real, like? The sugar she put in your petrol tank ... that fantasy sugar, Maxie?

CYRIL:	She's in the kitchen. That's good. I was hoping she would go straight to bed. Maxie . I can see you, now ... clearly. *(Touching him)* You're solid Maxie ... Listen what are you doing here?
MAX:	That's it Cyril ... What am I doing here?
CYRIL:	You're here to sleep with Gil. You came here to sleep with Gil? When are you going to do it Maxie? Did you see yourself sleeping with Gil, tonight?
GIL:	That what you fancy, Cyril? Coming up and watching us?
CYRIL:	Harry, what do you think? You reckon tonight would be as good a time as any ... while the iron's hot ...

MAX now beginning to prepare his retreat at last changing his position back to a Maxie position, a Maxie reality.

MAX:	You see ... Cyril ... Miriam ...
HARRY:	*(To Cyril)* What you on to now, Mack?
MAX:	You know Miriam, Cyril.
CYRIL:	Phone Miriam now, Maxie. Tell her you're doing an all night vigil for the blacks in S.A. in George Square.
MAX:	Not feasible, Cyril, the kind of woman Miriam is ... you know her ... she'd come down to George Square in the middle of the night with a flask of hot soup.
HARRY:	*(sarcastically)* Tell her it's a fast, Maxie. A vigil and a fast!
MAX:	*(taking him seriously)* That wouldn't stop her coming down to see if I was alright, Harry.
CYRIL:	You go up to bed now, Maxie.
MAX:	Basically, Cyril, it's not really practical, tonight, is it?
CYRIL:	You go up to bed together ... hand in hand ... I'm left down here. What do I do when you're in bed together, Maxie?
HARRY:	For fuck's sake, Cyril, man it's my problem, Gil and Maxie ... you'll be with Pat.
CYRIL:	*(to MAX)* You see, he doesn't know what's happening, does he Maxie?
MAX:	The kids are a factor, Cyril, aren't they, Gil?
CYRIL:	The world doesn't stand still for a single microsecond, Harry. Basic Marxism remember ... the time it takes you to solve one problem of life another hundred thousand have pulled up behind you.
MAX:	They're at an age when they notice things, Cyril ...
CYRIL:	The first thing is you'd undress Gil ... Gil ... do you fancy Maxie undressing you.

HARRY getting more and more distressed. CYRIL watching him.

PAT:	Cyril, pet ... Don't do that, honey ... Don't, pet ...
GIL:	We'd take up a bottle of wine, Cyril ... You think so, Max?
MAX:	What I'm talking about, Cyril ... Is ... If they woke up ... and didn't find me in the bedroom with Miriam, in the morning ...
CYRIL:	You'd get into bed together. First ... You'd slip your big fat body up the bed so that she could take your circumcised penis in her mouth ... While I'm down here, Maxie ... You've forgotten all about me ... I don't exist.

I'm down here, Gil ... You're sucking away at his circumcised penis ... and I don't exist. Lost in each other.

HARRY: That kills you, does it ... You not fucking existing ... while Gil's got some other cock in her mouth ... That's the fucking ultimate!

CYRIL: Max ... I can't have it. I'm not having it, Max ... I'm not having Gil taken away from me like that ...

MAX: *(moved)* Cyril ... I respect your feelings ... *(And relieved)*

CYRIL: I lean on her ... I lean on you, Gil ... I'm not having her move into a world with somebody else I'm kept out of ... I'm not having it, Max ...

MAX: I'm telling you ... I respect your feelings ... Cyril ... For Christ's sake ... I understand your position, Cyril ...

CYRIL: I lean on Gil ... I lean on you ...

HARRY: Swinging. Great. Fucking great scene ... You leaning people ...

GIL is silent. She is visualising this reality CYRIL has evoked and recoiling from it. As MAX recoils from the responsibility and commitment he is unable to feel.

PAT: Cyril. Pet ... It's not like that with Harry and me ... Even when we're making love, Cyril ... We're thinking all the time about the four of us ... aren't we, Harry? When you make love to me ... It's you making love to me, Harry ... and Gil and Cyril ... It's all of us being together ...

GIL: Do you believe that, Pat? I can't believe half the bloody things you come out with at times ...

PAT: Gil, pet ... It's true ... Max's helped us to a real understanding ... Cyril's right ... Do you not feel ... The four of us ... We're closer than ever together, Gil ...

CYRIL: That's a fog statement, Pat ... It's not real ...

PAT: If you'd just let yourself *feel* things out, Gil. Give in to your feelings.

GIL: We're in pieces all round the room, Pat, sweetheart ... And you're going on about us being closer than ever!

CYRIL: I'm not discriminating against *you*, Maxie ... I'm not having you *or* Harry sleeping with Gil ... I'm sorry ... I'm emotionally crippled ... I lean on Gil ...

HARRY: For fuck's sake! That's really moving into fucking orbit!

MAX: No, Harry ... That's not fair ... you can see, the way Cyril feels ... I'm exactly the same, Cyril ...

HARRY: Maxie ... I wish you'd fuck off home ... Honest to God!

MAX: I'm talking about the level of maturity you need to achieve before you can cope with your wife sleeping around, Harry ... You can see ... Gil ... with Cyril feeling like he does ...

GIL: Max ... I think you should go home, sweetheart ...

CYRIL: I'm a pervert, Maxie ... That's what it is ... I'll never know what real love ... and real sex are about ...

PAT: You're not, pet ... You're a lovely lover, Cyril ... Isn't he, Gil?

CYRIL: Not the big time stuff, Pat ... That Harry and the other revolution-of-the-body characters go on about ... That's me ... An emotional and sexual cripple ...

HARRY: You're acting, man! You're putting on an act.

MAX: I'm not kidding myself, am I, Cyril? It hasn't affected our friendship ... has it? We were all lost together, Cyril ... We were all groping for some kind of direction ... I feel we've moved closer together ...

CYRIL: Maxie ... I don't mind you, now ... I like you ... In time I think I could love you ... I think so ...

MAX: I feel this very much, Cyril ... We've been —

HARRY: Maxie ... I'm not pushing you out. But we've got problems to sort out here ... You can see that, Maxie ...

MAX: *(going)* We could still have an odd lunch together ... Couldn't we?

GIL: That'll be nice ... Max, I'd like that ...

    MAX looks to CYRIL for permission.

CYRIL: You could take her to the pictures, now and then, Maxie ... When we're stuck for a baby-sitter ...

MAX: *(standing at the doorway)* What it is ... You're right, Cyril ... It's losing contact with our inner voices, isn't it ...

HARRY: *(holds the door open for him)* Goodnight, Maxie ...

CYRIL: You'll give us a ring about Monty's car ...

MAX: I'll ring you ... Eh, Gil? *(Going at last)*

CYRIL: If I'm stuck I'll maybe take four hundred ...

GIL: yes, that'll be nice ...

MAX: I'll see what I can do, Cyril.

CYRIL: *(listening at the adjoining wall)* She's cooking one of her menus ... I can hear her ...

HARRY: *(getting down to business)* Right, Gil ... Great ... That's the scene with Cyril. He wants to move back to the womb. What about *you*? You want to move back with him?

PAT: Harry, I think we should all stop talking for tonight ... We're all tired out ... You can't settle a thing like this when you're tired, Harry ... I think we should all go to bed and have —

HARRY: That's the fucking point, Pat, for fuck's sake ... Who goes to bed with fucking who!

GIL: I'm sleeping by myself ... I'm going to bed with neither of you ...

HARRY: That's the scene then. You don't want to sleep with me. You want to sleep with Cyril.

CYRIL: I think I'll go into her while she's cooking ... That's the best way to tackle her ...

HARRY: You want to sleep with Cyril?

GIL: I've told you, Harry, I don't want to sleep with anybody.

    CYRIL switches off the heater.

HARRY: For fuck's sake, I gave you four fucking bob for it, man ...

CYRIL: I'm not doing it for the money ... I'm hot ...

HARRY: Then take your fucking clothes off, man! *(Switching it on again)*

CYRIL: I'm just going to be absolutely honest with her ... Like I was with Maxie ... I'll try and get her to work out with me exactly how we moved into this unreal situation in the first place ...

HARRY:	For fuck's sake, man ... What you on about now? ... You're hysteric ... You jump from one thing to another ...
PAT:	Cyril ... I'm frightened of her ... After what happened this morning ...
CYRIL:	*(going)* As she was this morning, Pat. Yes ... Of course ... you'd be frightened of her ... But that was a fantasy situation ... Pat ...
HARRY:	*(blocking him)* Christ! We're really moving back, now, Mack! To fucking ego-centered selfishness ... You have to go ahead with your fucking mystical, soaking wet christian missions to darkest fucking Africa.
	CYRIL pushes HARRY aside with violence ... HARRY backs away ... CYRIL goes out into the kitchen to ATARA.
GIL:	I'm going to bed ...
HARRY:	That's established, then, Gil. You don't want to sleep with me ...
GIL:	Or Cyril, Harry ... I'm not sleeping with either of you. Christ, somebody ought to tidy up this bloody room.
HARRY:	But you were ready to sleep with Maxie ... No fucking hang ups, about sleeping with fucking Maxie ...
PAT:	Harry, pet ... Honest ... If you leave it to the morning.
HARRY:	How's that like Pat ... Everything fucking resolved with the sun fucking coming out ...
GIL:	What are you doing now, Cyril?
CYRIL:	I'm camping out. Here.
PAT:	What did you say to Atara, Cyril?
CYRIL:	*(going out)* Atara's making poached eggs and toast and cocoa ...
HARRY:	Cyril, man ... I want to talk to you. What the fuck are you doing?
CYRIL:	I told you. I'm camping out ...
PAT:	What did you say to Atara, Cyril?
CYRIL:	*(moving HARRY)* Would you mind sitting over there. *(To PAT)* Atara turned on her death ray. I walked into the kitchen ... and she switched it on ... *(Making bed)* I'm going to read for a bit ... If you want to stay up a bit and talk, it's alright ...
HARRY:	I knew exactly what was going to happen, Cyril!
CYRIL:	*(to nobody)* It's exactly like when I sit with my guitar. *(taking down his trousers)* And I play it but nothing comes. I've nothing to say to it.
HARRY:	That's it, Cyril. You had fuck all to say to her. Except get the fuck out of my house, doll!
CYRIL:	I have reached a position where I cannot make a definite statement about anything. I have arrived at a position of intellectual impotence ... *(Putting on his pyjamas)*
GIL:	As long as it's nothing physical, honey.
PAT:	Cyril, love ... I want to sleep with you, tonight. I really do ... You understand, Harry?
CYRIL:	If I try to be absolutely honest with you ... Like explaining about me being an emotional cripple ... I see this ... This is just throwing my weaknesses at people, so that I can be excused of standing up as a whole, mature man ...
HARRY:	That's exactly what I'm saying, Cyril.

CYRIL: If I keep this to myself, I'm being dishonest and holding back important facts about myself ... Nobody knows where they are with me ... Least of all, myself ...

HARRY: It's simple, Cyril ... You do what you have to do ... You're doing what you have to do ... You can't live with Black Power ... You're booting her out ...

PAT: Can I, Cyril? Sleep with you, tonight?

CYRIL: You do what you have to do ...

HARRY: I'm telling you, Cyril ...

CYRIL: Like the whites in S.A. ... And the Nigerians in Biafra ... The Americans in Vietnam ... Hitler ... The Gestapo ... Buchenwald ... Dachau ... The Japs ... They were all doing what they had to do ... Maybe that's as it should be ...

PAT looks at CYRIL.

I'm sorry, Pat ... I just don't want to sleep with anybody, tonight ... I don't mean that as a statement of rejection, Pat ... In any case, the sleeping bag's too small ...

HARRY: *(to PAT)* I'm not sleeping on my jack, tonight. That's definite, Pat ...

PAT: Cyril's very upset, Harry. I've never seen him like this, before ...

CYRIL: What I really fancy doing is camping out in the highlands ... With the deer and the curlew round me, by a mountain loch.

HARRY: In ten feet of snow and twenty degrees of frost! Fucking swinging scene!

GIL: Why don't you camp out in your hut, Cyril?

CYRIL: Not enough leg room.

PAT: I really want to be with Cyril, tonight, Harry ... Not sexually, honey ... I'm not talking about sexualy.

HARRY: I'll tell you something, Pat ... You know who's taken the brunt of all this violence and these explosions in the last few months ... Fucking me!

PAT: Do you not understand how I feel, Harry ... Tonight, I feel I have to be with Cyril ...

HARRY: You don't realise how badly I've been hammered. That cunt there can get it all out of his system in the morning at his fucking typewriter ... What the fuck have I got?

GIL: Except fucking ...

PAT: Harry, sweetheart.

HARRY looks at GIL — desperate.

GIL: Harry ... Even if Maxie turned up, tonight, I'd throw him out of my bed ... even John Updike.

HARRY: I didn't fucking say anything to you. I'm talking to Pat.

CYRIL: Even this honesty, Harry ... This great truth kick ... What's that for? Me trying to be more honest than everybody else ... What for? So that everybody can say: Christ! That bugger's ruthlessly honest ...

GIL: *(kissing him)* Sweetheart, I leave you to your thoughts and your friends. I'm dropping on my feet. *(She goes out)*

PAT: Harry ... If it's only one way —

HARRY: Look at him! It's the fucking womb! He's back in the second womb! Jesus! Look what he's reading! WILLIAM IN TROUBLE!

PAT:	Harry, I really feel strongly about staying with Cyril, tonight ...
CYRIL:	I got it out of the library. You can get kid's books out with an adult ticket.
HARRY:	It's got nothing to do with fucking sex, Pat ... I mean ... It's a bit to do with it ... I'm a mass of anxieties, just now ... Tensions ... I need a warm human body beside me.
PAT:	If it's the only way, Harry ... This thing between us. I want what you want. But you don't always want what I want, Harry ...
CYRIL:	There's a world outside, Harry ... People are starving by the thousands ... Wars are looming up between east and west and west and east in all permutations and combinations ...
PAT:	Is it, Harry? One way? Do *you* think it is, Cyril?
CYRIL:	It's no use asking me, Pat. I've told you. I can't make a definite statement about anything whatsoever ...
HARRY:	For a character that can't categorically say whether one and one might be two or seventeen, Mack, you've got a fucking lot to say for yourself!
CYRIL:	It's like the Jews when they were thrown out of Spain: Whither shall we turn, the East casteth out and the West refuseth entry.
PAT:	Harry. Is that right, what I said about us?
HARRY:	I don't know ... I can't remember what you said. *(To CYRIL)* Cyril ... I want to get closer to Gil ... And she keeps pushing me away ...
CYRIL:	Looking at you, Harry ... I can't see that's important.
HARRY:	Everybody's going from me. I feel it. I feel the whole world is receding from me.
CYRIL:	At the speed of light.
PAT:	It's just that ... sometimes it feels right to go with Cyril, Harry. Sometimes with you ...
HARRY:	I'm telling you, Pat ... Go to bed ... If I fucking jar on you like that ... I'll sleep in the fucking bathroom ...
CYRIL:	The whole world is receding from you, Harry ... At the speed of light ...
HARRY:	Stop fucking saying that!
PAT:	Harry, pet ... You can't sleep in the bathroom.
CYRIL:	I'm sorry, Harry ... You're not sleeping here.
HARRY:	I'm not fucking sleeping, here, man!
PAT:	There's a mattress in the box room, Harry ... and spare blankets.
HARRY:	It's alright. I'm not coming into your room. Even if I have to walk the fucking streets till dawn. I won't bother you.
CYRIL:	All in the same boat, Harry ... whither shall we turn The East casteth out and the West refuseth entry.
HARRY:	Fucking hilarious ...
PAT:	*(kissing CYRIL)* Goodnight, pet. Have a nice sleep. *(Turning to HARRY uncertainly)* Goodnight Harry.
	He turns away from her.
HARRY:	Good fucking night, doll!
PAT:	Harry, pet ...

HARRY: Oh, go to fucking bed will you ... I love you ... Cyril loves you ... Everybody loves you. Go to bed, man!

PAT gives up and goes out.

CYRIL: You look old and red faced and a poor soul. I should feel sorry for you. Pat feels sorry for you ... I can't feel sorry for you, Harry.

HARRY at the wall ... listening to ATARA moving around.

HARRY: I'm sure I can hear her taking off her clothes, Cyril ... Fuck! I get an erection, man, thinking about it! Jesus! Those ebony tits of hers, Cyril!

CYRIL: She's unzipped something ... heard it ...

HARRY: Quiet, man, a minute!

There is the faint sound of a woman crying.

She's crying, Cyril. Listen.

CYRIL: She wants to. In her position, I would cry, too.

HARRY: *(looking at CYRIL with concern)* You reckon you might've burst a blood vessel in your brain, at the Tribunal this afternoon, Cyril?

CYRIL: I don't think so.

HARRY: You've undergone some major personality damage. I'm telling you.

CYRIL: Yes ... Atara's crying, Harry.

HARRY: I'm going into her. You can't leave her like that!

CYRIL: Before you go, Harry ... make sure you have everything you need. I'm going to snib the door and settle down for the night.

HARRY: I've got my smokes. Where's my lighter. *(In front of the mirror, combing his hair)* You're right. I don't look very hot, tonight. *(Putting on his dressing gown)*

CYRIL: If I could get Walter Scott finished by next week Harry ... I could bugger off to the highlands. You think I could do that, Harry?

HARRY: Shake yourself, Cyril ... Shake yourself out of this fucking trance, man! For Christ's sake! Where's my fucking lighter.

CYRIL: If I went up to Western Ross, Harry *(Getting out of his sleeping bag to let HARRY out)* And got myself a Highland woman.

HARRY: Where's my lighter?

CYRIL: That would give me confidence. I would know I still had it in me. Maybe I'm no good at getting. But why should I be?

HARRY: Where's my fucking lighter, man!

CYRIL: It's there beside the cooker ... Looking at you ... Harry, Beside you, I have definitely some real physical beauty.

HARRY: There's no doubt about that Cyril, man. You've got bloody physical beauty.

CYRIL: And I've had three women. And how many have you had, Harry?

HARRY: Christ knows! With a bit of luck, I might be notching up another one, this night.

CYRIL: *(escorting him to the door)* You sure you've got everything you need, now, Harry?

HARRY: Good night, son. I won't bother you again, tonight.

CYRIL: I can never understand how I didn't turn out a queer, Harry ... Not having a father figure, during the crucial years of my development. The only explanation I can think of, is my mother was masculine orientated lesbian.

HARRY: Could be, Cyril. Definitely could be ... *(Going with obvious excitement in his eyes)*

CYRIL snibs the door after him. He goes to the fridge and pours himself out a glass of ginger-beer. Unwraps a bar of chocolate and crawls back into his sleeping-bag. He takes up "William in Trouble" and settles down for his night's camping.

Scene Two

ATARA's room. ATARA in her underwear is sitting at the table crying. HARRY is standing at the doorway trying to work out some approach, her supper untouched is in front of her.

ATARA: To God! Don't think I'm crying about leaving this bloody house! I burned my toast and the water boiled over from my egg and spoiled it ... because bloody Cyril was standing watching every bloody thing I do. He doesn't say a bloody word. He keeps watching me.

HARRY going to the table and sitting opposite her.

HARRY: I know doll ...

ATARA: Harry ... you go to hell out of here! I know bloody fine whose friend you are!

HARRY: I'll tell you something, Atara ... I'm on my jack, I've got nobody ... not one bugger in the world cares a fuck for me ...

ATARA: I see you sitting at the trial not speaking to me not coming over to me, after everything is over ...

HARRY: Look at us, honey, I've got nothing.

ATARA: You never say one word to me after the bloody trial. You go straight to your bloody friend, Cyril.

HARRY: Purely as an objective comment, Atara, hen, you look fucking beautiful, just now ... I'm telling ...

ATARA: *(getting up and putting on a negligee)* I see you shaking hands with him!

HARRY: Atara, after the Tribunal ... you rushed out, honey you didn't give anybody a chance to talk to you ...

ATARA: What the hell do you want here, Harry. You fighting with bloody Cyril, now?

HARRY: I've got nothing ... wherever I turn, honey ... my work ... my wife's finished with me ... failure ... everywhere, doll ...

ATARA: What's this, Harry? You tell me this to make feel sorry for you? To God! *You* need people to feel sorry for you!

HARRY: You think you and I should go to the golf course, honey and fuck them all!

ATARA: Don't try and tell me you fight with your friends over me being thrown out on the bloody streets!

HARRY, taking her hand. She lets it stay in his passively.

HARRY: Atara ... nobody wants to throw you out ... honest ... honey I'm not saying ... after your performance this afternoon, Cyril wasn't a bit shattered.

ATARA: To God! I don't know what happened to me this bloody afternoon! A spirit took hold of me.

HARRY: I told him ... *You* were reacting to Cyril throwing you out ... *he* was reacting to your losing your control, a bit, this afternoon ... I'm not blaming you, doll ... it's understandable ... the whole fucking scene, there ...

ATARA:	When he came into the kitchen I want to tell him ... all I want to do is tell them all the bad things that happen to me in this house ... and my tongue runs away with me ... To God! these bloody people ... they throw me out on the street in winter and make me put all kinds of mortal sins on my head.
HARRY:	I explained to him, Atara ... he definitely got the message. The basic trouble, is he doesn't know where he is, just now, honey.
ATARA:	Not all the things I tell them about him at the court were lies!
HARRY:	I know, doll ... I know.
ATARA:	I'm bloody stupid. I still fool myself. I tell myself this is a big lie. All the bloody whites stick together in this country. I fool myself I will get justice in the bloody court!
HARRY:	He heard you crying, Atara.
ATARA:	I'm not bloody crying for him, that's certain. You tell him that!
HARRY:	He's infected Gil and Pat. He's gone completely against me ... And he's turned Pat and Gil with him. That's the fucking situation, Atara ... That's basically it, no point in fucking kidding myself ... I've lost my wife ... and my two closest friends in one night!
	Getting really sorry for himself. Almost crying as he realises the pathos of his position.
	I'm fucking forty ... Christ, to have to start all over again ... when you're fucking forty ... finding a wife ... friends ...
ATARA:	*(taking his hand, now)* To God, Harry! What's the bloody matter with you.
HARRY:	Christ, I don't know, Atara ...
ATARA:	I never see any man crying, before.
HARRY:	I'm not fucking crying!
ATARA:	Harry ... Pat is a kind woman ... she is a good friend to you. She is like my husband is to me. She would never leave you, Harry ... I wish I have my husband beside me. Like you have Pat, Harry.
HARRY:	I'm the kind of character, honey ... that only has a few friends. I can't be bothered with anything but real, deep relationships.
ATARA:	To God, I tell you about friends, Harry! I was in bloody Egbo's all night ...
HARRY:	We were worried about you, Atara. We didn't know where you were.
ATARA:	I tell you what Egbo do to me. I go to his house after the trial. Egbo is studying ... he has no time for me till he has finished his studies ... you know how bad the snow was tonight ... I say to him: Egbo I have a bloody heavy mind ... you take me to church. If I bloody don't make confession, I won't sleep all night. He says to me: his car is in the garage ...
HARRY:	*(stroking her hand again)* I know, doll ... I know the scene, exactly!
ATARA:	I go out to buy some aspirins for myself ...
HARRY:	You got a bad head, honey?
ATARA:	It's alright, now ... and I see Egbo's bloody car round the corner ...
HARRY:	I'll tell you something, Atara ... you and me ... we're simple honest people, we say what we fucking mean.

ATARA: I bloody tell him: your bloody car is round the corner. He says to me: Oh I forgot. I think I put it in the garage. All bloody night he's taking me to church. When he's finished his studies, all he wants, is to get me into bloody bed ... I say ... Now, you take me to church ... he says, Atara it's too late ... come to bed ...

HARRY: Listen, honey. If Cyril throws you out ... fuck him. You'll come to me ... we'll organise something to get you to college.

ATARA: I bloody run out of his house and go to Matthew's ... Matthew tells me the same bloody lies ... I tell him: do me a favour and drive me home to Cyril's. He says he's having trouble with *his* car. Snow's getting into the engine ... in the end, I have to get a bloody taxi ...

HARRY: It's feasible, honey ... Snow could cut out the engine ...

ATARA: Listen, don't bloody tell me! Matthew's a bloody liar! He is angry, I don't make love to him I tell him I have too bad a head to do anything ... I have no friends here ... At home, I have friends ... I have my husband ... and my mother and father, and my sisters ... and my brothers ...

HARRY: Atara, sweetheart, I'm your friend. I love you ... we're the same kind of simple, honest people, honey.

ATARA: I have nobody in this bloody country! I fool myself. Cyril is a good friend to me If I was a bloody Ibo, he would be my friend. He doesn't know what the bloody Ibos did to my family ... Some smart bloody Ibo, pushing his family into all the top places, takes my father's job on the railway from him ... he's turned into a beggar ... To God! He knows damn nothing about these bloody Ibos ... But because I am angry at what they did to my father!

HARRY: Doll ... listen ... I'll take you to the church, now ... Yes? If it's weighing on you, honey ...

ATARA: It's too late, now, man, I'll go in the morning. If I got a bicycle, Harry, I could stay in the golf course.

HARRY: I'll organise something for you, honey ... I won't let you down.

ATARA: Harry ... I'm hungry, I can't eat that rubbish ... To God! I have had nothing to eat all day.

HARRY: *(rising)* I'll get you something. I think there's some cold beef in the fridge.

ATARA: You're tired, Harry ... you need to go to bed.

HARRY: I'm great doll. Anyway ... I've got nowhere to sleep in this house. I'll get some wine, too, we'll have a midnight party, honey.

ATARA: I got something, Harry.

HARRY: *(kissing her)* You should see this beef Cyril has in the fridge, honey. We'll have beef sandwiches ...

ATARA: *I* make you a meal, the next time, then, Harry, I tell you.

HARRY: *(putting his arms round her for a moment)* We'll have a party, doll ... fuck Cyril, Gil and Pat!

ATARA: *(swaying as if she was dancing in his arms)* I'll put some records on ... we'll have a nice time ... we'll fill ourselves with good, happy spirits to throw out all the bad spirits of today.

HARRY: *(taking her hands for a moment and admiring them)* These hands of yours, Atara! Christ! They're beautiful. Jesus, honey!

Scene Three

The Jackson's living room. CYRIL is deep in 'William in Trouble' now and then he breaks off from his reading to take a drink or a nibble at his chocolate. The door is rattled, somebody is trying to get in.

GIL: *(from outside)* Cyril, Cyril, the door's stuck ... What are you doing in there?

            CYRIL hides the chocolate under his pillow, gets out of bed.

CYRIL: I've got the snib on. Wait a minute.

            He lets GIL in.

GIL: Where's Harry?

CYRIL: I'd just settled in for the night, Gil ... Harry's seducing Atara ...

GIL: You can get back to bed, darling ...

CYRIL: No ... I'll snib the door when you go.

GIL: I wanted to come down and tell you I love you, before you fell asleep ...

CYRIL: I should look into love ... I should do a whole series of plays examining the whole question.

GIL: I love Harry. And to some extent Max ... Nothing really with Max. But definitely not the way I love you.

            She finds the wrapping paper from the bar of chocolate. Picks it up. CYRIL looks at her, guiltily.

CYRIL: I was using it for extra sugar ... to feed my brain cells. Working on this book ...

GIL: *(lifting up his pyjamas)* Look at that belly, honey! You're going into a bad age, Cyril ... With all that fatty tissue.

CYRIL: As soon as the spring comes ... I'll start my running round the block again, Gil ...

GIL: That's what started me thinking about you, Cyril ... I was reading an article in one of Harry's Health Magazines ... About living into old age in the twentieth century ...

            CYRIL is marking his place in "William in Trouble"

            I'm telling you what happened to me, Cyril ...

CYRIL: I'm just marking my place ...

GIL: *(taking up the ginger beer bottle)* That's bad for you too, Cyril. Full of sugar ... I started thinking, honey I don't want anybody to die ... but I could stand Max dying and probably Harry ... I could do without them. But you, Cyril ... I couldn't think about myself without you ... I mean ... It's not being morbid or anything like that ...

CYRIL: It could be ... the measure of love is the degree of pain the fatality of the loved one causes in the lover ...

GIL: Cyril, honey!

CYRIL: I'm being serious, Gil ... yes ...

GIL: Do you feel that about me?

CYRIL: I never think about dying ... I never think about any period beyond the day after tomorrow ... that's about as far as I can see ... sufficient the day thereof.

GIL: That's just evading the facts of life.

CYRIL: It could well be. Yes.

GIL: Anyway ... it's nothing to do with dying ... it's just a way of understanding how much you need people ...

            CYRIL is on a line of thought ... obviously working on a new insight.

            It shows you the people you can't do without ...

CYRIL: I was like that with my mother.

GIL: I was like that with my mother and father. But not as much as with you ... *(Taking his hand)* Do you want to come up with me, honey ... Or do you really fancy camping out?

CYRIL: You want a night on your own, anyway, Gil ...

GIL: Yes ... but if you want to come up ...

CYRIL: *(looking at his sleeping bag)* I've got everything organised for the night now, Gil ...

GIL: I don't mind, honey ... I don't ...

CYRIL: I need to do some reading ... you can't sleep with the light on.

GIL: No ... honest ... I'm fine ... I'm happy I've worked things out ... I was dead happy when I found I knew exactly where I stand.

CYRIL: That's good, Gil ...

GIL: I know physically I'm not as attractive as Pat ... or as sexy ... but I know the one you could do least of all without is me ...

CYRIL: God! yes, Gil! definitely. I love you.

GIL: *(kissing him)* I'll never love anybody the way I love you ... Definitely ... Goodnight, sweetheart ...

CYRIL: Have a good sleep ... is Clair alright?

GIL: *(going)* She's fine. She had all her covers off ... I had to put them back on ...

CYRIL: We should pin them down or something ...

            Returns to his sleeping bag. Takes the bar of chocolate out then puts it down again. Takes a drink of ginger beer. Can't resist the chocolate and begins to eat it. Starts on his book again. At this point there is a light knock at the door, this time it's HARRY.

HARRY: Cyril ... for Christ's sake ... open the door, man. I know you're not sleeping ... the light's on ...

CYRIL: Go away, Harry. I'm studying.

HARRY: *(off)* Cyril. For fuck's sake, man! Let us in a minute ... I want to tell you something.

CYRIL: I'm in this trance ... I'm paralysed ... I can't get out of my bed son.

HARRY: Cyril ... stop fucking about, man! I'm making a fantastic breakthrough ... for Christ's sake! Look! Look Mack! If you don't open up, I'll fucking knock away here, till you do ...

He begins to knock in a steady rhythm on the door. CYRIL gives up and wearily goes to open the door.

(coming in) What are you doing here, Cyril ... locking yourself in like that!

CYRIL: You've been sweating, you smell, Harry. You should use a deodorant.

HARRY: *(at the fridge)* I'll just take a bit of this meat, Cyril ... I'll get you some more in the morning ... her father ... did you know her father was an educated man?

CYRIL sits, watching HARRY slicing the beef.

Her father was a clerk in Lagos. On the railway ... he was jacked out of his job because some smart, fucking Ibo was pushing his family into all the good places in the railway ...

CYRIL: When I was a laddie, I lived with my grannie, and many a hiding my grannie gave me, but now I'm a mannie, I hammer my grannie. It serves her right for hammering me!

HARRY: I'll just take this wine, Cyril. *(Going into fridge and bringing out bottle of Spanish wine)*

CYRIL: There's one opened.

HARRY: You can't take in an opened bottle, man ... I'll buy you another one in the morning ... Cyril ... *(This is a bit dodgy)* Do's a favour. Lend us a couple of condoms.

CYRIL stares at him. This is interesting.

HARRY: I don't want to fuck about here, too long, Cyril. Give us a couple of Durex, Cyril.

CYRIL: You're infertile, son. What do you need Durex for?

HARRY: You need them, man ... if you've got a girl who doesn't know you ... give us them, Cyril ...

CYRIL: Harry ... you're guaranteed one hundred per cent sterile ...

HARRY: Right, man ... I'm fucking sterile ...

CYRIL gets up and looks for the condoms.

A kind of spirit took hold of her, this afternoon, that's the way she sees it, Cyril.

CYRIL: *(finding the packet)* I've only got two, Harry.

HARRY: You don't need them, tonight, man!

CYRIL: They cost money, Harry.

HARRY: Give us them, Cyril.

CYRIL: What do you need them for, Harry? They cost money.

HARRY: I'll buy you some more tomorrow. For fuck's sake, Cyril ... she's waiting for us man ... if a girl doesn't know you ... she can't be sure you're sterile ... can she? You could be shooting her a line.

CYRIL waits for the rest of the explanation, his hand tightly gripping the packet.

It could put them off. You know ... when they know you can't make kids. *(Holding out his hand for them)*

CYRIL: I'll give you them on one condition, Harry. I don't see you again, till the morning. Right?

HARRY:	I'm telling you, Cyril ... I'm there ...
	CYRIL hands him the condoms. HARRY takes them as if they are some life-giving drug.
HARRY:	I'll probably be with her all night ... We're in orbit, Cyril ... she's got some Nigerian records.
	CYRIL escorts HARRY to the door.
CYRIL:	Do you think if I died, it would shake you badly, Harry?
	HARRY stops, knocked by this question.
HARRY:	If you died, Cyril?
CYRIL:	It would shatter you, would it, Harry?
HARRY:	What do you think, man? Christ, Cyril! I fucking love you, man!
CYRIL:	It's unrequited, Hary ... I'm sure it's totally unrequited. we are finally moving away from each other. Or anyway, I'm moving away from you ... do you get that feeling?
HARRY:	Cyril, I've got to go ... I'm telling you ... You don't know where you are, just now, Cyril. You're on some kind of fucking trip ... I've got to go into her, now, man ... the whole crisis is on the point of being resolved, Cyril. You sleep it off, Cyril.
CYRIL:	The whole crisis is being resolved with your penis ... That's an interesting concept, Harry. If anything can solve a problem, you're right, Harry, it's a sterile penis.
HARRY:	*(deeply hurt at this)* Fuck you, Cyril!
	CYRIL immediately reacting to the hurt he has caused. Moving into his own old role of pitying people.
CYRIL:	I said that out of envy, Harry. I did. I'm telling you, good night, Harry ... you got everything you need?
HARRY:	*(coldly)* Yes ...
CYRIL:	*(holding him back)* I did, Harry. I didn't mean it as a bitch. Do you believe us? I didn't, Harry!
HARRY:	I accept it, Cyril. Alright. Don't go into a fucking panic about it!
CYRIL:	You want to take the other half bottle, too, Harry?
HARRY:	No, I'm alright.
CYRIL:	I'm a bastard, Harry ... I don't appreciate people.
HARRY:	Good night, man ... I've got to go ... For all of our sakes.
CYRIL:	*I'm* the real bastard in the family. Definitely. Basically ... I love you, Harry.
	Looking at him, forcing himself to love HARRY.
	Definitely ... I'm sure of it.
	HARRY goes out. *CYRIL crawls back into his sleeping bag and takes up his book again. But he can't settle down to the simple innocent world of 'William' this time. He lies, staring up at the ceiling. The door is tried again. PAT comes in.*
PAT:	I waited. Till I was sure Harry was away for good, sweetheart.
CYRIL:	It's like queuing up for an audience with the Pope.

PAT: Harry's in with Atara. You know that? I heard him going in. I couldn't settle down with all the activity going on, honey. I thought if we had a nice cup of cocoa ... the two of us ... beside the fire ...

CYRIL: Ovaltine. That's what you should have, if you want to sleep. Not cocoa. Atara's got a tin on her shelf in the kitchen.

PAT: We can't take Atara's ovaltine, honey.

CYRIL: She's got your Harry. You can take her ovaltine.

PAT: Do you think he's making her, this time, Cyril? I hope he is. *(Going into kitchen)*

CYRIL: It doesn't do anything to me. I don't find the image erotic ... Her and him in bed.

PAT: *(returning with the tin)* It's nearly full, she won't miss a couple of spoons. *(Going to the field kitchen)*

CYRIL: I want two heaped teaspoons, Pat. I don't like it weak.

PAT: *(at the stove)* It's a real thing with him, Cyril, having a black girl. Different colours of skin. It really excites some people.

CYRIL: Are you making it with all milk?

PAT: Yes, I'm making it with all milk.

         She goes to the door and fastens the snib. She swirls round in her negligee.

         Do you like this one, pet?

CYRIL: It's nice. Yes ... do you think we're trying to outrun history, Pat?

         PAT opening her negligee and revealing the pair of men's pyjamas she's wearing underneath.

PAT: You think that's kinky, sweetheart?

CYRIL: *(obviously interested)* Sexy ... yes ... You look nice in them.

PAT: I saw them in Marks and Spencers. I fancied them.

CYRIL: I'm jealous of the kids, Pat, you see them going about with their swinging gear ...

PAT: I was thinking in bed, Cyril ... I love Harry. Very much. I'm sure of that. But just now I find you more attractive.

CYRIL: You see them in their long coats. Frilled shirts. No sex problems ... sleeping around with who they fancy ... the way they move ... they *flow*. They're going somewhere.

PAT: I don't know ... you don't know what they're really like, do you, honey?

CYRIL: You're right, Pat. I could be romanticising the whole scene! Yes. I definitely get this feeling of inadequacy when I see them marching down Regent Street in their greatcoats like the bloody Red Guards in Petrograd, 1917 ... I envy them ... you're right. Maybe there's nothing to envy there.

         PAT sitting down beside him on the sleeping bag, handing him a cup.

PAT: You understand what I mean about how I feel about you and Harry, honey?

CYRIL: Yes, I mean ... it was only my father, Pat ... who was going on about one man and one woman for life ... and God ... and adultery ... honouring your father and mother.

PAT:	*(taking off her negligee)* You don't know what your father believed in, Cyril. Obviously he didn't believe in till death do us part ... running away from your mother like that.
CYRIL:	I'm not talking about my father. I'm talking about our fathers. Men of wisdom, men of worth ... leaders by virtue of their knowledge.
PAT:	I loved my father and mother ... my father better than my mother. My mother wasn't as honest as my father.
CYRIL:	Every single thing our fathers said about morality can't be wrong! Some of it would be first class stuff ... like the concept of the family, maybe ... and we've thrown it all out with the rest of the bathwater. The problem is, what's worth keeping and what's worth throwing away.
	PAT has taken his hand and is stroking it. Intent on other things.
PAT:	See ... The mistake was to *talk* about it, Cyril ... As long as we didn't talk about it ... I know Harry ... If I just had a baby ...
CYRIL:	I mean this Black and White concept of life ... That's definitely not on.
PAT:	That's just stupid, honey ... If I ever had a baby ... He would just accept it ... He'd just leave it like that ... Maybe by some chance ... it was him ...
CYRIL:	But what about blackish and whitish ...
	She lets her hair brush against his face.
	Your hair smells nice.
PAT:	I washed it when I was in the bath.
	She puts her arm round him.
CYRIL:	You feel nice in these pyjamas.
PAT:	*(kissing him)* You look nice, tonight, honey ... I love your body ... and your hair.
CYRIL:	Pat ... before we get all worked up. Harry's gone off with my last two condoms.
PAT:	Isn't that funny, that? Harry having to use protectives with girls he doesn't know.
CYRIL:	I was just going to finally break with him. You know? Completely cross him out of my list ... he comes out with this.
PAT:	*(distressed)* Cyril, pet ... you wouldn't break with Harry ... would you?
CYRIL:	It moved me ... god knows why! I couldn't help it.
PAT:	He loves you, pet ... He looks up to you. If you ever finished with Harry ... in some ways ... he loves you more than anybody. Do you not know that, sweetheart?
CYRIL:	I *think* so ... yes ...
PAT:	*(almost in tears)* I want us to be together, honey ... the four of us ... for ever.
CYRIL:	*(comforting her)* It's alright, Pat. I told you ... as soon as he came out with that ... he was real again, to me. You're crying now ...
PAT:	I'm not ... I'm just ... moved ... like you.
	Kissing him. Both of them getting roused. CYRIL despite himself. PAT begins to unbutton his pyjamas.
CYRIL:	Pat, sweetheart.

PAT: Just a nice cuddle, honey ... before we go to sleep.

She takes off his jacket, then his trousers.

(taking off her negligee) I've got a new game for us.
(She puts it on CYRIL) Does that feel nice?

CYRIL: Yes ... Cool ...

She moves closer to him, kissing his chest, stroking his body. CYRIL is moving to the brink, beyond rational thinking.

PAT: I love you sweetheart ... I really do ... *(Her arms round him)*

CYRIL: *(making no attempt at resistance. Allowing himself to be pulled to her, a last cry)* Pat ... We've got no protection! ...

Gynt!

Characters

GYNT
PEER
FANTASY PEER
OLD PEER
BUTTON MOULDER
AASE, Peer's mother
PEDERSON
GIRL
GIRL'S FRIEND
SOLVEIG
SOLVEIG'S MOTHER
INGRID, Pederson's daughter
DANCING PARTNER
GUESTS
HERDMAN/TROLL KING
HERDGIRL/GREEN LADY
DOCTOR
BOYG
BOY
PRIEST
VIRGIN MARY
DOCTOR
CAPTAIN
GIRL
MATE
GERMAN GENERAL
VALET
ANITRAS
SHEIKH AMADHI
MAN
LAD
GRAVE-DIGGER

The edge of the moor.

Three figures come out slowly through the mist ... GYNT, carrying a suitcase ... PEER ... and the FANTASY PEER ... They stand, trying to penetrate through the mist across the moor ... As they are standing the BUTTON MOULDER begins to call GYNT ...

Gynt! ... Gynt! ... Peer Gynt! Peer Gynt!

(GYNT turns towards him)

GYNT:	Peer Gynt, you're looking for ... That's me ...
B.M.:	That's a relief. You coming without any trouble ... That's good. Makes things easier, all round, doesn't it?
GYNT:	I know your face, friend. Such a long time I've been away ... Nearly fifty years ... How are you? Never been much good at names ...
B.M.:	*(holding up his mould)* Clean ... You see ... All ready for the melting down ...
GYNT:	Nice and clean ... Yes ...
B.M.:	Button Moulder.
GYNT:	Yes ... You're the Button Moulder. How are you?
B.M.:	You know I'm here ... We don't need to get involved in these long tedious arguments I keep getting all the time with people I have to collect ...
GYNT:	Listen ... You know me ... The whole foundation of my life ...
B.M.:	They always upset me these arguments ... People fighting against melting down ...
GYNT:	Face up to the objective truth about yourself ...
B.M.:	Oh yes ...
GYNT:	The foundation of my whole life ... What I'm saying, Button Moulder ... However painful the truth about myself was to me ... You understand me ... Even if it negated in a way everything I'd done before ... I faced up to it ... What am I talking about ... I embraced it ... Totally ...
B.M.:	*(catching a word)* Yourself ...
GYNT:	Whatever that adds up to ... It gets more and more complicated every day, doesn't it ... All the things that adds up to that collective word: yourself ...
B.M.:	I thought it was going too well ... You're going to start arguing with me too about the significance of this great self of yours. The fact is if you had ever for one fraction of a minute, made the most minute impression on one other soul, Gynt, the ...
GYNT:	Touch of a butterfly's wings ...
B.M.:	That's a nice expression ... Yes, the touch of a butterfly's wings. The order to Melt would never have gone out ...
GYNT:	I see ... There is in fact an ORDER TO MELT.
B.M.:	*(showing him his order)* ORDER TO MELT.
GYNT:	I'm reading it ...
B.M.:	Gynt, Peer ... Sum total of life: Zero ... Melt.

GYNT: No question about it ... Through some kind of administrative error ... you are wandering around the moors here with an Order To Melt on Gynt.

B.M.: That's good. You accept that ...

GYNT: I keep telling you, friend ... Do I not keep telling you ... I am ready and prepared to accept whatever truth about myself I am confronted with ...

B.M.: That's alright, then ...

GYNT: What's so terrible, anyway, about ... Gynt being melted down into nothing ... If that has to be, it has to be ...

B.M.: That's a good point ... I'll make a note of that for future jobs ...

GYNT: Peer Gynt ended for eternity ... whatever that means ... No, I suppose that still does mean something ...

B.M.: Oh ... Yes ... For ever and ever ... Long time ...

GYNT: Plunged into blackness and nothing for ever ... Blotted out, worse things than that, isn't there ...

B.M.: Of course there is ... You've got the right attitude, totally ... You ready, then?

GYNT: Just one thing seriously troubles me ... Something that's been the whole foundation of my life ...

(BUTTON MOULDER about to remind him about his other foundation)

Apart from the truth about myself ... Justice ...

B.M.: Oh yes ... I like justice ... Justice is good ... I'm with you all the way there ...

GYNT: And it's on that point ... that I can't really agree to go with you ... Without looking into the Order to Melt a bit closer ... No ... If it is correct ... Not based on any administrative error or shoddy research work ... Honestly ... You won't need to look for me ... I'll come looking for you ...

B.M.: You've seen the Order ... Do me a favour ... Don't make any difficulties ...

GYNT: *(at order)* Totality of life; Zero ... Look at me ... does that sound a correct assessment of the kind of man I am ...

B.M.: Listen ... I'm telling you ... These appeals against Orders to Melt, they only cause more pain and misery ... Raising false hopes ... You have to produce witnesses and testimonies ... Open up old wounds, as the saying goes ... Re—live forgotten agonies ... Take my advice.

GYNT: That's all I want to know, Button Moulder ... You need witnesses ... Testimonials ... I'll get them for you ... In writing ... In duplicate ... triplicate ... Whatever you want ...

B.M.: Honestly, Gynt ... Be guided by me ...

GYNT: Be straight back to you ... As soon as I've gathered all my evidence.

B.M.: You'll have to keep reporting to me, Gynt ... The progress of your case ... I'll see you at the next crossroads ...

(GYNT turns to stride over the moor)

GYNT: *(stopping)* Yes. If that's the procedure. I'll see you at the next crossroads.

Outside PEER's house ... The young PEER is hoeing ... His MOTHER, AASE, sits, looking on.

AASE: Listen. There's no law of God against people failing.

PEER: *(stopping his work to listen for a moment)* Wedding fiddles, Mother. You not hear them?

AASE: People succeed and people fail. That's what happens.

PEER: *(looking at the groundsel)* I wish I could do something about the groundsel.

AASE: Listen. What's it got to do with me, son? What you do. You're not a boy any longer.

PEER: The garden full of groundsel ... Gives me even more pain than you. I know. You wouldn't believe that, Mother. It does. *(looking at the groundsel)* Does it?

AASE: Fiddles? I can't hear any fiddles.

PEER: No.

AASE: Wedding fiddles? The Pederson's are three miles away. On the other side of the hill ... How would you hear wedding fiddles from there?

PEER: You couldn't. You're right.

AASE: So ... It could've been *your* wedding night, tonight. The Pederson's girl could have been *your* wife ... So bang your head on the ground that we're not all living happily every after!

PEER: What is it, Mother? An hour's hard work. Getting rid of the groundsel, ploughing the north meadow. Two days at the most. And the groundsel stays. And the north meadow's to your waist in weeds ... That's not a good situation to be in, is it? I should be able to do something about it ... I should ...

AASE: *(turning her head to listen)* You've got *me* hearing wedding fiddles, now, you rotter!

PEER: *(throwing down the hoe)* When you think about it. The cabbages still grow between the groundsel.

AASE: All the months, going backwards and forwards to the father and mother ... Begging the girl for you. And she's marrying Jorgen Moen. I still can't understand that, son. To break into people's houses in the middle of the night. Stark naked.

PEER: I had my pants on.

AASE: It's like fits you get. Suddenly you break into a fit.

PEER: It was a warm night, wasn't it? I couldn't sleep. That's what happened.

AASE: The dowry Pederson's settling on that girl! God in heaven!

PEER: You're right about the groundsel, Mother. Cabbages might grow between them. But the groundsel takes food from the cabbages. Food taken from useful plants for useless ones. It's true ... *(she's looking at him, closely ... studying his face with concern)* What's the matter now, Mother?

AASE:	I was just thinking you looked a bit thin in the face ... there.
PEER:	*(worried)* Do I?
AASE:	Just probably the light ... I'll make you a bowl of bone broth for your supper ... *(listening)* It's the wind ... That's what your wedding fiddles are ... The way the winds blowing through the trees ...
PEER:	*(with sudden decision)* Mother. Listen. I'll tell you what we'll do. We'll go over tonight. To the Pedersons.
AASE:	That's right. They're waiting for us!
PEER:	*(sharply)* Are you listening to me, Mother? Mother! Listen to me. *(waits for attention)*
AASE:	I'm listening to you, madman.
PEER:	We'll tell Pederson: We've made up our minds. I'm going to marry Ingrid, after all. Alright? *(AASE turns to go into the house)* Where are you going now?
AASE:	I'm going to bathe my feet. In warm water. With salt in it.
PEER:	Mother. We're going to the Pedersons.
AASE:	I told you. I'm going to bathe my feet. For at least an hour ...
PEER:	*(taking her hand, holding her back)* Listen. She *loves* me. You know that ... And I don't fancy any other girls anyway ... All the trouble all over again. Getting round another girl ... I might as well just take her.
AASE:	Apart from her marrying somebody else, son ... They don't think you're right in the head, over there, now. Pederson said to me: You should get a medical opinion on that poor boy.
PEER:	You see ... It bothered me, Mother ... All the paper to be signed. And agreements ... And money ... Just for me and Ingrid to live together ... I was just going to run off to the forest with her.
AASE:	On a cold, wet July night ... Her in a thin nightgown ... You naked to the wind.
PEER:	It got a bit cold. You're right ... The trouble was I'd left my clothes nearly a mile back ... They were soaking when I got to them ...
AASE:	Oh, Peer, love ... What's going to become of you ... What's going to become of *us?*
PEER:	I'm going to marry Ingrid. Put on a new roof here with the dowry.
AASE:	Wake up, son ... Wake up.
PEER:	You see ... It was alright when I left the house ... Just when I got near the Pedersons ... It started to rain.
AASE:	She's got another man, now, Peer. A lovely strapping man. With land of his own. Money in the bank.
PEER:	If you start thinking of things like that, you're beaten before you started. The main thing is, Ingrid loves *me.*
AASE:	Do you love Ingrid, son?
PEER:	I had a very clear plan of action, that night, Mother. We'd build a hut in the forest. No shortage of wood to do that.
AASE:	*You* build a hut? You can't even put a hinge on that door there ... I had to do that.

PEER: For food ... We'd have picked wild mushrooms ... fish ... berries ... later on.

AASE: Peer, love *you* can't *find* mushrooms. There's some people who can find mushrooms, some people who can't ... You're one of those who *can't*.

PEER: Ingrid might've been the other kind.

AASE: If she wasn't, you'd have grown fat together, wouldn't you?

PEER: I love *you*, mother ... Whatever it is ... I know that ... *(looking at her ... trying to work it out)* Yes ... I love you. How's that, mother?

AASE: Why do the leaves fall from the trees?

PEER: Yes ... I suppose you can understand that ... I was part of you.

AASE: You're still part of me ...

PEER: If they'd had a bit of imagination ... The father or the mother ... They'd have come into the game with us, wouldn't they? ... Going hysterical ... and Pederson firing his gun at me ...

AASE: You never told me that ... The swine firing his gun at you ... You could've been killed, Peer, love ... That fat, over–fed swine ... Daring to lift his gun at my Peer ...

PEER: I dodged him quick enough ... At the most he fired a dozen shots at me.

AASE: God in heaven ... a dozen shots ...

PEER: You know how fast I am, Mother ... I jumped out of the window I came in ... Used all the cover and the shadows ... Pederson had a bit of luck ... Because the moon was nearly full ... But he only grazed me, once ...

AASE: Where ... show me, darling ... Oh, Peer ... You're all I have, love ... You know that ... If I lost you ...

PEER: Just a little scrape ... there *(showing her)*

AASE: The pig! ... My precious son's ... *(stops, recognising the scrape)* ... That's not a bullet ... You got that from me. That's my own nails that did that ... The time I lost my temper with you ... Last Wednesday ... For lying around ... listening to the cow crying to be milked and doing nothing about it ...

PEER: No ... That was another shoulder, mother ...

AASE: Where ... show me ... That's my own nails ... And I don't regret doing it at all ... You rotter ... You know how hard it is for me to milk ... with my arthritis ... when it's wet ... and you just lay there ... reading rubbish.

PEER: He didn't actually graze me ... That's right, Mother ... He missed me.

AASE: He never fired at you at all, swine ...

PEER: I was so upset, I'm not sure what happened ... He lifted his stick to me, Mother, definitely had a stick. Mother ... I'm sorry ... Look ... I'm going, now ... please give me your blessing, Mother.

AASE: My curses I give you, swine. Upsetting me like that!

PEER: Mother. I know ... I understand ... I'm sorry ... Will I put the water on for your feet ... before I go ... ?

AASE: Got the water on already ...

PEER: Listen ... I'll weed for ten minutes ... Will I ... before I go? That's what I'll do ... I'll do it in stages ... So that I can stand it ... ten minutes a day ... and I'll be finished in a week.

AASE:	Why do you do these things to me, Peer, love ... Torturing me like that.
PEER:	I'm sorry, mother ... honestly ... If you knew how I felt ... upsetting you like that ... Will you forgive me ... Mother ... Don't make me go away ... feeling terrible about you like this.
AASE:	Come here ...
PEER:	You know how I love you, mother. The idea of hurting you ...
AASE:	*(putting his head on her lap for a minute)* What can you ... if you love people? Listen ... If you're determined to go, son, go ... But tidy yourself up a bit ... And promise you won't take anything to drink ... And explain to Pederson ... It was a joke ... the whole business, that night, love ... the way you explained to me before ... be nice to both of them.
PEER:	I will, mother ...
AASE:	And don't be too disappointed if nothing comes of you going, love. They're going to church tomorrow, for God's sake ...
PEER:	No ... I won't, mother.
AASE:	I'd come with you, Peer ... But I'm very weary ... and anyway ... you're probably better just going on your own ... If it's going to happen ... It'll happen just because of what Ingrid feels for you ...
PEER:	You have a nice evening, mother ... I'll bring you back some cake from the Pedersons ... Will I?
AASE:	Peer ... Where are you going? I thought you were going to weed for ten minutes, first ...
PEER:	It's not a practical plan, mother, is it? ... Ten minutes a day ... It needs concentrated effort for two hours. In a day twice as many weeds will have come up as I can weed in ten minutes ... *(going)*
AASE:	*(calling after him)* Don't let them see you taking anything from the table ... But if you can manage to bring back some honey cake ... She makes beautiful honey cake, Mrs. Pederson ... Light like a feather.
	Outside the Pedersons' House ... The music and noise of the wedding takes place within ... PEER moves towards the house but is checked by the sounds.
PEER:	Let's face it, Mr. Pederson ... Everybody has their mad moments ... I apologise ... I'm sorry ... But you know what the world's About better than me ... Ingrid loves me, I love Ingrid ... You can't condemn her to a lifetime of unhappiness because of one mad moment ...
	... Right I'm back ... To hell with it ... If a man can't have a laugh now and then without everybody going hysterical and working themselves into a panic ... You know the situation ... Alright ... This other character's got a bit of money and land ... But is that the proper basis for two people committing themselves to each other for a lifetime ... *(sits down)*
	As he is sitting, the FANTASY PEER walks up to the cottage ... he is calm and totally indifferent to his reception or anybody looking at him ... he calmly takes a beer from the table and sits drinking and watching the proceedings, as PEDERSON approaches him.
PEDERSON:	Peer, lad ...

PEER: Thirsty, Pederson ... Heard the fiddles so I came in for a pint ...

PEDERSON: Listen, Peer, lad ... Come inside ... I've got that brandy you like so much ... Eh? Let's discuss the situation calmly.

PEER: I'm not interested, Pederson ... Am I? Listen ... I know exactly why you've turned right round, now you've heard I can fly ...

PEDERSON: Listen, Peer ... Congratulations ... Eric told me. He saw you last Thursday.

PEER: Nothing yet ... Three hundred yards ... Four, maybe ...

PEDERSON: It's a start, Peer ...

PEER: The important thing is, I've got the principle, Pederson.

GIRL: *(coming up)* Peer ... Would you like to dance with me?

PEER: *(considering her)* Different tune you were singing, the last wedding, wasn't it? ... I'll see ... Might ... Might not ... I doubt if I'm staying much longer here, anyway ...
                What's all the excitement here? Think somebody was getting married or something ...
                (GIRL turns away)

GIRL: *(to friend)* Did you hear something, just now?

GIRL'S FRIEND: No ... it's just the band getting ready for the song ...

PEER: I like that ... Yes. I'm not here ... Nobody is talking to you. How's things then, Karen?

GIRL: *(to friend)* Funny smell ...

GIRL'S FRIEND: Yes ... *(they move away)*
                (They gather round the FANTASY PEER, GYNT goes up to PEDERSON.)

GYNT: Mr. Pederson ...

PEDERSON: Who invited you here ... Turning up like a ghost at the wedding ...

GYNT: I just came ... You know why I came ... I came to apologise ... I had a –

PEDERSON: Alright ... I forgive you ... Get yourself a drink and sit down and behave yourself ...

GYNT: You haven't heard what I want ...

PEDERSON: *(going)* Quiet, man ... Somebody's going to sing ...

GYNT: I was going to tell you about my experiences in levitation ... You know of course, I'm working on the principle of flight ... In a couple –
                (PEDERSON has gone ... GYNT sits in a corner, rejected, lost ... FANTASY PEER in front of the band.)

FANTASY PEER: Alright ... If that'll stop pestering you ... I'll give you a song ...
                (FANTASY PEER sings the GYNT Song.)

                I sit all alone,
                Like a prisoner in a cell.
                Who I might be
                No one can tell
                No one can touch me
                You just can't touch me.

                Look through a crack
                At the prisoner next door,
                He looks back at me,

But there isn't much more.
That's what it means to be free
I can't touch you
And you can't touch me.

He taps out a message
Through the fifty feet wall,
"I know someone's there
Won't you answer my call.
And come and touch me.
Won't you touch me."

I tap back some answer
To let him know I am there.
I'm sorry for him
But I don't really care.
That's all I know of his soul
Another soul sending his call
Somebody drumming through a fifty foot wall
But never touching me
He doesn't touch me.

That's what it means to be free.
I can't touch you
And you can't touch me.

(As the applause for the song dies down ... SOLVEIG enters ... followed by her parents ... GYNT watches her as she enters ... the FANTASY PEER disappears ... SOLVEIG approaches GYNT.)

SOLVEIG:	Shouldn't everybody be happy at weddings?
GYNT:	*(his face lighting up)* I'm happy now ...
SOLVEIG:	Oh, I've never seen a face change so quickly before ...
GYNT:	I know ... I look like that ... When I'm not wanted ... I shouldn't have come here, really ...
SOLVEIG:	I was frightened. Coming here ... We've only moved here a month ago ... And I don't know anybody ... Do you get frightened at the idea of meeting people you don't know ... You shouldn't really ...
GYNT:	I could write a book about all the things that frighten me.
SOLVEIG:	Could you? ... So could I ... Did you come on your own ...? It's harder when you're on your own ... When I went to weddings and parties with friends ...
PEER:	Will we dance? I'm not a very good dancer ...
SOLVEIG:	I'm quite good ... But I could be better .. My mother says I could be much better ... She's looking at us, over there ...
PEER:	I see her ...
SOLVEIG:	I'm Solveig.
PEER:	I'm Peer Gynt.

(She starts for a minute ... checks him ... As he takes her in his arms to dance.)

What's the matter?

SOLVEIG:	You're getting that ugly look on your face again ... When you're not wanted ...
PEER:	I'm sorry ...
SOLVEIG:	I don't believe anything they say about you ... I don't ... I know. People say all *kinds of things* about you. I don't believe them!
PEER:	*(looking at MOTHER)* I bet your mother does ...!
SOLVEIG:	I know you were once going to marry the bride here ...
PEER:	That's finished with, years ago ...
SOLVEIG:	Did you love her?
PEER:	Come on, we'll dance ... Eh ...
SOLVEIG:	I know ... I knew the minute I came into the room and saw you sitting there ... with your face all screwed up ... and ugly ...
PEER:	I seem to dance a bit better with you ...
SOLVEIG:	You dance fine ... Light on your feet ...
PEER:	What did you know looking at my ugly face ... then?
SOLVEIG:	I don't know ... Just ... You were on your own ... and I wanted to be your friend.
GYNT:	Are you on your own?
SOLVEIG:	I have my mother and father ... And sisters ...
GYNT:	I've got *my* mother ...
SOLVEIG:	Yes ... I know you live with your mother ...
MOTHER:	*(pulling SOLVEIG gently but firmly out of GYNT's arms)* Excuse me ... But my daughter has been forgetting her manners ... *(to SOLVEIG)* Dancing before you were introduced to the host, Solveig ... Really dear ... I don't know what you're thinking of ... *(bustling her away)*
SOLVEIG:	*(to GYNT)* I'll dance with you later ... *(to MOTHER)* Can I?
MOTHER:	*(pulling her away ... clearly determined SOLVEIG will do no such thing)* We'll see, dear ...
	(GYNT leaves the dance floor ... stamping his foot in his fury and frustration)
	INGRID, the bride has been watching the scene, he's just about to run out when she blocks him.)
INGRID:	A new taste, Peer ... Schoolgirls just confirmed ...
GYNT:	What about yours. Red faced farmer's boys!
INGRID:	He's much better looking than you, Peer. Look at him.
GYNT:	Yes. I'm telling you. You're doing a much better deal with Jorgen than me ...
INGRID:	He's gentle, too. His whole nature ... Peer, can you just love one person ...?
GYNT:	You should have come with me ... That night ... Shouldn't you?
INGRID:	Why can't I love him like I loved you, for God's sake!
GYNT:	You should've just kicked their teeth in ... And come with me ...
INGRID:	I know ... I should've gone with you ... They wouldn't let me ... You saw them ...

GYNT:	You wouldn't let yourself!
INGRID:	I'll love him in time, won't I?
	(SOLVEIG dances past this time with another lad ... her MOTHER smiling.)
GYNT:	*(taking her hand)* Come with me, now, then ... I ... nobody's watching ... God's still to join you together ... Come on ...
INGRID:	*(clearly tempted ... this is what she's been after at one level all the time they've been talking)* Peer, darling ... I wish I could ...
GYNT:	You can, sweetheart ... Come on ...
INGRID:	Where can we go, love? ... They'll follow us wherever we go ... What will we do ...?
PEER:	You just go ... Don't you ... You want to go with me ... You go ... I want to go with you ... I go ... You don't start weighing and adding up sums ... Making a balance sheet out of giving yourself to somebody ... Do you?
INGRID:	You know that, Peer ... I love you ... I'll always love you ...
PEER:	*(taking her hand)* Right then ... Come on. *(they slip out of the room)*
	(SOLVEIG alone has seen them leave, her eyes on GYNT as her partner guides her round the room.)
DANCING PARTNER:	I know the place your father's taken, now ... Halster's Farm ...
SOLVEIG:	*(her eyes on the doorway)* Yes, Halsters ...
DANCING PARTNER:	*(continuing to make conversation)* You were confirmed last spring, then ...
SOLVEIG:	*(distressed)* Yes .. I was confirmed last spring ...
DANCING PARTNER:	That's good ...
GUEST:	*(at doorway)* Look ... on the hillside ... Peer Gynt ... with the bride!
PEDERSON:	My God! ... Look at him ... He's carrying her like a pig!
SOLVEIG:	*(to her partner)* I wore the same dress my mother wore for her confirmation ... My Grandmother wore it before her ... White Flemish lace ...

On the hills above the village ... PEER and GYNT are walking with INGRID.

GYNT:	No ... I am genuinely worried about my back ... Look at it ...
INGRID:	What about me having a baby?
GYNT:	I'm telling you. You definitely can't tell as soon as that ...
INGRID:	I *felt* it ...
GYNT:	You could get piles ... Getting wet like that ... You could ...
INGRID:	Anyway, I'm sure it should have been the other way round ... You on top of me ...
GYNT:	Then *you'd* have got piles ... You might have coped with them better than me, though.
INGRID:	I've read somewhere ... About him getting on top of her ...

GYNT: God, I'm cold! That wind cuts right into you, Ingrid. What are we going to do now?

INGRID: The main thing is we love each other ... Isn't it?

GYNT: Who was he? Getting on top of her?

INGRID: I'm cold, too ... If we put our arms around each other ... We'll be warmer ...

GYNT: (backing away) You'll get wet, Ingrid ... Putting your arm round me ...

INGRID: We'll go to your mother's ...

GYNT: Listen ... I don't deserve you ... All I think about is myself ... Dragging you up here ... In a moment of lust ...

INGRID: Love, sweetheart ...

GYNT: Not a thought about what we're going to do ... Just run off together ... Like madmen ...

INGRID: Peer, sweetheart ... Look at me ... Honestly ... I've never been happier in my life ... I love you ...

GYNT: I've got this tendency to bronchial infections, too ... Last winter ... I was in and out of my bed ...

INGRID: I'll give you my shawl, sweetheart ...

GYNT: Will you not be cold ...

INGRID: *Please* ...

GYNT: In all fairness ... Mind ... I didn't drag you away to be seduced by you ... That wasn't in my mind ... I don't think so ... Nothing was in my mind ...

INGRID: Everything was in your heart ...

GYNT: Heart's not hard talking, Ingrid ... Heart pumps your blood through your body ...

INGRID: Soul ... then ... Spirit.

GYNT: How can we go to my mother? I'll come trooping in: Hullo, Mother ... It's not enough you've got me to feed, I've brought a girl ... and the whole village is after me for running away with another man's bride ...

INGRID: What are we going to do, Peer? (it gradually dawns on her that PEER doesn't quite return her love)

GYNT: It's difficult to think with a soaking wet behind ... That's one of the problems. What I'm thinking is ... They don't know what we've been up to up here ... You go back ...

INGRID: Peer, love ...

GYNT: You say ... You broke away from me ... No ... That would still get me into trouble ... Just say it was a joke ...

INGRID: Like you coming that night to our house naked.

GYNT: I wish people would get their facts right ... I came ... naked to the waist ... I can produce witnesses ... that I had my underpants on ... No ... We just ran off ... For a laugh ... Yes ... Nothing happened ...

INGRID: Except I got a baby.

GYNT: If we did it the wrong way round like you make out ... Maybe you can't get a baby that way ... In fact ... That's why I did it ... Yes, I remember, now ... That way ... All that seed falls out of the womb ...

INGRID:	You don't love me, Peer ...
GYNT:	What else can you do ... You've got to go back, Ingrid ...
INGRID:	And go to church with Jorgen in the morning ...
GYNT:	If you are going to have a baby ... You're in the clear anyway ... You'll only be a day out.
	(INGRID ... crying ...)
	You know what I mean.
INGRID:	Peer ... if we told my father ...
GYNT:	He'd murder me ... Yes ...
INGRID:	He would just accept it ... He nearly did before ... You'd have the farm ... after him ... and my dowry ... And you know I'd make you a good wife ... I would ... wouldn't I, Peer?
GYNT:	*(trying to wriggle out of that one)* I'm telling you ... He'd be after me with an axe, the minute you told him ... With a shotgun ... Listen ... You go back to them ... Will you ... I've got to go ...
INGRID:	Where ... To your schoolgirl mistress ... Your new obsession ... With girls too young and innocent to make any demands on you ... Yes. That's the best kind of girls for you ... They won't even find out what a hopeless lover you are ...
GYNT:	I wish you wouldn't fight with me ... I hate fighting with people ... Especially fighting when you're parting.
INGRID:	Where are you going?
GYNT:	I don't know where I'm going ... I'm going ...
INGRID:	You don't love me ... You never loved me ...
GYNT:	If I don't ... I can't help it ... Can I?
INGRID:	*(covering her face)* It's horrible. The whole night. What did you need to come for, tonight? I would've been fine ... If you wouldn't have turned up ...
GYNT:	You should've come with me ... That night ... I came for you ...
INGRID:	I've come *now* ...
GYNT:	I know ... It's too late ... Ingrid ...
	(She runs from the sight of him)
	I can't help it ... It was too late ...

Outside the house ... PEDERSON is shouting ... AASE and SOLVEIG are straining their eyes, searching for some sight of GYNT.

PEDERSON:	Gynt! Gynt! I'm telling you ... When I get hold of him ... I'll massacre him! Gynt ...
AASE:	Listen, Mr. Pederson ... I know ... You're upset ... Things look bad ... But know my Peer ... It's always words with him ... All talk ... You know that ... He never *did* anything.
PEDERSON:	He's up there ... With my daughter, for God's sake ... He's *doing* something, now ...

AASE:	It's just another of his jokes. Mr . Pederson ... You know him ...
PEDERSON:	If I could get my hands on him!
AASE:	Listen ... Did you hear it ... A cry ...
SOLVEIG:	Just a buzzard ... Or a raven ...
AASE:	Peer ... Peer ... Where is he ... Sometimes ... his thoughts just run away with him ... He doesn't know what he's doing ...
PEDERSON:	I thought I saw something ... a white shape ... Up there ... Moving. *(going up)*
AASE:	*(to SOLVEIG)* Will you help me ... I'm no use when it comes to climbing.
SOLVEIG:	I'll help you ...
AASE:	God reward you, child ... You see ... I know ... Everything looks so bad for him ... All the talk against him ... But I know him better than anybody ... don't I? I've only known two good men in my lifetime ... His father and Peer ...
PEDERSON'S VOICE:	Spread out ... They're on the upland pastures ... I'm sure of it.
SOLVEIG:	I know ... I spoke to him, tonight ...
AASE:	Underneath all his talk and wildness ... There's such goodness ... and kindness ... I'm not saying that just because I'm his mother ... *(breaking off)* Listen ... What do you want to hear old women rambling on about their sons ... A child like you ... Wearying you like that ...
SOLVEIG:	Please. Tell me everything about him. You would weary of the telling long before I would of the listening ...
AASE:	*(leaning on her)* You've strength in you ... Haven't you ... Even though you're such a little one.

The hut of the HERDMAN ... GYNT and PEER are sitting with him and his daughter, being entertained to supper ...

HERDMAN:	What do you think, then? ... Solves everybody's problem all round ...
PEER:	I'm not sure if I could get on with the goats ... What do you think?
HERDMAN:	First thing is the girl.
HERDGIRL:	I'd like to see him without his clothes first ...
PEER:	It's a bit cold ...
HERDMAN:	I'll blow up the fire ...
PEER:	*(to GIRL)* I like you ... Very much ... I could look at your face all day ...
HERDMAN:	You'd need to do more than that ... for her, squire ...
HERDGIRL:	You get used to the goats ... Don't you?
HERDMAN:	Goats stink ... No question about it ... But up here ... Stinks don't stay long ...
PEER:	*(as GIRL strips)* What is she doing ... ?
HERDGIRL:	I'm showing you myself ...
HERDMAN:	Want to see what you're letting yourself in for, don't you?
HERDGIRL:	He wouldn't be like *you* would he, Da?

HERDMAN: That's a point ...

PEER: Is your mother dead?

HERDGIRL: That's what we're talking about ...

HERDMAN: No question about it ... It's not a bad life up here, is it?

HERDGIRL: With a man ... It's perfect ... It's a perfect life ...

HERDMAN: You keep your eye on your goats. Milk them ... Drop the cans of milk at the end of the path ... for people to pick up. They leave money and food and soap ... Got a first class place to live ... You don't need to talk to anybody from one year to the next ... When did I last talk to somebody? ...

HERDGIRL: I remember a man coming up here ... What I was six ...

PEER: That would suit me ... I'm not much use at dealing with people ...

HERDMAN: Mother left me when she was a baby ...

HERDGIRL: Da' says they're quite nice. *(showing her breasts)* What do you think?

HERDMAN: She ran after me night and day, her mother ... Till in the end I gave in to her ...

HERDGIRL: Da' ... I'm showing him ...

HERDMAN: Yes ... They're alright ... What do you think?

HERDGIRL: And don't say you could look at them all day ...

PEER: I don't know what to say ...

HERDMAN: I like doing it myself, you see ... That's the trouble.

HERDGIRL: That's why mother ran away from him ...

HERDMAN: She didn't like it ... Thought it was something wrong with her ... You're not like that, are you?

HERDGIRL: *(now naked. Going to PEER)* Oh ... I don't think so...

HERDMAN: Now and then I gave her it ... I didn't mind her being around to look after me ... But she wouldn't leave me alone ... Got a wife ... she kept moaning at me ... What do you need to do that for ...

PEER: I'd help you with the goats ... and everything ...

HERDGIRL: All the goats'll be mine ... when he goes ...

HERDMAN: Seventy goats ... *(to GIRL)* ... with you two looking after the goats ... I could get on with finding the people.

HERDGIRL: There's people ... Up in the mountains.

PEER: Thought he didn't like people ...

HERDMAN: These people down there ... Yes ... Civilised people ... Nobody can stand them ...
Wild people ... we're talking about ... Up there ...

PEER: I don't fancy milking goats ... I was never much use at milking our cow ...

HERDMAN: *(showing him a Stone Age arrow head ... and other implements)* ... That's them ... See?

HERDGIRL: I'll milk the goats, darling ... Come on ... It's warm enough now. Take your clothes off ... and show me ... Da' won't mind ...

HERDMAN: You ever tried it with lads ... *I* did. I don't like their bodies ... Too hard and boney ...

PEER:	*(looking at the Stone Age weapons)* They're dead ... Millions of years ago ...
HERDMAN:	They're up there ... I know ... I keep finding their stuff they leave lying around ...
PEER:	It's another age ... I'm telling you ...
HERDMAN:	That's one theory, yes ... I've heard that before ... I don't believe it ... Wait, till I bring one of them in here ... Seeing's believing.
HERDGIRL:	*(having stripped off PEER's shirt)* Oh ... I think I'm going to like him, Da ... He's nice.
HERDMAN:	That's good ... Yes. It's a good life here, lad. Peaceful ... Don't need to kid you're anybody but yourself ... You can piss where you want ... Shit in the sun ... *(GIRL fumbling with PEER's pants)*
HERDGIRL:	Oh ...
HERDMAN:	What is it, now ...
HERDGIRL:	Nothing ... *(looking at PEER and kissing him)*
HERDMAN:	I can't understand people locking themselves up to shit ... Can you? *(The scene moves into the Troll King's Palace ... the HERDMAN becomes the TROLL KING ... the girl, the GREEN LADY ...*
	The FANTASY PEER comes in ...
	The GREEN LADY is singing a sentimental Love Song to F. PEER ... as she leads him into the throne room):
GREEN LADY:	Oh honey don't you leave me, Cause you'll make me blue ... I've been your baby, So good and true ... Every couple have their bad times, They just ride them through ... Oh, honey you're leaving and I'm grieving ... Cause I'm still in love with you ...
TROLL KING:	*(to F. PEER)* If you look into the history of courts and Kings and that kind of thing ...
GREEN LADY:	Father, I have found the love of my life ... The discovery is mutual ... Tell him:
FANTASY PEER:	King ... I have found the love of my life in your daughter ...
TROLL KING:	*(grabbing F. PEER ... Throwing him to the ground ... Taking out a dagger to him)* Pig's arse! Die!
FANTASY PEER:	King ... Ask your daughter ... My intentions ...
TROLL KING:	No ... Not a dagger ... Stamp on the swine! Pig's arse ... Keep still while I stamp on him ... *(to daughter)* Would you care to join me, daughter ...
GREEN LADY:	You know that's not my scene, Father, dear ...
TROLL KING:	You should try once or twice ... It's a change ...
FANTASY PEER:	I want to marry her ... My intentions ...
TROLL KING:	*(moving away from him)* You'll read of Court Astrologers ... Court Musicians ... What's he doing, lying there for ...
GREEN LADY:	Get up, darling.
TROLL KING:	Oh ... Did he think I was serious ... My dear lad ... I'm sorry ... Forgive me ...
FANTASY PEER:	No ... It's me, King ... I can never get used to the idea that what people *say* isn't necessarily what they mean.

TROLL KING:	Stop that analytical rubbish. I will not have it in my palace! You hear me ...
GREEN LADY:	Look at his eyes, darling ...
TROLL KING:	Yes ... Beautiful eyes.
GREEN LADY:	And he kisses so well, darling ...
TROLL KING:	Yes. I can imagine ...
FANTASY PEER:	I don't believe in underselling yourself, King ...
TROLL KING:	Let me see, boy ...
FANTASY PEER:	I want your daughter ... She wants me ...
KING:	I said ... Come here, boy ...
FANTASY PEER:	What does he want?
KING:	Kiss me ...
FANTASY PEER:	I'm a man with ability ... I know. When the time comes for you to go ... King ...
KING:	Kiss me ...
FANTASY PEER:	You?
GREEN LADY:	Go on, my love ...
FANTASY PEER:	You don't mind ...
KING:	Get on with it, man ... *(waits for a kiss ... F. PEER kisses him on the cheek ...)* That's not a kiss! *(he takes F. PEER's head and plants a kiss on his mouth)*
GREEN LADY:	Isn't he nice, father?
KING:	*(throwing him off)* He might brush his teeth before kissing kings ...
FANTASY PEER:	When the time comes, for you to hand over your Kingdom ...
KING:	Court Painters ... Court Philosophers ... You know the kind of thing ... Gynt?
FANTASY PEER:	I'm saying ... You couldn't find a better man to hand over to than me ...
KING:	*(to GREEN LADY)* Is he not interested in what I have to say?
GREEN LADY:	Yes, he is, darling ... Very ... Aren't you ...?
KING:	But no Court Pornographers ...
FANTASY PEER:	The minute I met your daughter ... Sir ... I couldn't believe in my happiness ... I stood there ... Saying to myself: That beautiful, wonderful woman is looking at me ... obviously admiring me ...
KING:	How many times have I got to tell him ... Stop that ... Stop that ... Watching yourself in mirrors all the time!
GREEN LADY:	*(to F. PEER)* Try to get out of that habit, darling ... For both our sakes.
KING:	I'll cut it out of him ... No question about it ... Obviously he's in desperate need of an operation ... I'm talking about the innovation I'm about to make as a King ... I'm going to be known as the first King to Introduce Court Pornographers ...
FANTASY PEER:	Congratulations.
TROLL KING:	Thank you! *(to GREEN LADY)* What about him? ... Could he double as son-in-law and Pornographer ...?
FANTASY PEER:	Could I just say ... Not that I've much experience of erotic books and pictures ...

KING:	In that case he's out. We'll have to look further afield ...
FANTASY PEER:	But the reasons it may be Kings had no pornographers ... was the plentiful supply of the real article at hand, King ... They didn't need a substitute ...
KING:	*(to GIRL)* He's a good thinker, that lad ...
	Absolutely ... *(to F. PEER)* I admire you, boy ... You're quite right ... There is no substitute for good pornography ... Listen ... This is the deal. Half the kingdom and my daughter while I'm alive ... Other half when I snuff it ... Now ... A quick test, to check if you need the usual operation ... *(to GREEN LADY)* Ready, dear ...
GREEN LADY:	*(lying on couch ... Lifting up her dress)* Yes, father ...
KING:	Good. *(to F. PEER)* Kindly oblige me by having sexual intercourse with my daughter on the count of ten ... One ... Two ...
FANTASY PEER:	You know that, King ... I couldn't ... That's the one way to put me off completely ...
GREEN LADY:	What way, darling?
FANTASY PEER:	Doing it in front of people, sweetheart ...
GREEN LADY:	I don't mind, dearest ...
FANTASY PEER:	In front of your father ...
GREEN LADY:	*(to father)* Yes ... Darling ... I'm afraid I see what you mean.
KING:	Thought so ... *(ringing bell ... The surgeon enters ...)* Everything ready, Doctor?
DOCTOR:	At all times, King.
FANTASY PEER:	What's he going to do?
DOCTOR:	Just lie on the couch please ... *(producing instruments)*
GREEN LADY:	It's alright, my love ...
KING:	If you're not a troll ... How can you marry my daughter ...?
DOCTOR:	Just a simple painless operation to convert you into a troll ...
FANTASY PEER:	Yes ... Well ... I'm not sure about that, King ... I think I'd be better staying as I am ... From your daughter's point of view, alone. You understand ... She's fallen in love with *me*. If he starts messing about changing me ...
GREEN LADY:	No ... Just minor improvements, darling ... To make me love you all the more ... and you me ...
FANTASY PEER:	No ... That's definite ... No man could love a woman more than I love you ...
DOCTOR:	Ah, but wait till I'm finished with you, Gynt ... *(to KING)* Eh?
KING:	Indeed ... Indeed ...
FANTASY PEER:	I'm not even sure what a troll is ...
KING:	That's simple enough ... What is the purpose of the Universe?
FANTASY PEER:	... Tricky question that ... If you believe in God, of course –
KING:	You see ... One difference immediately: A Troll would answer without hesitation: Who cares?
FANTASY PEER:	Yes ... I can see the point in that answer ...
KING:	Are people essentially good or bad?
FANTASY PEER:	I'm thinking about that ...

KING:	A Troll wouldn't give it a minute's thought: They're people ... That's a Troll's answer ...
FANTASY PEER:	There's sense in that approach, too ...
KING:	How did the Universe begin?
FANTASY PEER:	Troll'd say: who cares ...
KING:	Nearly ... Troll answer would be: We'll never know ... Life is short enough without wasting precious minutes worrying about useless rubbish like that ...
FANTASY PEER:	Yes ... I can see the point in that answer, too ...
KING:	I'm telling you ... You're nearly a Troll already, my boy ...
DOCTOR:	If you'll just lie down ... Gynt.
KING:	Won't take a minute ...
DOCTOR:	It's a simple operation ... Just a nick in your spinal column. Absolutely painless ...
FANTASY PEER:	But what does it do?
DOCTOR:	Then a minor incision in both eyes ... Nothing but a scratch on the lens ...
FANTASY PEER:	I'm asking you what the effect is ... If I'm going to let you get on with this operation ... I want to know what I'm letting myself in for ...
KING:	The whole business will give you a totally improved outlook on life, my boy ... After the eye operation, you'll be able to see only what you want to see ...
DOCTOR:	No more ugliness. Only beauty ...
GREEN LADY:	I'll be as beautiful to you as the first minute you saw me ... for all our life together ...
FANTASY PEER:	The spinal incision will totally eradicate this tendency of people to be continually looking at themselves ...
DOCTOR:	And at the same time, cut out the questioning circuit in the nervous system.
KING:	No more stupid, pointless questions ... A tree will be a tree, Peer ...
GREEN LADY:	Your loving wife, your loving wife.
DOCTOR:	Complete surrender to the beauty of every minute of your life ... *(bending over him)* Steady, now ...
FANTASY PEER:	*(jumping off the table)* No ... I'm not having it ... That's out ... You take me as I am ... or I'm off ...
KING:	Get back on that table, Pig's arse!
GREEN LADY:	Is that how much you love me?
KING:	Is that Pigeon's Prick saying there is something wrong with my outlook in life! Doctor. Cut off his balls!
GREEN LADY:	Father ... Don't run away with yourself ...
FANTASY PEER:	King ... I admire you ... Totally ... I only wish I had your attitude in life –
KING:	That's what we're going to give you, isn't it, Monkey's Cunt! ... Get on that table!
FANTASY PEER:	You see ... You're *you*, and I'm *me*.
	(The KING and the DOCTOR are forcing him back on the table ...)

GYNT! 127

	(breaking loose) I'm not having it! ... Open that door ... Let me out ...
KING:	Pigeon's Prick! Are you defying me!
GREEN LADY:	Grab him, father ... Smash him to bits on the rocks!
KING:	Cut off his balls!
GREEN LADY:	Tear out his eyes!
FANTASY PEER:	King ... Sweetheart ...
GREEN LADY:	Tear out his lying tongue!

(They all converge on him. F. PEER desperately backs away ... jumps up on the rocks ...)

KING: Come down from there, Pig's Arse! ... I'm warning you! Come down here and get your balls cut off!

(F. PEER climbs out of their reach ... higher and higher ... Their screams subside ... He finds himself in a dark cave ... From the floor the BOYG rises ...

The BOYG rises up and embraces F. PEER ... F. PEER breaks its grip. But it fills the cave and rises to grip him again ... The BOYG speaks only to itself ...

FANTASY PEER: Listen. Put that out of your mind. I am not going to die. You hear me!

BOYG: Temperature?
Minus eight ... Going down. High wind.

FANTASY PEER: I'm not giving in like that ... *(lunges at the BOYG)*

BOYG: Subject's physical condition?
First stages of exposure. Pulse below normal. Respiration in thin atmosphere difficult.
Laboured breathing. Body temperature falling rapidly ...

FANTASY PEER: The thing is to find out who I'm up against ... Once I've found that out, I'll know how to tackle you ... *(peering at the BOYG)* Tiger ... Yes! Can see now ... That's what I'm up against ... Tiger ... Get me by the throat ... No ... Waiting to spring ... *Waiting* to get me by the throat ...

BOYG: Long term future?
Daily struggle for survival ...
Body temperature?
Still falling ...

FANTASY PEER: Alright ... Now we know what we're up against ... That's what I've been doing all my life ... Keeping you at bay ...

BOYG: Prospects of happiness
Minimal ...
Capacity for love?
Minimal ... Deeply disturbed personality ... Fragmented ... Character's defects beyond maximum tolerable level ...
Pulse?
Continuing to fall ...

FANTASY PEER: Yes ... Got the tactics ... tactics are obvious, aren't they? ... Spell it out to me I've nothing to live for ... And I just lie down and let you spring on top of me ... But listen ... Where there's life there's hope ...

BOYG: Pulse continuing to fall ... Body temperature falling ...

FANTASY PEER: Where there's life, there's hope ... Yes ... I'm not an idiot ... I know the tiger's more complicated than that ...

BOYG: Subject beginning to embrace the blackness.

FANTASY PEER: No I'm not ... I'm not ...

BOYG: Subject beginning to accept the state of perpetual unconsciousness ...

FANTASY PEER: I can see that ... The Tiger comes from me ... Right ...? Part of you ... No doubt about it ... *Comes* from me ...

BOYG: *(moving forward with a black velvet sheet to finally blot out F. PEER ... He makes a last effort ... throws off the blackness ...)*

Subject's pulse rate rising ...

Regaining consciousness ...

Regaining consciousness ...

Another time, then ...

Another time ...

(GYNT is moving over the moor ... The BUTTON MOULDER rises up, blocking him)

BUTTON MOULDER: I've got to pick up the statements you've got so far, Gynt ... *(holding out his hand for them ...)*

GYNT: Listen. This order ... That's what I meant to ask you ... Who gives the order ...?

B.M.: The order goes out to melt and the Button Moulder melts ...

GYNT: You don't know *who* gives the order?

B.M.: The leaf falls from the tree ...

GYNT: Who decides the sum total of somebody's life is zero? That's basically what I'm getting at ...

The leaf falls from the tree?

B.M.: On to the forest bed ...

GYNT: I'm not all that mad on poetry, friend ...

B.M.: It rots ... The leaf ... Becomes the earth ... Who orders the leaf to rot ... and become part of the earth ...

GYNT: I'm working that out ... You've got a good mind ... See what you're getting at ... Same process a man whose life adds up to zero ...

B.M.: *(holds up mould)* Ends up here ...

GYNT: It's good that ... Got a touch of profundity to it ... I don't know what profundity's worth ... But it's entertaining, isn't it?

B.M.: The other line of approach ... You could try ... I'm just passing this on, as hint ... This is off the record ... But it might be easier ... if you want to avoid this ...

GYNT: Injustice.

B.M.: Whatever ... To look into the negative side ... You could've been a significant winner ... I'm just telling you this because I find your whole case very interesting ... Because of the insights it seems to throw on the whole question of melting.

GYNT:	Sinner ... I'm not sure about ... I don't basically know what it means ...
B.M.:	Some evil action ...
GYNT:	No use, either, you see ... I'm not sure about good and evil ...
B.M.:	Difficult ... Good and bad?
GYNT:	There's bad actions. Absolutely ... I give you that ... But if somebody does something bad ... It's something wrong with that person isn't it?
B.M.:	*(at loss)* What's usually done ... Is you go to a priest ... Confess to him ... And leave him to give you the certificate of sinning ...
GYNT:	Eerr ... But if you don't *believe* in it, man ...
B.M.:	Other levels besides intellectual, Gynt, aren't there?
GYNT:	That's it ... You're right ... Listen ... That's a good idea. I'll get hold of a priest ... and have a long talk with him ...
B.M.:	If you could get one on the road ... That would help ... To give the appearance that you're genuinely taking action on your appeal.
GYNT:	Look for one straight away ... Bound to be one somewhere on the road. I'll get a statement from him ... and bring it to you to see what you think ...
B.M.:	Try to make it the next crossroads, Gynt ... Will you ... If you haven't heard anything by then ... It could be difficult ...
GYNT:	Will do, Friend ... Listen ... Don't worry about it ...
	The Forest outside Peer's Hut ...
	PEER chopping wood ... Suddenly turns in a panic to the cottage ...
PEER:	Solveig! Solveig! ...
SOLVEIG:	*(at the doorway)* I'm not here!
PEER:	*(still frightened)* Solveig, love! *(reaching out to her ... she moves out of his reach)*
SOLVEIG:	You see. I'm not real. You can't touch me.
PEER:	*You're* joking about it! ... Solveig ... Come to me, a minute.
SOLVEIG:	I'm watching my stew, dear ...
PEER:	Solveig ...
SOLVEIG:	*(going to him)* Everything is perfect in a dream, Peer ... That's how you can tell the difference ...
PEER:	*(stroking her hair)* Can't touch people in a dream.
SOLVEIG:	Can.
PEER:	Can you ...
SOLVEIG:	And be touched ...
PEER:	Don't, Solveig ... Don't tease me like that.
SOLVEIG:	Will I not?
PEER:	Once I told my mother I was going to build a hut in the forest ... She laughed at me ...
SOLVEIG:	She was quite right, Peer ... You didn't build it ...
PEER:	I cut down the trees.
SOLVEIG:	If I told my mother, I'd build a house, Peer! I don't know how I did it ... It looks nice ... doesn't it ... Like a real house ...

PEER: It was wet ... We had to build it.

(Going to it ... laying his hands on the wood ... to make sure it's real)

SOLVEIG: *(watching him)* If it was a dream, Peer ... Your mother would be with us ... And you wouldn't be worrying all the time about her ...

PEER: Wouldn't have rabbit every day for dinner ...

SOLVEIG: *(rising ... looking around)* I wish you'd chop the firewood away from the house ... *(taking a broom and sweeping)* Do you not like it yourself ... when everything's clean outside our door ...

PEER: What it is, Solveig ... Listen ... I'm a coward.

SOLVEIG: *(looking at him)* You just don't want to die, love.

PEER: What else is that? That's a coward.

SOLVEIG: Nobody wants to die. Do they?

PEER: That's true, Solveig ... That time I was nearly finished ... On the mountain ... I was free for a month or so ... Once you've nearly died ... That's it ... You know you can stand it ... Wore off months ago ... Solveig ... Why should it be so difficult for me ... Making a hut?

SOLVEIG: You're not a hut maker, Peer.

PEER: It's not all that bad dying, in a way ... Just get blacked out ... It's just leaving you ...

SOLVEIG: And your mother ...

PEER: You think they would shoot at me? The minute I showed my face down there ... Yes ... They would.

SOLVEIG: The whole valley, Peer ... Good, kind people ... If you knew how gentle and kind my father is ... But when he used to talk about you ... It's like all the hate of the whole valley is centred on you.

PEER: Don't even have one brother ... Or a sister ... That's me. On top of everything else, I have to be an only child.

SOLVEIG: Poor boy! The whole world's against you.

PEER: It is, Solveig! It's a big responsibility ... Being somebody's only child, isn't it ...

SOLVEIG: In the spring, Peer –

PEER: Most of her life's burnt up, isn't it? That's not a good thought to live with. Last bit of her life ... And she hasn't even the company of her only son.

SOLVEIG: In the spring, I'll go down and bring her up. If you met us halfway ... We could make some kind of stretcher ...

PEER: That's what I'm talking about! Having to do all these things ... Making stretchers ... Going in the night ... To see my own mother!

SOLVEIG: *(calming him)* It's only two months, love ... And the snow will all be gone.

PEER: *(taking her hands)* I don't know why I went down for you ... I knew you'd never come with me ... I was sure of it ...

SOLVEIG: I was waiting for you ... I wasn't living ... I knew you'd never come ... But I kept waiting ... That was funny, wasn't it?

PEER: Solveig, why have you always got to be frightened of something? Before I was frightened I'd never find you ... Now I'm frightened of losing you.

SOLVEIG:	*(comforting him ... like a child)* Peer, love, you're just a *man* ... Like everybody else ... People are always frightened ... That's people ...
PEER:	I've got to stop it. That's not use to anybody ... Going about frightened all you life. *(SOLVEIG rises)* Is it?
SOLVEIG:	I'm going to look at the stew, dear. And finish the tidying up.
PEER:	That's right, Haus Frau. Leave me for your house.
SOLVEIG:	It's for you as much as me, Peer ...
PEER:	*(holding her back. Kissing her)* Listen ... I love you. For what that's worth.
SOLVEIG:	*(turning to him)* It's worth *everything*! You know that. If we love each other ... *(going)*
PEER:	Solveig ... *(she turns to listen)* There's no reason why we shouldn't live here for ever ...
	(SOLVEIG goes into the cottage ...
	As he stands looking round ... The GREEN LADY confronts the FANTASY PEER ... she wheels an old pram ... her former beauty is distorted)
GREEN LADY:	So there he is! *Glowing!* In his prime ... A bit more flesh on his bones ... Mr. Gynt! Listen, darling ... I haven't come to hold grudges against you. That's the world, isn't it. I accept it ... If you can get away with murder, you get away with it ... Congratulations.
FANTASY PEER:	You see ... I don't accept that ... People are not like that ... Not at all ...
GREEN LADY:	Quite right ... Some people don't, in the end, get away with it ... *You*, for example ...
FANTASY PEER:	I need that ... To be challenged like this ... That's the only way you can develop your thinking and arrive at some kind of objective picture of the world ... Absolutely ...
GREEN LADY:	*(to pram)* Dear me, he's getting worse than ever in his old age for intellectual conversations ... *(to F. PEER)* How is the other side of your personality, darling ... Are you performing any better in bed? I'd hope so for the sake of the little girl you've picked up to keep you company ...
FANTASY PEER:	Your child's very quiet ...
GREEN LADY:	Are you?
FANTASY PEER:	I might be wrong ... But basically, from my experience, people prefer to do good ... They prefer to like and be liked ...
GREEN LADY:	*(to baby)* Doesn't he dodge the important questions, love ... *(to GYNT)* What about your performance? ... Are you improving as a lover?
FANTASY PEER:	That's another thing ... I've never been able to look on the act of love.
GREEN LADY:	The act of love!
FANTASY PEER:	If you'd let me finish ... The act of love as some form of athletics ... Where one competed with others ...
GREEN LADY:	Where one competed with others ...
FANTASY PEER:	Excuse me ... I can see ... There are some people ... who just can't communicate with other people ... Not a reflection on yourself ... or me ... Just accidents of chemistry ...

GREEN LADY: Sweetheart ... You're not looking into my eyes ... Look into the pram, darling ... Can you not recognise your own dear flesh ... Don't run away, now, Mr. Gynt ... You were talking about the need for challenges.

FANTASY PEER: *(briefly looking ... repelled)* There's something wrong with the child.

GREEN LADY: True, indeed ... As there is something wrong with his father ... *(to baby)* There you are, tiny love ... Your dad's worried about you.

FANTASY PEER: Where did you come from?

GREEN LADY: Isn't he repulsive, Peer ... Baby and me ... The two of us ... You turn your head at the sight of us ... don't you, darling ... And not all that long ago ... you were covering my body with kisses. You surely remember the hair ... My hair is as beautiful as the days when you spent an hour of ecstasy combing it for me ...

FANTASY PEER: Now ... Wait, now ... I'm with you, now ... We're talking about an offer made to me by your father, The Troll King ... Yes ... Which I rejected totally out of hand ... You were there ... There's no question about that ... You have no claim on me whatsoever ... If it will help ... Certainly ... I might be able to give you some produce now and then ...

GREEN LADY: Darling ... I'm as ugly as your feelings for me ... You know that ... *(pointing to pram)* This is the child of the time when you tempted me on the hillside ... Remember, darling ...

FANTASY PEER: Listen ... That was another man ... Look at me ... Then ... and now ... That Gynt's dead ... You can see that ... That Gynt ... and me ...

GREEN LADY: You remember, how beautiful I was to you ...? The way we opened out all our secret desires to one another ... and the way I answered yours ... You'll get nothing like that from your little house frau in there will you?

FANTASY PEER: Please ... Go away ... I'll bring you food ... From time to time ... I can't give you any money ...

GREEN LADY: All you have to do, love ... To have me as beautiful as our first kiss, is send that schoolgirl home to her mother ... Get her out of your sight and your mind ... Do that, my love ... I promise you ...

FANTASY PEER: *(lifting an axe)* I'm warning you! ... Get away from me, witch! ... I'll break your head in!

               (Out of the pram the BOY jumps out ...)

BOY: Touch her and I'll break *your's* in, father.

GREEN LADY: Now, now, darling ... What a clever, brave little boy ... You're growing up to be just like your daddy!

FANTASY PEER: *(horrified at the sight of the ugly boy)* I love her ... Do you understand that ... How much I love Solveig ...?

GREEN LADY: I know, darling ... Isn't it too bad ... How there is neither rhyme nor reason in what happens to people ... *(GYNT takes an axe to her)*

BOY: *(menacing him)* Watch it, Daddy!

GREEN LADY: Sometimes good is rewarded, sometimes bad ... Sometimes the guilty suffer, sometimes the innocent ...

FANTASY PEER: Listen ... You tell your mother ... You can't force yourself to love people ... What will she accomplish ... Forcing me to go back to her ...

               (BOY pulling at him)

GREEN LADY:	What's he doing now?
FANTASY PEER:	He wants you take him a walk ... *(to BOY)* That's right, darling ... Daddy will take you a nice walk ... while I cook the supper ...
	(The FANTASY PEER is dragged off by the BOY ... The GREEN LADY makes a turn ... and confronts PEER ... She is transformed into the HERDGIRL ... carrying a baby ...)
HERDGIRL:	We were getting on alright, weren't we?
PEER:	I know ...
HERDGIRL:	What do you think of the kid? Not much, is he?
PEER:	As soon as the goats start breeding ... I'll pay him back ... Your father ...
HERDGIRL:	He was upset, the old man ... He liked you ...
PEER:	It's difficult to explain to you ... You know?
HERDGIRL:	No ... He said right away ... He'd enough goats not to miss the dozen or so you'd stolen ... He said ... If you had to steal them ... That was it ... Just he misses you ...
PEER:	I'm going to give him them back ... Just really a loan ...
HERDGIRL:	The old man said that ... You'd probably turn up one day with them ... We had good times together, didn't we, Peer?
PEER:	Yes ... We had ...
HERDGIRL:	She nice ... this other woman you have, is she?
PEER:	Don't think I don't like you ... I like you very much ... I appreciate everything you did for me.
HERDGIRL:	See ... I don't mind coming here with her ... Or taking her back with us to the old man ... I don't get worked up about these things ... Your man having two girls ...
PEER:	You see ... We're all settled here ...
HERDGIRL:	Yes ... Your hut's fine ... I could come here ... The old man could easily build another hut near here, couldn't he ... Good goat pasture all round here ...
PEER:	It would be no use ... It's too difficult ...
HERDGIRL:	*She* wouldn't have it.
PEER:	Difficult all round ... I'd feel funny, too ... Wouldn't you?
HERDGIRL:	We wouldn't need to sleep all in the same bed, if she didn't want it ... One night you could come to me ... one night go to her ... I wouldn't even mind if you spent more time with her ... I just miss you, Peer ... And the kid should have his father around, shouldn't he?
PEER:	I wish you weren't so nice!
HERDGIRL:	You still think I am ...
PEER:	If we could do that ... it would be good ... All of us live together ...
HERDGIRL:	I don't want to make you miserable ...
PEER:	I'm telling you ... Stop being so kind and understanding to me, will you!
HERDGIRL:	Don't shout at me! ... I don't want you to be miserable ... because you'd only make me miserable ... That's all there is to it ... If she's one of these characters who must have a man all to herself ... *(PEER is standing there ... waiting for some great revelation)* ... You could at least give me a kiss ...

PEER:	Having the baby's made you different ...
HERDGIRL:	I don't mind you just coming over to me ... From time to time ... If that's all you can do ... It's stupid just to cut yourself off from me ... I'm not angry with you ... Dad isn't ...
PEER:	Your figure ... It's different ...
HERDGIRL:	Why don't you kiss me, Peer? I haven't had a kiss from you for ages ...
PEER:	(kissing her ... She puts her arms round him) ... Why has everything got to be so complicated for me! Your figure's nicer ... I don't know what it is ...
HERDGIRL:	My breasts are ... I think ... Look, sweetheart ...
PEER:	(his hand on her breasts) Oh ... For God's sake! They're lovely.
	(They both slip to the ground ... She rises again as the GREEN LADY)
FANTASY PEER:	Listen! Tell your mother. You can't force yourself to feel the right feelings ... What good will she accomplish ... Forcing me to go back to her?
	(BOY pulling at him ...)
PEER:	(to GREEN LADY) What's he doing now?
GREEN LADY:	He wants you to take him a walk ... (to BOY) That's right, darling ... Daddy will take you a nice walk while I cook the supper ...
	(The FANTASY PEER is dragged off by the boy ... The GREEN LADY goes into the hut to make the supper ...)
	(PEER watches her as she goes ...)
SOLVEIG:	(from inside) Peer ... Peer!
PEER:	Solveig ... No ... Don't come out ... I want to speak to you through here ...
SOLVEIG:	Peer, love ...
PEER:	No ... It's just something I fancy ... Solveig ... Remember I told you ... How I used to live with this old man ...
SOLVEIG:	The goat herd ... You're going to give him back what you took from him ... You can't carry your guilt for ever like that, darling ...
PEER:	Can't you ...
SOLVEIG:	I want to come out to you ...
PEER:	(holding the door) No ... I just want to imagine your face, just now.
SOLVEIG:	I want to hold you ... I think you need me to hold you for some reason.
PEER:	The old man ... Listen ... You know what Ingrid and I did ... That night I ran off with her, Solveig ...
SOLVEIG:	Love, that's melted ... All that ... Like last year's snow ...
PEER:	Yes ... The old man's daughter, Solveig ...
SOLVEIG:	Peer ... I love you ... Whatever happened before I came to you ... You know that ... Everything ... Was wiped out with our first kiss ... wasn't it ... If you did love the old man's girl once ...
PEER:	Yes ... (giving up ... at the impossibility of it all)
SOLVEIG:	It's finished ...
PEER:	Solveig ... I've never loved anybody like I love you ...
SOLVEIG:	Peer, love ... Can you not tell me? What you want to say ... I'll stay behind here ...

PEER:	I think ... If I go up in the hills a bit ... It might help ...
SOLVEIG:	You know that, love ... Whatever happens ... Whatever you tell me ... I love you ... You can tell me anything, Peer ... Peer ... You're not going to go away from me ...
PEER:	Listen ... Solveig ... Be patient with me ... will you? Sometimes, I don't know what's happening to me ...
SOLVEIG:	I'll always be patient, love, with you ...
PEER:	Remember that. Whatever happens ... I love you ... I'll always love you ... *(going)* Solveig ... Listen ... Wait for me ... Will you ... Please, love ... Wait for me ...
SOLVEIG:	I'll wait, Peer ... You know that ... I'll wait for *ever* for you ...

(PEER slips into the night ...)

A path through the Moor. GYNT is climbing ... Ahead of him a PRIEST ... GYNT trying to catch up with him ...

GYNT:	Father! ... Father!...

(The PRIEST checks his pace for a moment ... GYNT reaches him)

	I can see you're in a hurry, Father ... But if you could just spare me a few minutes ...
PRIEST:	Are you a Catholic, my son ...?
GYNT:	There's a certain order but ... You understand ... Against me ...
PRIEST:	An Order to Melt ...
GYNT:	Without grounds, Father ... There's no question about it ... I have committed ... I can't describe it as sins ... That would be dishonest ... Not believing in sins ...
PRIEST:	If you don't believe in sin, there's nothing I can do for you ...
GYNT:	How about "acts of immorality", Father ... Would that do, do you think?
PRIEST:	You believe in morality, then?
GYNT:	I'm not sure ... I'm trying to be honest with you, Father ...
PRIEST:	You believe in honesty?
GYNT:	Yes ... I see what you mean ... To some extent ...
PRIEST:	What do you want from me, my son?
GYNT:	It was clear in my mind up till now ... You understand ... the idea was to find a priest ... and put it to him ... If I can get a certificate ... establishing that I have committed serious sins ...
PRIEST:	You believe in God, then?
GYNT:	I told you ... I'm not a believer ...
PRIEST:	Sins against who ... if not against God?
GYNT:	You know that ... Against people ... against men ...
	In your terms ... There didn't seem to be any doubt about it ... I'd done some monumentally bad things ... and ... Well ... in my philosophy ... good things ...
PRIEST:	Oh ... You have a philosophy, then?
GYNT:	I thought I had ... I'm not exactly sure ... It could be my philosophy is I have no philosophy.

PRIEST:	I see ... Excuse me ... *(taking off his cloak ... and revealing a pair of angel's wings)* That's better ...
	(PRIEST lifts his arms ... and a choir of angels sing some appropriate psalm)
GYNT:	First class voices ...
PRIEST:	Fair ... Ah ... Here she comes ... Could you possibly bow your head, a little ...
	(The choir swells and the VIRGIN MARY approaches ...)
VIRGIN MARY:	Now what appears to be the trouble, Mr. Gynt?
PRIEST:	The usual, My Lady ... Bad case of spiritual disorientation ...
GYNT:	That's about it ...
MARY:	And such a nice man ... Huge, warm eyes ...
PRIEST:	Yes ... Indeed ...
MARY:	*(stroking GYNT's head)* Such a hot head ... Troubled brow ...
GYNT:	You can say that again, lady ...
MARY:	And *all* the things you've done *all* your life, dear boy ... Didn't you know if they're good or they're bad ... or even if such terms have any meaning ...
GYNT:	No question about it ... It takes a woman to understand you ...
MARY:	Now, dear boy ... If you tell me *all* about it ...
GYNT:	Could we talk as we go ... I'm still trying to find ...
MARY:	Yes, of course, dear boy ... Take my hand, now ... What a lovely, strong manly hand ...
GYNT:	*(going off with her)* Is it ... Do you think so?

Aase's House. Night ... AASE is huddled on a couch, clearly dying ... PEER, himself in a bad way, enters shivering against the cold ... hungry ... wearing thin, torn clothing ...

PEER:	Mother ... Mother ... are you sleeping?
AASE:	*(stirs)* Peer, darling ... Peer ... You shouldn't have come, dear ...
PEER:	You see ... I'm not with Solveig, just now ... That's how it took me so long to come ... Till I got your message.
AASE:	Come here, love ... Give your old mother a kiss ... Listen. You're cold. You're shivering.
PEER:	No ... I'm fine.
AASE:	Going about in summer clothes like that ... No wonder you're shivering ... Is that all you have, Peer?
PEER:	No ... I came out in a hurry ...
AASE:	*(rising)* I'll make you a hot drink ... Put that jacket on over there ... Over, Peer ... Are you hungry? What I am asking for? I can see ...
PEER:	I'll just cut myself some bread, mother ...
AASE:	I've got everything waiting for you, Peer ...

PEER: Lie down, Mother ... You're ill.

AASE: I'm getting your supper, aren't I? What are you talking about? Lie down ... Look ... I've got everything ready for you ... Pickled herring ... Salami ...

PEER: Mother, I can get it ...

AASE: Will you put that jacket on, for God's sake! You'll get pneumonia. The way you're shivering like that!

PEER: *(frightened at the thought ... quickly throwing the jacket over him)* I'm cold mother. I fell in the snow. You know how the snow soaks into you ...

AASE: I'll make you a hot water bottle. Listen ... Lie down in my bed there, Peer, darling ...

PEER: Mother, I'll have to go soon. You know that ... I can't stay long here.

AASE: God! That's my miserable luck! I've got one only son and he can't even visit me without him risking his life.

PEER: I'm not getting anything like pneumonia, mother. *(clearly convinced he is)*

AASE: I'll give you some of my medicine. That might help. It's for my cough.

PEER: I could try it, mother. Yes.

AASE: *(giving him a spoonful)* Oh, you're so thin, son. Are you alright? Have you been coughing much?

PEER: *(coughing)* No ... I don't think so ... It's just the medicine mother ...

AASE: There's a bottle for you. Wrap these blankets well round you. I've got some soup on ... I'll give you that first.

PEER: Soup would be good.

AASE: *(serving him)* Your old mother knows how to look after you, doesn't she?

PEER: Mother, I'm pushing you out of your bed.

AASE: I'm fine. I'll sit by. Your Auntie Kari brought in the soup ... What's it like? To tell you the truth, I can't stand her cooking. But what can I do?

PEER: It's good.

AASE: *(drinking in the sight of her lad taking in good nourishment)* You didn't get a priest for you and Solveig. It doesn't matter, dear. If you love each other, God will bless the marriage.

PEER: We'll get one, mother.

AASE: That's the one right thing you've done in your life. Found the right woman for you. You've a nice hut up there ... I hear things ... And she keeps it beautiful. *(she leans back ... watching him eating)*

(... the FANTASY PEER enters with the DOCTOR)

DOCTOR: I'm moved, sir ... I doubt if there is another moment in my professional career when have been so deeply moved ... This is the dear lady, your mother ...

FANTASY PEER: Mother ... My friend, Doctor Maier ...

DOCTOR: I'm so honoured, madame ... The mother of the great professor Gynt. Benefactor of humanity ...

FANTASY PEER: He's come to give you an injection, mother ... My life serum ...

DOCTOR: Just a moment's work, madame ...

AASE: If you knew how kind my boy is to me, Doctor ...

FANTASY PEER:	A few minutes for the serum to take its effect ... And a surprise ...
DOCTOR:	Indeed ...
AASE:	Another surprise ... Every minute of the day, my son is showering surprises on me ...
DOCTOR:	If you would draw up your sleeve, please ... Thank you ... My feelings, Professor ... I'm overwhelmed ... That, of course, is a man's dearest wish ... That he keeps his mother by him in good health for as long as he lives ... And here I am ... Privileged to give the serum which makes this possible to the mother of the man who has given this miracle of science to the world ...
FANTASY PEER:	Doctor ... You overestimate the genius involved in the discovery ... Once the first deductions were made ... And that ... To be honest with you more accident than design ... sir ...
DOCTOR:	Not at all, sir ... I've read your papers ... and your book thoroughly ... *(dabbing AASE's high arm with alcohol)* Just relax, Madame ...
AASE:	I'm fine ...
DOCTOR:	*(injecting the serum)* There you are! Work of a moment ... *(bringing out watch)* In sixty seconds ... we should begin to see the effect ... A wonderful moment, Professor ...
FANTASY PEER:	How are you, mother?
AASE:	I'm excited, Peer ... Will this really give me back my health?
DOCTOR:	More than that ... as you'll see ...
	(... The DOCTOR bends over her ...)
	Taking effect, now ...
AASE:	Can I have a mirror?
FANTASY PEER:	No ... Not till you've gone behind the screen ... and put on the surprise I have for you there.
AASE:	I feel strange ...
	(The mask of age is peeled from her as the DOCTOR bends over her ... She rises ... a young girl)
DOCTOR:	*(covering his face)* ... Oh ... Forgive me, Professor ... I'm overcome.
AASE:	Is it working, dear?
FANTASY PEER:	Look behind the screen, mother ... *(she goes ...)*
AASE:	*(a cry of delight)* Peer ... But I can't wear that ... That's for a young woman ...
FANTASY PEER:	Put it on.
DOCTOR:	What a moment in history, Professor ...
FANTASY PEER:	*(bringing out a mirror)* If all our dreams could come true like this, doctor ...
	(AASE comes out in a ball gown ... A young woman ... she looks in mirror)
AASE:	Peer, darling!
DOCTOR:	My God! It is ... It's beyond bearing ...
AASE:	It's like looking at a photograph of yourself ... Forty years old ... Peer, love ...

(FANTASY PEER holds out a chair for her ... She sits ...)

DOCTOR: Like a young queen on a throne!

(The DOCTOR and FANTASY PEER ... turn around ... and dissolve into the background)

FANTASY PEER: Mother ... Mother! ... Could I have some water ... The herrings have made me thirsty ... Mother ... *(AASE is slumped in her chair ... dead ...)* Mother! *(rising to go to her ...)* Auntie Kari ... Mother ... I'm sorry ... You know how I sometimes get lost ... Thinking ... Whatever I did ... It was just the way I was pulled ... Mother ... You know that ... I always loved you ... Do you know that ...

It was just ... You know how my mind wanders ... But I was dreaming About *you*, mother ... all the time about you ...

The Moor.

The VIRGIN MARY is wrestling with GYNT's spiritual problems over a cup of tea ...

VIRGIN MARY: Another cup of tea, Mr. Gynt?

GYNT: It might stimulate the brain cells ...

VIRGIN MARY: The trouble is one takes to you, Mr. Gynt ... Such a charming, likeable man.

GYNT: You think that might be it.

VIRGIN MARY: So far, anything might be it ... It's such a complicated mesh of accident and design.

GYNT: You think we might have to put it to your son?

VIRGIN MARY: If I can't handle it, dear boy, *he* certainly can't ... So much easier if you were in the faith, dear ...

GYNT: I could try ...

VIRGIN MARY: Could you?

GYNT: Maybe it's an acquired taste ... If I try long enough ... I'll believe in it ...

VIRGIN MARY: Isn't that rather self-conscious, darling ...

GYNT: You mind ... If we go on a bit ... The walking seems to help me to think ...

VIRGIN MARY: Not at all, dear boy ... Have you had enough tea ...? Another bickie?

GYNT: Maybe later, lady ...

VIRGIN MARY: Yes ... Do shout if you want anything ... I'll take your arm, dear boy ... The road's so uneven underfoot isn't it ...?

(They walk on ...)

A Ship's Cabin. Copenhagen ... PEER enters with the CAPTAIN ... The CAPTAIN in a glowing, relaxed mood after a night in the pub ...

CAPTAIN: Cabin ...

PEER: It's nice.

CAPTAIN: *Captain's* Cabin.

PEER: Comfortable ...

CAPTAIN:	You like it?
PEER:	Very much ...
CAPTAIN:	*(looking around)* Yes. I can see people taking to it ... The bunk's very good ...
CAPTAIN:	Do you like me?
PEER:	*You*, captain?
CAPTAIN:	I think you do ... You've taken to me ... haven't you? Admit it?
PEER:	You're a first-class, open kind of man ... That's the kind I like.
CAPTAIN:	Bring out the ring.
	(PEER produces the ring ... puts it on the palm of his hand ... displaying it so that it catches the light ...)
	Yes ... Family heirloom, that was it, wasn't it?
PEER:	My mother's ...
CAPTAIN:	Family fallen on hard times.
PEER:	Just till I get enough money for a passage to America.
CAPTAIN:	What a lad you are, aren't you! ... Oh ... You're a joy to listen to ... Aren't you, lad? You stand there, with your glass ring with a bit of glass in it ...
PEER:	Yes. Copenhagen's full of confidence men ... You do right ... Not to accept anybody at their face value ...
CAPTAIN:	Rambling on about how you're the son of some Duke or something in Norway ...
PEER:	If you want to see my papers ... They're in my lodgings ... If you give me twenty minutes –
CAPTAIN:	I've got your papers, my little duke ... *(throwing him a wanted notice ...)* Peer Gynt ... Wanted for ... Oh, dear me ... The things you are wanted for, Mr. Gynt ... Listen ... Sit down. Have a bev.
PEER:	I didn't know these had reached Copenhagen ...
CAPTAIN:	I'll tell you something ... I'm a smart lad ... Gynt ... Am I?
PEER:	Smarter than I thought.
CAPTAIN:	No ... Listen ... I'd have bought that bit of glass from you ... The way you told your story ... I was nearly giving you a tenner for that bit of glass. Till I remembered your papers here ... You're a bright lad, Peer ... With a future ... Provided you get out of Copenhagen ... fast enough ...
PEER:	You know how easy it is to make out a case against –
CAPTAIN:	Listen ... Look at me. Look at my eyes ...
PEER:	Yes.
CAPTAIN:	You know what this ship's used for?
	You're on a Slaver, Gynt ... Down there ... we pack 1200 human beings in the hold ... It's alright ... You don't need to hide your disgust from me ... *I* know it ... *You* know it ... It's a crime against humanity ... Could be the worst crime ... Using human beings as commodities in the market ... Listen, Peer ... You've got to help me ... You hear me? ... If there's one man in this world who can help me with this thing ... It's you ... The things *you've* done ... and you *can* live with yourself.
PEER:	I'm not a filthy, murdering slaver!

CAPTAIN:	We're sailing in the morning ... Africa ... Load cargo ... Then to the West Indies ...
PEER:	What do you want from me?
CAPTAIN:	*(at paper)* Been on the run now ... three years, Gynt ... Crossing from one frontier to another ... Sweden ... Denmark ... Finland ... Back to Sweden ...
PEER:	I have no sailing experience ...
CAPTAIN:	Listen ... I know I can't be as bad as I think I am ... Can I? I need somebody to tell me. I'm not really an evil, immoral, murdering monster ... I'm not ... Am I?
PEER:	You sail in the morning ...
CAPTAIN:	You can write ... can't you ... You can be Captain's secretary ... I hate paper work ... There's all kinds of ways you can be useful, Peer ...
PEER:	*(indicating flute case)* What's that?
CAPTAIN:	That's my flute ...
PEER:	You can't be all that bad ... If you like music ...
CAPTAIN:	Sometimes ... In bad seas ... with a full hold ... It gets on my nerves ... The noise they make ... It shuts up the noise.
PEER:	You've obviously got a conscience ...
CAPTAIN:	I make up little songs, too. From time to time.
PEER:	You like animals?
CAPTAIN:	I like cats ... But I'm not interested in these crumbs of comfort, man ... I need more than that ... I need a purpose in life ... To justify the horrible way I make a living ... *(PEER is lost in thought ... CAPTAIN looks at him)*
PEER:	I'm thinking ...
CAPTAIN:	I hate it! The whole idea of slavery! My God, Peer, sometimes I can't stand it! I have to come back here ... and drown myself in two bottles of brandy ... To get over the day ...
PEER:	Captain ... Give me a beer ... will you?
CAPTAIN:	Take ... my boy ... Take ... Whatever you want ...
PEER:	The abolition of slavery ... That's what you're working for ...
CAPTAIN:	I wish I could ... I wish I could afford it, Peer.
PEER:	Listen ... It's not your fault slavery is still legal ... You're not in the government ...
CAPTAIN:	You think they might ... Declare it illegal ... My God ...
PEER:	Let me finish ...
CAPTAIN:	I need the money, Peer ... I haven't any other connections ... If you knew what a cut-throat business the everyday cargo trade was ...
PEER:	Yes ... That's what you can do best ... Run slaves ...
CAPTAIN:	I look after them ... No doubt about it ... I don't even let the men near the women ... I have one myself ... naturally ... But you've got to establish your position as commander of the ship.
PEER:	Until it's made illegal ... If *you* didn't do it ... there's a hundred others ready to.
CAPTAIN:	My God, yes! That's the whole point! Christ, you've got a brain lad!

PEER: And if you have anything to spare ... Ten or twenty quid ... At the end of the voyage ...

CAPTAIN: Listen ... Don't think there's any fortunes to be made in the business ... The way people talk about slavery ... You'd think we'd be millionaires after a couple of trips ...

PEER: Just if you have anything to spare ... You give it to the Abolition of Slavery people ...

CAPTAIN: Where's the brandy ... Peer, lad ... It's somewhere on the shelf ... Get the brandy ... What thinking Peer ... son ... Give it ... to the abolitionists ... yes ... Listen ... I will ... The minute I get back ... I'll give them ... Ten percent of all the profits ... Definitely five ...

PEER: Something ... substantial ...

CAPTAIN: Christ! That's it ... We are working for the abolition of slavery ... This is the quickest way of raising funds to win the battle ...

PEER: I can write pretty well, Captain ... No doubt about it ... I could make a good secretary ...

CAPTAIN: Listen ... Boy ... I don't mind *you* having one of the girls from time to time ... Providing you keep it quiet ... You can have them in here ... with me ... That would be nice ... The two of us together with our black juicy little virgins ... I'd like that very much ... That's being real pals ... I've never had a pal to do that with me before ... Listen ... I'll give them *ten* percent ... Twelve ... Definitely ten ...

                The Moor ...

                ... GYNT, tired, but pushing himself hard ... The BUTTON MOULDER shouts after him ...

BUTTON
MOULDER: Gynt!

GYNT: Things are moving.

B.M.:   Listen ... What I forgot to tell you ... Is practically everybody anyway ends up here. *(holding up his mould. GYNT waits for the revelation)* Everybody ...

GYNT: What do you want me to do about that?

B.M.:   No ... But that does not make it easier alright ... You're in the same boat as billions ...

GYNT: I don't get your reason, Moulder ... What are you trying to prove? The situation's completely changed, anyway ... Changing every second ... You're behind the times ... I don't even *think* about that order, now ... I'm trying to *understand* ... What's happened ... and what's happening ...

B.M.:   What's happening's easy ... There's an order To Melt out on you ...

GYNT: If I can even get the meaning of one *action*, man ... That would be a start, wouldn't it?

B.M.:   You see ... I'm beginning to know you, Gynt ... That worries me ... Give you any kind of a start at all ... and you're off, pushing on to the bitter end ...

GYNT:	That might help ... Is there an end? Apart from the obvious one ...
B.M.:	I just thought ... You mightn't take it so bad ... If you knew you weren't the only one who ended up in this ...
GYNT:	God ... It's cold ... That wind, isn't it? *(going)*
B.M.:	Is it? Yes it is ...
	(putting up his collar ... and going) ... It is cold ... I just thought I'd let you know.
PEER:	*(going)* Thank you ... Thank you very much. That's very kind of you.
	A Street in Paris ... The CAPTAIN, *very much down on his luck, is singing for coppers ...*
CAPTAIN:	*Pity the fishes,* *Deep in the sea,* *They can be drowned,* *As well as we.*
	Pity the stars, *Crowding the sky,* *They can be lonely,* *As well as I.*
	(The OLD PEER *approaches with a* GIRL *on his arm)*
GIRL:	What a banal, sickly song!
CAPTAIN:	*(clearly not recognising the* OLD PEER*)* You like it ... I'll sing you more ...
OLD PEER:	*(holding the* GIRL *back)* No ... It's got something to it.
CAPTAIN:	To be honest with you, I'm a master mariner ... Sailor first ... Musician After that.
GIRL:	You can say that again, Sailor!
OLD PEER:	The tune ... I like the tune ...
CAPTAIN:	Think there's something in the tune. Do you, sir?
	Yes ... Not all that long ago ... I had my own ship ... My best pal bought it from under me ...
GIRL:	*(trying to pull* PEER *away)* We're not to listen to the story of his life, are we?
OLD PEER:	Maybe he *wasn't* your friend, Captain.
CAPTAIN:	Wouldn't have any girls with me. That's true enough. Slunk off to have them on his own ... in his cabin.
GIRL:	*(to* PEER*)* What do you mean? He wasn't his friend.
CAPTAIN:	*(agressively to* PEER*)* What do *you* know about it, anyway? Know who he was ... My best pal ... Won't believe this ... Mr. Gynt ... Peer Gynt ... Richest man in the world, today. One of them, anyway.
GIRL:	And he owes all his success to you.
CAPTAIN:	Listen ... He was drowning. If I wouldn't have stretched out my hand to him at the right minute ...
GIRL:	And this is the thanks you get ... Poor man!
CAPTAIN:	I'm not complaining. That's people ... Look at you, having to run around with an old man twice your age.

OLD PEER:	How long did he spend with you, Captain. Nine years ... Ten?
CAPTAIN:	I've got plenty of other songs. Take your pick.
	(sings)

> *If I was a tree,*
> *I would stand in the square,*
> *Watch all the people,*
> *And breathe in the air,*
> *I'd watch all the people,*
> *And look at the sun.*
> *And I would be wiser before I was done.*

	Spent nearly ten years with me ... If you knew the pal he was to me ... And me to him.
OLD PEER:	What I'm saying, Captain ... A great man like Mr. Gynt ... And you, Captain ... Warm-hearted ... and generous ... *and*, of course, musical, as you might be ...
CAPTAIN:	Yes ... I see what you're getting at ... I was lucky to have him for a pal for ten years ... You're right ...
OLD PEER:	All those years you were together ... Basically, you might never have really communicated. You see what I mean ... Talking ... Yes ... but he'd never really be able to get through to you.
CAPTAIN:	You should've heard us when we got going. Talking about everything under the sun ... Monkeys ... Did Monkeys love each other like people ...
GIRL:	And of course the slave girls ... That would be another topic in common.
CAPTAIN:	We had everything in common. You're quite right.
OLD PEER:	What I'm saying ... Is ... At real depths ... You never knew him.
CAPTAIN:	You calling me a liar, mister!
OLD PEER:	What I'm saying is, you only knew a small part of him. Most of his personality ... You understand. He wouldn't be able to show you. He'd have to shut it out.
CAPTAIN:	He showed me everything. I wouldn't say he was all that well hung. He wasn't bad, but ...
GIRL:	No ...
OLD PEER:	So ... in the end ... What I'm saying ... is if he left you ...
CAPTAIN:	He bought my ship from under me, I'm telling you. That was the start of his slaver fleet.
OLD PEER:	It would be understandable. Him leaving you ... Because, in a sense, he'd never been near you. He was nothing to you.
CAPTAIN:	I can give you a tune on the flute. If you fancy it.
OLD PEER:	If that was the case ... Peer Gynt having to shut out most of his personality for ten years, Captain ... A great man ...
CAPTAIN:	The greatest. No doubt about it ... I don't hold it against him. Dropping me in the shit. That's people. If he walked across the street this minute, I'd have my arms round him the next minute ...
GIRL:	Not kick in his balls!
CAPTAIN:	What's she saying? Girls, these days! Watch your language, please, Miss.

OLD PEER: A great man ... Having to act like an ordinary person ... For all these years ... I would still think he might have dreams about these years, Captain.

CAPTAIN: No doubt about it ... Got plenty to dream about ... Him and me ... We had some happy times together ... The girls ... It was beautiful.

OLD PEER: It was honest, wasn't it? There were no illusions about it. It was an open, honest relationship ...

GIRL: They knew what you wanted – and they had to give you it.

CAPTAIN: They loved you in the end ... These girls ... Didn't they?

GIRL: Better than some of these frigid white cunts!

CAPTAIN: Would you please tell your long lady to watch her language, sir. She's upsetting .

OLD PEER: What I am saying, in the end ... You never knew Mr. Gynt ... At any depths ...

CAPTAIN: Look, mate ... If ever two men were real pals ... When he was away ... I didn't know where to put myself, till he came back ... Or if I went away from him ... Couldn't get back to him quick enough.

GIRL: What a pity you stopped short of physical relationships.

CAPTAIN: Now you mention it ... That's another thing. He never pissed with me.

OLD PEER: Do you think the warmth was enough? Even though you got near his mind ... The goodwill ... and friendly feelings ... I don't know ...

CAPTAIN: I don't like pals shitting with you. But an odd piss together ... Brings you closer, doesn't it

GIRL: *(pulling PEER away)* Are you coming ... ?

CAPTAIN: *(taking up his flute)* How about the Irish Washerwoman?

OLD PEER: *(emptying his pockets into the begging tray)* that's alright, Captain. Another time.

CAPTAIN: Thank you, sir. That's very generous of you. Yes. Very generous of you, indeed ... Listen ... Don't think he threw me off his ship empty-handed, Mr. Gynt ... If I'm on the street, here today, it's not his fault ...

GIRL: *(going to PEER)* The fantasies people have, darling!

OLD PEER: Yes ... Amusing but ... For a few minutes ...

(The CAPTAIN continues his song as they go)

CAPTAIN: *Pity the rich,*
Warm and secure,
They can be hungry,
As well as the poor.

Pity the seeing,
Cold and unkind.
They can be sightless,
As well as the blind.

(... Sound of a storm as he finishes his song ...

... The FANTASY PEER is clinging desperately to the keel of an upturned boat ... The CAPTAIN is trying to reach the keel, stretching out his hand to grasp it)

FANTASY PEER: Get off!

CAPTAIN:	Peer ... For Christ's sake!
FANTASY PEER:	*(lifting a spar)* I'll smash you hands!
CAPTAIN:	I've got my old Mother, Peer ...
FANTASY PEER:	Let go, will you! I'll sink with two ... You'd drown both of us ...
CAPTAIN:	Waiting for us ... I'm all she has ... My old mother ...
FANTASY PEER:	*(lifting the spar ... about to bring it down)* Let go!
CAPTAIN:	Peer, lad ... I'm drowning ...
FANTASY PEER:	Talk to God, man. Up there ... Wasting your time, talking to me.
CAPTAIN:	God ... Please ... Help me ... Oh God ... Please help me ... *(sinking ...)*
FANTASY PEER:	The Lord's Prayers, man! To help your reception when you get up there ... If you do reach there.
	(CAPTAIN drowns ...)
FANTASY PEER:	*(swinging himself up on the keel)* ... Well ... Mr. Gynt ... Where there's life, there's hope ... Eh?
	Captain's Cabin ... PEER at a table, working on the books. The FANTASY PEER is lolling on the bunk near him. The CAPTAIN comes in, happy, relaxed and smiling ...
CAPTAIN:	Alright ... So score off another male, there, Peer ... Plenty more where they came from, eh?
	(PEER looks up coldly ...)
	... Yes ... Had a bit of an accident.
PEER:	Working out the figures on a ten percent mortality basis ...
CAPTAIN:	*(at book. Emotionally)* That's people there! Flesh and blood! ... Not figures in a book.
PEER:	If we can *keep* it to ten percent we'll end up about sixty percent on our investment this trip.
CAPTAIN:	Altogether ... Since we left ... Right? I've had four accidents ... That's all ... Listen ... Where's that salami ...
PEER:	*(handing him it)* I don't like violence. You know that.
CAPTAIN:	That's your trouble ... You're right. You don't like hitting people ... Want some salami ...?
PEER:	Take a bit ...
CAPTAIN:	*(cutting him a slice)* See ... *You* don't hear them ... They've been moaning away for hours there ... and you just sit at your books ... They were getting on my nerves, Peer ...
FANTASY PEER:	*(to CAPTAIN)* I've worked it out, Franks ... Yes? You listening? I've tried very hard to find a place for you on this ship. Out of humanity ... But you've got to go.
CAPTAIN:	They always get like that in heavy seas ...
PEER:	They're not sailors ...
CAPTAIN:	You're right, Peer ... They're not sailors ... It eats into your nerves ... That's all you can do, isn't it? Go out and bash them ... Go off your rocker sitting there listening to them.
PEER:	Didn't like his face?

CAPTAIN:	I don't like any of their faces. The girls are alright. But there's something about a black man's face, isn't there?
FANTASY PEER:	All this liberal shit about improving the quality of slavery! ... Slavery's slavery, man! ... Give them an extra cubic inch of air ... Another ounce of mealie ... Honestly, Franks!
PEER:	If you packed another couple of hundred in the hold ... Could easily do that ... Next trip ... knock it up to 70 percent.
CAPTAIN:	That's out, Peer ... I'm not having that ...
PEER:	And the money we waste on food ... I've worked out a diet here ...
CAPTAIN:	I'm telling you, Peer ... All you see is figures ... You don't *hear* them ... I shouldn't have given you a percentage ... You were hard enough before ... That was a mistake ...
PEER:	Apart from anything else ... You're throwing good money overboard ... Killing off your stock ...
CAPTAIN:	They give you these dirty looks ... I'm shouting to them. Stop that moaning ... Stop it ... Just keep on ... And this tall blackie pops his head up to the grill ...
FANTASY PEER:	If you had some *purpose* in what you were doing, Franks.
PEER:	You're not in all that good a financial way ...
CAPTAIN:	I get the mate to bring this blackie out ... You know how I get ... when somebody gets my back up like that ... I just had to bash him down to the deck ... If you knew the relief it was to bash into that stupid, black face!
PEER:	I've been with you nearly ten years, Albert ...
CAPTAIN:	You know that, Peer ... I can't help it ... You should understand that ... I feel bad enough about the rotten busines I'm in ... without you rubbing it in ... What's the matter with you? ... In the old days ... you used to help us ... Used to have some great nights ... didn't we ... After I'd had one of my accidents ...
PEER:	Been with you ten years, now, Albert ...
CAPTAIN:	Stop saying that ... I don't like you saying that, Peer ... The way you say it ...
	Anyway ... it does everybody the world of good ... Bashing one of them now and then ... They all shut up the minute he fell to the deck ... You know how this business weighs on me, Peer ... You don't grudge me a couple of hours of peace ...
FANTASY PEER:	*(coming down from the bunk)* Alright ... Fair enough ... You're going nowhere ... What about *me*?
PEER:	Just now. Are you listening?
	(The CAPTAIN is pissing through a porthole)
CAPTAIN:	Peer. Come on. Have a piss with us.
PEER:	I'm speaking to you. That's all I can do just now ... Stuck here ... But I'm not going to do it all my life.
CAPTAIN:	I can't stand pals shitting with you. But a pal who never pisses with you.
PEER:	I don't need to.

CAPTAIN:	You never need to when I do.
PEER:	All this soft, sentimental shit, Albert ... Crying every time you have one of the girls ...
CAPTAIN:	I've got a heart ... That's right ... Hold it against me ... I've got a heart!
FANTASY PEER:	I'm facing up to the reality of my situation. That's the crucial difference between us ... I don't make up any fairy tales about us making our money out of *crucifying human beings* ... People, Captain ... Like you and me ...
PEER:	What we're doing ... Is making a living from sucking the lives out of human beings ... *People*, Albert ... You know that?
CAPTAIN:	Peer ... You know the kind of life they lead in their jungles. It's not as if we were taking them from civilised homes. A lot of them ... You know that ... End up with Jesus ... They all have to go to church ... that's doing something for them, isn't it?
FANTASY PEER:	*(confronting CAPTAIN)* I'm not putting myself above you. Yes ... I am ...
CAPTAIN:	*(going to PEER)* Listen. Leave your books alone, a minute. We'll have a sing song ... Eh ...
	Pity the fishes, *Deep in the sea ...* *They can be lonely ...* *As well as we ...*
	(PEER ignores him) ... PEER ... Don't ... It upsets me ... When you're angry with me like that ...
PEER:	Do you know that, Albert? What we're doing, is climbing up on tens of thousands of black corpses ... I'm not saying it's bad or good ... It's what we're doing.
CAPTAIN:	In all ... Listen to this ... I've had maybe twenty accidents in the sixteen years I've been Captain ...
PEER:	No ... *You're* not even *climbing* ... You're going nowhere ... *I'm* climbing ...
FANTASY PEER:	But I can see *exactly* what I'm doing ... That's something ... Isn't it? That's one step forwards.
CAPTAIN:	What I should do ... Is not tell you ... When I have these accidents ...
FANTASY PEER:	Where am I climbing? Difficult ... Somewhere ... Until I have enough capital ... I can't really get moving ... Next thing is to get a *fleet* of slavers ... Then move out ... To something quick and sure ... Arms is a good business ...
PEER:	Even the girls ... We've got to have all these violins and sentimental crap ... Every time, they end up loving you ...
CAPTAIN:	They do ... It's the white prick ... Go mad over a white prick ... you know that.
PEER:	They *hate* you, Albert ... Hate! There's nothing they can do about it ... They have to give you it ... Then they hate you even more.
CAPTAIN:	Look ... I'm telling you ... I know ... They end up loving me ... I know better than you ...
FANTASY PEER:	*(holding up a pistol)* So that's it, Captain. *You* used me. *I used you* ... I *don't need you any more* ... Goodbye, Captain Franks ...

PEER: Mate!

CAPTAIN: I don't want the mate, Peer ... Listen ... We'll get a couple of girls, eh ... Have a nice night ... Wine ... women ... song ... eh ...

Pity the rich,
Warm and secure.
They can be hungry
As well as the poor ...

(The MATE enters)

MATE: Sir!

CAPTAIN: I don't want you ...

FANTASY PEER: Lower a boat and load it with enough supplies to make the nearest landfall, mate.

PEER: Lower a boat with enough supplies to make the nearest landfall.

MATE: *(going)* Aye, sir ...

CAPTAIN: Peer, man ... Listen ... What's the matter with you ... It was just an accident ... You're taking it too much to heart. Listen ... I promise ... I'll watch myself ... Peer. You can't leave me ... You're the only real pal I have ...

PEER: *(lifting a pistol to him) You're* leaving *me*, Captain ... I'm taking over the ship ...

Battlefield ... Shellfire ... The FANTASY PEER, dressed as a Commerical Traveller, is carrying his case of samples. FANTASY PEER is being guided respectfully through the battlefield by a GERMAN GENERAL ... Shells are continually flying overhead and exploding.

FANTASY PEER stops to study a line of trenches.

GERMAN: Interesting, Herr Gynt?

PEER: Profitable.

GERMAN: *(to FANTASY PEER)* I'll take another couple of gross of the sixty millimetre ...

FANTASY PEER: I'd take four, General. In short supply. One of our best lines.

GERMAN: Four then.

PEER: They stand there ... In a ten foot slit in the clay, firing at another ten foot slit.

GERMAN: Ah, but Herr Gynt. You know this better than me. Yes? A great philosopher like yourself. Any human activity under the sun can be reduced to absurdity.

PEER: I'm saying. It's one way of passing a couple of months of your life. Good luck to them.

GERMAN: Thank you.

FANTASY PEER: How are you off for grenades?

GERMAN: That's right. Badly down in grenades. *(to PEER)* Down Herr Gynt!

PEER: *(dodging a shell)* Not *reduced* to absurdity. It *is* absurdity. All human activities.

GERMAN:	That's interesting. Of course, any statement from an intellect of your calibre is interesting.
PEER:	Is it?
FANTASY PEER:	You see. It doesn't worry me, particularly ... How many lives do you estimate are going to be lost as a result of our little business transaction? Twenty thousand? Thirty?
PEER:	Another six months ... If you can carry on this war for About that time, General ... That should do me.
GERMAN:	To make Herr Gynt's fortune ... Anything to support genius, Herr Gynt.
FANTASY PEER:	You ask me why it doesn't weigh on my conscience, General? All these lives ... It doesn't bother me, because basically we're a blight. People are a blight on the earth ... A disease.
GERMAN:	Ah ... You speak of the English ...
FANTASY PEER:	English ... American ... Spanish ... German ...
GERMAN:	German, Herr Gynt?
PEER:	All a blight. As soon as we're all wiped out ... The earth'll be able to get on with its business in peace ...
GERMAN:	You, too, Herr Gynt ... You see yourself as part of the general disease, humanity?
PEER:	No reason why I should be any exception. I wasn't talking about my fortune ... Made that years ago ... No ... Another six months ... And I should be financially impregnable ... Safe, General ...
GERMAN:	(dodging a shell ... and stepping over a corpse) One must respect the views of a deep thinker like yourself. But ... Human life, Herr Gynt ... Human life is very precious ... Human life is very sweet.
FANTASY PEER:	Not many new lines, this trip, General ... But we've brought out a new gas cylinder ... Chlorine ...
GENERAL:	Looks interesting ...
FANTASY PEER:	I can give you a special quote for quantity in this line ...
GENERAL:	(bending down to indicate a flower growing in the battlefield) Now here, Herr Gynt ... Exactly what I was trying to say ... (breaking into Schubert) Once a boy Found a rose. Growing in the hedgerow, Petals opened to the day. Held the eyes of the boy on his way
PEER:	It's a daisy.
GERMAN:	Of course, it's a daisy ... But the general principle. The general principle still holds. The rose needs a Goethe to appreciate its beauty and significance.
PEER:	Yes, I can see now why they made you a general!
FANTASY PEER:	I can see that. You take all these things seriously. Imaginary lines across countries. Boundaries ... Territories ... God's justice and so on ... I know. They're very real to you ... It's just ... I can't understand these kind of abstractions ... I can't grasp the concepts ...

GENERAL: *(as they go ... passing him the cheque)* But you can grasp the cheque
                alright, Herr Gynt? Yes? ... *(PEER takes the cheque)* ... I make a little joke
                ... You don't mind ...?

PEER: *(looking at the cheque)* Yes ... I can grasp that fine ...
                *(... PEER bows ... The GENERAL salutes ... A bugle plays a fanfare ...
                which changes into a PRIEST calling the faithful to prayer ...
                PEER moves over to the Sahara Desert. The FANTASY PEER strips as
                they go, down to a striped bathing suit ...
                The Desert. A VALET enters with all the equipment Peer will need for his
                retreat in the desert. A deckchair ... table ... paper ... typewriters ... drinks
                ... While it's all being set up FANTASY PEER enters ... followed by
                PEER)*

PEER: Anitras!
                *(ANITRAS enters in Arab gear with a shorthand notebook. Looks
                round)*

ANITRAS: Arid.

PEER: That's the whole idea. *(snaps his fingers, dismissing servant)* Exactly what
                we're looking for. Nothing grows here. No water. No plants ... Nothing
                for the blight to feed on.

ANITRAS: *(turning to SHEIKH AMADHI)* But still they keep coming!
                (SHEIKH prostrates himself on the ground)

SHEIKH: My father! King ... Prophet. Prophet of prophets! *(PEER pours himself
                out a brandy)* ... How are you keeping? What a pleasure and an honour to
                have you in our midst. *(offering him a box)* Cigar? Turkish Delight?
                Cheese and Cucumber sandwich ...?

FANTASY PEER: Told you! Doesn't matter where you go. Never get rid of Jews.

SHEIKH: *(alarmed)* Jews? Where ...?

PEER: Nothing personally against them. Just ... We'd have been better off
                without them.

SHEIKH: The poetry that comes out of your golden mouth.

FANTASY PEER: Bad enough for Greeks. With their self-conscious navel contemplation.
                But we might have got over them.

SHEIKH: I know ... I know ... I know ... I know ...

FANTASY PEER: But then the Jews saddling you with their liberal, pathetic humanism ...
                What chance had we?

PEER: On the other hand, you could say without the Jews we might have ended
                up even worse off. Who knows?

SHEIKH: Prophet. I know exactly why you have come to my desert.

PEER: Oh ... It's his desert.

ANITRAS: This *all* your sand. How nice.

FANTASY PEER: Make a fortune in the building trade.

ANITRAS: I thought you'd given up making money.

FANTASY PEER: Just a thought.

SHEIKH: Father. Listen. Stay here. Please, sir. You are welcome for the rest of your
                life. I make you a present of it. This desert.

PEER: That's an idea. We could settle down here.

ANITRAS:	I'm not living here.
FANTASY PEER:	Pipe a water supply. Organise a regular camel run ... Build an air conditioned bungalow ... You could be happy for life. ... No tigers here, are there?
SHEIKH:	If you wish a tiger, sir ... I could get you a tiger ...
PEER:	Tell you what I really want.
SHEIKH:	Ask, sir ... And your wish be granted.
PEER:	Go away.
SHEIKH:	I see.
PEER:	Thank you. Goodbye.
SHEIKH:	I know why you have come here, sir ... To confront yourself ... To come face to face with your own mind and self. And to write the final volume in the world's greatest statement ever to be made since Mohammed and Charles Dickens ...
ANITRAS:	Will I take him behind the Pyramid?
PEER:	I need you for dictation, Anitras.
SHEIKH:	What I have in mind, sir ... Listen to this, please ... Then I'll go ... A Pan Arab Conference ...
PEER:	I'll *take* a bit of your Turkish Delight, while you're here ...
SHEIKH:	Thousands of my brothers ... Gathered in the desert. To hear the prophet of prophets.
ANITRAS:	Obviously he hasn't kept up with your books. *(to SHEIKH)* Mr. Gynt's given up people, making money, talking, reading and sexual intercourse.
SHEIKH:	Listen to me, please, sir ... We have everything now ... Thanks to God's goodness and the demands of modern technological society ... Only one thing we lack. Happiness. We want to be happy, sir. Please ... Teach us to be happy.
PEER:	What's he talking about?
ANITRAS:	He wants to be happy.
PEER:	Should be a song about that, shouldn't there ... I'd Be So Happy If I Could Be Happy ...
SHEIKH:	All my brothers ... Please, sir ... Address us ... I know ... It's no use offering you money ... *You* can offer *us* money ...
ANITRAS:	How about a Pyramid ...
SHEIKH:	Yes ... Please ... Take a Pyramid, sir ...
FANTASY PEER:	I don't like Pyramids ...
ANITRAS:	Put it up somewhere ... For a monument ... After you've gone.
PEER:	Admit defeat. Only thing I can leave is this ponderous monument on top of me.
FANTASY PEER:	*(jumping up)* It gives me great pleasure to declare this Pan Peer Conference now open.
PEER:	I have lived ... what ... sixty odd years ...
FANTASY PEER:	Long time ...

SHEIKH:	He's going to deliver an address ... Listen ... The Prophet's inspired ... Look at him ... Listen ... Get your notebook out ... We don't want to lose a word.
PEER:	Shut up, will you! I'm trying to speak!
FANTASY PEER:	Where do I stand? I stand on sand.
SHEIKH:	My God! You know what this is? This is the *New Koran!*
FANTASY PEER:	Take people ... Odd people I don't mind ... I can stand ... But the species as a whole ...
PEER:	*(in disgust)* Humanity. The word puts me off ...
ANITRAS:	I don't mind people, but humanity makes me reach for my revolver.
SHEIKH:	That girl! My god! She's bright!
FANTASY PEER:	Wake up one morning. Sun shining ...
PEER:	Nice day.
FANTASY PEER:	All your physical functions operating at optimum level ...
SHEIKH:	The range of his thought.
FANTASY PEER:	Look out the window at the world. Read the papers ... Things are moving ... New discoveries in medicine. More humane attitudes all round. The value of human life at its highest level in history.
PEER:	Conclusion for a sunny day: the world is moving forwards.
SHEIKH:	It is. He's right. That's what the world wants to hear ... a fanfare. Victory is in sight ... Oh, yes, sir. Indeed!
FANTASY PEER:	Wake up another day. Grey ... Wet ... Liver not so good. sympathetic system not functioning so well.
PEER:	World doesn't look so good this morning. No ...
FANTASY PEER:	Violence and greed turning the world into a jungle ... Fathers and mothers deserting children ... Children deserting fathers and mothers ... Nine tenths of the world starving while the other tenth's stuffing themselves to death ... Everything totally out of control.
SHEIKH:	It's so true ... Every word he says ...
PEER:	The sun shines – the word's "love" ... Cloudy – the word's "survival" ... So where do you go from there?
FANTASY PEER:	All that concern to remedy the world's evils ... Escapism ... Trivia ... From the central dilemma ... Yourself ...
PEER:	At the same time ... Sitting on your arse contemplating your navel ... No solution either ...
FANTASY PEER:	Retreat to digging your garden and leave everybody to their madness ... Bastards'll be knocking down your walls before you've got your seeds in ...
PEER:	Get back to the basic biological drives ... Man as an animal ... Trouble is I'm not mad about that word either 'man' ...
ANITRAS:	I like men, but when I heard the word 'man', I reach for my revolver.
SHEIKH:	That woman. She's so bright!
FANTASY PEER:	Even truths you think you've found about yourself. You don't even know what's happening inside yourself.

PEER:	Used to dream about having a girl make real demands on me ... instead of just lying down and submitting to what was coming ... Time I got round to that ... Couldn't cope with it ...
ANITRAS:	That's what I mean, darling ... The way we are is much nicer ... We make no physical demands on each other ... We can be real friends.
PEER:	She does it to herself ... I do it to myself.
ANITRAS:	In the end, you can only experience your own orgasm ...
PEER:	I don't even know about *that*, now.
FANTASY PEER:	You act out a lie for some reason ... And end up finding out it's a buried truth. Deep need you never realised you had.
PEER:	Or acting it out ... you make the lie a truth ...
ANITRAS:	*(jumping about in delight)* All this, is first class stuff. My mind's reeling!
PEER:	*(sitting down)* Hot isn't it? ... Would be, of course ... In the middle of the desert ... *(takes a handful of sand ... and lets it slowly run through his fingers ... FANTASY PEER watches closely)* ...
FANTASY PEER:	A heroic lonely figure, in the middle of a great desert, sifting through the totality of his life for some grains of truth ...
PEER:	Nice feeling. Letting the sand run through your fingers.
FANTASY PEER:	Time running out ... Life ...
PEER:	Hot ... The sand.
FANTASY PEER:	Life running out.
PEER:	Clean ... Very clean, sand, isn't it?
FANTASY PEER:	Time ... Life ...
PEER:	Nice to sink into ... Very pleasant ... Sitting here in the hot sand ... in the middle of the desert ...
FANTASY PEER:	*(looking round)* Man's history. A Desert ...
PEER:	Funny thing, a desert ... Hot ... Sandy ...
	(... ANITRAS and the SHEIKH retreat ... as the conflict mounts ... PEER and FANTASY PEER are left on their own)
FANTASY PEER:	*(looking round)* That's my life. A desert.
PEER:	Could get on your nerves after a bit, mind ... A desert ...
FANTASY PEER:	My life ...
	... Yes. Alright for an hour or so ... A desert ... Probably better without the Pyramids ... Spoils the view ...
FANTASY PEER:	*(turning to the Pyramid)* A futile finger pathetically raised to the sky to dispute its own insignificance and irrelevance ...
PEER:	A futile, pointless, ugly pyramid. Jars.
FANTASY PEER:	The trace of a butterfly's wings on the sands ...
PEER:	Totally pointless waste of energy ... A Pyramid ...
	(PEER lies back to back with the FANTASY PEER ... Somehow, if this is possible, in such a position that the OLD PEER can be behind them ... to rise up in their place ...)

FANTASY PEER:	A magnificent heroic figure ... Fighting to my last breath for some truth that will outlast these pyramids. A lonely figure in a great desert ... Tiny ... But dominating the barren landscape ...
PEER:	I've got heartburn ... It was the pineapple I had before. God ... I'm tired ... I'm all in ...
FANTASY PEER:	A great man ... Fighting to the last for the truth.
PEER:	See ... I give you that ... Keep taking heavier loads on your back ... You can make it stronger and stronger ... But comes a point when you're heading for breaking your back ... I'm not breaking my back ... Bad enough I'm growing old and losing my teeth and I've got heartburn ... Listen ...

(He slowly gets up ... This time as the OLD PEER ... The FANTASY PEER and the YOUNG PEER have joined to make this New Peer)

OLD PEER:	See I don't want to go to the stars ... Or find out why daisies come up every year ... I want to go home ... That's what I want to do ... All these years ... I've always wanted to go home. The day I left ... It was buried in me ... *(turning to an empty stage)* ... So that's what I'm going to do ... You hear me? ... I'm going home ...

(... The sound of church bells ... He walks on into the village ... The BUTTON MOULDER is waiting for him)

OLD PEER:	These damned bells!
B.M.:	I know ...
OLD PEER:	I'll show you ... You'll see ... Even though I've been gone fifty years ... Just up here ... The farm ... You see? ... My grandfather's grandfather's farm ... *His* grandfather's ...
B.M.:	*(looking)* Farm?
OLD PEER:	The house was here ... Just to the north of the copse ... *(searching ... desperately)* This is where my mother sat out in the summer ... Looking at the hills ...
MAN:	Looking for something?
OLD PEER:	The old farmhouse ... I lived here ... The Gynt's farm ...
MAN:	Farm? Here ... Might've been ... I'm not sure ... Gynts ... Gynts ...
AASE:	Listen ... There's no law against people failing ...
OLD PEER:	You hear that?
MAN:	Excuse me ... ?
OLD PEER:	*(bending down)* Look ... There's the groundsel ...
PEER:	What is it mother ... An hour's work ... Getting rid of these groundsel ... Ploughing the north meadow ... Two days at the most ... And the groundsel stays ... and the north meadow's high as your waist with weeds ...
OLD PEER:	*(to BUTTON MOULDER)* You can see them, can't you?
B.M.:	*(gently pulling him away)* Come on, Gynt ...
OLD PEER:	... There's the Pederson's house ... See ... Old Pederson'll remember me alright ... *(going to door)*
	(BOY answers)
OLD PEER:	I'm looking for Mr. Pederson ...

BOY:	This is Anderson's house, sir ... there were Pedersons ... here before us ... But they're dead ...
OLD PEER:	Not all of them ... There was a daughter ... Younger than me ...
BOY:	I'm sorry, sir ...
OLD PEER:	Listen ... You know who I am ... You won't believe this ... I'm Peer Gynt ... I bet you you've heard stories of me ... Eh? ... The terror of the village ...
BOY:	Peer Gynt?
OLD PEER:	That's me ...
BOY:	I'm sorry, sir ...
OLD PEER:	Look ... That's the barn where the wedding dance was ...
PEDERSON:	Who invited you ... turning up like a ghost at the wedding ...
PEER:	I just came ... You know why I came ... I came to apologise ... I had ...
PEDERSON:	Alright ... I forgive you ... Get yourself a drink and sit down and behave yourself ...
OLD PEER:	That was him ... *(to BOY)* That was Pederson ...
	(The BOY has gone inside)
	(to BUTTON MOULDER) That night ... we went up that path ... You see ... into the mountains ...
B.M.:	The path's there, Gynt ...
INGRID:	*(covering her face)* It's horrible! The whole night ... What did you need to come for, tonight? I would've been fine ... If you wouldn't have turned up ...
PEER:	You should've come with me ... That night ... I came for you ...
INGRID:	I've come *now* ...
PEER:	I know ... It's too late, Ingrid ...
OLD PEER:	She can't be dead, Button Moulder ... She was four years youngers than me ... At least ... Listen ... Come up here ... There's the Goat herd's hut ... That man ... He'd the strength to live to a hundred ... and the girl ... There was a kid I had by her ... That's something, isn't it ...
	(A YOUNG MAN comes out of the hut)
	That's probably him ...
	Listen, young man, I want to speak to your grandfather ...
LAD:	Do you want a drink, old man?
OLD PEER:	Or your mother ... You'll never guess who I am ... But if I'm right ... I can smell your trade's a goat herd ...
LAD:	I look after the goats ... My mother went away ... A long time ago ... After her father died ... That's right ...
OLD PEER:	Did she ever speak to you about your father ... Peer Gynt ... ?
LAD:	She went away with my father ...
OLD PEER:	No ... If you look in a mirror ... *(to BUTTON MOULDER)* ... You can see ... His eyes ... That's Gynt eyes ... and the nose ...
LAD:	My father was Olson ... Willie Olson ... They went away ...
OLD PEER:	Why was that? Why did they go away ...

LAD:	They wanted to ... Will I give you a drink ...
OLD PEER:	*(giving up going)* ... No ...
HERDGIRL:	Don't shout at me ... I don't want you to be miserable, because that would only make me miserable, wouldn't it? That's all there is to it ...
OLD PEER:	*(to BUTTON MOULDER)* Listen ... We'll go to the cemetery ... That's what I should've done first ... Visit my mother's grave ...
B.M.:	If you think it'll be any use, Gynt ...
OLD PEER:	*(searching)* ... Look ... It'll be somewhere round here ... Help me to read the headstones ...
GRAVE-DIGGER:	Looking for the grave of a loved one, sir?
OLD PEER:	Good ... You can help me ... My mother ... Gynt ... Aase Gynt ... Died ... Oh ... nearly fifty years ago ...
GRAVE-DIGGER:	Gynt ... Aase ... Trying to place it ... I haven't come across any grave with that name, sir ... Have you any idea what stone was used ... Granite ... Marble ...
OLD PEER:	I didn't see the stone ...
GRAVE-DIGGER:	No ... Nothing here, sir ... Of that name ...
OLD PEER:	Listen ... She died here ... In the Parish ... Where else was she buried ...
GRAVE DIGGER:	Were you at the funeral, sir?
OLD PEER:	Gynt ... Aase ... No, I missed the funeral ...
GRAVE-DIGGER:	No offence, sir ... But it might have been ... Accidentally, maybe... She was buried over there, sir ... In the Paupers' graves ... If she died in bad circumstances ...
OLD PEER:	Over there...
GRAVE-DIGGER:	That's it, sir ... Nice sunny spot ... You get a lovely show of celandines in the spring ...
	(GYNT stands by the mound ... The GRAVEDIGGER leaves him)
OLD PEER:	I can imagine ... It must be nice ... The celandines in the spring ...
	(The church bells boom out again ...)
	These damn bells!
B.M.:	I know ...
OLD PEER:	Listen ... the hut over the moor ... Somebody said there was a Solveig lived there ... Did you hear him ...
	(He runs towards the hut ... A GIRL comes out ...)
	(going to her) Excuse me ... I was told there was somebody living here ... Solveig ... Gynt ... maybe ... I'm not sure what name she was using ...
GIRL:	That's me ... I'm Solveig ... sir ...
OLD PEER:	She'd be an elderly lady by now ... About my age ...
GIRL:	She's gone, sir ... Last Autumn ... My aunt, sir ... Not really my aunt ... But she looked after me ... since I was a baby ...

OLD PEER: Solveig ... Solveig Gynt ...

GIRL: Solveig Gynt, sir ...

OLD PEER: Dead ...

GIRL: She died sleeping, sir ...

OLD PEER: No relation, you said? ... You look very much like her ...

GIRL: My parents were killed, sir ... In some avalanche ... They saved me ...
                 You're not Peer Gynt, sir, are you? Her husband ...

OLD PEER: *(to BUTTON MOULDER)* There you are, man! You see ... Listen ... did
                 she tell you about me ...

GIRL: She never tired telling of you, sir ... and I never tired of listening to her ...
                 Sometimes ... at nights ... I lie in my bed ... thinking about her stories ...
                 Like a book, sir ... In my head.

PEER: The old man ... Listen ... You know what Ingrid and I did ... that night I
                 ran off with her, Solveig?

SOLVEIG: Love, that's all melted. All that. Like last year's snow ...

PEER: The old man's daughter, Solveig ...

SOLVEIG: Peer ... I love you ... Whatever happened before I came to you ... You
                 know that ... Everything ... was wiped out by our first kiss ... I'll always be
                 patient love, with you ... Remember that ... Whatever happens ... I love
                 you ... I'll always love you ...

GIRL: Sometimes I got angry with her ... Being so patient with you, Mr. Gynt ...

OLD PEER: Yes ...

GIRL: But when she started talking about it ... She said it didn't matter what
                 you'd done before you married her ... or after when you had to leave her ...
                 The time you were together in the mountains was so good ... It was worth
                 a dozen lifetimes ... When she said it ... I could understand it then ... The
                 way she said it ... Listen ... It's cold now ... I was just going a walk ... Come
                 in and I'll make you some tea ... The fire's blazing ... I can make you some
                 eggs for supper, if you're hungry ... and we can talk about her ...

OLD PEER: *(going in)* You see ... I couldn't come back ... I don't understand that ... I
                 wanted to all the time ... but it got buried in me ... the want ... so deep ...
                 under so many things.

GIRL: I've made some scones, too. Would you like some fresh scones and cream
                 cheese ...

OLD PEER: *(looking round for the BUTTON MOULDER ... but he has slipped away
                 into the night ... going in with her)* Yes, I would like that ... I'd like that
                 very much ...

                 (They go inside)

You Are My Heart's Delight

Characters

DAVID
JANET

A cottage in the borders of Scotland. Recently modernised by the estate management. Telly in the corner. Modern fireplace, contrasting with the heavy, old-fashioned furniture. A fish tank.

JANET is dividing her time between preparing the tea and cutting out figures from a mail order catalogue. She sticks the pages to odd pieces of cardboard and after they have dried, cuts out the figures. Completed figures are displayed all round the room, on the mantelpiece, on the sideboard as ornaments.

It's late spring. Evening. JANET hears DAVID approaching and concentrates on her cooking. DAVID enters. He carries a shot-gun, which he puts down carefully.

He takes off his coat and boots, then begins to clean his gun, watching JANET. He is clearly disturbed about something.

DAVID:	Good smell. *(DAVID looks at the catalogue on the table)*
JANET:	Mince roll.
DAVID:	Andrew told me he'd brought you a new catalogue.
JANET:	Some bonnie things in it, David. *(showing him)* I just cut that out ...
DAVID:	There's something left in the bottle, isn't there?
JANET:	You know better than me what's left in the bottle.
DAVID:	*(going over to the sideboard and pouring himself a glass of whisky. His hand is shaking)* You couldn't say I had any temper to us, could ye? That's one thing nobody could say against me.
JANET:	All you need to do, David. I told you ... Is get Sir Malcolm on one of his clear days. And tell him how much that gate's bothering you. He'd put —
DAVID:	It's nothing to do with the gate, woman! Who says it's anything to do with the gate!
JANET:	Look at you, just now. Going at the spirits.
DAVID:	I said to Mr. Charles. Last year. We're losing partridges by the hundred along the Berwick Road. Getting mowed down, right, left, and centre. If we rented the shooting rights to a syndicate, we'd have enough money for proper fencing along the whole of the estate running by the Berwick Road.
JANET:	Did Andrew tell you he had to stop Sir Malcolm driving through the village, this morning?
DAVID:	Sir Malcolm's saner than you or me. His mind's sharper than ever. He's over much on his mind, that's the problem. Mr. Charles has him running round in circles ... the way he's mucking about with the estate ...
JANET:	Sir Malcolm was driving on the wrong side of the road. Half on the pavement ...
DAVID:	He's a lawyer, Mr. Charles. What the hell does a bloody lawyer know about running an estate like this!
JANET:	Andrew said Sir Malcolm probably thought he was driving in France or somewhere ... Where they drive on the wrong side of the road.

DAVID:	I never wanted a tar road up to the cottage. It happened, exactly as I told Sir Malcolm it would ...
JANET:	Will I give you your soup now, David?
DAVID:	I haven't finished my gun, have I? Ye want me te put it away with all the filth of the day's work.
	... I told him; you put a tar road up to the cottage, and you'll have every Tom, Dick and Harry coming up to the moors ...
JANET:	*(watching the gun being cleaned)* If you told Sir Malcolm how that gate's getting on your nerves, David ... It wouldn't cost all that much to put a cattle grid in its place.
DAVID:	Tearing up the land on either side of the road. All that disturbing the earth. We haven't had a snipe on the moor, now, within a mile of where they've been working ... Took near a year to get the badger back again.
JANET:	I mean. There's no need for it, David. Coming back every night, all worked up like that. Over the gate. When all you need to do is to tell Sir Malcolm –
DAVID:	I'm not worked up about the gate, woman! I told you! It's nothing to do with the bloody gate! *(finishing cleaning his gun)*
JANET:	*(eyes on the gun)* Did you thin the coots on Sweethope?
DAVID:	*(putting the gun away)* I'll take my soup now, Janet.
JANET:	Aye ... Have it now, David. I'm starving. Waiting for you ...
DAVID:	*(holding gun for a moment, before he replaces it in the gun cabinet)* I took seventy coots from Sweethope ... Single handed ... Mr. Charles wouldn't dirty his hands on a job like that. Doubt if he can shoot anyway. There's still forty odd left. Wasted half the morning spelling it all out to him, why the loch needed thinning out. Left to him, he wouldn't have taken one!
JANET:	I can understand him. I like the sight of the loch full of coots. They've *life* in them ... Haven't they David? *(putting down his soup)*
DAVID:	It was *Mr. Charles* that gave me the van. Sir Malcolm would have never given me a van. I never wanted a van.
JANET:	You know what we had at the table this morning, David? A nuthatch ...
DAVID:	I can'ne *talk* to *Him*! You can'ne get through to him. He keeps shouting about natural control ... Coots'll control themselves in the end. The Partridges that've learned the trick of crossing the Berwick Road without getting flattened by heavy lorries'll go onte raise chicks with that knack, too. He's driving everybody like mad. Planting the woods. Draining fields. Building new roads. Paying me to keep his estate. And he keeps on shouting about *natural control!*
JANET:	*(apropos of the soup)* Ye like it?
DAVID:	It's fine ... See ... He can'ne grasp it. This is not a *natural* estate. Is it? Any estate. It's not natural.
JANET:	He came right on the table ... The nuthatch ... Bonnie, David ...
DAVID:	He's due about, now ...
JANET:	Was he no' a wee bit later last year. Have ye had words with Mr. Charles, then?
DAVID:	Benny Hill's on the night, is he?

JANET:	Tomorrow night ... *Softly Softly's* on ... That you like.
DAVID:	One of these days ... These Catalogue people. They'll get on to ye. Won't they? Ye keep getting them to send ye catalogues ... and ye never buy anything out of them.
JANET:	I like them. I like looking through them, David.
DAVID:	They could get ye for that. Couldn't they? They talk about the catalogues being worth four or five pounds ... don't they ... They could ask the money for them.
JANET:	*(protectively at her catalogue)* It says ... when you write away for them. Under no obligation.
DAVID:	I was going to shoot at this lorry ... for God's sake, Janet ... on the Berwick Road ... God knows what the hell stopped us. Had the safety catch off.
JANET:	At a man? Ye were never going to shoot at a man, for God's sake, David?
DAVID:	I never said I was shooting at a man. At a lorry. I said. I was aiming at his tyres. Couldn'e tell ye te this minute what the hell stopped my finger on the trigger ...
JANET:	He must've riled ye, David. To shoot at him.
DAVID:	God, maybe. Something ... beyond us ...
	(She waits for him to continue. He indicates his empty soup plate)
	I'm ready for my mince, Janet.
JANET:	I'm getting it for you ...
DAVID:	You could buy something from them ... couldn't you. For once ... From the catalogue. To stop them from taking it up. You getting catalogues and never buying anything.
JANET:	What did you take your gun to him for, David?
DAVID:	To the Lorry Driver ... Streak of evil ... answering, evil ... That's what it was ... Some of the things that happen on the Berwick Road. They're accidents plain and simple ... But some of them ... it's a streak of evil.
	I'm walking along the big field ... skirting the Berwick Road. A few minutes back. I just found a sandpiper with a full clutch ... by the river ... Just going through the gate. Back to the road and my van. And there's this hen partridge. Twelve chicks on her tail. Crossing the Berwick Road.
JANET:	David ... I can'ne stand hearing about things like that ...!
DAVID:	You asked me to tell you what took my gun to my shoulder ... didn't you ... Ye know how partridges take their time crossing ... Dawdlin' across. One chick stuck on the bank. The mother callin' her. Half a mile off. This big lorry. Quarter a mile. Dry road. Clear sight of her. That bit ... The road's straight near a mile ... isn't it ... Belting ... Sixty an hour. Seventy ... maybe ... this wee raft of chicks ... and the mother ...
JANET:	David!
DAVID:	He couldn't miss seeing them. A line of them. If his eyes were on the road, he couldn't miss seeing them. See from his face, woman, he'd the sight of them. And I was there. With my arm up, shouting to him to stop. Hen started panicking ... then, now ... could see ... Putting his foot down harder ... more like it ... then taking it off ... Bloody ploughed right through the raft of chicks – Right through them ...

JANET:	It's just killing ... People killing ...
DAVID:	That wee raft of life. On the road ... Him just throwing himself at it. Never even stopping for me. Had my gun up ... and my sight on his back tyre ...
JANET:	You could've killed him. If he had a burst at that speed, couldn't you ...
DAVID:	Was'ne thinking of anything ... But putting a cartridge inte that bloody monster ... Stinking exhaust ... spittin' filth and noise ... just filling the air with filth and noise ... wherever it went ... and killing ...
JANET:	You could've, couldn't you ...
DAVID:	God knows how ... The mother came out of it ... and four chicks.
JANET:	Thank God, David, you never fired ...
DAVID:	See ... The minute before he turned up ... It was such a bonny afternoon ... wasn't it?
JANET:	Like summer ...
DAVID:	And I'd been watching the sandpiper on her eggs ... And then seeing the partridges ... Watching them with their mother ... All that life jumping in them ... In wee things like that ... There's so much life jumping inside of them ... Isn't there? ... And that bastard comes along with his bloody monster!...
JANET:	At least there's four of them left, David. And the mother ...
DAVID:	A wee bit salty. *(indicating mince)*
JANET:	Is it? ... Should'ne be ...
DAVID:	It's alright ...
JANET:	Do you want to see what I got in the order from Patterson's ... Wee treat for you ... *(going to sideboard)* Wee box of chocolates ... the dark ones ... you like ...
DAVID:	You like the milk ones ...
JANET:	I don't mind either ... Thought we'd have a treat ... While we're watching *Softly, Softly* ... eh, David?
DAVID:	It's no' my birthday ... Is it?
JANET:	You know fine it isn't ...
DAVID:	I lose track of it ... It's soon ...
JANET:	Soon ...
DAVID:	I'm over it, now, Janet ...
JANET:	I know.
DAVID:	It was being so near to shooting at him ...
JANET:	De ye think I *should* maybe get something from the catalogue, David? For once?
DAVID:	If there's something takes your fancy. Why shouldn't you?
JANET:	What do you think I should get?
DAVID:	You know what you need yourself, don't you?
JANET:	No ... But the way you were talking before ...
DAVID:	Just a change ... From these dresses and that you get at Coldstream ... That's all I was thinking about ... Some of them ... Ye cut out ...

JANET:	Like one of these. *(indicating the cut out models around the room)*
DAVID:	Just whatever ye fancy ...
JANET:	They're just for young lassies, David!
DAVID:	Not all of them ...
JANET:	If folks saw us in one of them ...
DAVID:	Who'd see you here ... Eight miles up the hills ... Anyway?
JANET:	Would you like to see us in one of these, David?
DAVID:	It's up to you ... I don't know anything about dresses ... Be a change, wouldn't it?
JANET:	I'll make you a cup of tea, now ... Will I?
DAVID:	*(looking at the chocolates)* Isn't there chocolates ye can buy ... milk and plain ... *(as he is talking the lights go off)* I think I saw them on the television ... What have ye done there, Janet? Put the light on, woman!
JANET:	Have'ne touched it, David ... It's just gone out ...
DAVID:	He ye fused it. Putting in the kettle.
JANET:	Just filling the kettle. I'm no' near the plug.
DAVID:	Be a fuse somewhere.
JANET:	*(with a torch)* I'll get the fuse-wire.
DAVID:	I'm sure there's these chocolates. Dark and white.
JANET:	Have you been at the fuse wire, David? It was in the top drawer here.
DAVID:	Wait a minute. I was using it for the van. For a bad connection. I brought it back in again.
JANET:	I've got a screwdriver ...
DAVID:	God! Where the hell did I put it?
JANET:	I'll light one of the lamps, just now ... *(she gets out an oil lamp, and lights it)*
DAVID:	I'll just use some of this flex ... See ... Strip it down ... and use that, the now ... Do. Till the morning.
JANET:	Sure. It'll be safe.
DAVID:	Got the wire cutters ...?
JANET:	They're all in the top drawer ...
	(DAVID strips the wire, separates the strands)
	I'll get the steps.
	(JANET brings out step-ladders, puts them against the wall to let DAVID reach the fuse box)
DAVID:	That'll do.
JANET:	I'll hold the ladder ...
	(DAVID mounts the ladder, screwdriver in hand, wire)
DAVID:	Can ye hold the torch right up ... Higher ... That's fine. *(takes out a fuse and examines it ...)* NOT that one ... *(replaces it, about to take another one when he draws back his hand)* Janet ...
JANET:	Have'ne given yersel' a shock, have ye?

DAVID:	I'm just thinkin' ... Will we leave it, the night? ... Just for the night *(he looks at her)* We've got the lamps ... We've had the electric light night after night. Nine months running ...
JANET:	Just ... Not fix it, David? ...
DAVID:	Night after night.
JANET:	What about the kettle ... David? Ye have'ne had yer tea, yet?
DAVID:	We've got the old kettle ... Haven't we? ... Look at the room ... in the light of the lamp ...
JANET:	It's bonny ... Soft ...
DAVID:	We can do without it for one night ... *(climbing down)*
JANET:	Ye'll miss *Softly Softly*, David ...
DAVID:	*(taking away the step-ladder)* To hell with *Softly, Softly*!
	(JANET brings out the kettle, goes about organising the tea. DAVID stands by the gun case)
DAVID:	There's two pair of Jays, now. In the Bygate woods.
JANET:	*(looking at the guns in the case)* They look nice ... In that light.
DAVID:	Can'ne take two pair of Jays. That wood. Bad enough with one ...
JANET:	They're so bonnie.
DAVID:	You have'ne seen them tearing away at a nest to get at the eggs or the chicks.
JANET:	I saw them at that wren's. Two summers ago. Didn't I?
DAVID:	I like the smell. Of the oil.
JANET:	I don't mind it.
DAVID:	Good smell. There's no other way ye can do it. Keep an estate ... Is there? ... Thinnin out the coots, this afternoon ... It had to be done. Loch would've been covered with them. In a couple of years' time ... No room for anything else.
JANET:	There's your tea. Do you want a chocolate, now, David?
DAVID:	I might have. One or two.
JANET:	Last year or two ... Sometimes ... When you turn your head ...
DAVID:	Ye get led astray by the bonny feathers. You know what the Jay is in a wood ... A Jay's death.
JANET:	You look like Father ... Just a wee bit.
DAVID:	How ... Like ... In the last year or two ... What happened in the last year or two to turn me looking like him.
JANET:	I just said ... Just ... a hint ... A wee bit ... like ... It's maybe ... getting that wee bit older, David.
DAVID:	*(disturbed at this)* You said that yourself ... Something you keep saying ... Age doesn't mean a thing ... It doesn't ... The kind of life we have here. Probably does it. I never feel old. Never at any time in my life have I ever thought of you as anything but a young woman ...
JANET:	We're not old, David. I'm no' saying we're old ... We're no' young, either.
DAVID:	The way you move about the house. And outside. You can run up Murton Law like a young lassie ... for God's sake ... Can't you.

JANET:	I didn't say we were old. Do you like your chocolates?
DAVID:	They're fine. Got a better taste to them. Take one.
JANET:	Bought them for you.
DAVID:	Janet, woman.
JANET:	I'll take one. Is there a nut one?
DAVID:	Taste it. *(getting up)*
JANET:	Aye. They're nice.
DAVID:	Wish we'd had our tea in the oil light. *(from bedroom)* Have you shifted the gramophone, Janet? I put it under the bed.
JANET:	That would be nice. I put it on top of the wardrobe. The records are in a box inside. I'll light you another lamp.
	(She goes to light another lamp, and takes it to him)
DAVID:	I don't feel old ... Janet ... Do you? *(from bedroom)*
JANET:	You managing it ...
DAVID:	I'm fine.
	(He brings in an old acoustic gramophone, sets it on the table)
JANET:	I didn'e mean ... You were anything like father ... In *nature*, David. You Know That.
DAVID:	I'll get the records.
JANET:	We're both like mother ... aren't we ... Thank God ... We both get our nature from mother.
DAVID:	How long are you going to bear a grudge against a man dead near twenty years, for God's sake.
JANET:	That's not bearing a grudge. What I'm saying ...
DAVID:	Twenty years dead ... and you only had nine years of him ... anyway ... hadn't you ... I had over twenty ... You got away soon enough to grannie's ...
JANET:	David ... Honest ... Whatever he did to us ... It's forgiven and forgotten long ago.
DAVID:	Look at the dust covering it. *(opening gramophone lid)*
JANET:	I'll get a duster.
DAVID:	God! The things he did to me. When I was a *man* ... never mind when I was a *boy*, for God's sake ... The last time I sat at his table ... He threw a plate of scalding broth at us.
JANET:	Forgot we had so many records.
DAVID:	What it was, was he was jealous. At us ... Getting out of Blantyre. Not getting sucked inte the pits like him. Ye couldn't blame him, could you? Him stuck in Blantyre. Down the pit six days a week. Me going off to Northumberland. Living in the hills. Out in the sun all day.
JANET:	I'm telling you. I've forgotten and forgiven him years back.
DAVID:	What do you want on?
JANET:	I'll have a look. *(turning over the records)*
DAVID:	There's nothing to forgive. Even when he was leathering inte me when I was a boy ... I knew that ...

JANET:	I just said ... at odd minutes ... in the light.
DAVID:	He was like chained up, woman. To the pit. The pit had him.
	(JANET has put on a record of Kathleen Ferrier singing 'Blow the Wind Sotherly'. She stands, listening to it, lost in the song's images)
	He was like me. You can't tie me up. There's some folks that can be tied up. I'm not saying it's natural to anybody ... but some can stand it. Like some animals or birds that can be tamed ... isn't it? *(JANET is listening to the record)* He was bursting out the pit ... pulling away ... That's what made him like he was ... that's all ... Tearing himself away ... and the pit never letting go its hold of him.
JANET:	She had cancer when she made that record.
DAVID:	That's all his hammerings amounted to ... isn't it?
JANET:	She died not all that long after ... of cancer ... Kathleen Ferrier ...
DAVID:	Oh ... *(sits listening to the record)* Never been keen on that. Depresses you ... to listen to it ...
JANET:	Not me ... Nothing like that. Other way round.
DAVID:	*(when record is finished)* Put something on more like it. *(puts on Tauber's 'You Are My Heart's Delight')*
JANET:	Oh ... that's lovely ...
	(DAVID has gone to the sideboard and is pouring two drinks out from the whisky)
JANET:	Still got my tea, David.
DAVID:	Need something better than tea for that.
JANET:	We have'ne had that out *(indicating gramophone)* ... since we got the electricity ... Have we?
DAVID:	Television set ...
JANET:	I never asked for one, David.
DAVID:	Couldn't refuse it ... could you? Sir Malcolm coming all this way to bring it to us.
JANET:	I'm not bothered with it ... If it broke down tomorrow ... I would'ne lift a finger to do anything about it.
DAVID:	*(listening to Tauber)* Get nothing like that on the television.
	(JANET listens and drinks)
DAVID:	You see ... You're cramped up in the van ... In the morning ... Driving away down the road ... And then you come up to the gate ... Driving along without stopping for miles ... and then you have this gate ...
JANET:	It's just the one gate, David. I know ... It gets on your nerves ... But at the same time.
DAVID:	You have to stop the car ... brake ... get out ... Open the gate ... Start up again ... Stop when you're through ...
JANET:	But before you had the van. You had to walk near eight miles. What I mean ... Is – are you no' letting your imagination get the better of you ...
	(For a minute DAVID sits back, listens to Tauber, thinking)
DAVID:	To hell with that bloody van!
JANET:	You've father's bad language ... That's one thing you have from him ...

DAVID: Just leave it in the garage ... Or give it back to Sir Malcolm ... I don't want it ... What the hell do I want a van for ... Been here twenty years without one ...

JANET: It was Mr. Charles that gave you it ...

DAVID: What the hell use is it to me ...? What use is a game keeper, that keeps to the roads all his time, for God's sake.

JANET: Would you give him it back ...

DAVID: I'm telling you. The time I go into Coldstream. It takes any pleasure you have out of going there.

JANET: I enjoy the bus. Seeing folk in the bus.

DAVID: If he wants, Mr. Charles can give us a pony ... But I wouldn'e use that, all that much. Aside from the gate ... You can see nothing from a van. The noise of it – frightens anything miles ahead of it.

JANET: David. You know something ... I really feel happy ... just at the idea of it. Getting rid of it ... like something was taken off our backs ...

DAVID: I'm telling you ... I'll take it back to the estate office, in the morning.

          (Record finishes)

          (to JANET) Have that again, eh?

JANET: It's lovely ... Could never have enough of that.

DAVID: Lifts you right up, doesn't it. *(winding up gramophone and putting on Tauber, again)*

JANET: Do you know what I think it was, David ... I think it was the electric light. Making you look like father ...

DAVID: Shut up in the van ... You don't get any feel of the summer. All ye get is the smell of petrol ... and the noise of the engine.

JANET: If you explain to Mr. Charles you can do your work better without it, David ...

DAVID: Or the winter ... or any of the times of the year ... do you?

JANET: They're nice chocolates.

DAVID: Listen, Janet. This ... Just now ...

JANET: I like it. I've always liked the light from oil ... That electric ... It hammers on your head ... Doesn't it?

DAVID: We don't need to fix that fuse, Janet. *(she looks at him, this is something she would never have thought of)* We can leave it. As it is ...

JANET: For the night, David, like?

DAVID: Never fix it ... leave it as it is ... We've plenty lamps ... Easy get oil delivered again ...

JANET: *Never* fix it.

DAVID: We don't need it ... We don't need the van ... and we don't need electricity ...

JANET: What about the television?

DAVID: Do you need the television?

JANET: It doesn't bother me one way or the other ... If it's on, I'll watch it ... if it isn't ... I've plenty other things to do ...

DAVID:	We're doing fine without it, just now, aren't we?
JANET:	It's lovely ...
DAVID:	Can'ne hear yersel' speak at times for it, can ye?
JANET:	Would you do that, David ... Just leave it off ...
DAVID:	He had a good week ... A few months before he died ... Father ...
JANET:	I know ...
DAVID:	He could've stayed here with us for ever. Had the time of his life. That was his place. Out here ... with green all around him.
JANET:	He was entirely different here ... wasn't he?
DAVID:	I'm telling you ... He never raised his voice once ... did he ... the week he was here.
JANET:	I'm happy enough ... David ... To do without the electricity.
DAVID:	Sir Malcolm and Mr. Charles meant well, with all these things ... improvements.
JANET:	I forgot all about that week ... father was here, David. Is that not funny. Till you spoke about it, just now.
DAVID:	When you think about it. I'm saying ... I know he meant it for the good of us ... But the last year ... Since we've had all these improvements. I'm thinking about it. Can you remember one thing about it ... That stands out in your mind.
JANET:	Can'ne remember much about the summer. No ...
DAVID:	That's what I mean. Nor the spring. I can remember dozens of things the summer before.
JANET:	We had a picnic in Cocksburnpath ... and you were swimming. That was the year before wasn't it? That was the year ... there were wild strawberries ... covering the place.
DAVID:	That night we went down the road ... and found these two badger bears wiring into each other.
JANET:	I remember it was a bad summer ... That's all I can get.
DAVID:	It was a *bad* year ...
JANET:	And the year before ... two years back ... I mind things from that ...
DAVID:	It was miserable, wasn't it? That's the only word for it. There was no joy in it. I can'ne call to mind one scrap of joy in the whole year!
JANET:	Do you think so, David? *(thinking)* It wasn't all that bad, David.
DAVID:	Think yourself ... Neither bad ... Nor good. There was nothing.
JANET:	*Maybe.* The electricity ... and the van and that. And the gate getting on your nerves.
DAVID:	And the room Mr. Charles built on.
JANET:	My room.
DAVID:	We didn't need another room. We were fine as we were, weren't we? We'd been in that room together since we first came here, for God's sake!
	(JANET shaken by the depth of feeling in David's voice, sensing where all this is leading)
JANET:	Mr. Charles was just doing it for us. To make us more comfortable.

DAVID: We were fine. Weren't we? Tell you the whole thing. All these changes they've thrown at us. You know what they're doing. They're going to make us old before our time. That's what they're going to end up doing! Everything they've given us ... has turned the whole year sour ... But the worst was shutting us out from each other with these walls they built ...

JANET: Do you think they did ...

DAVID: I've been on my own all last year, Janet ... So have you ... I cann'e stand lying all night on my own ... I'm cold ... body and spirit ... I'm shivering all the night.

JANET: David. So am I ... I'm the same.

DAVID: Are you?

JANET: I'm telling you.

DAVID: That soured the whole year. I'm out all the day, away from you ... And then being cut off from you at nights.

JANET: See — when you go into one room ... at night ... and I into the other — it cuts into me.

DAVID: Goes right into my stomach.

JANET: We'll use that room ... for storing things ... eh ... will we?

DAVID: You need somebody beside you at night. It's natural, isn't it?

JANET: Listen, David. Will we go to bed ... now ... and talk ... like we used to do?

DAVID: Are you tired ... Janet?

JANET: Just to talk. It's nicer and easier talking in bed. I'll make you some cocoa, later ... like we used to do, and we'll have it in bed.

DAVID: They're mad ... aren't they ... Some of the things folk do to themselves.

JANET: I'll get my night things.

DAVID: Will we get ready for bed, here?

JANET: That's what we always used to do.

(DAVID goes and fetches his pyjamas. JANET returns with her nightie. She puts on a record — Schubert's 'An Die Musik'.

DAVID comes in, a bit shy. They turn their backs on each other, undress and put on their night things)

JANET: *(when she's ready)* I'm ready, now ...

DAVID: Nearly ...

(As he is unbuttoning his jacket, the light suddenly comes on. JANET still doesn't look at DAVID. He hasn't given the signal. Instead ... she quickly pulls a chair to the main switch, climbs on it and switches the current off)

I'm ready ... *(they turn to each other)* You see ... when you're walking ... The time you get to that gate ... You've been right through that cut in the Bygate woods ... And you come up to the gate ... You're full of the thirty minutes you've been walking ... The gate's like the gate to another place ... with the woods ending there ... and the fields and the hills stretching down to the river. It's a pleasure when you're walking with feet feeling the ground underneath you. It's a pleasure to go through it.

JANET: *(touching his hand lightly)* Come on, Davie ... We'll talk about it in bed.

(She turns down the lamps, takes one, and they walk together into the bedroom)

To Be A Farmer's Boy

Characters

AUCTIONEER
PETER
MUM
GEORGE
ERIC
CLAIR
DOROTHY

ACT ONE

1980

*QUEEN'S HOTEL ... ASHBURTON ... ROOM SET UP FOR AUCTION ... LIGHTS
ON AUCTIONEER PETER ... DOROTHY ... CLAIR ... ERIC ... GEORGE ... BIDDING
REACHING ITS HEIGHT ... TENSION ...*

AUCTIONEER: 277,000 pounds ... Seventy-nine ... Eighty ...280,000 pounds. Any advance on 280,000 ... No more bids ... 280,000 offered for this graceful 300 acre farm ... 280,000 pounds.

LIGHTS ON PETER ... DIM ON AUCTION ...

PETER: Sitting there ... in the Queen's Hotel ... Watching them auctioning away my life ... I'm happy ... I am ... That shouldn't be ... I should be happy like this ... Should it? What it is ... It's like a story ... That's it ... I'd like to get the drift of it ... If three is any ... Is there? ... Any drift in anybody's story ... Definitely funny things happen to me ... My wife falling for me forty odd years after we're married ... That doesn't happen to many people ... does it ... That would be interesting to get the hang of ... Probably entirely me ... The peculiar kind of a chap I am ... Who isn't a funny kind of chap? Always been mad ... I can never fit in ... That's something to do with it ... I've never been able to act like a husband does ... or a father ... Or a *son* to Mam ... Wasn't *too* bad before the pony ... I mean, I know it couldn't just have been the pony ... Could it? But it *seems* that was the start of me going downhill ... After the pony ... Early in life, that, wasn't it ... To start going downhill at *twelve* ...

Scene 1 1932

... Pony was me being a fool ... I'm always a fool ... Less a fool then ... when I was twelve ... than now ... Like a snowball ... You pick up more and more rubbish with the years, don't you ... Get rid of some, too ...

MOTHER APPEARS

PETER: Mum came downstairs ... funny eyed ... Still in a daze ... After feeding Betty ... Her nineteenth kid ... There was about *forty* kids in the house ... That's why I'd given up talking to people ... You could never *talk* to her ... She was always feeding babies ... I exaggerate ... she had *eight* ... What was I reading this afternoon ... I'd realised what a fool I'd been ... and I was running away from myself in a book ... Reading about other fools ... I liked my books to be full of people making a mess of things like me ... What was the book? *(FINDS BOOK IN HAND)* ... "Pride and Prejudice" ... That's right ... I'd got it for Mum at the library ... that day ... That was the first thing she said to me when she came down ...

MUM: Peter ... Don't you start getting into that book ... It's *my* book ... And I don't want to start fighting with you over it ...

PETER: There wasn't any need to answer that ... was there? ... Anyway, George was waiting to pounce on Mum the minute she showed her face ... with his consumption ...

GEORGE: Mum ... I want to talk to you ...

PETER GETS UP

MUM:	Peter ... I want to talk to you ... Where are you going?
PETER:	*(TO HIMSELF)* ... That was the interesting thing about her ... she never wanted to talk to the people who wanted to talk to her ... *(TO MUM):* ... I'm going upstairs to read ...
MUM:	I don't want you to get into that book ... Get another book ...
PETER:	*I* got you that one, Mum ...
MUM:	What's that got to do with anything ...
PETER:	It has nothing ... I'm just saying ...
GEORGE:	Mum ...
PETER:	He's got consumption, Mum ...
MUM:	Peter ... What have you done with Trixie ...
PETER:	I'll tell you about it after George's told you about his consumption ...
GEORGE:	I haven't got that ...
MUM:	George, what's the matter with you ... Why do you have to keep having all these imaginary illnesses all the time ...
GEORGE:	I don't, Mam ...
PETER:	He's spitting blood into his handkerchief ... That's T.B. ... That's a sure sign of consumption ... Spitting blood into handkerchieves ...
MUM:	Are you dear? ...
GEORGE:	Mum *(GOING TO HER FOR COMFORT)* ...
MUM:	Let me see ...
PETER:	What you do, George is look at the *worst* that could happen to you ... You see ... Then you'll be all right ...
MUM:	What have you done with that pony, Peter ...
PETER:	Did *you* tell her about the pony, George? ...
GEORGE:	What's the *worst*, Peter ...
PETER:	Did *he* tell you about the pony, Mum ...
MUM:	I can see it's not in the damned field, can't I ...
GEORGE:	What's the worst that can happen to me ...
PETER:	You just *die* ... That's what happens with consumption, isn't it ... You *die* ...
MUM:	What have you done with her ...
PETER:	That's all ... If you look at it sensibly, George ... All these millions of people in the world ... You're just one person out of all these millions dying ... Aren't you? ...
GEORGE:	Mum ...
MUM:	You're not dying ... You know what Peter's like ...
PETER:	I've been a fool with that pony, Mum ... That's all ... I don't want to talk about it ...
MUM:	You tell me, *now*, boy ... What you've done ...
GEORGE:	*You* damned well wouldn't want to die, would you? ...

PETER:	I don't know ... I don't know what it would feel like ... *I'm* not dying ... It's *you* that's doing the dying ...
MUM:	Stop it ... Let me see *your* handkerchief ... How are you spitting blood ...
GEORGE:	Mum ...
PETER:	How would *you* spit blood ...
MUM:	You go and get that pony back ... This minute, boy ...
PETER:	I told you ... I've been a fool ...
MUM:	Where's your handkerchief, child? ... The last time ... Last week ... You had a broken leg ... When you fell in the yard ...
GEORGE:	I thought I had a broken leg ... Mum ... It *felt* broken ...
PETER:	Time before that ... he had cancer ... with that boil ... Of course ... One of these days ... He is going to be right ... He is *going* to have some *deadly disease*...
MUM:	Let me see your handerchief ... George ... What have you done with that pony ...
GEORGE:	It's upstairs ... Mum ... My handkerchief ...
MUM:	Get it ...
PETER:	I don't think there's much for us to talk about, Mum ... about that pony ...
MUM:	What have you done with her?
GEORGE:	Mum ... I haven't got that ... have I?
MUM:	Get your handkerchief ... George ... will you ...
PETER:	He just *spits* it ... It doesn't come out in gushes ... That would be the last stages ...
GEORGE:	*ESCAPES TO GET HIS HANDKERCHIEF* ...
MUM:	What kind of child have I brought up, with you, Peter ...
PETER:	I know ... I don't know ... Am I funny ... I don't *feel* funny ... I probably am ...
MUM:	My oldest and strangest ...
PETER:	What happened, Mum ... Do you want to know what happened about the pony ... I worked out ... I couldn't let her be sold ... That's understandable ... She's *my pony* ... I'm like her friend ... Amn't I ... I don't want her to be pulling a butcher's cart down the town ...
MUM:	Peter ... Peter, child ...
PETER:	That's what I worked out *before* ... Why are people such fools, Mum ...
MUM:	Like *me*, do you mean?
PETER:	I took her up to the Moor ... after school ... that seemed to be the best idea ... Save her from the butcher's ... What do you think ...
MUM:	Peter, fetch me over my purse, there ...
PETER:	I took her up the road ... To the Moor ... We had this stupid conversation ... What kind of a conversation can you have with a pony ... I treat her as a person ... *She's* a pony ...
MUM:	Give me my purse ... I don't understand it ... How have I brought a child like you into the world ...

PETER: What's the matter with me, Mum ... I know there's *something* wrong with me ... What do you think it is ... Do you know? ... Don't worry about it, Mum ...

MUM: Have you turned the pony out on the Moor ...

PETER: I'm going up the road with Trixie ... Having this talk with her ... Don't worry, Trixie, I'm not letting my best friend be sent down the town ... I'm going to save you ... rubbish like that ... There's your purse ... I believed in it at the time ... Trixie didn't know *what* I was talking about ... She *wouldn't*, would she? ...

MUM: Empty out my purse ... go on ... child ...

PETER: Mum, if you're going to tell me what a stupid thing I did turning the pony out on the Moor ... I *know* ... You don't need to tell me ...

MUM: Count the money ...

PETER: when we got on to the moor ... I took off her bridle ... I was really miserable, Mum ...

MUM: Peter ... I hope you haven't lost that damned pony ... Have you lost her child? ... Count the money ...

MUM: Where's *George*, gone ... George ...

PETER: He doesn't want to show you his handkerchief ...

MUM: Is it as bad as that? ... George ...

PETER: If he doesn't show you it ... It's still not settled ... If he *has* T.B. or he *hasn't* ... Once he shows you it ... He's *doomed* ...

MUM: He hasn't got consumption ... You know that ... George ... I want to see your handkerchief ...

PETER: You've two shillings and fourpence, Mum ...

MUM: What day is it, today? ...

PETER: I'm telling you about Trixie ... Goodbye, Trixie ... You're free, now ... I said that to her ... and turned my back on her ... Daft thing just followed me ...

MUM: She'd be bound to ... wouldn't she ...

PETER: I know that ... animals can't understand English ... or German ... or any language ... I *know that* ...

MUM: What day is it? ...

PETER: I know animals don't understand ... I'm a fool ... But not that big a fool ...

MUM: It's Tuesday ...

PETER: Yes ...

MUM: George ... Bring down that handkerchief ...

GEORGE: *(OFF)*: Coming, Mum ...

PETER: "Get away ... you stupid thing" ... I shouted to her ... She got me in a terrible temper ... You see ... Mum ... Still followed us ... I threw stones at her ... Go on ... Get off ... One of them got her flank ... It started to bleed ... She ran for her life from me ...

MUM: I know how you loved that pony, Peter ...

PETER: Then I got really stupid ... Mum ... Because I was angry with her and me and sorry for her and me at the same time ... The whole thing was just a stupid messed up muddle, wasn't it ... There she was running for her life onto the Moor ... I was standing there ... watching her ...

MUM: Peter ... I've two and fourpence to feed the ten of us all week ...

PETER: That's what I'm saying to you, Mum ... I'm standing there watching Trixie run off into the Moor ... And all I can think of is where has that got me? ... It's got me I've lost Trixie ... I haven't a pony to ride any more ... and you've lost the money we'd get for her ...

MUM: Your father's getting seven pounds ten for her ...

PETER: You see ... All that money's gone running for its life on to the moor ... Why have I got to be such a fool ... That's stupid ...

MUM: If you go back, now ... I'll come with you ...

GEORGE: There's my handkerchief ... Mum ...

MUM: Let me see, George ... Get your coat on ... we're going out to look for that pony ...

PETER: If we don't find her, Mum ...

MUM: We've *got* to find her, Peter ... we're desperate for the money ...

PETER: I could give up my violin lessons ... That would save a shilling a week ... In a year ... that's over two pounds ...

MUM: *Peter* ...

GEORGE: What do you think, Mum? ...

MUM: I'm talking to Peter, just now ... Peter ... Listen to me ... Are you listening to me ...

PETER: We'll find her Mum ... There's still plenty of light ...

MUM: I'm not talking about the damned pony ... I'm talking about your music ... Don't ever say that again, Peter ... You hear me, boy ... Don't ever say anything like that again ... to me ... I'll lift my hands to you ... I *will* Peter ... give up your music ...

PETER: I like it, Mum ... It was just the money ... To save us the money ... It's alright ... Don't get upset about it ...

MUM: That's a *gift* we've been given ... Our family ... That's worth more than anything ... hundreds of acres ... thousands of pounds ... Anything ... that *gift* ...

PETER: Yes ... You're probably right ... It's good ... Playing the fiddle ... Another thing for you to do ... isn't it ... going out on the moor ... Looking for nests ... taking the dogs for a run ... playing the fiddle ...

MUM: Peter ... I don't know what we can do ... It's an ungrateful farm ... Whatever blood and sweat your father puts into it ... It's a bottomless sack ... I knew it was ... I knew it was ungrateful land ... It was like that when your father took it over from your Uncle ... and his father before that ... A gift like that ... that you have, Peter ... You can lean against ... whatever bad times you have to pass through in your life ... That's something you have to lean against that can keep you on your feet ... Do you understand me ...

PETER: I *do*, Mum ... I've just told you ...

GEORGE: Mam ... Is it bad ...

MUM: I'm sorry child ... Let me see ... *(TO PETER):* Never say that again to me, Peter ... will you ... Give up your music ...

PETER: I just *said* it ... I don't think I meant it ...

MUM: *(AT HANDKERCHIEF):* Is that all ... That little speck ...

GEORGE: Is it alright ... Mum ...

PETER: You might *live*, yet, George ... That would be a nice surprise ...

MUM: It's just your catarrh ... child ... I get that from time to time, too ... It's nothing ...

GEORGE: Do you, Mum ...

MUM: Look at you ... How could you have consumption ... With that healthy look about you ... All that fresh air you have ... Look at the flesh on you, child ...

GEORGE: Should I take a couple of lumps of sugar with us, Mum ... To tempt Trixie back ...

MUM: Yes ... Take a lump or two of sugar George ... Yes ...

PETER: If we can't find her ... I mean ... I think we *will* find her ...

MUM: We'd better find her, child ...

PETER: If we don't ... We've still got plenty of teddies ... We won't die and the cow's milk ... We won't die of starvation, Mum ... It'll be alright ... And you've two sacks of flour ... and vegetables ... It's alright, Mum ... Honest ... it is ...

MUM: Is it, Peter?

PETER: *(HAND ON HER WRIST ... SOOTHING HER):* It's alright, Mum ... It's *good* ... It's not *Bad* ...

MUM: Come on ... You'll have me talked out of it ... we won't even need to sell that damned pony, at this rate ...

PETER: Not only that ... George isn't going to *die* ... For the minute ...

MUM: Come on ... Let's go and find that Trixie of yours ...

PETER: That proves what a stupid thing she was ... She was grazing up the road ... half a mile from this house ... No, she wasn't a *fool* ... She was a *pony* ... Better eating there than on Dartmoor ... Found herself a lovely clump of clover ... white dutch ... Dad sold her the next morning ... I didn't say another 'last goodbye' to her ... Because I had to deliver my milk before school and there was never any time for anything else ... I got new trousers and stockings ... that week ... Grey trousers ... They were nice ... It was nice putting on new clothes for the first time ... That was good ... That was real happiness ... new clothes ... Smell and feel of them ...

Scene 2 1977

PETER: *(TO HIMSELF)* I got it entirely wrong with Clair ... I'm always getting it wrong ... I was working on the basis of her being *my* woman ... I was saying ... Taken you sixty-odd years to find the right woman for you ... Better late than never ... Eric got it right ... *Clair* got it right ... *I* never know *what's* happening ... First feeling for her was sheer naked violence anyway

... Beautiful day ... Eric and I going up to have a look at our sheep on the Moor ... And this woman ... Trampling my damned corn ...

PETER:	Hey *you* ... You! ... *(TO ERIC)* Eric, give her a shout ... Look at her ...
ERIC:	Hullo ...
PETER:	*(TO HIMSELF)* Could never depend on the boy *(TO CLAIR)* Get out of that *cornfield!* Get *out* ...
CLAIR:	You don't need to shout ... I can hear you ...
PETER:	Get damned well out then ... Get *out!* ...
CLAIR:	*(TO ERIC)* Tell that man to stop shouting at me like that ... I hate people shouting at me ...
ERIC:	*(TO CLAIR)* Boss ...
PETER:	Lady ... That's a *cornfield* you're trampling through ...
CLAIR:	*(TO ERIC)* Will you tell that bad tempered boss of yours that I *know* it's corn ... and if he looks he'll see that I'm *not* trampling through it ...
ERIC:	He's my father, really ...
PETER:	Get out of that damned cornfield! ... You're trespassing ... You have no right to be in it ...
ERIC:	What are you doing in it anyway ...
CLAIR:	I'm looking for my cat ...
PETER:	I'll come and *drag* you out of it ...
CLAIR:	*(TO ERIC)* What's he shouting like that for? Can he not see I'm walking round the edge ...
PETER:	What are you doing in this field? ...
ERIC:	She's looking for her cat, Dad ...
CLAIR:	I *told* him that ... Can he not *hear* ...
PETER:	I understand the language, you know ... What's your *cat* doing there ...
CLAIR:	I don't know ... I'll ask him when I find him. I've been carefully going round the edge ... Making sure I don't graze one single stalk of your corn ... I know *farmers* ... How neurotic they are about their bit of *grass* ... I don't mean that ... *(TO ERIC)* ... But you know what I mean ...
PETER:	It is ... You're right ... It's like somebody touching me ... Somebody touching my crops ...
CLAIR:	There's probably a female in heat somewhere around ... He changed personality as soon as he got within range of her scent ... He shouldn't really be into sex anyway now ... I had him doctored years ago ...
ERIC:	Maybe after a partridge ...
CLAIR:	I get a bit panicky ... at the idea of losing him ... I mean ... He's the only thing close to me in the whole of Devon ... Maybe in the world ...
PETER:	A *Cat*?
CLAIR:	You're not Peter Brent ... You *are* ... Oh! ...
ERIC:	Peter Brent ... Is that bad? ...
CLAIR:	It's not *good* ... It's not good at all ...
PETER:	Only thing you have in the world ... a Cat?
CLAIR:	Why not a cat? What's wrong with being close to a cat?

PETER: Was the *cat* close to *you*?

PETER: *(TO HIMSELF)* God knows what it was ... face ... Look of her ... Voice ... Who knows? ... I was saying to myself ... That's my woman ... Not in the words ... But it was there ...Sixty-two and that happens to you ...

CLAIR: I'm just moved in ... This week ... Broom Cottage ... I've been coming over to talk to you ...

PETER: You and the cat ... In Broom Cottage ...

CLAIR: You know cats ... Cats aren't close to anybody ...

PETER: Just *you* close to the cat ...

ERIC: You keep asking her that, Dad ...

CLAIR: Cats aren't close to anybody ...

PETER: You were coming to see me ...

CLAIR: He's still my only close friend in Devon ...

ERIC: Kind of early days, isn't it? If you've just moved in here ...

CLAIR: That's a great start ... Isn't it. *(TO PETER)* To you and me ... That's finished it, altogether ... Me and you fighting over your corn ... *(TO ERIC)* Why doesn't he sell me that little bit of land? It's only a little bit, isn't it ...

PETER: I'm not selling it ...

CLAIR: You've got all that land ... and you won't sell me ... what is it ... half an acre ... an acre ...

PETER: It's a third of an acre ...

CLAIR: Is that all it is? ...

PETER: It's taken me all my life to get it ... I'm not giving you it ... It's unreasonable ... not to sell you it ... I know that ... It's only a field ... I can't sell you it ... Forces beyond my control ... I don't know ...

CLAIR: Your solicitors have stopped answering my letters ... Nobody even talks to me when I phone ... It's very important to me ...

PETER: It's more important to *me* ...

CLAIR: It's *nothing*, is it?

PETER: I'm telling you ...

CLAIR: Just a patch of land ... To let me have a garden ... That's all ...

ERIC: It's a deep thing, Dad has ... About land ...

PETER: You don't know *what* I have, son ... I *should* sell you it ... You're quite right ... But I'm not going to ...

CLAIR: Can I take you over to the cottage and just show you what I mean ...

PETER: It's to do with it taking all my life to get what I have ... Bit by bit ... You see ... Till I built up my farm ... It's *probably* to do with that ...

CLAIR: I'll show you the tiny bit I want ...

PETER: I *know* what you want ...

CLAIR: Just let me show you ...

ERIC: I think it's like a bit of his body ... Parting with a limb ... I get that feeling sometimes ... Dad ... Your land ...

PETER:	*(TO HIMSELF)* Yes ... That was important ... I said to her ... and Eric ... He was getting on my nerves ... Explaining *me* to *her* ... She was *my* woman ... wasn't she ... *(TO CLAIR)* I've built the farm to what it is now ... you see ... And I have to keep it exactly as it is ... It seems to be a deep thing with me ... *You* pushing me to sell that field ... Disturbs me ... I wish it didn't ...
CLAIR:	*(TO ERIC)* Why does he wish it didn't?
PETER:	Why has she to ask you questions about me?
ERIC:	I don't know ...
CLAIR:	I don't know ...
PETER:	I'm not selling you any land ...
CLAIR:	I'm Clair ... Let me show you what I want ...
PETER:	I know the bit you want ...
CLAIR:	Can you not spare five minutes to look ...
ERIC:	Give you anything ... Dad ... Except a bit of his land ... It's no use ...
PETER:	Teacher ... are you?
CLAIR:	Just come over and have a look ...From my room window please ... I'm sorry for fighting with you over the corn ... I didn't touch one stalk ...
PETER:	What do you teach?
CLAIR:	I got this job teaching music at Ashburton ... I'm not really a teacher ... I'm a player ...
ERIC:	I can never play well enough for him ... I had piano lessons ... So he would have somebody to play with ...
PETER:	That's right ... Haven't played with anybody for years ...
ERIC:	I play too mechanically for him ... I do ... He's right ... I can't get my soul into playing ... I don't know why ...
PETER:	You might get her to give you lessons ...
CLAIR:	Come and look at this bit of land ... I've got a piano in the cottage ... It's not bad ...
ERIC:	He won't sell you any land ...
PETER:	*(TO HIMSELF)* That's right ... The phone was ringing ... When we got to the cottage ... Before that ... There'd been a funny moment ... Both of us ... Eric and me ... We'd both rushed to help her over the barbed wire ... I'd touched her hand ... just for a second ... I felt the smooth warm skin of her hand ... I didn't think about it at the time ... It excited me ... Touching her hand for a minute ... I doubt if she noticed it ... The phone kept ringing as we went in ...
	PHONE RINGING ...
CLAIR:	Oh ... God ... Listen ... Would you help me ... Would you answer the phone one of you ... It's Michael ... My husband ...
PETER:	What do you want me to say ...
CLAIR:	Do you mind?
ERIC:	I'll answer it ...
CLAIR:	Yes ... I think it might be better if you answer it ... You have the younger voice ...

ERIC:	What do I say?
CLAIR:	I'll get you a drink in a minute ... Would you like a drink ... Just ... *(PHONE STOPS)* He'll ring back again ...
PETER:	How do you know it was your husband?
CLAIR:	If you look out from that window there ...
PETER:	How do you know it was your husband?
ERIC:	Dad likes to know these things ...
CLAIR:	*You're* not bothered?
ERIC:	*I* just move in a straight line ...
CLAIR:	You don't ... Why do you say that all the time ...
ERIC:	*He's* the strong man in the family ... *I* just *work* with him ... Don't I, Dad?
CLAIR:	I don't believe that ... Do you?
PETER:	He's a good farmer ... I can tell you that ... Nearly as good as me ...
ERIC:	I went to college ... I am better than you ... In that respect ...
CLAIR:	When he phones ... Just answer it ...
ERIC:	What will I say ...
CLAIR:	It's dead simple ... I lost a baby ... when she was four months ... That's probably why I get into a panic about my cat ... I don't know ...
PETER:	Not good that ... losing a baby ... No ...
CLAIR:	I'll get another one ... when I need it ... It's alright ... It's just Michael wants to come down here ... and have one last try at getting me to come with him ... He's going back to Nigeria ...
PETER:	It's dead simple ...
CLAIR:	It is ... He's going to come down ... I keep telling him I have another fella ... but he doesn't believe me ... because every time he rings ... *I* answer the phone ... Once, he knows I really have somebody else living with me ... He'll just go away ... He'll be happy ... You see ... There's nothing to be done about it ...
ERIC:	But you haven't *got* anybody living with you ...
CLAIR:	Look out the window, Mr. Brent ...
PETER:	Looking at your piano ...
CLAIR:	I've lived all my life in towns ... I've never had any space ... Like ... a square foot of back garden ... All I want is just a bit of space ... you understand ... That's my own ... Did we not offer enough ... I mean ... I'm getting over five thousand a year at the school ... I'll give you more ...
PETER:	You offered too much ... Stupid money ... A thousand pounds for a third of an acre ...
CLAIR:	I'll offer you more ... Two thousand ...
ERIC:	What do I say when your husband phones ...
CLAIR:	I don't know ... What should you say ... do you think? ... Michael's a beautiful man ... He's lovely ... He's got this thing about the Third World ... Have *you* ... *I* haven't ... You have things about all kinds of things ... haven't you? ... I've never been into the Third World ... He has it about the debt he owes to the Third World ... He's going out to Zaria to kind of pay it off, by ripping off the natives for about fourteen thousand a year,

running the English Department at this University ... he's not an idiot I think it's good ... I do ... It's just ... I can't help bitching against things ... I'm not into ... It's a habit ...

PETER: Nice view ...

CLAIR: But that fence ... I'm fenced in ...

ERIC: Dad's land ...

CLAIR: There's no way you can get a decent garden out of that stupid ribbon of land in front of me ... is there ...

PETER: When He rings ... What do you want me to say to him ...

CLAIR: I think Eric's better ... He's younger ... And you're *married* ... Aren't you ...

PETER: Eric's *engaged* ...

CLAIR: That's alright ... *You're* married ...

PETER: True ... yes ...

CLAIR: I wrote after this job, in the Music Department ... I told him ... But he didn't believe I was actually going ... *I* didn't ... I think it was the idea of going to Africa ... I mean ... That was him, losing the baby he has to go to Africa ... If he had wanted to go to America ... California would have been nice ... wouldn't it ... One of those nice sunny hippy universities in California ... But Africa ... Water tasting of T.C.P. and insects like out of horror movies ...

PETER: I wish I could sell you the land ... I do ... You know that ... I can see that ... That fence ...

             PHONE RINGS ...

ERIC: What will I say?

CLAIR: Say 'hullo' ...

ERIC: *(LIFTING PHONE)* Yes ... *(INTO PHONE)* Hullo ... Yes ... This is Eric ...

CLAIR: Say I'm having a bath ...

ERIC: *(INTO PHONE)* Clair's having a bath ... Will I get her to ring you back ... No ... Alright ... Yes ... Eric ... She's fine ... Yes ... Great ...
             (PHONE DOWN)

CLAIR: That was good ... How did he sound ...

ERIC: Down ...

CLAIR: He'd be defeated ... For the minute ... But he'll work it out alright ... That'll let him throw me out of his mind ... Now he's really rejected ... I feel really happy now ... That's good ... Thanks ...

CLAIR: Tea or coffee? ...

PETER: We're going up to check some fencing ... It's alright ...

CLAIR: What can I do to get that bit of land off you ... Could I offer to buy all my milk and eggs ...

ERIC: Milk goes to the tanker ... No eggs for sale ...

CLAIR: What can I do? ...

ERIC: Offer to play some music with him ... Might help ...

PETER: No ...

CLAIR:	I'll still play music with you ... if you want ... We could play the three of us ...
ERIC:	I told you ... I'm no use ... I can't get my feelings into it when I play ... I just get on Dad's nerves ...
CLAIR:	*I'll* help you to get your feelings into playing ... if you want ...
ERIC:	I know me ... I know what I can do and what I can't ...
CLAIR:	Why does he think he's so *useless*? ...
PETER:	Probably is ...
ERIC:	I said ... I *know* what I can do ... Somebody sets me on a course ... and I go along it ...
PETER:	That's him ...
ERIC:	Dad was a farmer ... So I'm a farmer ...
PETER:	Gil, a farmer's daughter turns up and he gets engaged to her ...
CLAIR:	I'll make you some tea ... while you're fighting ...
PETER:	We're not fighting ...
ERIC:	We never fight ... I never fight with anybody ... I like what I'm doing ... I like farming ... But I just went into it ... That's me ... I never feel strongly about going into anything ... That was there ... and was as good as anything ... I'm telling you ... It's like my music ... Isn't it ... I never can feel strongly about anything ... Not like Dad or Uncle George ... Or you ... I can see she feels strongly about things ... Like that field ... The way you want that field ... When Dad gives me the farm ... I'll give you it ... That's a promise ...
PETER:	Clair ... Isn't it? Show me how much you think you need ...
CLAIR:	I'm making the tea, now ...
PETER:	Come out and show me what you want ...
ERIC:	Are you going to sell her it? ...
PETER:	Come out and show me ...
PETER:	*(TO ERIC)* You stay and make the tea ... I want to talk to Clair ... *(TO HIMSELF)* Outside ... The sun was burning now ... The way it sometimes does on the Moor ... A curlew was calling ... Something disturbing her ... Be young by now in her nest ... I said to her *(TO CLAIR)* Curlew *(TO HIMSELF)* As if I was giving it to her ... Like a present ...
CLAIR:	Yes ... I know ...
PETER:	That's Lambsdown ... *(POINTING TO A FIELD, BELOW)* Can you see it ... That big green ley down there ...
CLAIR:	Yes ... I see it ... I just would like ... If it could go up to about ... these stones are there ... I'd build a wall there ... I *hate* that barbed wire ... *I'd* build it ...
PETER:	That was the first field I opened up ... When I took over Furzeland ... There was five little plots, all hedged in ... Nothing but thistles ... My father had given up fighting ...
CLAIR:	The light on it ... The way the sun's on it ... It shines ... Doesn't it ...
PETER:	You can see that Ley from all round the Moor ... It's the one thing that will outlast me and Eric ... People who know say its already ... They point out ... Peter Brent made that field ...

CLAIR: That's good ... That's nice ... If it gives you a high ... Looking at that field ... That's good ... I like that ... *I* feel this is *my* place ... I know I've never lived anywhere really ... But this is *my* place ...

PETER: You're probably a hill person ... That's what it is ... That's right you're a hill person ...

CLAIR: If that makes you happy ... I might be ... I don't know where my father came from ... Because I don't know who he was ... One of my mother's great secrets ... She had a lapse in her girlhood ...

PETER: Clair ... I'm not selling you it ... Can't sell you it ... I'll *rent* you it ... Half an acre ...

CLAIR: I wish you'd *sell* me it ...

PETER: I *can't* sell you it ...

CLAIR: Be good for you ...

PETER: Probably would ...

CLAIR: Sell me it ...

PETER: No ...

ERIC: *(A BIT JEALOUS)* Tea's ready ... Want it out here ...

CLAIR: Yes ... We'll have it out here ...

PETER: Alright? Deal?

CLAIR: A Deal ... But I still wish you'd sell me it ...

PETER: Showing her Lambsdown ...

ERIC: I thought you might be, Dad ...

CLAIR: They're nice ... Big rolling fields ... I like small fields, *too* ... with hedges all round them ... They're one of my things, as well ... Nice, little hedged in fields ...

Scene 3 1942

PETER: *(TO HIMSELF)* He kept getting in my way ... Eric ... That first meeting with Clair ... exactly the same thing happened first time I saw Dorothy ... That's funny that ... isn't it ... George getting in my way with Dorothy ... No ... me getting in George's way ...

          DOROTHY APPEARS ...

PETER: Don't know *why* I went on these nature rambles ... Hundreds of people tramping the countryside ... looking for wildlife ... Yes ... That was the other way round, wasn't it ... I was fighting with him ... Dorothy was *George's* woman ... I got the signal ... *(LOOKING AT HER)* She was nice when she was young ... Had a nice dress on ... even though it was still wartime ... and you couldn't get decent clothes ... She always seemed to wear nice clothes ...

DOROTHY: We're losing the others ...

GEORGE: You're right ... They're ... losing us ...

DOROTHY: It's a bit rude ... leaving them like that ...

GEORGE: They left us ... Didn't they leave us, Peter ...

PETER:	You see ... I want to *talk* to you ... That's what it is ...
DOROTHY:	You're daft ... The pair of you ...
PETER:	I know that ...
GEORGE:	Farmer's boys ... The sun gets at your brain ... Working in the fields all day ...
PETER:	Does it? ... It does get at your head ... I put a handkerchief over mine ... Don't you ... I want to talk to her ...
GEORGE:	What about? ...
DOROTHY:	What about? ...
GEORGE:	Up along that hedge there ... Redstart ...
DOROTHY:	Is it? ...
PETER:	I'm not sure ...
GEORGE:	Redstart ...
PETER:	That's good ... I'd put that down in my notebook ... But I haven't got one ...
DOROTHY:	I've never seen a Redstart before ...
PETER:	I've never seen *you* before ... That's the two of us ...
GEORGE:	Do you like dancing? ...
PETER:	*(TO HIMSELF)* Never seen George like that before ... Grabbing her ... Minute he saw her ... *(TO DOROTHY)* He reckons I can't dance ... I would say I *can* dance ... would you ...
DOROTHY:	I wouldn't know ... would I?
PETER:	Why not? ...
GEORGE:	She hasn't *seen* you ... Has she? ...
PETER:	Generally ... Talking generally ...
DOROTHY:	What is he talking about? *(TO GEORGE)*
GEORGE:	It's the sun on his brain ...
PETER:	I'm talking about everybody being able to dance ...
DOROTHY:	Can they? ...
GEORGE:	I haven't seen you at the dances at Buckfast ...
PETER:	I would dance more often ... But he keeps saying I can't dance ... I wish you'd stop saying that, George ...
GEORGE:	You can't dance ... You can play the fiddle ... But you can't *dance* ... You know you can't dance ... Got two left feet ...
PETER:	When I think about it ... I'll be honest with you ...
GEORGE:	You don't get to the dances at Buckfast? ...
PETER:	She's only here three weeks, man ... I'm being honest with her ...
GEORGE:	That's right ... You're just here from Torquay ...
DOROTHY:	Torbay ...
PETER:	To be honest with you ...
DOROTHY:	Apart from anything else ... It is my first outing with the Natural History club ... It's bad manners ... Just to wander off like that ...

PETER:	It is ... You're right ... Apart from what else? ...
GEORGE:	They've got a good dance at Ashburton ... Next Thursday ... Do you like country dancing ... Nice crowd go there ...
DOROTHY:	I'm not very good at dancing ... I'm afraid ...
PETER:	That's good ...
GEORGE:	Why is that good? ...
DOROTHY:	I wish I *was* better ... I'd like to be ... I'm not really good at anything ...
GEORGE:	You're good at your job in the library ... You must be ... Otherwise they wouldn't have given it to you ...
PETER:	She's just a week in it ... Early days yet ...
DOROTHY:	*Three* weeks ... Shouldn't we go on ... *(TO PETER)* What did you want to talk to me about?
GEORGE:	You don't need to have a medal or anything for dancing up there ... Half of them can't tell a Dashing White Sergeant from the Duke of Perth ...
PETER:	How about finding her a wren's nest ... George ...
GEORGE:	Go on ... Have you ever seen a wren's nest ... It's a beautiful thing ... isn't it, Peter? ...
PETER:	George, I'm not interested in nests ... It's just hit me ... Talking to you just now ...
GEORGE:	What are you doing on a Natural History outing then ...
PETER:	That's a joy ... You see ... In the course of the day ... coming across a bird ... or a stoat ... or a nest ... I enjoy that ... That's a great joy ... But *hunting* them out ... I don't want to *do* that ...
DOROTHY:	You're *not* doing it ...
GEORGE:	Have you seen a wren's nest ...
DOROTHY:	I've seen a wren's nest ... They're lovely ...
PETER:	I don't go in for too many people, do you? ... Like ... That army out there ... *thousands* of people ...
GEORGE:	Eighteen ...
PETER:	I said '*eighteen*', eighteen ... That's why I don't go all that much to dances ... Apart from the fact that I can't dance ...
DOROTHY:	I thought you thought you could ...
PETER:	I think I can ... Yes ... That's right ... I ... I don't know what to *say* to hundreds of people ... Do you? ...
GEORGE:	Wouldn't be much use as a public speaker ... would you? ...
PETER:	One I don't mind ... One's fine ... Three gets a bit too much ...
DOROTHY:	I'll leave you two then ... To get on with it ...
PETER:	Do you know why I come on these outings? ... I know why I come on these outings, George ...
DOROTHY:	I'd better go and catch up with the others ...
GEORGE:	*(TO DOROTHY)* If you like ... We could go to the Thursday night dance together ... It's in the school hall ... A good band ...
PETER:	George ... She doesn't dance ...

DOROTHY:	I don't dance all that *well (TO GEORGE SMILING)* ... If you could put up with me ...
GEORGE:	I'm no great shakes either ...
PETER:	*(TO GEORGE)* That's up to you ... Why I put up with all these nature types ... I know why ... It's to see you ... *You're* the naturalist in the family ... When I come to think of it ... You're the *everything* in the family ... I do nothing but till the fields and plough and sow ...
DOROTHY:	You play the violin ...
PETER:	I play it very well ... I could play better ... If I had the time to practice ... He enjoys my playing ...
GEORGE:	He's a lovely tone ...
PETER:	I tolerate all these nature characters ... I don't dislike them ... I might do ... Sometimes I don't like people ... How do you get on with people ... *(TO DOROTHY)*
GEORGE:	It's alright ... You'll get used to him ... He's always been like that ...
PETER:	I get worse ... Do I? ...
GEORGE:	*(TO DOROTHY)* Would you like to go, then?
PETER:	I'm *talking* to you, George ...
GEORGE:	I'm listening to you ... I'm just asking about the dance ...
PETER:	Just because of you ... I come out here ... I talk to you ... Rest of the week ... We're miles from each other ... I seem to like being with you ... God knows why? ...
GEORGE:	We like being with each other ...
PETER:	So that's it ... isn't it ...
GEORGE:	It's only once a month ...
PETER:	It's too much ...
GEORGE:	I enjoy it ...
PETER:	I know you do ... That's what I'm saying ... I've no idea *why* ...
DOROTHY:	*I* enjoy nature outings, too ...
PETER:	That's good ...
DOROTHY:	I thought you said a minute ago it wasn't ...
PETER:	I know ... I was telling you something ... When I was talking about wanting to talk to you ...
GEORGE:	We're talking about Thursday night, just now, Peter ...
PETER:	No ... we're talking about what I wanted to talk to her about ...
DOROTHY:	*(TO GEORGE)* I'm not very good at some of the complicated dances ... I could probably manage a *Barn* dance or Strip The Willow ...
PETER:	What I was going to say ... If you want me to be honest with you ...
GEORGE:	They start about half past seven ...
PETER:	Tell you what ... What we could do is ... I could come, too ... couldn't I ... and talk to you ... during the complicated dances you can't do ... Do you like reading? ...
GEORGE:	She works in a library ...
	DOROTHY IS LISTENING TO SOMETHING ...

PETER:	She's listening to something ... What do you hear?
DOROTHY:	I'm sorry ... It's just the water ... We lived on the shore ... Since I was a baby ... I always lived with the sound of the sea ... It was always there ... I miss it ... I don't really know if I can stand being away from it for very long ... I'll have to go back one day ...
PETER:	Yes ... I can understand that ... Since I went to work away from Dartmoor ... Being parted from the moor ... Bit like being separated from a sweetheart ... isn't it ... I need the hills ... I need to be in the hills ... George is lucky ... He got a job on the moor ...
GEORGE:	*(TO DOROTHY)* Would you like to come, then?
PETER:	Do you like reading?
GEORGE:	She works in a library ... Night jar ...
DOROTHY:	Where? ...
PETER:	Just over there ... That dead branch ... By the beech ... What I was saying was ... To be honest with you ... When I said I wanted to talk to you ... I didn't know what about ... I hadn't any particular thing in mind ...
DOROTHY:	I can't see anything ...
GEORGE:	Look through the glasses ...
PETER:	What I'm talking about is ... I'm not all that much use talking to girls ... That's what I'm talking about ... George is ... It's all the dances he goes to ...
DOROTHY:	Look at it ... Like a part of the tree ...
PETER:	Better back away ... Quiet ... So we don't disturb it ... That's what it is ...
DOROTHY:	I've never seen a nightjar before ... It's beautiful ... isn't it ...
PETER:	It's beautiful ... Beautiful bird ... I like all birds ... Like the colour of a nightjar ... See it flying ... Lovely, flying ...
GEORGE:	Like a big moth ...
PETER:	So ... when it comes to it ... I don't really know what I particularly want to talk to you about ... I want to talk to you ... Do you see what I'm getting at ...
DOROTHY:	I think so ... I do ... Will we go on ...
PETER:	You like reading do you ...
DOROTHY:	I read all the time ... Yes ... My mother says I read *too* much ...
PETER:	We could talk about reading then ... *What* could we talk about reading? ...
GEORGE:	He reads all the time ... Takes his books out into the field with him ...
PETER:	Reading a good book just now ... Of Mice and Men ... That's keeping me going for the next week or so ... That Book ... Does it keep *you* going ... Had a bad day yesterday ... *(TO GEORGE)* had us out with plough from light to dark all day yesterday ... George ... Making up for lost days ... What kept me going was getting back to my book ... Getting up to bed with my book ...
DOROTHY:	I've heard of it ... He's a good writer ... Steinbeck ...
PETER:	Got it out the library ... I'll hold on to it for you ...
GEORGE:	You don't need to, man ... She works there ...
PETER:	I'll hold on to it for you ...

DOROTHY:	I'll read it when you bring it back ...
PETER:	Yes ... Read it ... Will you ... I'd like you to read it ... Yes ... Listen ... if you're interested in books ... There's a good club in Ashburton ... I sometimes go ... *(CORRECTS HIMSELF)* ... I go odd times ... I don't go *every* time ...
GEORGE:	When you've nothing better to do ...
PETER:	Somebody talking next month ... about Bernard Shaw ... If you fancy going ...
DOROTHY:	I think Bernard Shaw's wonderful ... The clear mind he has, hasn't he ...
PETER:	Has he? ... I can't get all that interested in him ... Might be him being a vegetarian ... I can't understand vegetarians ... That's *me* ... That's nothing to do with vegetarians ...
GEORGE:	Clever man ... Too clever for me ... They're all too clever for me ...
PETER:	George ... You are ... You're a very simple man ... I wish I was a simple man ... You always were a simple man ... That's good ... It's *excellent* ...
DOROTHY:	Are you, George *(GROWING INTEREST IN HIM)*
GEORGE:	He's right ... *I* just work and dance ...
DOROTHY:	*(CLEARLY RESPONDING TO HIM)* I'd love to go to the dance ... I really would ...
GEORGE:	Will I call for you ... You live above the newsagents in Fore Street, don't you ... Your dad's taken over Rhodah Graham's shop ...
DOROTHY:	My auntie ... He's taken it over from her ...
GEORGE:	Thursday night ... about seven ...
PETER:	*I* might come, too ... Will I? ...
DOROTHY:	Yes ... That would be nice ... *(EYES ON GEORGE THOUGH)*
PETER:	You see ... What I was going to talk to you about ...
GEORGE:	Thought you didn't know *what* to talk to her about, Peter ...
PETER:	What I was going to talk to you about was ... I don't know how much longer I can stand being away from Dartmoor ... Like you from the sea ... Hits me ... Every time I come back here ... and going away from it again ...
DOROTHY:	Yes ... I know ... I have that feeling, too ...
PETER:	*(TO HIMSELF)* ... How long did we go like that ... The three of us ... My God! ... Must've been nearly *two* years ... Dorothy waiting for George to make a move ... George married to old man Andrews at Muirfield ... Allowed out one night a week ... and the rest of the time ... stuck in playing dominoes and listening to the radio with him ... and the cat ... Me waiting for the pair of them to come to some conclusion ... No doubt about it ... Look on Dorothy's face ... that day ... though ... watching George ... Her eyes ... Bad minute that for me ... Shows you, doesn't it ... Never predict anything with people – *how* they're going to end up ... Mad, people ... Do anything ... *Stand* anything ... can't they?

Scene 4 1934

PETER:	*(TO HIMSELF)* Could never make up their minds about anything ... Mam and Dad ... That chance of a job coming up for me in Briar Farm ... Dad talking about it all Sunday morning ... Mam ran out of the house, in the end ... In the middle of getting the dinner ... That was what she did ... When things got too much for her ... Ran out of the house and made for the Moor ... Sunday was very good for running out *(UP CHURCH BELLS)* ... You had the bells on Sunday ... they soothed her down a bit ...
MUM:	*(COAT ON)* I'm going up the road to listen to the bells ...
PETER:	*(TO HIMSELF)* That was the only time you could get her on her own ... Not a good time ... Apart from anything else it was a bit dangerous ... being too handy when she was in one of her moods ... She might throw something at you ... She did that morning ...
MUM:	*(THROWING TURF AT HIM)* Go away ...
PETER:	It's anybody's road, isn't it ... You can't drive off people from public highways ...
MUM:	Don't come up here and start your clever arguments with me, boy ... *THROWS TURF* ... Go away ...
PETER:	You could *hurt* people, throwing things at them ...
MUM:	*(MORE TURF)* Go away ...
PETER:	I've come up to listen to the bells ...
MUM:	Listen to them somewhere else ...
PETER:	This is the best place to listen to them ...
MUM:	You're not listening to them *here* ... You're not listening to them here ... Go away! ...
PETER:	*(TO HIMSELF)* I moved away a bit ...
MUM:	Can't you leave me alone a minute ... The damn lot of you ... *(NO ANSWER)* Can't you ... I'm speaking to you ...
PETER:	I thought I hadn't to talk to you ...
MUM:	*Stop watching* me ...
PETER:	I'm *not* watching you ... I *am* watching you ...
MUM:	Can't I have a blessed minute to listen to the bells in peace ...
PETER:	Mum ...I want to take that job over Briar Farm ... I want to, Mother ...
MUM:	Go away ...
PETER:	Talk to me a minute ... then you can listen to your bells in peace ...
MUM:	What do you all want from my life!
PETER:	I don't know ... I don't want anything ... Do I?
MUM:	Can't I have *one* thing I *want* in this damned world?
PETER:	Yes ...
MUM:	*(TURNING ON HIM)* What?
PETER:	*I* don't know what you want ... You're bound to have had *something*...
MUM:	*What* have I had?

PETER:	*I* don't know, Mum ...
MUM:	What did you say I had for then ...
PETER:	Mum ... I want to talk to you about the farm ... I know you want me to stay on at school ...
MUM:	Do what the hell you like ...
PETER:	Dad wants me to take the job, too, Mum ...
MUM:	I've given up ... I told you... It's finished ... There's nothing I can do about it ...
PETER:	Yes ... That's the best way, Mum ...
MUM:	What do you mean its the best way? ... What do you know about anything ... You're just a child ... Just lie down and die ... Is that the best way to live? ... You want to be a teacher ... They said at the school ... You had it in you ... You could be a teacher ... You could maybe even get to a university ...
PETER:	Mother ... It's alright ... If I can't be a teacher ... I'm not worried ...
MUM:	You know that ... I don't want you to be a damn *farmer* ... I want you to better yourself, I've had farms enough with your father ... That's enough to put up with for half a *dozen* lifetimes ...
PETER:	I'll be getting a pound a week ... and my keep ...
MUM:	What are you *doing* to me, Peter ...
PETER:	I'm talking to you about going to Briar Farm ...
MUM:	You're *not* talking to me ... That's *not* talking to me ... What are you *talking* about? ...
PETER:	Mum ... I want to ... I really want to go, Mum ... *Look* at me ...
MUM:	I can't bear looking at you, just now ...
PETER:	*Look* at me ... *(THRUSTS HIS FACE IN FRONT OF HERS)*
MUM:	Will you go away and let me listen to the bells in peace ...
PETER:	No ...
MUM:	You're a proper devil ... You are ... the oldest and the worst ...
PETER:	I know ... I am ...
MUM:	Why do you say that, boy? ...
PETER:	BECAUSE I am ... It's the truth ...
MUM:	You're not ... That was just my temper ...
PETER:	I am ...
MUM:	Peter ... Come here, child ... I didn't mean that ...
PETER:	Look at me a minute ... Mum ...
MUM:	What's there to see ... Looking at *you*? ...
PETER:	Look at me ...
MUM:	What's the *matter* with you, boy? ...
PETER:	It's alright ... Can't you see, Mum ... I'm happy ... Look at me ...
MUM:	*I'm* not ...
PETER:	I am ...
MUM:	What's happened ... then ... You're happy ...
PETER:	I'm always happy ... Most of the time ... I'm a happy character ... aren't I ...

MUM:	You're sort of … I am, too … when I'm not miserable … I could be a very happy person …
PETER:	You know that … It'll be better for everybody … If I take this job, Man … I'm fourteen … We've no money … It's one less to feed … and I can bring some money home …
MUM:	*Oh*! …
PETER:	What do you mean 'Oh' …
MUM:	I'm not having that … I'm not having people sacrificing themselves like that … I don't believe in it … I know that … Sacrificing yourself like that doesn't do anybody any good … You're staying on another year at school … You *hear* me …
PETER:	*(TO HIMSELF)* Then I heard the stoat … That's right … In the middle of Mum going on about sacrificing … Coming from the hedge … I went over to it … Mum said to me …
MUM:	What is it? …
PETER:	Stoat …
MUM:	Leave it alone … Bite your blooming head off …
PETER:	It's stuck …
MUM:	That's his bad luck … Can't be much of a stoat, letting itself get stuck in a hedge …
PETER:	Might've been chased … I might have frightened it …
MUM:	Boy, leave it alone …
PETER:	I'm trying to push back that branch … To let it go …
MUM:	Wait a minute … You need a heavier stick than that … *LOOKING ROUND … BREAKING OFF BRANCH* … Listen to it … We're just trying to save you, you stupid creature …
PETER:	Give it to me Mum …
MUM:	Peter … Careful, now …
PETER:	Come on! …
	PUTTING HIS FOOT INTO GAP …
MUM:	Don't do that … He'll bite right through your boot leather …
PETER:	He's out … Look …
MUM:	Buntings … He's probably been after the buntings nesting round here, the swine …
PETER:	*(TO HIMSELF)* … I had that thing, then … hadn't I … Can't remember when I didn't have it … When I think about it … It's like … shaking myself … and finding out what's underneath everything … all the rubbish you hide under … where you are … What you want to do … where you want to go … Times I grate my teeth at the kind of things I find out about myself … Sitting there on the gate after we found the stoat … It came to me … I was a bit of a swine … I had a bad streak in me … Mam … Listen … I've a rotten streak to me … I know … I have …
MUM:	What do you say that for, boy?
PETER:	I have … Could be everybody has …
MUM:	Me, included …

PETER:	I'm *sick* of here, Mum ... I'm really looking forward to going to Briar Farm ... I really am ... I woke up this morning ... Really happy ... Saying to myself ... Couple of weeks time I'll be working and earning wages ...
MUM:	Getting *away* from me ... *Leaving me!* ...
PETER:	I'm coming back Saturday afternoon ... For the whole weekend, Mum ... Let me take it, Mum ... Please ... Go on ... I'll bring back at least fifteen shillings a week ... Go on ... I'd only keep five for myself and the bus ... You'd have fifteen shillings Mum ... to help things on *(TO HIMSELF)* I was like fighting ... It was like fighting for survival wasn't it ... Getting away from Furzeland ...
MUM:	Will you go away ... I'm trying to listen to the bells, child ... Just leave me in peace for one minute ... You've had your say ...
PETER:	Alright then Mum *(MAKES TO GO)* ...
MUM:	*(AFTER HIM)* I'll talk to your Dad again about it ... We might let you give it a try for a few months ... But you'll have to promise to me ... When things get better here ... You'll go back to school, finish your schooling ... You'll have to swear *that*, Peter ...
PETER:	I will, Mum ... I'll swear it ... I'll go back to school ... if we can afford it ...
MUM:	You'll swear *that* On The Bible, Peter ...
PETER:	*(TO HIMSELF)* She turned her back on me and drifted off to the bells ... I had this feeling ... Yes ... Good feeling ... I was *free* of her, now ... Going down the road ... Then she shouted after me ...
MUM:	You want to watch yourself with them stoats boy ... You're lucky he didn't have your finger off ...
PETER:	*(TO HIMSELF)* I was going to answer her ... That I knew all about stoats and weasels ... But she turned away again ... Towards the bells ... Going home ... I was thinking all the way ... How I was going to spend the first money from my wages ... Books ... I was definitely going to buy some books ... I'd never had any books of my own ... Always out of the library ... and music ... I wouldn't mind some music ... Walking down the road ... singing away ... Larks ... all round me ... It was like the whole future was in front of me ... Waiting for me ... It was the sun, I think ... too ... Funny the way the sun works on your mood ... The way it was shining ... in front of me ...

Scene 5 1977

CLAIR:	You're just in time, Peter ... I'm making hamburgers ... Will I take some out of the freezer for you ...
PETER:	Clair ... What's he doing out there? He's supposed to be going to Cambridge today ...
CLAIR:	He got a chance of a J.C.B. Roger or somebody ... He had it free for today ... Somebody's cancelled it ...
PETER:	*(TO HIMSELF)* ... I didn't know what I was doing ... that day ... did I? Going over to Clair's cottage ... Do I ever know what I'm doing? *I* don't know ... Eric being there irritated me ... *He's got* his woman ... that's right

... That's exactly what came into my mind ... when I saw his car outside the cottage ... It didn't come to me I've got *mine*, too ... I didn't think about Dorothy ... What it boils down to is ... I'm just not very good at women ... am I? Speaking to them ... When it comes to getting close Eric seemed to be alright at it ... Eric could probably come out with it ... You fancy going to bed with me? That's the generation ... isn't it ... Anyway ... It wasn't a simple case of that, was it? ... Sleeping with her ... That was in it ... But that was only *part* of the story ... That's what I thought, anyway ... I didn't know how to go about getting closer to her ... Words or anything ... Difficult that ... Offering yourself to a woman ... I was giving her a present ... That was the easiest way ... God ... I was saying to myself ... I've really fallen for that woman! ... Look at her ...

CLAIR: Do you want a hamburger ...

PETER: *(SEEING A BIRTHDAY CARD)* Birthday?

CLAIR: From Michael ... I forgot about it ... Since I reached thirty ... I don't like birthdays ...

PETER: Should be in Cambridge ... Gil's expecting him ...

CLAIR: He's going this afternoon ...

PETER: Look at it ... That's a *lake*! Not a *pond* ...

CLAIR: do you mind ... I'm sorry ... I've always wanted a garden with a pond ...

PETER: It's a *lake* ...

CLAIR: It isn't is it?

PETER: *Big pond* ...

CLAIR: Will I fill it in ...?

PETER: I wanted to talk to you ...

CLAIR: That's alright ... Talk over a hamburger ...

PETER: *Eric's* here ... I'm saying ...

CLAIR: Eric's digging ...

PETER: He should be on his way to Cambridge ... To his girl ... He's getting married in a couple of months ... What is he doing digging ponds ...

CLAIR: I've got some wine ... Take a drink ... and settle down ... a minute ... Eh? ... Is it bothering you ... Digging the pond ... It seemed alright ... when I asked you about it ...

PETER: *(LOOKING)* I don't think it bothers me ... No ...

CLAIR: That's alright ... I want to plant a few trees round it ... Rowans ... Do you think?

PETER: I just came round with a present for you ... *(WITH ENVELOPE)* ...
ERIC ENTERS ... PETER HIDES THE ENVELOPE ...

ERIC: Going this afternoon, Dad ... Don't panic ... I phoned Gil ... It's alright ...

PETER: What are you doing with all the soil? ...

ERIC: Rockery ... Do you think? ...

CLAIR: Rockery would be great ... Wouldn't it, Peter? ...

PETER: Just thinking ... You could do with some topsoil for *your* garden ... *(TO CLAIR)* She's a trained gardener ... Gillian ...

CLAIR:	I know ... Eric was going to get her to come round when he brought her back, next week ... *(TO ERIC)* Have you decided where do you want to go then? *(TO PETER)* Talking about his honeymoon ...
ERIC:	I don't want to go anywhere ...
PETER:	You're going to *Crete* ...
ERIC:	I'm talking about ... what I *want* to do ... I'm happy to stay here ... And get settled in our house ...
CLAIR:	Is there really nowhere in the world you're dying to go to? ...
ERIC:	I *know* ...
CLAIR:	No ... That's alright ... If you're happy here ...
ERIC:	I'm happy digging that pond just now ...
PETER:	Better get on with it, then, and on your way to Cambridge ...
ERIC:	I was telling Clair, Dad, the difference between you and me ... If you had this 300 odd acres ... When you were my age ...
CLAIR:	I'm making you a hamburger ...
PETER:	Dorothy'll have something for me ...
ERIC:	You know what I mean ... If you'd had a farm like this ...
PETER:	Are you going to dig that damn pond, boy ...
ERIC:	I'm going ... You would have to end up with it doubled ... wouldn't you ... Seven hundred eight hundred ... Dad ... That's the difference between us ...
PETER:	You'll end up with damn all!
ERIC:	I'll stick with the three hundred ...
PETER:	Eric ... Gil's taken off two days especially for you to get things for the house ...
ERIC:	I got the chance of Roger's J.C.B. ...
PETER:	Go and use it, then ...
	(ERIC GOES)
CLAIR:	What's the matter with you, Peter? Are you angry with me? digging that pond ... You *are* ... aren't you ...
PETER:	I've got this present for you ...
CLAIR:	I got a cheque from Michael too ... He's a nice man ... isn't he ... He's stuck in that campus just now ... He can't teach or anything ... There's some student riot ... They've shot six students ...
PETER:	End up getting shot himself, if he doesn't watch out ...
CLAIR:	He might do ... Yeah ... What is it? ...
PETER:	It's not my land now ... Leasing it to you ... I've done without the last four months ... since you've had it ... I can do without it ... I'm *giving* you it ... There you are ...
CLAIR:	You can't *give* me it ... What's the matter with you, Peter ... Giving your land away ... I'll *buy* it from you ... I'm not *taking* it ...
PETER:	I don't care if you take it or not ... The transfer's made out ... It's yours ...
CLAIR:	How can I take *that* off you ... Peter ... Don't be stupid ...
PETER:	What are you going to put in it ... Your lake? ...

CLAIR:	Peter ... I'm going to pay you for it ... Please ... It'll spoil it between us ... It will ... Giving me it ...
PETER:	I want to give you a present ... What's wrong with giving you a present ... I damn well like you ... don't I ... If you want ... you can say I'm paying you for music lessons ... You are ... That's what you're doing ... Every time we play something together ... I learn something from you ... that's a big thing to me ... You know that ... Having somebody to play music with ...
CLAIR:	I'm still not taking it ...
ERIC:	*(COMING IN)* Taking what? ...
PETER:	You finished? ...
ERIC:	Just came in for a drink ...
CLAIR:	There's a lager in the fridge ...
ERIC:	Good ... What's she not taking ... Secret? ...
PETER:	Secret ...
ERIC:	Alright ... *(TO CLAIR)* You think it's alright ... Me being like that ... I ... I don't know ... That's me ...
PETER:	You're a happy lad, for goodness sake, Eric ... Just relax and enjoy yourself ... I'm a happy man ... That's good ...
ERIC:	I am ... He's right ... Isn't he? *(CLAIR DOESN'T ANSWER)*
ERIC:	*You* not think I'm happy, Clair? ...
CLAIR:	Probably ... *I* don't know ... How would *I* know? ...
ERIC:	What do you think's wrong with me, then? ...
CLAIR:	You keep asking me what I think is wrong with you ... I've never said there *is* anything ...
PETER:	I wish you'd get that damn pond dug, Eric ...
ERIC:	No. I know, Clair ... You think there's something seriously wrong with me ... You're probably right ... You usually are ...
CLAIR:	Eric ... Go and be happy and dig my pond ...
PETER:	How are you going to line it ...
ERIC:	Heavy gauge polythene ...
PETER:	Not concrete? ...
CLAIR:	Too permanent ... We thought it would disturb you ... concreting it ... like for ever ...
ERIC:	Too dear ... Getting the right stuff ... *(GOES)*
PETER:	What are you saying to him? ... You've got to be careful what you say to that boy ... I know, he's my son ...
CLAIR:	Honest ... I say nothing to him ... He's a friend ... He's my *friend* ... *You're* my friend ... I'm not taking it ...
PETER:	It doesn't matter if you give me that bit of paper back or not ... I've got rid of that land ... It's not mine any more ...
CLAIR:	Peter ... Don't ... Please ...
PETER:	I want to *give* you it ...
CLAIR:	I know ... I don't want to take it ...
PETER:	Go on take it ...

CLAIR: I'm going to have big fat goldfish in the pond ...

PETER: The herons 'll love it ... You'll have to re-stock it every day ...

CLAIR: They won't ... Will they?

PETER: You'll have to scare them off ...

CLAIR: Peter ... I don't want to take it like that ... Please ... How would you scare the herons off ... In any case I'd rather have herons at my pond than goldfish ...

PETER: *I'd* rather have Herons ...

CLAIR: Do you think they'd come ...

PETER: Place is isolated enough ... If you stocked it with goldfish ... Yes ... Till they'd eaten all your goldfish ...

CLAIR: Peter ... Let me *buy* the land off you ...

PETER: I'll tell you what we'll do ... You and me ... We've never been out on our own for a meal ... the four months we've known each other ...

CLAIR: I don't think so, Peter ...

PETER: Let me finish ... woman ... for goodness sake ... We'll go out somewhere on the coast ... And talk about it ... This week ... One evening this week ...

CLAIR: Peter ... I don't think so ... I'm happy the way we are ... You see ... That's really good ... The way we are just now ... You and Eric ... The both of you ... You've both really lifted me ...

PETER: I just want us to go out for a meal ... The two of us ... A Birthday dinner ...

CLAIR: Why not with Eric and Gil ... and Dorothy ... the five of us ...

PETER: Clair ... What do you think I'm trying to do ... I would just like ... Now and then ... The two of us to be together ... Relaxing ... Go out together ... I'll *tell* Dorothy ... It won't be behind her back ... You know that I don't go in for that kind of thing ...

CLAIR: I know ... I know the kind of person you are ... I know that ...

PETER: What's the problem ... Don't you want to go ... Alright ... Forget it ...

CLAIR: You know that ... I'd like to ...

PETER: Will I book a table ... then ... Where do you fancy ...?

           ERIC ENTERS — PETER BREAKS OFF ...

ERIC: I don't want to interrupt you ...

PETER: You're not interrupting anything ... What are you talking about, son ...

ERIC: I've dug the hole ... Do you want to see it ...

CLAIR: Yeah ... I'll come out in a minute ... that's fantastic ... Eric ...

ERIC: It's the machine ... No fantastic skill digging a pond ...

PETER: You've left the motor on ...

ERIC: God ... I have ...

CLAIR: I'll come out in a minute ...

ERIC: Alright ... Looks good ...

PETER: Clair ... What's the problem ... You know what Dorothy and me are like ... She's been going out dancing every week with George ... *Before* we were married ... She's not going to mind me taking you out for a meal ...

CLAIR:	Can we not just keep us like this ... I'd like to keep it like this ... Couldn't we, Peter? ...
PETER:	Yes ... If you want that ... Yes ...
CLAIR:	Just now ... Peter ... Could we just keep it like it is ... Having some music together ... You helping me in the garden ... Me coming up to see you and Dorothy ... Could we? ...
PETER:	Alright ... Yes if you'd like it like that ... sure ...
CLAIR:	I haven't hurt you ... have I? ... I'm not pushing you away ...
PETER:	You could make it up a bit ... And take that Deed ... without arguing ... that would make it up a bit, Clair ...
CLAIR:	I don't want to ...
PETER:	I know ...
CLAIR:	I'll take it ... Thank you ... Thank you very much, Peter ... *(KISSING HIM)*

Scene 6 1946

GEORGE COMING IN WITH SUITCASES, FOLLOWED BY DOROTHY ...

PETER:	*(TO HIMSELF)* Funny wedding night we had ... Wedding night was very strange ... Got very confused on my wedding night ... Drink affecting me ... and George having to drive us back to the farm ...
PETER:	*(TO GEORGE)* I have to sit down for a minute ...
GEORGE:	Are you alright, Peter ...
PETER:	Just the wine ... Going to my head ... *(TO HIMSELF)* Sitting there looking at Dorothy and George ... I had this feeling ... Like the three of us were married ... Together ... Could be we were ... I was going to come out with it ... Watching them ... I never did ... Ever ... What I was going to say was ... To Dorothy ... I know you're marrying me as your second choice ... He never got down to asking you ... That's alright ... Is that what it is ... That's what it is ... It's alright ... Was it alright? ... I couldn't have been alright ... She seemed to keep looking at him ... I didn't like the way she kissed him, either ... Coming out of the church ... Funny kiss for a bride to give to a best man ... Dorothy didn't seem to be able to handle the situation either ... Top of everything else ... One of our two cows was calving ... that damn night ... George said again ...
GEORGE:	You're alright, then? ...
PETER:	*(TO HIMSELF)* All Dorothy could think of was tea ...
DOROTHY:	Will I make you a cup of strong tea, Peter? ...
	(SOUND OF COW — FROM THE BARN)
GEORGE:	Better be off then ... Good wedding eh? ...
PETER:	You want a cup of tea, before you go? ...
DOROTHY:	It's late ... George wants to get to his bed, Peter ...
GEORGE:	To tell you the truth, Dorothy ... I know this is a funny kind of wedding night ...

DOROTHY: George ... Nothing surprises me with the Brents ...

GEORGE: That cow ... you see ... Going to calve any minute ... and you and Peter wanting a good night's rest ... Maybe I should sleep on the couch down here ... just in case ...

PETER: It's alright, George ...

DOROTHY: You get back to Mr. Andrews, George ... Peter and I'll probably have the night in the cowshed, to keep her company ...

GEORGE: Probably be the morning before she manages it ...

PETER: Want a cup of tea, before you go off ...

GEORGE: Better get back to the old man ... *(LOOKING ROUND)* Got the old house lovely, Dorothy ... Different place entirely ...

PETER: *(TO HIMSELF)* The cow was moaning ... George was standing there, looking at Dorothy ...

PETER: Might get you up to help me ... if I've any problems with her calving ... *(TO DOROTHY)* Better than a vet ... George is ... Aren't you? ...

GEORGE: Let me know if you need me ... *(GOES)*

PETER: Make you a cup of tea? ...

DOROTHY: Come here husband ... *(HE GOES)* ... *(PUTS HER ARMS AROUND HIM ... KISSES HIM)* Despite all your Brent ways ... You ignoring everything I wanted for my wedding ...

PETER: Not true ...

DOROTHY: I *still* love you ...

PETER: I just wanted George for the best man ... That was all ...

DOROTHY: And to come back here ... instead of going away ... for even one night ...

PETER: You like the house, then? ...

DOROTHY: I wish that damn cow would shut up a minute ... It is nice ... yes ... Should we go to bed? ...

PETER: Yes ... I'll have a quick look and see if she's alright ...

DOROTHY: Do you not feel a bit funny ... Peter ... Coming here ... I still can't get over the feeling I'm living in your mother's house ... When I was cuddling you before ... For a minute ... I thought ... I'd better watch it ... in case she walks in and finds us kissing ...

PETER: You'll get over that ...

DOROTHY: Still I wish you could've found another Best Man, my dear ...

PETER: I'll go and see the cow ... and we'll go to bed ...

DOROTHY: I'll get ready ...

PETER: I'll bring you up some tea .....

DOROTHY: I read a book about love ... But I don't understand it all that much ... The physical side ... Do you? ...

PETER: We'll manage, won't we? ...

DOROTHY: ... Yes ... A cup of tea would be nice ... You'll bring it up ... The house is nice ... It's really nice ...

(SHE TURNS ... PETER IS BRINGING UP A TRAY)

PETER: I'll have to go back to her, Dorothy ... She's started ... Brought you some tea ...

DOROTHY: Should I get dressed and help you ...

PETER: It could be *hours* ... Doesn't matter ... I'll be alright ... You go to sleep ... You look lovely, now ...

DOROTHY: I do ... I should probably come down and be with you ... Now I am a farmer's wife ... I should learn about calving and things like that ...

PETER: You will do ...

DOROTHY: Will she be alright ..?

PETER: Good healthy animal ... No reason why she shouldn't ...

DOROTHY: It's a funny wedding night ... isn't it? I *thought* it would be a funny wedding night, though ... with you?
(COW MOANS)

PETER: *(CUDDLING HER)* I'll be back soon, Dorothy ...

DOROTHY: You'd better go to her, poor thing ... I might come down and see her ... If I don't fall asleep ...

PETER: *(KISSING HER)* I know that ... What a stroke of luck it is ... Getting you for a wife, Dorothy ... Don't think I don't ...

DOROTHY: *(KISSING HIM)* I know you do, love ...

(... SOUND OF COW ...)

DOROTHY: *(GETTING UP ... PUTTING ON DRESSING GOWN)* ... Peter ... Peter ... Is that you? ... *(GOING TO HIM)* ...

PETER: Just one calf ... But a *beauty* ... You want to see it ... Everything's alright ... Proper heffer calf ... Had to get George in the end ... Calf was lying wrong way round ...

DOROTHY: It's raining ...

PETER: Bit, not much ... Light's beautiful ... Come on and I'll show you your calf ...

DOROTHY: And then we'll have breakfast in bed ... will we?

PETER: We could *do* that ... I've never had breakfast in bed in my life ... Put that coat over you ... *(PUTTING COAT OVER HER)*

DOROTHY: The air ... Peter ... *(THEY STAND FOR A MINUTE IN THE DOORWAY)*

PETER: I know ...

DOROTHY: I've never been up here so early in the morning ... and the stillness ...

PETER: *(HIS ARM ROUND HER ... LOOKING OUT AT HIS FARM)* It's what I've always wanted ...

DOROTHY: *(DRAWING HIM CLOSE TO HER)* I love you, Peter ... I really do ...

PETER: I love you ... You know that ... It is, Dorothy ... It's what I've *always* wanted ... *(LOOKING ROUND AT HIS LAND)*

ACT TWO

Scene 7 1952

PETER: *(TO HIMSELF)* All the way to Muirfield that night ... only thought I kept getting is old man Andrews dead ... and George is the first Brent to get his hands on his own land ... Jealous ... Absolutely ... Injustice ... Me sweating blood year in year out, to make something of Furzeland ... for Sir Roy and his damned heirs ... And George just falls like that into his own farm ... And George's mind on something entirely different ... Apart from him thinking he'd killed the old man ... It was the old man after all not loving him ... wasn't it? ... That was what bothered him ... In a strange mood ... too ... Never seen that bit of George before ...

PETER: What do you keep saying you killed him for, George?

GEORGE: I'm telling you I killed him ...

PETER: What do you mean you killed him ...

GEORGE: Want a cup of tea ... I'm having a cup of tea ...

PETER: Did you *hit* him ... What did you do to him? ...

GEORGE: Have a look and see, Peter ... I couldn't see any life in him ... You have a look ...

PETER: *(GOING TO LOOK)* I would take a brandy ... Have you any brandy in the house, George ...

GEORGE: I've whisky in the house ... Do you want some whisky ...

PETER: I'd better take a look at him ...

GEORGE: He's over there ...

PETER: Switch off the radio, for God's sake, George ...

GEORGE: We were just listening to a play ...

PETER: What did you do to him? ... He looks alright to *me* .

GEORGE: Is he living? ...

PETER: He's dead alright ...

GEORGE: I thought so ... There's your whisky ...

PETER: *You* take it, man ... You've had a bad shock ... I'll phone the doctor ...

GEORGE: Can't see what good the doctor can do ... if he's dead ...

PETER: George ... Sit down ... Take it easy ... Now ... You didn't kill him ... It's not in you ... what are you talking about ...

GEORGE: He had a rotten death, Peter ... Old swine that he is ... Mean, sly old devil ... I'm sorry I gave him such a bad ending ... I'm genuinely sorry ... That's a shame ... We had words ... That's what I'm saying ...

PETER: Shouldn't we take him into the bedroom ...

GEORGE: He's alright there ... Past hearing what we say about him ... poor old miserable soul ...

PETER: He was seventy odd, wasn't he ... *More* .

GEORGE: Seventy-five ... I'm not saying he wasn't on the brink of the grave anyway ... I'm saying ... I gave him a bit of a push to hurry him on ...

PETER: Now ... listen ... George ... I can't see any sign of violence on him ... He could've died naturally ...

GEORGE: Stroke ...

PETER: He could've easily have died from a stroke ... absolutely ... there's no need ...

GEORGE: I'm telling you he died from a stroke ... anyway ... that's the end of that chapter ... I'm finished with this place ... I'm going to get a place of my own ...

PETER: You had words ...

GEORGE: Kettle's boiling ... *(LOOKING AT HIM)* I don't bear him any grudges ... Not all that many ... You can't help it, if you're a tight miserable old sod ... can you? I liked him in a way ... You want a cup of tea ...

PETER: Did you hit him? ...

GEORGE: First thing tomorrow, I'm going out to see what's on the market ... not too big ... about a 100 acres ... Like ... Furzeland ...

PETER: Did you damn well hit him, man? ...

GEORGE: We were listening to a play ... About a blind woman ... Don't ask me why he suddenly came out with it at that minute ... I don't know ... I'd made him a mug of cocoa ... He was sitting there ... with his mug of cocoa ... and a tea biscuit ... He leans over to me ... George ... I'm leaving you a thousand pounds ... Cash ... Is that alright? ... It's possible the old so and so had signals he was on the point of going, anyway ...

PETER: A thousand pounds ...

GEORGE: With the bit I've got I'm in a good position to take on a farm ... Get a nice bit of stock ... machinery ...

PETER: He hasn't *left* you Muirfield? ...

GEORGE: That's what I'm telling you we had the fight over ...

PETER: George ... You're not saying he hasn't left you the farm ...

GEORGE: He hasn't left me the farm ... That's it ...

PETER: Listen ... I can't get over that ... How could he not leave you the farm ...

GEORGE: Too late to ask him, now ... isn't it ... If I can ... I'd like somewhere not too far from you ... We've been nearby each other too long ... for me to be easy a long way from you ...

PETER: Did you strike him ... then?

GEORGE: He has a nephew ... Did you know the old so and so had a nephew, Peter? ... In London in the Civil Service ... High up ... He's got this nephew ... Blood thicker than sweat ...

PETER: I didn't know he had any family ...

GEORGE: He got a Christmas card every year ... Now I think about it ... Nice card ... Can't remember who signed it ... I might be able to find them ... He kept all his cards and rubbish in that chest of drawers here ... *(LOOKING)*

PETER: George ... Wait a minute ... You had a fight ...

GEORGE: I'm trying to find the card ...

PETER: It doesn't matter about the card ...

GEORGE: It matters to me ... I might buy a few calves off you ... If you've any to spare ... I was thinking of Fresians ... Good herd of Fresians ...

PETER: I can't get over that ... Not leaving you the farm ... I always said to Mother ... That'll at least be one Brent to end up owning his own land ...

GEORGE: It wasn't me, you see, wanting the farm so much ... It was ... What it was, was the idea of this Civil Servant ... Londoner ... Being left it ... and apart from him not needing it ... Selling it ... off to some stranger ...

PETER: He'll sell it off ... will he? ...

GEORGE: He's a top grade civil servant ... he doesn't want a *farm*. He's a *town* man ... He can't stand country ... First time I shouted at him ... in the fifteen odd years we've been together ... "All the blood and sweat and love I've poured into that land ... and you're throwing it away to somebody who doesn't give a damn for the place or the country" ... All he kept saying was "I'm not ungrateful ... I appreciate everything you've done ... I'm leaving you a thousand pounds" ... I kept shouting at him ... "Keep your thousand pounds" ... Good job he died when he did, in a way ... because that would probably have been the end of my thousand pounds too ...

PETER: You didn't hit him ...

GEORGE: I *should've* hit him ...

PETER: Give yourself a shake, George ... You had a bit of an argument ... Excitement ran a bit high ... and it was too much for the old man ... He was going anyway ... If it had not been the fight you had ... It would've been something else ... He couldn't have been in all that shape ... if a few words ... killed the poor soul ...

GEORGE: I'm saying ... He was dying anyway ... I said that ... I gave him a bit of a push ... that's all ...

PETER: God, George ... Nobody could blame you, losing your temper ... all the years ... and work ... you've spent building up the farm ...

GEORGE: Lately ... You know ... He'd been cold at nights ... You know that ... last year or so ... I've had to go into bed with the old misery ... Nights ... To keep him warm ... Do you know that ...

PETER: Listen, if they're selling the farm ... George ... *You buy* it, then ...

GEORGE: He got frightened at nights ... Last few months ... trembling ... had to hold him like a child at times ... Do you know that ... How could I buy Muirfield, Peter? ... 140 acres of good land ... They'll want ten thousand for it ... *More* ... I've got a thousand pounds ... I don't want it anyway ... I'm *finished* with it ... Keep your 140 acres, you old misery, you ...

GEORGE: I was in Ashburton this afternoon ... and got some kippers ... want one? ...

PETER: You could do with a doctor ... too ... you know *(TO HIMSELF)* Couldn't wait, but, to get my hands on that land ... Listen ... George ... An idea's just come to me ... Now ... Tell me straight ... If you're not happy about it ... Tell me ... Say 'No' ... Outright ... How would you feel if *I* bought Muirfield? ...

GEORGE: *(LOOKING AT HIM)* I *thought* you'd a pile of money stacked away somewhere ...

PETER: We all did alright in war ... We were lucky ... I haven't got ten thousand ... but I could get a loan ... But *only* if you would be happy about it ...

GEORGE: It's 140 acres ... and buildings ...

PETER:	I'm saying ... I could raise a loan ...
GEORGE:	What are you thinking about ... Giving me Furzeland ... I'm not having that ... I don't want that place ...
PETER:	I'm holding to that ... What I'm thinking ... There's only that strip of Bob Hendy's land ... between Furzeland and this ... No more than a parcel of 40 or 50 acres ... If I could get him to sell that parcel, one of these days ... You see what I'm getting at ... Joined on to Furzeland ... That's nearly a 300 acre farm ...
GEORGE:	Kept me up half the night, that old misery ... last few months ... going back and forward to the toilet ... On top of everything else ... he had a weak bladder ... Everybody has, when they get old ... I'm not getting any younger, either ... am I? ...
PETER:	What do you think about that, George? ... Would you feel bad about it ... If *I* had Muirfield ... George ... I'm asking you? ...
GEORGE:	How do I feel about *you* taking *my* farm ... All that blood and sweat ...
PETER:	I *know* . George ... I know that ... It is ... By right and justice ... It's your farm ...
GEORGE:	What do you want me to say, Peter? ... I never dreamt you were making money ... like that ...
PETER:	You know how much *he* was making ...
GEORGE:	What for? ... Look at him ... When you think about his life ... Hell ... I'm sorry for that poor old soul ... He didn't deserve me shouting him into his grave did he? ...
PETER:	Wouldn't it be better ... than going to a stranger? ...
GEORGE:	I'll tell you something ... Peter ... I'm jealous, envious ...
PETER:	Everybody is ... That's people ...
GEORGE:	I know that's a bad attitude ... It's a rotten attitude ... But I'd rather see a *stranger* having it ...
PETER:	Yes ... I can understand that, George ...
GEORGE:	That's a lousy attitude ... A bad, rotten attitude ... I'm sorry Peter ...
PETER:	I'm saying ... I understand your feelings ...
GEORGE:	There you are, then ... It's no use asking *me* ... Is it? ... What's it got to do with me ... I don't own the farm ... I've given the best twenty years of my life to it ... True ... But that's nothing ... What's that? ... That's nothing ...
PETER:	I know ... I can understand you being bitter about it ...
GEORGE:	I'm flattened by it ... That man there ... doing a thing like that to me ... I was his *son* . wasn't I, Peter? He was more a father to me than father ... Though mind that wound't have been all that hard ... So what are you asking me, for? What's it to do with me ...
PETER:	I'll phone the doctor ...
GEORGE:	You might as well ... While I have my kipper ... What do you think you're doing? Peter? Talking to me like that ... What are you talking to me like that for ...
PETER:	How am I talking to you? George ... What are you talking about? ...

GEORGE: You know that ... You've your mind set ... You're going to bid for this farm ... whatever I say ... I *know* you ... What are you trying to kid me for, Peter? ...

PETER: We'll talk about it again, George ... Just now ...

GEORGE: You know that ... In the end ... The two of us ... The way we're close to each other ... And me being Dorothy's friend, too ... What will I do? I can see ... You've always been jealous of this place ... I can understand that ... You've got these big plans for the farm of your dreams ... What kind of position is that you're putting me in ... I'm going to block you from the farm of your dreams ... For a bit of envy and jealousy ... What are you *talking* about ... You and me ... We don't talk like that with each other ... Do we, Peter, my dear ...

PETER: Yes ... You're right ... Like in the Bible ... I've coveted Muirfield since you started working on it ... I have ...

GEORGE: I *know* that ...

PETER: I'm sorry ...

GEORGE: You can't help it ... You're a human being ... You can't help being a human being ... I can't help being a human being ... That old swine, he can't help it, either ...

PETER: We'll talk about it, after ... It could be they might not even sell in the end ...

GEORGE: Don't worry, my dear, they'll sell ... *(BENDING OVER – PICKING UP FALSE TEETH)*

GEORGE: What are you doing? ...

GEORGE: It's the poor old soul's teeth ... They fell out when he had his stroke ... I'm putting them back for him ...

Scene 8 1979

GUNSHOT ... PETER AIMS AT A PIGEON ... FIRES ...

PETER: *(TO HIMSELF)* He wouldn't know I'd fallen for her ... Would he? ... How *would* he? . And taking me out on a *freezing* cold day ... to break it to me ... No question about it ... Definitely lacking in imagination, that boy ... Bringing me out on a freezing March morning, with the wind cutting right through me ... And in any case ... It always put me in a bad mood, shooting with Eric . He knew that ... Had one of those eyes *made* for shooting ...

ERIC AIMS ... FIRES ...

ERIC: *Got* you! No more of my corn in your gizzard ...

PETER: Two up on me ...

ERIC: Better shot ...

PETER: Better gun ...

ERIC: *You* have it, then, Dad ...

PETER: Then I won't have an excuse ... Eric, I'm *freezing* .

ERIC: Like some tea, Dad? ...

PETER: *(PICKING UP BIRD HE'S JUST SHOT)*

ERIC: Quid's worth of our corn's gone to fattening him ...

PETER: You *hate* pigeons, don't you, boy? ...

ERIC: Hate them ...

PETER: I love them ... Look and sound of them ...

ERIC: Waking you up at five o'clock in the morning ... Dad ... I got you out shooting ... To talk to you ...

PETER: Curlew ... Hear it? ...

ERIC: I like the curlew ... lovely bird the curlew ... wonderful call ... I've been in trouble ... you see ... Dad ... I'm alright now ... I mean ... I'm through it ... You don't need to worry about me ... Time Gil came over a couple of weeks ago ... To look at the house ...

PETER: You over it, now?

ERIC: I'm alright, now ...

PETER: I didn't *want* to go shooting ... Did *you* want to go shooting ... Eric ... Why get me out on a cold damn freezing day like this to talk to me? ...

ERIC: I know ...

PETER: I could've talked to you in the *house* ...

ERIC: I know ... You know what I'm like ... It's a difficult thing to talk about it ... I find it difficult ...

PETER: About Gil ...

ERIC: About everything ...

PETER: That's not so bad ... If it's about the whole world ... That's alright ... I don't even *like* pigeons ... Eating them ...

ERIC: You're getting old ...

PETER: *How* am I getting old? ...

ERIC: You're *not* getting old ...

PETER: What is it, then? ...

ERIC: You should maybe get that Thermal underwear in the Radio Times ...

PETER: About you ... In trouble ...

ERIC: I'm alright, now ...

PETER: That's good ... You're alright, now ... I'm alright, too ... If I was warmer ... So you're alright ...

ERIC: I'm on the road to it ...

PETER: You've got me out in the cold to shoot pigeons to *talk* to me ... You're *not* going to talk to me now? ...

ERIC: Yeah ...

PETER: Go on ... Talk to me ... I'm listening ...

ERIC: You see what I mean ...

PETER: What do you mean? How can I see what you mean ... When you don't damn well *say* anything ...

ERIC: I'm saying ... It's difficult to talk about it ...

PETER: I'll try and help you ... It's about Gil ... You've had a fight with Gil ... What about Gil? ...

ERIC: I like Gil ... I'd never have a fight with her ... I could never *see* me having a fight with her ... What is it ... I've got an idea now, what Clair thinks is wrong with me ...

PETER: There's nothing wrong with you ... What's wrong with you? There's something wrong with everybody ... Something wrong with me ... Something wrong with Clair ... What is this you've developed ... There's something wrong with you ...

ERIC: You're not letting me tell you ... The last few weeks ... Till Gil turned up ... I was in trouble ... I couldn't work out who I wanted ... between Gil and Clair ... *(PAUSE ... PETER ABSORBING THIS ... NO RESPONSE)* ... You know what I'm getting at, Dad ... I was falling for Clair ...

PETER: Was she falling for you ... *(TO HIMSELF)* Getting worse and the *cold* on top of everything else ...

ERIC: Yeah ... She was falling for me ...

PETER: She told you? ...

ERIC: I *know* . You *know* ... When that happens ... Don't you ... You know ... But it's alright now ...

PETER: She's gone off you ...

ERIC: When Gil came over that weekend ... It was alright ... While we were going round the house ... The two hours or so we were in the house together was too long ... You see what I mean, Dad ...

PETER: Let's go home ... We'll talk on the way home ... I need a hot bath ...

ERIC: The two hours in the house ... Going around the house ... It was a *long* two hours ... You see what I mean ... I think for Gil, too ...

PETER: *You've* gone off *Gil* ...

ERIC: I've never been on her ... Have I? ...

PETER: That's why you're marrying her ...

ERIC: That's what's wrong with me ... I'm telling you ... I just go along whatever way people push me ...

PETER: Invitations are out, Eric ... For the wedding ...

ERIC: I know ...

PETER: Presents are coming in ... Your house is organised ...

ERIC: That's why it was hard to talk to you about ...

PETER: I'll tell you something ... I'm not worried for myself ... Whatever you do ... You're your own man ... aren't you ... You're twenty-eight ... I can't keep on worrying for you all my life ... *Marry* Gil ... *don't* marry her ... I'll be honest with you ... I like Gil ... Good girl ... Best wife you could get ... to help you with the farm ... But it will not *kill* me ... Eric ... if you don't marry her ... If you break off the engagement ... If you *don't* have the wedding *(TO HIMSELF)* Kill me a bit if he marries Clair, but ...

ERIC: That's great, Dad ... That's fine ...

PETER: Damn well upset your Mother, but ...

ERIC: I know ...

PETER: She's still hanging on to you ... Still her boy ... Aren't you ...

ERIC: Will *you* talk to her ...

PETER: Listen ... Clair's thirty five ... Do you know that ... She's nearly ten years older than you ... Do you know that ...

ERIC: She looks twenty ...

PETER: She's thirty five ... Whatever she looks like ... Her body and mind are thirty five, son ...

ERIC: I knew she was kind of thirty ... I knew that ...

PETER: Thirty *five*, Eric ... Five years to forty ...

ERIC: You can't help who you fall for ... Can you? ...

PETER: Has she told you ... It's a great requited love then ... *(TO HIMSELF)* God, she couldn't have fallen for him ... Could she ... *Could* have, *God*!

ERIC: I *know*.

PETER: The other problem, Eric ...

ERIC: Dad ... I'm telling you ... I've never felt like this before ...

PETER: Did you tell *Gil* . Or do you think *she knows* too ...

ERIC: Dad ... She knows ... It was just drifting into getting married ... The two of us ... I'm talking about wanting something ... I really *want* something.

PETER: To go to bed with Clair ... Or have you done that already ... *(TO HIMSELF)* Probably ... Why not ... God in heaven! ...

ERIC: What's the matter with you, Dad ...

PETER: I don't know ... What do you want me to say to you ... I'm not a *father* ... I don't know what fathers *are* . I've only *had* one kid to practise on ... It's not a lot ...

ERIC: It's not about that ... Not about sleeping with her ... Hasn't got near that, anyway ...

PETER: Yes ... I know ... It's not about that ... It's beyond that ... I'm sorry ... Yes ... Eric ... She's married ...

ERIC: I know ... She's finished with her husband ... I *think* she is ... Isn't she? ...

PETER: Do you think you'd marry her ...

ERIC: I'm saying ... If I could ... Yes ...

PETER: That's it then ... She's fallen for you? Why shouldn't she fall for you ... A good natured nice looking young chap ... What about Gil? ... Will *I* talk to Gil ... and your Mother ...

ERIC: I'll talk to Gil ...

PETER: Has she said ... She feels the same about you ... Has she said that ...

ERIC: You know what Clair's like, Dad ... She wouldn't say anything like that ... while I was engaged ...

PETER: She hasn't said anything? ...

ERIC: I know you think it's my imagination ... Dad ... But I *know* . You must've known ... when Mum was falling for you ...

PETER: Did I? ... No ... I didn't ... I didn't know ... Not that I can remember ... no ...

ERIC: Anyway ... I can't go on with Gil ... now ... Can I? ... *Whatever* happens with Clair ... Can I? ...

PETER:	Eric ... I'm not putting you off ... If she was sixty, and had a false leg ... It's up to you ... Whatever takes your fancy ... She's nearly *forty* ... *married* ... Strange woman in many ways ... But that's up to you ...
ERIC:	I knew I'd upset you ...
PETER:	You haven't upset me ... How have you upset me? ... I love you ... You're the only kid I have ... I love you ... But I can't feel along with you the way your Mother seems to ... it's *your* life ...
ERIC:	I don't know what it is ... It gets me ... upsetting you ... more than upsetting Mum ...
PETER:	You probably love me more than you love your Mother ... That's alright, boy ... I'm not upset ... Yes I am upset ... I'm upset ... It doesn't matter ...
ERIC:	I do Dad ... I feel like I've suddenly come to life ... I've come alive ...
PETER:	That's good ... That's very good ... That's first rate, Eric ... I am, I'm glad for you ... I am ... I think I can see it ... Yes I can ... I am ... I'm really glad for you ...
ERIC:	But I've upset you ...
PETER:	Eric ... It's nothing to do with you ... Why I'm upset ... In a way ... Yes ... I don't want to tell you why I'm upset ... It's not *directly* you ... Alright ... *(SHIVERING)* I'm cold ... Freezing ...
ERIC:	I shouldn't have brought you out in the cold ...
PETER:	I'll be alright when I've had a hot bath ...
ERIC:	We'll go home ... Eh ...
PETER:	What I was going to say to you ... Was ... I'll tell you something ... Strictly between you and me ... Are you listening ... In a way ... That woman ... Clair ... She's a very giving woman ... You know what I mean ... She gives out a lot of feeling ... I'm saying ... Don't build up your hopes too high ...
ERIC:	Mum's the problem ...
PETER:	That's a *disaster* area ... It's a proper calamity ... Your Mum and Uncle George ... Uncle George was all set to be the chairman at the wedding ... It *might* kill your Mother ... It'll certainly upset her ... That's a consequence you'll have to face up to ...
ERIC:	It's going to be difficult ... I know that ...
PETER:	We'll just have to ride that, boy ... It's up to *you* and her ... There mightn't be such a thing as maturity ... Eric ... But the one sign I've found of an adult person ... is he has to more or less accept the responsibilities for his actions ... I know ... Difficult that ... But you try ...
ERIC:	I really have, Dad ... I've fallen for her ... You've no idea ...
PETER:	I hope it'll be alright for you ... I do ... It doesn't *look* as if it'll be ... But I damned well hope it works out exactly as you want it, Eric ...

Scene 9 1977

PETER:	Can never predict what I'm going to *feel* about anything ... That's what happens ... doesn't it ... What gets me is never getting *used* to it ... Getting down over getting down at something you'd never think would get you

down in the first place ... that should lift you up ... Never get used to these ups and downs in myself ... Day they signed over Furzeland to me ... the last 60 acres was mine ... twenty eight years to get my farm together ... For *God's* sake! I should have been jumping, shouldn't I? A three hundred odd acre farm ... Just as I wanted it ... That last 60 acres, I always saw it as an island ... Not mine ... *Never* be mine ... *(TO HIMSELF)* ... So I should have been flying high, shouldn't I? ... That day ... Spring afternoon ... just back from the lawyers at Ashburton ... lovely, sunny, spring day ... And I feel *down* ... What's the matter with you, man? You've realized your damn dreams and you're *down* . I park the car ... come into the yard ... the sun hits me ... that's always a great minute, isn't it ... the first time in the year when you feel the sun at last warm on your face ... the spring really hitting you ... Dorothy was feeding her hens ... Real farmer's wife ... except that she *wasn't* . I told her ...

PETER:	Hit me, just now ... Did you feel it? That sun ...
DOROTHY:	Cuckoo's been calling this morning ...
PETER:	Do you know what I never told you ... I don't know why I didn't ... Just came to me ... Day I was born ... the cuckoo called all day ...
DOROTHY:	You remember it do you?
PETER:	Old woman down the road ... Mrs. Carr ... everytime she saw me with my Mother ... I mind the day Peter was born ... cuckoo called all that day ...
PETER:	*(TO HIMSELF)* All I wanted was for her to come with me and walk Lapdown field ... Not much for a wife to do for a husband ... It was very important to me ... that we walk it together ... the interesting thing was I couldn't tell her why it was so important to me ... she got it out of me in the end ... Why I couldn't come out with it right away ... something about me ... I didn't want anybody to know ... that weakness ... that was it ... I had that deep seam of superstition in me ...
DOROTHY:	I don't feel like walking with you, just now ... that's all ...
PETER:	Are you upset because I didn't tell you I was going to buy it before? ...
DOROTHY:	Why should I be upset over that? I'm used to that ... aren't I ... Farm's nothing to do with me ... is it? ... It's never had anything to do with me ... I'm not interested in it ... it's you – the farm ...
PETER:	I was worried that it wasn't going to come off ... that's why ... When Sir Roy died ... I wasn't sure what the estate was going to do ...
DOROTHY:	I just want to sit in the garden and write for a bit ... First day we've had I can sit in the garden ...
PETER:	*(TO HIMSELF)* That kind of diary she was always writing in ... started it first year she was married ... never liked it ... bound not to ... Never knew what she was damn well writing in it ... *(TO DOROTHY)* Just round Lapdown field with me ... that's all ... Then you can get back to your diary ...
DOROTHY:	I don't know *what* I feel about it all ... I never know most of the time *what* I feel, Peter ... Do you think I *exist*? ...
PETER:	*You*? ...
DOROTHY:	Don't you think sometimes I'm just a figment of your imagination? ...
PETER:	I'm looking at you ... *I imagine* you? ...
DOROTHY:	It could be the last nail ... that bit of land ... You buying it ...

PETER:	In my coffin ... You going on about *dying* again. ...
DOROTHY:	Yes ... it could be that's the last hope ... gone down ...
PETER:	I was telling you about that a moment before ... when the sun warmed my face ... there ...
DOROTHY:	Yes ... That's right ...
PETER:	It *lifted* me ... I was down ... I can understand, Dorothy, you not wanting to walk Lapdown with me ... I can see that it's a big thing to you this minute ... I can understand how you feel ...
DOROTHY:	Just watching you and listening to you ... You try so hard to be open and honest with me ... with anybody close to you ... Don't you? ...
PETER:	Yes ... I *think* I do ... Yes ...
DOROTHY:	Everything's so *open* about you ... All these words to explain how you feel ... Letting people right into your mind ... Isn't that nice of you ... It's very honest of you ... It gets on my *nerves* ... that's what it is, Peter ... it gets on my damned nerves ...
PETER:	I'll stop it then ... you should've told me before ...
DOROTHY:	I've no idea *why* it gets on my nerves ... why *should* it get on my nerves? ...
PETER:	Things get on people's nerves, Dorothy ... I'll try and stop it ... with you ...
DOROTHY:	The sun warmed your face ... it's warming mine now ...
PETER:	*(TO HIMSELF)* I looked at her ... the sun was on her face ... I still was moved at times by her ... the look of her ... I could've done with putting my arms round her, that second ... but it passed ... she asked me ...
DOROTHY:	What did you see ... then ... when the sun was warming your face that moment? ...
PETER:	It lifted me ... There was a hedge sparrow singing ... on the hawthorn there ... always nest around there, every year ... It started to sing same time as the sun fell on me ... That probably started it ... I had this insight ... I can think and control a few things ... But in the end I'm caught up with the damned earth same as any other creature ... or living thing.
DOROTHY:	Peter ... Why do you come out with things like that? ...
PETER:	Should I *not*? ...
DOROTHY:	I didn't mean that ...
PETER:	That's what I felt ... it lifted me ... the whole thought ... If you don't want me to come out with my profound thoughts ... I'll watch that too ... Maybe I shouldn't say *anything* ... "Pass the salt" ... "Nice day" ...
DOROTHY:	Sometimes ... I get the feeling ... If I went away from you ...
PETER:	*(TO HIMSELF)* That bothered me ... First time she'd ever talked about that ...
DOROTHY:	Don't get that look in your eyes ... I can't understand what you damn well see in me anyway ... I'm not thinking of leaving anybody ... Where would I go? ... I'm trying to say ... when I think about it ...
PETER:	You think about it ... bound to ... Things people think about ...
DOROTHY:	*You* wouldn't think about it ... because you're married first to the farm ... That's you ... You're married to the farm ... Like those monks down at the Abbey ...

PETER: Yes ... You're right ... I *think* so ... I'm not sure ... You might be right ... I'm married to the farm ... but the farm's for you and Eric ... As far as I can picture it ... without you and Eric the farm would be damn all ...

DOROTHY: It's important to you, isn't it ... that you get me to walk that damn field with you ... I should ... shouldn't I? ...

PETER: Not if you can't stand doing it ... I feel you should ... yes ...

DOROTHY: I don't seem to be able to make the effort, Peter, to do it ... why is that? ...

PETER: Do you think of going off ... that runs through your mind? ...

DOROTHY: It's not serious, Peter ... Where would I go to? Who with ... It's a fantasy ... Everybody has fantasies ...

PETER: Yours is going away from me ...

DOROTHY: I'm trying to say ... sometimes I think, if I went away from you, I'd cease to exist ... I wouldn't exist ... I don't ... have I? ... I don't have any real thoughts of my own ... opinions ... All I am is Peter Brent's *Wife* ... and Eric Brent's *Mother* ...

PETER: That's just Women's Liberation ideas getting to you ...

DOROTHY: Is it? So that's not my own, either ...

PETER: I wish you'd walk that field with me ...

DOROTHY: I know ...

PETER: *(TO HIMSELF)* I was working out how I was going to tell her ... Her walking Lapdown with me was more important even than me keeping to myself one of my last places ... Every time I bought some land ... ever since Muirfield ... Dorothy had walked it with me, same day I bought it ... Was it like her blessing it. God knows ... I had the conviction that if we didn't walk it together, there would be no joy in the land ... I *know* I'm mad ... People are mad ... It could even be true ... There *could* be something in it ... What am I talking about ... As far as I was concerned, there *was* ... It *was* damn true ... Telling Dorothy ... I took her hand ... and had a last try ...

PETER: *(TO DOROTHY)* Come on ... Let's walk Lapdown, eh? ...

DOROTHY: That's the end of a kind of hope I had, you see, Peter ... Last hope ... gone down ...

PETER: Yes, I know that ...

DOROTHY: What do you know? You *don't* know ... I haven't damned well *told* you, have I? ...

PETER: No ... you're right ...

DOROTHY: I know that ... that island we were living in ... belonging to Sir Roy ... I know it was getting on your nerves ...

PETER: Bad ...

DOROTHY: I think I had a fantasy in my mind ... you see ... One of these days it would get so much for you ... you would get so sick ... you'd say: Damn it, I'm going off ... I'm selling out ... And we'd go off somewhere ... might even buy a small place by the sea ... I was always hoping we would get back to the sea ... That's one thing I have ... I've held on to ... that's me, isn't it ... this has never really been my place ...

PETER: Yes ... I know that ...

DOROTHY: So ... that's the end of my dreams, you see ... You've got your farm complete now ... You'll *never* leave the damn place ... I can understand that ... I can ... I don't blame you ... This is *your* place ... It's not mine, Peter ... It's *never* going to be mine ...

PETER: *(TO HIMSELF)* That was what got it out of me in the end ... not to get her to walk Lapdown with me ... That wasn't important for the minute ... be important the next ... What was getting me now ... was this feeling we were separate ... I was separated from her ... A gulf, would you call it? I couldn't stand that ... So I offered this thing that I was ashamed of ... deep in me ... to her ... To get us back that bit closer together ... When I told her ... she didn't move any closer ... she didn't take my hand ... or anything ...

DOROTHY: You're a funny man, dear, aren't you? ...

PETER: I am ...

DOROTHY: I'm a funny person too ... we both are ...

PETER: *(TO HIMSELF)* Then she said that funny thing ... No idea why she said it ...

DOROTHY: Do you think you're *wiser* than me, Peter?

PETER: What's it mean ... wiser ...

DOROTHY: ... We'd better go then, hadn't we ... And make sure your new land is going to be fruitful, and grateful ... and God ... or whoever, or whatever it is who looks after these things, smiles down on it ...

PETER: *(TO HIMSELF)* God ... She made me walk every acre of these 60 odd acres I'd bought ... The sun shone all the time ... and the larks were shouting their heads off ... I didn't hear one damned cuckoo all day ... At least another week before I heard it ... Damned Dorothy heard it every day ... a week before me ... and saw a nuthatch on our bird table ... I never saw one at all that year ...

Scene 10 1979

PETER: *(TO HIMSELF)* I went to Clair when it hit me ... I wasn't going to be around much longer ... I didn't go home ... To Dorothy ... I came off the moor ... Exhausted ... It was cold up there enough to freeze a snipe ... and walked half a mile out of my way to Clair's cottage ... I couldn't talk to anybody else, anyway ... about dying, could I? ... Trouble was, on top of finding out I was going to die ... I had to cope with facing up to Clair being Eric's woman ... Never going to be mine ... No ... That was probably good ... A bit closer to reality ... Whatever that is ... What am I saying that for ... It's *something* isn't it ... She's *not* my woman ... is she? ... I'm not sure ... In a sense ... maybe she is ... Knocked for about two minutes at the door ...

CLAIR'S COTTAGE SUMMER

PETER: Knocking at Door ...

CLAIR: *(OFF)* I'm coming ...

PETER: It's just me ...

CLAIR: (IN DRESSING GOWN) Just having a shower ...

PETER: I don't like getting people out of baths ...

CLAIR: I've had a *shower* ... are you coming in? ...

PETER: Just been up on the Moor ...

CLAIR: Eric's here ...

PETER: In that case ... I'm going home ... Is he having a *bath*, too ...

CLAIR: He's *showering* ...

PETER: I'll see you later ...

CLAIR: Peter come in ... You want to talk to me ...

PETER: I don't want to *talk* to *Eric* ...

CLAIR: He's showering just now ...

PETER: He'll not be showering for the next *hour* ...

CLAIR: Have you got to talk to me all that time ...

PETER: I'm keeping you at the door ... It's cold ... I had a funny experience just now ... I'll tell you later ...

CLAIR: Come in and talk to me ... I need to talk to *you* ...

PETER: No herons turned up yet? ...

CLAIR: Gulls ...

PETER: They like goldfish, too ...

PETER: *(LOOKING OUT OF WINDOW)* You've got a Sandpiper there ...

CLAIR: Have I? ...

PETER: I'll tell you what I found out ... Just now ... Up on the Moor ... I'm going to die ... What do you think of that ...

CLAIR: Like you've got a deadly *disease* ...

PETER: Have I? ...

CLAIR: Have you? ...

PETER: I don't *think* so ... Brent's bodies are all built to last ... No problem the bodies ... Emotionally – could be better – not *bad*, but ...

CLAIR: *(SHOUTING)* Your Dad's here ...

ERIC: *(OFF)* ... Oh ...

PETER: *(TO ERIC)* I thought you were mending that gate ...

ERIC: *(OFF)* I've done it ...

PETER: *(TO CLAIR)* I think I'll go home ... Leave you with Eric ...

CLAIR: How are you going to die?

PETER: I don't like it ...

CLAIR: Peter ... I love him ... I can't help it ...

PETER: I thought you might ... THAT's what I mean ...

CLAIR: What are you talking about ... Dying ...

PETER: I know that's the trouble ... I know ... *You* and *me* ... The pair of us ... we *know* . It's not all that good *knowing* . Is it? ...

CLAIR: How do you mean, dying? ...

PETER: I discovered I am not going to go on for ever ... I got this insight ... just now ...

CLAIR: A shock. Finding out a thing like that ...

PETER:	You're doing *something* to him ... He's not Eric now ... That's definite ... Don't know if it's good or bad ... Musically ... *bad* . He's taking music books out the library and trying to *play* them ...
CLAIR:	Peter ... He's getting better ... Now he is ... isn't he ...
ERIC:	*(FROM SHOWER)* You talking about me ...
PETER:	Just get yourself showered, boy ...
CLAIR:	I've got him doing a lovely version of *Frère Jacques* with two hands ... *(TO ERIC)* Eric ... when you're dressed play *Frère Jacques* for your Dad ...
ERIC:	Not playing anything for him ...
PETER:	Thanks ... You're a good son to your Dad ...
ERIC:	What do you say ...
CLAIR:	Get your shower ...
ERIC:	I'm nearly finished ...
CLAIR:	Shower a bit longer ... I want to speak to your Dad ...
PETER:	That was interesting up there ... Finding out I was going to die ...
CLAIR:	I don't *feel* thirty-six, Peter ... I don't *look* it ...
PETER:	Clair ... I hope it works out for you ... The two of you ... It *might* do ... You never know ...
CLAIR:	*You* don't think so ...
PETER:	How would *I* know? ... I don't know ... I've never been involved in these great passions ... have I ... Never have thought Eric would've had it in him ... He's surprised me ... I wish he wasn't here, for the minute ... I want to talk to you ...
CLAIR:	I think it *could* work out ...
PETER:	That's good ... I'm glad ... I am ... I do ... I really want it to ...
CLAIR:	Dorothy doesn't ...
	ERIC COMES IN ...
ERIC:	I've put in new posts, Dad ...
PETER:	I'll tell you something, Eric ... I've got a new lease of life ... What do you think of me? ...
ERIC:	I don't know ... Have you? ...
PETER:	Maybe the Pixies have got hold of me ...
CLAIR:	Eric ... Go and make some coffee, will you? ...
ERIC:	How has he got a new lease of life ...
CLAIR:	He found out he's not going to live for ever ...
PETER:	Eric ... I want to talk to you in a minute ...
ERIC:	Alright ...
PETER:	Mist up there ... Like a wall ... like pushing through a hedge ... couldn't see your hand in front of you ...
ERIC:	I noticed ... Sandpiper at the pond ...
PETER:	I saw it ...
PETER:	Tell you what ... *Frogs* might bring the herons ... You could put in some frogs ... *(TO ERIC)* Yes ... Go and make some coffee ...

CLAIR:	I love *you, too (TO PETER)*
PETER:	I've been wandering around up here in that mist for nearly an hour ... Pixie Lost ... Going round in circles ... I got myself in a right state ... I came to these stones ... you see What I did ... My handkerchief ... I kind of jammed it between a stone ... I went off again ... Thinking I was moving down towards here ... Twenty mintues later ... Another pile of stones ... The handkerchief was there ... It got cold ... When that mist comes down ... No idea how cold it gets ... I had this picture of me breaking a leg ... or collapsing with exhaustion ... You see ... and dying ... That was alright ... I didn't mind the dying ... What I minded ... was the stupid idiot I was ... I was going to die ... with all that property and land ... And I hadn't made a *will* . I *can't* make a will ...
CLAIR:	*I* couldn't make a will ...
PETER:	*You* haven't all that much to will anyway, have you?
CLAIR:	I've got this ... and your third of an acre ...
PETER:	"Stupid idiot ... You've gone up her in a mist ... risked your life and ... and left all that damn mess to be sorted out over your dead body on top of Eric and Dorothy being upset about you dying ... You've left them in trouble ... You have no idea the complications of some stupid idiot dying with 300 odd acres and no damn will ...
CLAIR:	You have a different feel about you ... You're right ...
PETER:	I'm telling you ... I've woken up again ... Do from time to time ...
CLAIR:	Are you *going* to make a will ...
PETER:	Clair ... I can't it's a deep thing ... It disturbs me ... the whole idea ...
CLAIR:	Yeah ...
ERIC:	Coffee's ready ...
PETER:	What are you going to do then, Eric?
ERIC:	I told you ... We're going to get married ...
PETER:	Eric ... She's *married* already ...
ERIC:	*She'll* organise that ... won't you?
CLAIR:	I'll organise it ...
ERIC:	I'm going to live here ... Dad ... That is what we're talking about ...
PETER:	It's up to you ... What about your Mum? ...
ERIC:	We were thinking of me moving in here ... next month ... some time ... To let Mum get used to the idea ...
CLAIR:	If she knows we are going to get married ... Do you think, Peter?
PETER:	This smell I had ... Coming down from my encounter with death ...
CLAIR:	He was Pixie led in a mist ... *(TO ERIC)*
PETER:	I had this echo ... You know ... Getting up on a spring morning when I was a young lad ... Going to get the horses in to harness them up for the day's work ... You've no idea the feeling you had ... It wasn't like jumping onto the tractor and turning the engine on ... you went with the horses ... Harnessed them ... a whole ritual ... talked to the horses ... conversations with my horses ... you're always in touch with horses ...
CLAIR:	Peter ... You're going off with the fairies ... again ...

PETER:	No ... You don't know about that, Clair ... I'm not making up any fairy tales ... Eric'll tell you ... He's worked horses a bit ...
ERIC:	It's a good feel ... Yes ... Team of horses in front of you ... He's right ...
PETER:	So I'm going to start again ... That's what I'm going to do ... What do you think? I'm going to get thirty or forty acres ... near the sea ... for your Mother ... use horses ...
ERIC:	Could come back ... Horses ... Price of diesel, Dad ... Yeah ... who knows ...
PETER:	There's nothing more for me to do at Furzeland is there, Eric? I'm finished with it ... I'm going to sign it over to you ... Alright, boy?
ERIC:	That's what you want ... It's alright ...
PETER:	I'm telling you ... There's no more I can do with it ... I don't ... I get no damn joy out of the place at all now ... *You* take it ...
ERIC:	If that's what you want to do ... Dad ...
PETER:	I'm going to phone Grey, now ... from here ...
CLAIR:	Before you talk to Dorothy?
PETER:	That's exactly what she wants ... to go back to the sea ...
ERIC:	Gull's got one of your goldfish ...
CLAIR:	Hell ... There'll be none left the way they're going ...
PETER:	Just keep restocking it ... Not all that dear goldfish ... If you buy them in quantity ...
CLAIR:	I don't *want* my goldfish *killed*
ERIC:	It's a big farm ... Dad ... 300 odd acres ... You think I'll handle it alright ...
PETER:	Not if you keep having showers halfway through the afternoon with your lady love ... No ... But you get over that stage ... don't you ... I'd *think* so ... Not that I've ever been through it ...

Scene 11 1979

PETER:	George 'phoned up ... I was having my usual struggle with Bach and my fiddle ... Nothing else to do, anyway ... with that rain hammering down ... I didn't even realise Dorothy wasn't in the house ... George 'phones up ... In a *George* panic ... First I thought he was looking for Dorothy ... Had one of these cross conversations ... "I'll go and get her for you ... Probably in the front room ... No ... She's with me ... She's here" ... George panic ... Dorothy's turned up in his house with a suitcase ... He's phoned the world ... to help him to cope with the situation ... Me ... Eric ... Clair ... Right, I say to myself ... on the way ... that's it ... The worst has happened ... Wait all your life for the worst to happen ... and it does ... Looking at them all in George's kitchen ... Dorothy sitting with her suitcase beside her ... George looking very guilty ... Why *shouldn't* he look guilty ... Eric trying to add it all up ... Clair? ... Clair ... I came out with it ...
PETER:	You wait all your life for the worst to happen to you ... and one day it does ... Doesn't it?
CLAIR:	You *die* .

PETER:	Who's *dying*? Could be *worse* than dying ... That's you blotted out ... When you die ... Finished ... When this happens ... You're still damn well there ...
GEORGE:	You cancelled the Combines ... Eric told me ...
PETER:	George ... What are you talking about damn farming for? It's not your fault ... It's all right, George ... I mean ... it's not all right ... it's *disastrous* . Dorothy ... Do you know what it is ...
DOROTHY:	I think so ...
PETER:	I don't think you do ... Does she? ... I don't know what to say ... I can't think of anything to say to you ... that's a funny thing, isn't it? ... You run away from me ... after 28 years together ... Should be able to say something ... Why shouldn't you run off ... twenty years is a long time to hang around one character ... better late than never ... It's a free country ... you should be able to run off with whoever you want to ... I don't believe that ...
CLAIR:	Of course you don't believe it ...
PETER:	I'm just saying it ... I don't know what I'm saying it for ...
DOROTHY:	You're upset ...
GEORGE:	Peter, listen to me ... It's nothing ...
PETER:	You look guilty George ... It's all right ... Why shouldn't you look guilty ... You'd probably be better to hold your tongue, George ...
GEORGE:	I want to tell you something ...
PETER:	I know ... But I don't want to listen to you ... As a matter of fact, looking at you, I don't like the look of you just now ... That's a bad attitude ... You're my brother, for God's sake ...
ERIC:	Dad, I think it's more complicated than that ...
GEORGE:	I just want to damn well say ... It's nothing like that ... that's all ... I don't know what the hell you're thinking, Peter ...
DOROTHY:	George ... what did you need to phone everybody for?
GEORGE:	Peter phoned me ...
DOROTHY:	You know that, George ... It's no use you trying to tell lies ... you can't *tell* lies ... There's definitely something *doomed* about me ... isn't there? I can't even run away in peace without an army following me ...
CLAIR:	Would you like us to go away, Dorothy?
DOROTHY:	I'm not sure ... I don't think I'm away an *hour* ... am I?
PETER:	I'm not sure ...
DOROTHY:	You wouldn't have known I was gone at all ... if damn George hadn't have phoned you ...
PETER:	I was playing my fiddle ...
DOROTHY:	I know you were ...
PETER:	If you look at George ... Clair ... Look at him ... He's younger than me ... A year ... But objectively speaking, Clair ... time's dealt better with me ... hasn't it? What's that got to do with anything?
GEORGE:	Peter, I'm very upset ... you've upset me ... Can you not see that ...
PETER:	I can understand that ... Dorothy ... I can ... you wanting to leave me ...

DOROTHY:	Can you? Is that what I'm doing?
GEORGE:	You're not ... How can you do anything like that?
PETER:	She's not dropped in for a cup of tea, George ... with all that luggage ...
DOROTHY:	I've just the one case ...
PETER:	That's right ...
	(TO HIMSELF) Eric was going on ... He *knew* what it was all about ... Didn't help any ... But he *knew* .
ERIC:	Mum ... It's no use kind of saying you're sorry ... What's the point, people saying they're sorry ... I can't work Furzeland any more ... I don't want to, Mum, I can't stand it ...
DOROTHY:	I know that, Eric ...
PETER:	He is sorry ... *(TO HIMSELF)* That damn rain ... Everything crashing down it started very well ... The Combines were going to start on the Barley ... and the damn heavens opened up ... Eric had come over first thing in the morning ... That was what set everything off ... The last year since he had the farm ... That was the ritual, wasn't it? Come over to the house before starting the day's work ... In the middle of talking to me ... It hit him ...
ERIC:	What do you think, Dad? Tell them ... not today ...
PETER:	Thought they'd be on the phone to us ...
ERIC:	It's just getting flattened ... Look at it ...
PETER:	*(TO HIMSELF)* Looking out the window ... watching the rain driving across the Barley ... he stood there for at least five minutes without saying anything ... Then he turned round to me ... What did he say ... What were his words ... Simple ... They seemed to come out of the blue ... To him and me ...
ERIC:	Dad ... I don't want to *do* this ... It just hit me ... I don't *want* it, Dad ... You see what I'm getting at ...
PETER:	If I *knew* what you didn't want, son ... Yes ... phone them ... You can't cut in this ... and the forecast ...
ERIC:	*You* don't want it either ...
PETER:	*(TO HIMSELF)* Got deeper that boy, definitely since living with Clair ... I was beginning to have hopes for him ... *(TO ERIC)* I'm beginning to have *hopes* for you ...
ERIC:	Not too high, Dad ...
PETER:	Not all that high, yet ... no ...
ERIC:	I'm talking about the *farm*, Dad ... You don't *want* me to work it ... do you ... You're not letting me anyway ... *You* were supposed to be going off six months ago ...
PETER:	I was ... you're right ... I worry you'll make a mess of it ... You probably will ...
ERIC:	I know that, Dad ... That's what I'm saying ...
PETER:	No, you won't ... I have every confidence in you as a farmer, boy ... I just can't trust you ...
ERIC:	It's yours, isn't it ... *I* might have it on *paper* ...

PETER: It's mine ... yes ... it is ... yes you're right ... What do you think we should do?

ERIC: Even if you *gave* me it ... and you went off ... Dad ...

PETER: *(TO HIMSELF)* He went back to the window again ... as if he was checking in his mind, trying to come to grips with his feelings for Furzeland ...

ERIC: I don't *want* it ... No ...

PETER: I've just damn well given you it, boy ... I know ... I *haven't* ... But on paper I damn well have ... Cost me a fortune ... signing it over to you ...

ERIC: I don't *want* it, Dad ... Might be something to do with Clair losing that baby ... Is it? I don't know ... She only carried it a few months ...

PETER: I know ... Upset your Mother ... very much ... Me ...

ERIC: We'll get another one ...

PETER: You will ... Why shouldn't you ... Once you know how it's done ...

ERIC: I think we'll go away, Dad ... for a bit ... You can get somebody in ... couldn't you ...

PETER: Isn't it just the rain ... waking up on a day like this ... Affects *me* days like this ...

ERIC: I could get a degree ... couldn't I? ... instead of that useless bit of paper ... from the college ... Might get into Cambridge ... and do the agriculture degree ... I don't *know* enough ... do I ...

PETER: You fancy doing that ... You *want* to do it ... That's you taking a real step forward ... wanting to do something ... *(TO HIMSELF)* That was too much, I suppose, to expect ...

ERIC: I don't know ... I *might* do it ... I'm not sure, Dad ... Could be ... Stuck here all my life ... Hardly seeing anybody but you and Mum and the young Farmers ... maybe, that's why I don't know ...

PETER: Or maybe you just don't know ...

ERIC: Maybe never know ...

PETER: What are you going to do, then ... *(TO HIMSELF)* The rain was battering down my barley ... My son was *leaving* me ... and I was happy ... I was getting my farm back. What a character I am ... At that minute ... the sky was full of rainbows ...

ERIC: Think I might get into Cambridge, Dad ...

PETER: Why *shouldn't* you ...

ERIC: Could you spare me for three or four years ...

PETER: Eric ... If you *want* ... I want you to do what you *want* ... Or have a try at finding out if there *is* anything you want ... Probably isn't ... But have a look ...

ERIC: I want to sign that farm back to you, Dad ... That's definite ...

PETER: I've got it, anyway ... You're right ... I never *gave* it to you ... The paper is neither here nor there ... is it?

ERIC: I think I'd have to have it on paper, too, Dad ... Back to you ...

PETER: If you have to ...

ERIC:	It's not mine ... If I work *another* farm ... It'll be mine. *If* I work one. I don't know ...
DOROTHY:	That was all I could think of doing ... I had to do something ...
PETER:	I can understand that, Dorothy, yes ...
DOROTHY:	I couldn't see anything left for me to stay for ... Can you?
PETER:	I'm thinking about it ...
DOROTHY:	You're stuck in Furzeland for the rest of your life ... Clair's lost her baby ... waiting for her baby would've been something ...
CLAIR:	I'll get another one ...
DOROTHY:	That was all I could think of ... Pack my bag and go to George's ...
GEORGE:	I was glad when you came to me, Dorothy ...
DOROTHY:	Why, George?
PETER:	Why shouldn't he be? ...
GEORGE:	That's what friends are for ... Isn't it ... When you're in trouble ...
PETER:	George ... if you can't *talk* . speak to *people* ... It doesn't matter ... that happens to people ... It's all right ... It's a difficult situation ... I can understand you not knowing what to say ... *Why* should it be a difficult situation? When you think about ...
DOROTHY:	Do you not think it is ...
ERIC:	You make a situation what you want of it ...
GEORGE:	Peter ... I'm very upset ... You won't let me say anything ... Any time I try to explain the situation ...
PETER:	George ... Why *can't* she go off with you ... For God's sake that's terrible ... If the pair of you want it all that much ...
GEORGE:	Damn well let me speak ...
PETER:	I'm talking to you ... Run off to Torbay or somewhere nice ... the pair of you ... For a week or two together ... I should be able to *stand* that ... shouldn't I ... At our age ... I *can't* . I know ... That's up to me ...
GEORGE:	Listen ... Peter ... Damn well listen to me ...
PETER:	It's all right, George ... I understand you, man ... Things you can't talk about it ... Things you can't talk about, better not trying ... End up making a bigger mess than ever ... Mess it all up with the wrong words ... You're right ...
GEORGE:	I'm damn well telling you nothing was further from my mind ... than what you're talking about ...
CLAIR:	Do you mean that George? Is that how you really feel about her? ...
GEORGE:	Clair ... What do you know about the way we work these things ... you're in a different age ... your generation ...
DOROTHY:	I was in the front room ... you see ... Peter ...
GEORGE:	Are you listening to me, Peter ...
ERIC:	He is ...
DOROTHY:	I was listening to you playing that Bach thing, ... over and over again ...
PETER:	Bound to get on your nerves, that ...

DOROTHY: And I was watching the rain sweeping down ... I couldn't *stay* there ... could I? I had to ... Apart from your damn fiddle ... The whole idea of going on with a normal afternoon ... bringing you in tea ... And ... *God* . I couldn't stand it ...

PETER: That's it ... You're right ...

GEORGE: Peter ... I'm talking to –

PETER: How about *you* and George?

DOROTHY: I'm not *sure*, Peter ...

GEORGE: Peter ... Dorothy knows what I feel about her ... one of the closest friends I have ... She knows that ... don't you?

DOROTHY: We have, George ... Haven't we? ... We've been close to each *other* for all our lives ... haven't we? I've always felt that ...

PETER: What do you want to do, George? Do you want to do that, George ... Go off with her somewhere ... to the coast ... Scotland ... *I* don't know ...

GEORGE: How could I do that ... my brother's wife ...

CLAIR: *Dorothy*, George ...

PETER: Is that what you want to do, George? *(TO HIMSELF)* Dorothy was watching him ... I couldn't stand that picture ... George going off with Dorothy ... me left to work Furzeland ... That would be me finished ... I knew that ... But I kept hammering away at him ...

PETER: Do you want to go *off* with Dorothy, man ...

DOROTHY: Peter ... Leave him alone ... He's upset ...

GEORGE: I honestly do feel ill ... you can see that ...

CLAIR: I'll get you an aspirin ...

PETER: *Do* you?

GEORGE: How could I do something like that, Peter ... Come between a man and wife ... What are you talking about ... You know that ... You know the friendship we have ... How much I look up to ...

PETER: *(TO HIMSELF)* That's what I was looking for ... I knew that ... I knew he was going to say that from the beginning That was what I was looking for ... That's what I wanted ...

GEORGE: You know that ... You're the closest friends I have ... you and Dorothy ...

PETER: *(TO HIMSELF)* she was lost, now ... Dorothy ... I could see that ... lost and isolated ... Nowhere to turn to ... I was lost myself ... Looking at her ... I couldn't stand that ... making her like that ... Taking her back to the farm like that ... waking up every day for the rest of our lives ... with that between us ... I said to her ... *(TO DOROTHY)* You see ... I don't think I could *do* that, Dorothy ... Could I, ... You know that ... the grip Furzeland's got on me ...

DOROTHY: I *know*, Peter ...

PETER: I can't stand that ... I can't stand making you miserable like this ... And blocking you ... you know that ...

DOROTHY: I'm saying ... I know ... what do you *want* me to say, Peter ...

PETER: I don't know what to do, Dorothy ... God ... The whole idea ... when Eric spoke to me about it this morning ... getting it back ... living out my days here ... I know that ... It's not a good situation ... I can see that ... The old game ... Your joy is my sadness ... My sadness your joy ... How can we get out of that. I *want* to ... you know that ... If we *could* get out of that game, Dorothy ... Clair ... How do you get out of a situation like that? ...

GEORGE: Peter ... I'm talking to you ...

CLAIR: You don't, do you ... You ride them ... I think ...

PETER: You wait ...

GEORGE: I'm *talking* to you ... Peter ...

PETER: God ... I love you, George, I do ... You're a good man ... The goodwill you have in you ... to people ... I wish *I* had some of it ...
George ... come here a minute ...

GEORGE: Peter ... come on ...

PETER: You are ... a brother in a million ... You damn well are ...

GEORGE: You don't think I made any suggestions to Dorothy, Peter? Dorothy'll tell you ...

PETER: It doesn't matter ... George ... I love you as much as I can love anybody ...

GEORGE: It *does* matter, man ...

CLAIR: You can't help your feelings, George ... There's nothing wrong with them, anyway ... What's wrong with them ... I think it's great ... You've had this thing for Dorothy all your life ...

GEORGE: Dorothy ... Tell them ... I don't understand them ... God knows *what* they're thinking ...

DOROTHY: It's all right, George, dear ...

ERIC: Uncle George ... Nobody's blaming you ... don't worry about it ...

PETER: It's not important, that, George ... we're not talking about that ...

GEORGE: How is it not important ... That's the whole point, man ... you thinking I was trying to steal your wife ...

ERIC: He *knows* now, Uncle George ... You weren't ...

GEORGE: Do you understand that, Peter? ...

PETER: George, come here ...

GEORGE: I'm very upset, Peter ... Leave me alone ...

PETER: I want to say something to you ... It's all right, all right George ... It's all right ... you understand ... I understand ...

DOROTHY: You raised my hopes again, Peter ... When you signed it over to Eric ... You see ... we were getting away from here ... It's *never* been *my* place ...

PETER: That's not right either, is it ... Had good times and bad times here ... Have that anywhere ... that's people ... what happens to them ... isn't it? Happens to them ... isn't it? Happens to me ... I'm having a bad time, just now ... I had a good time this morning ... Might have a good time, tomorrow ... Some time I will ... *(TO HIMSELF)* And a revelation from Eric ... another revelation ... I was getting to have faith in that boy ... My God ... that was my damn son! ...

ERIC: Dad ... I still have the farm ... You see ... haven't I ... I still have ... I know ... *You'd* never be able to do it ... I know that ...

PETER: *(TO HIMSELF)* What was he going to come out with next? ...

ERIC: What I've got to do ... is sell the bastard, haven't I, Dad? Haven't I? ... *I've* got to *sell* it ...

GEORGE: Eric, just leave that alone, just now ... everybody's a bit excited just now ... They don't know what they're doing ...

ERIC: I've got to do it ... You'd never be able to get rid of it, would you Dad ... *I* can ... it's still mine ... I've got all the paper ...

PETER: Good day this ... rain battering down my barley ... my Wife leaving me ... My lad selling my farm over my head ...

CLAIR: You don't believe that ... do you Peter? ...

PETER: The rain's damn well battering down the barley ... Dear Jesus ... you *are* . you're going to sell the farm, Eric ...

GEORGE: Peter ... Don't take him seriously, man ... You know the wild ideas the young people come out with ...

ERIC: I'm going to put it up for sale ... Uncle George ... I'll phone the auctioneers from here ...

GEORGE: You won't damn well use *my* phone for that, boy ...

PETER: *(TO HIMSELF)* That was the revelation of a day of revelations ... The boy was selling my farm ... I'd put my life into it ... I was saying that when it came to me ... *(TO ERIC)* I've put my damn life into that farm ... building it up ...

ERIC: You've still got a *bit* left, Dad ...

PETER: *(TO HIMSELF)* and I was still there. my boy was selling my farm ... If anybody would have asked me what is the foundation of your life, Peter Brent ... I'd have said to them ... Furzeland ... I put my life into it ... and I could not ... I could not work up any anger towards him ... or a sense of loss ... I tried picturing my field ...

CLAIR: You're right ... You are, Eric ... That's right ...

DOROTHY: Would he sell it, do you think Clair?

PETER: He's *selling* it ...

CLAIR: Now you're talking about selling it, Eric ... The idea of leaving it ...

ERIC: I know ... That's what I *want* to do ... All right?

CLAIR: Yeah ... all right ...

ERIC: I mean ... I don't want the money, Dad ... After it's sold ...

PETER: I might need some ... get a place by the sea ... Fancy that, Dorothy? Thirty acres ... Twenty's enough ...

DOROTHY: Eric ... you shouldn't my dear ... You can sell it ... some time. Not just now ... Not while your father's with you, Eric ... don't do that to him ...

PETER: He's telling you, Dorothy ... he's selling it ...

GEORGE: You're not going to sit back and let a boy ...

PETER: George ... It's his ... I gave it ... It's out of my hands ...

GEORGE: I *told* you, Peter ... I *told* you to hang onto it ...

PETER: You might've been right George ... Who knows ... Eh ... You're probably a wise man ... I wish I was a wise man ... I would think it would be good that ... to be a wise man ... Come on, Dorothy ... We'll go home ... will we?

ERIC: It's the best thing, isn't it, Dad?

PETER: You *know*, son ... I wouldn't have thought you'd know ... But you do, don't you? I love you ... I love you, too, Clair ... God ... I'm in a hell of a loving mood, aren't I, *(TO HIMSELF)* Outside ... Dorothy slipped her arm into mine ... she said a very strange thing ... There was a look in her face ... I don't think I'd ever seen it before ...

DOROTHY: Peter ... I want to tell you something ... Listen my dear ... I didn't know what I was doing going off like that, this afternoon ...

PETER: It's all right ... you do things like that ... People do ...

DOROTHY: *(MOVING CLOSER TO HIM)* I love you, you know ... at the bottom of everything ... I really do love you ...

AUCTIONEER: For the last time £280,000 *(HAMMER DOWN)* ...

                    LIGHTS ON PETER'S FACE ...

DOROTHY: You know that, dear ... I really do ...

PETER: (TO HIMSELF) God? She did! Oh God ... She did!

Bring Me Sunshine, Bring Me Smiles

Characters

TED
CAROL, *TED'S WIFE*
LINDA
JACKIE
PETER, *TED'S SON*
MART
PATTERSON
LES
WENDY
JAGUAR
OLD IDIOT
ANNIE

TED:	*(TO THE WORLD)* Started very funny with me. .. That Friday night. Got back from Belsay tip to make me cornbeef and onion pie for everybody. Just bringing it out....... *(UP SIREN.)*
	..I've got this saying.. You need a few sayings to keep you going, don't you? Always expect the wost and you've a chance now and then of being pleasantly surprised ... Minute I hear that...: "Jesus!" I says to myself. Minute I hear that. "Christ!" That's it, isn't it? End of the world."
	UP SIREN..
	(WITH HIS CORN BEEF PIE. TO THE WORLD) ...When I was in my second year's apprenticeship at the yard..This bloke..In America.. They'll all come from America these blokes.
CAROL:	Did you really think that, pet?...
TED:	What else could it have been, Carol .. ..Bound to come one of these days.. ..Isn't it..
CAROL:	Like you thought your last hour had come..
TED:	Me last four minutes...
LINDA:	That's why there's not enough pie to go round..
TED:	That's what I told you, you see.. ... It was nearly half an hour before you came back from work ... That bloke I told you about. .. He's prophesied the end of the world this day..at ten past eleven...Could've been..Never know..
LINDA:	It was lovely pie..what there was of it..
TED:	*(TO THE WORLD)* Eleven o'clock.. Ten minutes before the end of the world.. ...All the lads went off to the toilets.. ...To have a last fling... *I* didn't.. ...I wouldn't have minded... But you can't go off in front of the whole yard..To do what everybody know's you're going to do..
CAROL:	Teddy!
TED:	*(TO WORLD)* So. There I am.. Getting me pie out of the oven.. When I hear this bloody siren...Screaming its rotten head off...
	UP SIREN..
	(TO THE WORLD)
	Normally, when I hear that..I mean what it was was one of them fire alarms or something going off by accident.. Normally when I'd hear that, I'd think nowt of it. Quite right.. But Jackie and me..Driving over to Belsay that day, there was this thing on the radio..About the Russians and Americans at each other over Afghanistan...The way this bloke was talking..Like one of them characters you used to see walking round Newcastle in Crombie coats with placards: Prepare to Meet Thy Doom ....I could see it..Got Jackie upset..Spoiled his day for him..

LINDA:	*(HAULING AT A PIECE OF JUNK):* Come on Ted. Give us a hand. There's something big underneath here.
TED:	*(TO THE WORLD)* Working this tip in Belsay..Good tip, Belsay. We started on that game, raking the tips, couple of months after they finished us at Swan Hunters.. Raking the tips for old bikes and whatever else we could find..Doing them up..and flogging them.
JACKIE:	It's a big un..
TED:	Get the spade, man..
JACKIE:	Don't want to damage it...
TED:	Give me it, Jackie.
JACKIE:	Something bit there.. Stupid sods burying it under a load of shit..
TED:	*(TO THE WORLD)* So...I'm digging away.. Clearing off old suitcases..mattresses.. and all the other shit..Lovely day in the month of May. *(TO JACK)* Lovely day in the month of May..
JACKIE:	That's it.. It's not a bike..
TED:	Bastard!
JACKIE:	Rotten pram.
TED:	Wait on, man..It's not in bad fettle.
JACKIE:	Need new wheels.
TED:	Cannie pram..Get two or three quid for it..
JACKIE:	What do you think? .. Right..isn't it?
TED:	Might even get a fiver... Paint it up...
JACKIE:	Want a drink?
TED:	Lovely tip this..Beautiful position..
JACKIE:	You're right..
TED:	Surrounded by trees and fields and cows.. Always look forward to coming out here.. Good class of people dump here.. don't they..
JACKIE:	You see... I don't *want* Afghanistan... Ted..See what I'm getting..Do you want it?
TED:	No use to me.. Nuh..
JACKIE:	I don't even know where the bastard is.. ...In India.. ..Is it?
TED:	That's it..
JACKIE:	They wouldn't blow the world up with their bombs, would they..The Russians and the Americans..over Afghanistan...I know they're off their nut, Ted..but they're not as off their rocker as much as that... are they?...
TED:	*(TO WORLD)* ...That happy day in the month of May..with all the birds singing..sun shining..flowers blooming..me..and Jackie enjoying ourselves and at least three quid in.. ...I could not pat him on the back..my mate..Been together at Swan's..since we started as apprentices..like in the

Boer War.. ...I could not say to him "It's all right. I guarantee you the stupid bastards will hang back on the end from throwing nukes at each other".. ...I cannot guarantee you, my friend..we will see out the eighties..*Could* be..*Probably* will..But could *not*...You don't talk shit to a mate like Jackie..do you..What's the point in having a mate.. ...If you have to talk *shit* to him.. I could guarantee him a *week*.. I reckon the situation was good for a week.. We'd see out the Howdon Carnival...
....

...That's what I said to him.
...He said..

JACKIE: Not all that much..is it..A *week*..

TED: Could be *ten days*.. a fortnight..Talking about *guaranteeing*...

JACKIE   ... Live for today..That's the best policy.. ...Eat and drink and be merry and gay.. ...For tomorrow we may die..

TED: *(TO THE WORLD)* Had to check him there.. *(TO JACKIE)* Not *gay*... Jackie.

JACKIE   See what you mean..Yeah...
              ..Fancy stopping off at Throckley..see if anything's doing there..

TED: Got to get back to make the tea for everybody.. ...Making corn beef and onion pie..Don't want to get back too late.. ..Try and keep a bit for you, after the practice tonight..You like that pie, don't you..?

JACKIE: Cannie Pie maker...Better than my lass...

TED: You alright, now, Jackie?

JACKIE: Nowt wrong with me..

TED: Bothers me. You worrying like that.. ...Shouldn't. It's up to you..if you worry or *don't* worry...

JACKIE: I'm not worried... man..
              ...What's to be, 'll be.. Right?

TED: I'm not *sure* about that..

JACKIE: No..

TED: It's alright..don't worry about it..

JACKIE: Don't keep saying that..Ted, man.. It worries us.

TED: You're right..*(TO WORLD)* Bound to worry anybody..that.. People keeping at him all the time.. telling him not to worry..*(TO JACKIE)* Not to worry, Jackie..

JACKIE: You get the van started..I'll manage the pram meself..

              UP SIREN

TED: *(TAKING PIE OUT)*
              Perfect...Lovely golden brown crust..
              ....Now you'd never have thought that..would you ....I'd be a better cook than Carol or Linda.. Look at that pastry...... ..I'll tell you something.. .....I know.. It's not a thing you could've told most of the lads at the Yard..could you.. But I am very happy in my own little house..Making a pie..Peeling the potatoes..Gets on yer nerves times... But gives us a real lift..When you turn out something like that pie.. ..Watching Carol and Linda stuffing themselves with it..

....I'm taking the pie out..., the oven.. Admiring me handiwork... Good thing about pies.. You can see the result of your efforts in a couple of hours.. Bloody ships.. Be on for a year... and then you'd end up with an empty hulk that looked like nowt..

....So this four minute warning sounds..*(SIREN)* ...I say to myself: What's that..Jesus..God..Bugger of hell..Oh..God..Jesus..That's it..it's come.. Bound to come one of them days..The Ruskies and the Yanks have started throwing it around..O Jesus..

....I went white.. You'd go white..Anybody'd go white.. ...I was enjoying mesel..I was happy..but these stupid bastards were going to finish us off... ...That's what I shouted..Stupid, rotten bastards! ...Kept shouting that ..to the air.. ....Jesus..Oh..Jesus Christ..Dear Jesus Christ.. ....Wait a minute I says to myself. You've only four or five minutes left.. and you're burning them up swearing at these stupid bastards who can't hear you anyway...

...So I sat down.. with me pie..
(DOES THIS)

LINDA: You ate a whole half of a pie, Teddy..

TED: ....I'd ate it all.. But the siren stopped...

            ...*(TO WORLD)* I was working it out.. eating my pie.. If I'd known this was going to happen.. ...I could had Jackie come back with us and share the pie... Never said a proper goodbye to him..Or Carol... Me lad... Linda...

            (TO CAROL) I was thinking. You see...I know, the daft things that come into my head..What I was thinking...Was...The stupid bastaddin sods could at least have had the decency to tell us the night before... Then you could've taken the day off... And we could've had a last long-lie-in... Long time since we had a long-lie-in..Me and Carol.

CAROL: Did you think that.. Teddy..

LINDA: He'd be bound to..

TED: What's wrong with thinking that?

CAROL: Did you really do that, love? You went upstairs to have a look at our wedding photograph...

LINDA: It's just what he would've done, isn't it Carol?

TED: Would I?

CAROL: You did... Ted, pet ...

LINDA: He's that kind of a man, isn't he? ..

CAROL: Like you thought your end had come...And you wanted to be looking at our photograph...Ee...Ted ...

TED: *(TO WORLD)*.. I went into our bedroom and had a look at our wedding photo...Last look..Still eating me pie.. ...Like a last farewell...To tell you the truth...it put us off a bit..It spoiled my atmosphere..Like Goodbye Carol..We will never see each other again..But in that photograph..God knows what people do when they photograph Brides..She looked a bit cockeyed.. She isn't.. Look at her..So I went into Peter's room.. ...Our only lad..Never see our little lad again.. Jesus..Daft Bloody thoughts that come into yer head when you let your imagination run away with you.. ...Looked at his bed..It wasn't made, yet... ....So I made it.. Then I stopped myself. What am I doing making his bed..when he'll never get home again..It's all finished.. That really had us worked up..Tears coming into my eye...

I was standing in his room. Looking at his Sid Vicious wall...Had this poster of Vicious Sid taking up half the wall...He did, too...Looked a right vicious bastard, when Peter turns up... With a carrier bag of L.P.'s... drugs, Durex and booze...Like all his necessities for the week... Doesn't ask me what I'm doing there...Starts emptying his carrier bag...

Watch him emptying the vodka's and Southern Comforts... and Pernods onto his table...Got a funny sense of what's his and what isn't, my lad...Whatever he can pinch and get away with it is his...Must've seen something in me eye...because he says to me...

PETER:	Paid for most of this, Dad...You know? Out me Giro... Want a Pernod?
TED:	Give me a vodka...
PETER:	Want a vodka and Pernod?
TED:	Just give me a vodka, son...

(TO WORLD) Pours me out this mug of vodka, and puts on one of his records..We're sitting there, on his bed, the two of us, not saying a word..Drinking his booze.. I'm thinking of the time he was working..Lucky to get a half pint out of him, those days...Now, he's on the dole, and he's pouring out mugfuls of vodka for me... More, if I want it...

(TO PETER) Just thinking..When you were working...

PETER: Yeah...
...Couldn't keep on in that bastardin place.. could I..Dad.. I mean.. you know..

TED: I know, son..You're right..
(TO WORLD) ..That's me..you see.. A very understanding character.. I understand everybody.. Citizens Advice Bureau.. They all come to me, to understand them.. I do.. Understand everybody except meself..
...Comes to me.. This Thursday night.. Peter..

PETER: Dad.. Fancy a jar.. eh..?
TED: Always fancy a jar..
PETER: Want to talk to you, Dad..
TED: (TO WORLD)
So we go down to the pub..
And we're standing at the bar...Everybody is watching *The Good Bad and The Ugly* on the telly for the hundredth time.. Even the barmaid was too busy watching it to serve anybody... You felt like.... You had to apologise for disturbing her.. ...

Excuse me miss.. I'm sorry to disturb your telly watching.. ...When you've a minute.. or the next commercial.. Give us a pint of Scotch..will you..please...

...Peter gets the drinks, anyway.. and we're sitting there, I know he's trying to tell me something very important... Because he said...

PETER: Dad... Tell you what.. Know what I mean, ... It's difficult to kind of explain this to you.. ...Know what it is..

TED: No.

PETER: No.. I'm telling you..

TED: Yeah...

PETER: Know this bloke.. Marty..

TED: No..

PETER: That's right..
..Works beside me
..You see..
.. What happens .. Marty.. Tiger.. Shark.. Leper.. ...

TED: *(TO WORLD)* Mostly animals, Christ knows what their *real* names are...My son's mates...Not *all* animals...There's a couple of characters from Snowhite and the Seven Dwarfs ...*(TO PETER)* How's Dopey getting on these days?

PETER: ... I didn't sleep in the house last night ... You see... You wonder where I was...?

TED: That's right ...*(TO WORLD)* ... I never know *where* he sleeps ... I never know *what* he does ...

PETER: I wasn't with Wendy or anything ... You wonder where I was ...?

TED: I did ... I wondered where you were ...

PETER: Yeah ...

TED: *(TO WORLD)* Why did I con him like that ... That's not good to con your own lad like that ... is it? I more than *like* him ... I love him ... Do I? ... I more than *like* him ... What it is, is I don't like disappointing him ... If he *thinks* the whole world revolves round him ... And we're interested in every move he makes ... You don't want to disappoint him ... do you?...

PETER: I thought you'd wonder where I was ... I was at Shark's.
I took Marty to Bingo's

TED: All your mates? It's very difficult to piece this all together, son.

PETER: *(EDGY)* If you just rotten *wait* till I *tell* you ... I'm rotten trying to rotten rotten tell you something for shit's sake...

TED: *(TO WORLD)* After a couple more pints he got it out at last... The three of them had gone off to the Town Moor to pick some kind of mushroom or something ... Gone back and doped themselves to the eyeballs with them...

PETER: It was very heavy, Dad...man...You've no idea ... What it is... You know, very heavy ... Know what I mean ... I'm alright... You know...

TED: Bloody killed yourself, you stupid bastard, Peter ... Could've been poison.

PETER: Telling you ... I'm *alright* ... *Right?* ... You *see* ... I'm rotten alright ... I'm telling you...

TED: They're bloody poisonous.

PETER: Telling you ... I'm cool Dad, man ... Not talking about that ... That was alright .. Got a book ... about mushrooms.

TED: Putting your fist through Shark's window ...Running up West Road ... Dancing in your bloody underpants ... You could've been had for indecent exposure ...

PETER: I had my pants on ... I told you, Dad, man. That's not what I'm talking to you about ... See ... What happened ...

TED: *(TO WORLD)* Jesus ...What was coming next ..Knocked up some bird in the middle of the road and was up for rape or something... I've got to definitely do something about this thing I have ... Thinking the worst....

PETER: Marty ... and me ... You see ... Shark had flipped out ...Right?... This morning ... We're still kind of spaced ..you know ... This is the bad bit ... Dad .. ..You know what I mean ... We go into work...Jesus. That Place... Blows yer rotten mind... All these dead frozen chickens and we're still tripping ... And Marty has some stuff to smoke ...You know...

TED: You've lost you job ...

PETER: Tellin you .. Right? Rotten listen to me ... We're working away ... Right? In the Freezer room..Packing all these frozen Gateaux... And I find this Alien Gateaux... *(MAKING RED ALERT SOUND)*
               Whoo..Whoo..Whooo..alien on board space ship
               (TO TED) Alien detector's going mad...

MART: Where?

PETER: Alien Gateaux .. *(TO TED)* Like we found this Chocolate Gateaux hiding away in the middle of all them Black Forest Gateaux...

MART: *(GRABBING ALIEN GATEAUX)* ..Right .. Right.. Come here you rotten alien shithole!

PETER: Trying to land in Wallsend under cover...

MART: Right, then.. Show you what we do to shithole Aliens... ..Gona fill you in...

PETER: Get him out his space suit, Mart, man... first...

MART: *(TAKING GATEAUX OUT OF BOX)*... Right ... You rotten black bastard... You're gonna get it... *(THROWS GATEAUX ONTO FLOOR .. BOTH OF THEM ARE JUMPING ON IT .. KICKING IT ... HAVING THE TIME OF THEIR LIVES.. PATTERSON COMES IN QUIETLY AND STANDS WATCHING THEM...*

PETER: *(TO TED)* So .. We're just putting the boot into this Alien Pear Gateaux ... Right. Rotten Patterson turns up ... Two of us ... Jumping on the bastard.. Grinding him into the ground ... And he's standing there ...Not talking... *I* see him first...

PATTERSON: 'S Alright, lads ... Get it out of yer system ...

PETER: It just ... you know ... fell ... and we were having a laugh ...

PATTERSON: Go on, lads... Enjoy yourself ...

MART: Fell down ... That's it Mr. Patterson...

PATTERSON: What do you think then, lads?

PETER: Pay for it ...

PATTERSON: I wouldn't worry about it, Peter ... It's *my* money ... It's not *yours*, lads ...

PETER: *(TO TED)* ... Know what I mean ... Tell by his voice knew ... you know ... Shithole's going to rotten finish us ... Tell that ... Says to myself ... won't care a rotten shit ... Stuff the rotten soddin bastard ... Mart's looking the same ... Pair of us ... Mart says.

MART: Get something and clean it up ...

PATTERSON: In a minute, Mart ... It's alright ... No panic ... Sit down, lads ... Have a fag ... Want a cigarette?

You think I'm angry with you? I'm not angry with you. I know, lads ... This is no job for kids like you full of energy ... and life ... Stuck all day in this freezing shithouse ... It might be *my* business, lads ... but I know what it must be like for you ... Not so good ... is it?

PETER: *(TO DAD)* I was saying nowt ... Mart neither ...

PATTERSON: Packing dead chickens ... Orange Duck ... Gateaux all day ...

MART: 'S alright ...

PATTERSON: It's not alright for lively, full of energy kids like you and your mate ... *I* don't like it ... I can't *help* it ... I'm in this business ... and I need the money ... I've two wives and five kids...

PETER: *(TO TED)* Some bastards are lucky, aren't they ...

PATTERSON: But what it boils down to ... Is I can't afford, lads, to keep you on any longer ... It's not *your* fault ... you're not capable of doing a fair day's work for a fair day's wage ...

MART: You gonna finish us ...

PATTERSON: I think it'll be better for you in the long run, Marty ... It's not your job ... is it, now ... or Peter's ... Your heart's not in it ... Why should it be ... You'll get yer dole money ... and find something more suited to your talents and ability ... Right ... Tell you what I will do... I'll give you a month's notice...Give you time to look for something else ... I know ... these days.. Jobs aren't hanging on trees ... But two keen lads.

PETER: *(TO TED)* That kind of ... you know ... Dad... That got ME ... Rotten blew... You know ...Taking me all my time to get Wendy to marry Me... way things were, just now...When she finds out I've got the boot..

TED: Jesus ... You didn't fill him in, too ... did you? on top of his gateaux.

(TO THE WORLD) So we're sitting on Peter's bed.. Me thinking back to the time Peter was finished at the Freezer factory ... And it hits me... got something to pull him out of his drugged fog he lives in... *(TO PETER)* Just thinking about that time you worked in the Freezer Factory. Know why you got the push, Peter...Just hit me...You got the push, because you got yourself so doped up, you couldn't tell Frozen Gateaux from Martians.

PETER: Aliens.

TED: Aliens...See what I'm getting at, Peter..Drugs.. ...Fogs up yer brain so much, you don't know if you're on Venus or Planet Earth...

(TO WORLD) Now watch this ... This is my bloody problem. I end up seeing *everybody's* point of view ... I get turned round by people into seeing what they bloody see. He says to me.

PETER: It was rotten mortuary, man... A shittin' dead house ... Dead chickens and dead ducks flying backwards and forwards over yer head ...

TED: *Dead chickens flying over yer head ...?*

PETER: On *hooks*, man.

TED:	*(TO THE WORLD)* I saw what he was getting at... It was like a nightmare, ... Hit me for the first time ... My lad spending his life in that frozen bastard bloody mortuary... He was attacking me, now ... Getting stuck right into me ...
PETER:	Tell you something... Right... You don't try and tell me what to do about dope... Right? You know shit all about it ... *I* know ... I take it ... Right ... That's what I want to do ... I'm sick of characters going on to me about taking dope Right... That's what I like doing ... That's what makes me feel good .. I smoke a couple ... or take a few pills ... I feel good ... I put on an album ... and I smoke... I could go to the pictures... Or go with Wendy ... Times I do ... ...Times I turn on .... Right ... So I'm telling you ... Right just rotten lay off getting on me for taking dope.
LINDA:	Pet.. I want to talk to you ...
TED:	Just going into the kitchen to get the apple crumble, Linda ... *(TO WORLD)* See what I mean.. Citizens Advice Bureau... The whole word wants to talk to me,. Followed me into the kitchen and watched me taking out my apple crumble... Something seriously wrong with me... Could be standing in St. James Park, watching the Lads.. not that I stand about there much, them days... But I could be standing there... and some bloke'll catch my eye... and tell his life story...
LINDA:	*(WATCHING HIM TAKE OUT CRUMBLE)* Looks lovely, Ted.
TED:	*(TO WORLD)* I liked to give everybody a good dinner on Friday night... It was a heavy night for them... Their main Jazzband practice... She was standing there, watching me, waiting for me to say something.
LINDA:	Teddy...
TED:	*(TO LINDA)* ..You never get any older, Linda...
LINDA:	Ee.. You're the nicest chap I've ever known.. you know that... Not because you say that..
TED:	I know..,
LINDA:	I like you,... You're just a real canny chap..
TED:	You don't think there's something wrong with us.. The way everybody likes me..
LINDA:	Wish people liked me, Ted, pet,. .,Like that.. I mean they fall for us.. ...I've always been like that.. I attract men like flies.. Even nowadays,.
TED:	You do..
LINDA:	You're a right daft bugger.. Thinking the bombs were coming, before.. Listen. I want to talk to you. But that's not what I want to talk to you about, just now.. I mean, pet.. *I* need to talk to you, too .. About something very important..
TED:	*(TO WORLD)* It wasn't as complicated as it sounds.. When I straightened it all out.. What it was was me.. Linda wanted to talk to me about Carol wanting to talk to me.. *(TO LINDA)* Oh...

LINDA:	Get her on her own a minute before she goes to the practice, pet. She's in a funny mood...
TED:	I'd miss you, if you took that flat in Longbenton.
LINDA:	I want to talk to you about that, love... But your wife comes first...
TED:	*(TO WORLD)* Trying to work out in me mind why I never wanted to have a go at Linda... Lovely, sexy woman like her... Look at the way Jackie was all over her... Didn't bother him being married to Sheila. Didn't hold him back... Did I fancy her?... Looked at her in her tight sweater and skirt... Oh.. Jesus... ...Lovely woman.. She is...Hair... Mind Jackie doing a line with her put me off a bit... Running around with the same lass your mate is going with... Could be that... Don't know... Odd times... Been nearly grabbing her and giving her a bit of a cuddle... ..But every time.. Like one of them force fields round her.. or me... Stopped us... Gave her an odd kiss Christmas .. and New Year.. But even kissing her.. not touching her...
LINDA:	Tell you something... You and Carol.. Good friends to me.. ...Never let you down.. Pair of you...
TED:	Time yet..
LINDA:	I know, man.. You won't..
TED:	*(TO WORLD)* I don't know why Linda needed to tell me Carol wanted to talk to me.. ...Because after tea.. while Linda was washing the dishes... Carol says to me..
CAROL:	Ted, pet... Come upstairs a minute. I want to talk to you about something, love.
TED:	*(TO WORLD)* So we go upstairs and I flop down on the bed... To tell you the truth, I was hoping she might lie beside us for a minute.... Just for a cuddle... or even holding my hand for a minute. ... ..Instead she went to the wardrobe and started throwing out her whole wardrobe, looking for something to wear...
CAROL:	What do you think I should put on tonight?
TED:	*(TO WORLD)* Always had that problem... Band practice nights... and Carnivals...
CAROL:	How about that black skirt and top...
TED:	Nice ... *(TO WORLD)* ... How *is* that? ... You can say to her "Do you fancy going to the pictures?"... Or "Make me a cup of tea..." Or "Will *I* make you a cup of tea?" But "Give me a cuddle..." You can't say... *I* can't say... I can't come out with it... Something wrong there, isn't there... My bloody wife... and I can't come out with it... Give me a cuddle... When I'm desperate for one.
CAROL:	*(REJECTING OUTFIT)* ... No ... I don't like it... It makes me look like one of them old biddies that run Jazzbands... *(TRYING ON ANOTHER OUTFIT)*.
TED:	*(TO WORLD)* Kept looking at me ... Like *she* was trying to come out with something to me ...
CAROL:	God. I wish I wasn't so fat.
TED:	You're alright...

CAROL: I'm *fat*, man. Look at all that horrible bloody flesh. It's you... Making us all these fattening meals.. Pies.. and apple crumble...
(LOOKING AT HIM) Ted. You're so bloody calm about everything!

TED: I know... There's something wrong with me... ...Calm about *what*...?

CAROL: I take you up here.. and say I want to talk to you... You're not bothered..

TED: I like talking to you..

CAROL: You don't know what I want to talk to you *about*..

TED: I know, man...

CAROL: What do you know...

TED: You're right ... I don't know..

CAROL: Stop bloody *agreeing* with us!

TED: Right..

CAROL: You're still agreeing with me. Will you let me flaming fight with you, for Christ's sake.. ... Just for once, let's have a real, wild, screaming match!

TED: Alright... What about?
(TO WORLD) Stood in front of the mirror, looking at herself... Like talking to her reflection in it ... she comes out with it...

CAROL: Ted ... We've had this same weekend routine for years, haven't we? ... Every weekend, Linda and me sleep up here... and *you* sleep in the spare room..

TED: Yeah ... Friday night you need a good night's rest to be fresh for the Carnival Saturday, you need a long lie on Sunday to recover from it ... ...That's understandable...

CAROL: Is it?

TED: It's *me*, Carol, *man*. Isn't it... Getting up at five o'clock in the morning ... I can't *help* it... It's like when you chop off a chicken's head and it still keeps running ... I have to get up at five o'clock in the morning like I was still going into the Yard...
(TO WORLD) she came over to me ... In her petticoat and put her two hands on my face ... ...Looking into my eyes... Without talking ... ...Like she was looking for something in them... *(TO CAROL — PAUSE)* What do you think, then?

CAROL: *(LETTING GO OF HIS FACE)* I don't *know*, love.

TED: Yeah ...

CAROL: What I'm saying, Teddy, is I get up at seven o'clock every morning to go into that bloody old age home, during the week.

TED: *(TO WORLD)* That bothered me ... *(TO CAROL)* I know ... I don't know what to do about that, Carol, man ... *You* working to keep ME ...That's not all that good ... That *bothers* me ... I know ... That's the situation... There's work for *you* and there's no work for me ... If they'd let us ... ...*I'd* go into old age home.

CAROL: I'm not talking about that, man.

TED: *(TO WORLD)* I *knew* what she was bloody talking about ... I got this anti-Carol feeling ... ...Suddenly... From wanting her to cuddle me to wishing she was a hundred bloody miles away ... ...Said to myself ... "Go and piss off to your stupid bloody Saints and watch them marching round and round Pendower Playground ... Stupid bloody bitch..."

She bloody started it all ... didn't she...? What the hell's she getting on to *me* About ... I want to go and sit with me cabbages and onions in peace in me allotment ... I didn't say that to her ... ... Good job I didn't ... Minute passed. ...Urge to kick her in the teeth went ...

CAROL: Ted ... You're a lovely man to me ... I'm lucky ... To get somebody like you ... I appreciate you...

TED: *(TO HER)* Am I?

CAROL: Bloody telling you ...

TED: Good ... You're not a bad wife, man ...

CAROL: What I'm saying is ... Have you lost interest in Me? ...That's what I mean ... In these two years... Every weekend ... You've let me go upstairs with Linda... Friday night and Saturday night ... without a grumble. Oh ... I'm just putting on that skirt and top ... That'll have to do ... I've *no* bloody clothes...

TED: I see what you're getting at ...

CAROL: I just wonder... You're so bloody nice ... and agree with everything ... Been so bloody calm since you finished at the Yard ... It's like you've got to hit you over the head with a hammer to get you to even say ... "Do us a favour and don't hit me over the head with a hammer..."

TED: I still fancy you ...

CAROL: I just wondered ... Our only chance of a long lie in ... At the weekends ... and I'm upstairs with Linda ... in bed ... and you're in the spare room...

TED: We still have our like ... moments ... haven't we?

CAROL: *Seconds* ... more like it ...

TED: I see what you mean ... *(TO WORLD)* I saw what she meant ... I mean ... I *thought* I saw what she meant ... because when I said to her ... *(TO CAROL)* Will we ask Linda to sleep in her room, tonight ... *(TO WORLD)* She said...

CAROL: How could we do that. ... We've got to go to Darlington tomorrow morning ... Early start for everybody...

TED: Yeah ...

CAROL: Got a real chance of getting a first tomorrow... You know that...

TED: Yeah...

CAROL: We need to be fresh...Everybody...
           In any case, Linda would be a bit hurt... All of a sudden... Me not sleeping with her...

TED: Yeah...

CAROL: She *would*...

TED: I'm saying, 'yeah', man...

CAROL: Will you stop being so bloody understanding about everything!

TED: I can't help it if I bloody under*stand*, can I?

CAROL: You bloody *don't*!

TED: I know ... I don't ...

CAROL:	You're bloody *still* doing it!
TED:	*(TO WORLD)* Went down to answer the door. It was Les. Stood there in his Sergeant Major's uniform. Smiling at me ... Dead nice bloke, Les ... Friendly. Lovely nature ... *Hated* the *bastard*!
LES:	Bit early, Ted ...
TED:	*(TO WORLD)* Always wore his uniform on a Friday night Band practice ... Because he was a sharp bloke a nice bloke... and a sharp bloke... and a straight bloke... Beautiful man altogether... And I hated his rotten guts... No... I didn't hate his *guts*.. I couldn't get myself to like him...Why he wore his uniform Friday nights... according to him... anyway... I asked him once...
LES:	Get that bit extra discipline in the band ... When they see me ....Standing there in me uniform... And I give the command ... "Band ... INSTRUMENTS UP" ... Minute they see me...
TED:	I can see that, Les ... *(TO WORLD)* Personally ... I reckoned he was putting on a show for Carol and Linda ... He was a straight bloke... He admitted he was always on the lookout for a bit of talent on the side when it was going. Cup of tea Les...
LES:	God ... Give us a cup of tea ... Ta ... Ted ... God ... You got a minute ... I want to talk to you, Teddy.
TED:	*(TO WORLD)* Jesus. Another customer for the Citizens' Advice Bureau. *(TO LES)* Always got minutes, Les, man ... Whole life's minutes ... *(TO WORLD)* Thing about Les was, he put his arms round people ... Men ... women... Something to do with him travelled around the world ... *I* don't know ... Put his arms round me a minute ...
LES:	Good to *see* you, Ted ... Always good to see you ...
TED:	*(TO WORLD)* I never know what to say to him when he comes out with things like that ... Then he says to me ... Sitting at the table ...
LES:	God ... I *like* you ... You *know* that... Christ knows the characters I've come across Ted. But *you* I like ...
TED:	*(TO WORLD)* Got a kind of way of dodging that ... I said to him *(TO LES)* That's good ... *You* liking me ... You're right ... I'm a very likeable character ... *I* find that too ...
LES:	... God ... Close the door a minute, Ted ... ... Where are they all ... ... Got five minutes on our own ... Christ! ... You won't believe this ... ... Listen.. You got a whisky or anything ... ... Teddy ... I'm down ... I'm not in good shape.
TED:	Got some South African Sherry ...
LES:	Give me a glass ... Teddy, man ... ... Come Here ...
TED:	I'm getting you the sherry ...
LES:	Sitting here ... Ted ... No idea ... The *peace* ... ...Oh ... The week I've put in, Ted ... The *week* ... Jesus ... Telling you ... Rather be in the jungle in

bloody Malaya with the wogs spraying you with machine guns ... and rockets ... Than the week I've put in with Irene .. I can't understand that ... Can *you* understand that ...?

TED: You haven't told me ...

LES: I want to talk to you ... Ted ... That sherry's *diabolical* ...

TED: I know ...

LES: I want to take you out for a drink after the practice. You come out for a drink with me ... I need to talk to you ... My *wife* ... I can't understand my wife going round the bend like that ... can you?

TED: Oh ... She going round the bend ...

LES: Out of her *mind*! .... Out of her *total mind*! ... You don't know ... her ... Do you? ... No. You don't know her ... You should meet her ... She'd like you ... She'd fancy you ... Fancies all kinds of queer characters ... I mean ... I don't mean ... she'd fancy you because you're a queer character ...!

TED: *(TO WORLD)* You see ... That woman ... Carol ... She's such a straight, honest woman ... The way she lets me in on what's happening from the very first smile Les gave her ... Every cup of coffee she has with him ... Minute he smiles at her ... She comes back and tells me about it ... Comes in from work, that afternoon, ten months ago, full of it, ... Never seen her like that for year's. Like a young lass ...

CAROL: Ted, pet ... You'll never believe this ... I've *scored* ... This afternoon ... A Sergeant Major.

TED: Fell for the uniform ...

CAROL: No ... He doesn't do anything for me ...

TED: *(TO WORLD)* For the *minute* ... wait on ...

CAROL: *He* fancies *me* ...

TED: That's good

CAROL: He lives in one of the houses across the road from the home ...

TED: Made yer day ...

CAROL: Listen to me ... I'm going into the home ... This morning ... He's coming out of his house ...Lovely and smart ... He's got a red Maxi ... Lovely car... All dolled up in his uniform

(LES APPEARS, AS SHE'S DESCRIBING HIM)

Sees me across the street ... And gives me this smile ...

(LES SMILES AT HER)

TED: Oh ...

CAROL: That's all ... It was probably being like with the street between us ... Him smiling at me .... You could imagine like music ... in a picture ... couldn't you...?

TED: Could you?

CAROL: You know what I mean ...

TED: Love at first sight ...

CAROL: He just smiled at me ... Are you getting jealous, pet? ... Eee ... You're not getting jealous ... Just a smile ...

TED: I don't think so ... *(TO WORLD)* Bloody *was* ...

CAROL:	I smiled back at him ... That's all ... ... Listen ... Don't get jealous.
TED:	Right ...*(TO WORLD)* How do you do that?
CAROL:	Are you not ...
TED:	No.. .
CAROL:	You are ...
TED:	I don't know ... *(TO WORLD)* ...Week later ... Mind... I was getting *worried* ...
CAROL:	*(TO TED)* ... I don't know how he found out I was Secretary of a Jazz Band ... I was coming out the home ... He was just getting out of his car ... This time ... He crossed over to me ... Eee ... I didn't know *what* he was going to say ... It was a bit like fate ... Ted, love ...
TED:	*(TO HIMSELF)* Oh ... Jesus ... Oh ... God ...Bloody hell ... What's happening now ... *(TO HER)* Fate ..?
CAROL:	Listen to this, Ted ...
TED:	Fate ...?
LES:	Excuse me ... You're Mrs. Dunn ... Aren't you? ... I hope you don't mind me talking to you like this.
CAROL:	*(TO TED)* I didn't know what was coming next ..But it was ... Listen ... It was just like ...he'd come just at the right moment ...
LES:	I heard ... You run a Jazz Band, Mrs Dunn ... I wanted a word with you about it ...
CAROL:	*(TO LES)* That's right ... The Saints ... We've been running it for nearly seven years ...
LES:	I've just got back to Newcastle ...
CAROL:	Oh ... I thought I hadn't seen your face before ...
TED:	Interesting conversation the pair of you had ...
LES:	I'm working in a Recruiting Office ... They were saying ... You run a Jazz Band ...
CAROL:	That's right ...
LES:	To tell you the truth ... Mrs Dunn ... I'm Les ... by the way ... Les Bilbert ... Am I keeping you back ...
CAROL:	Just on my way home ...
TED:	What is he after.
CAROL:	*(TO TED)* I'm telling you, it's like fate ... Do you know what he wanted ... You'll never believe this ...
TED:	I've got a good idea!
LES:	To tell the truth. Mrs. Dunn. You'll find that ... I'm a straight bloke ... come right to the point ... Few Saturdays ago ... I was judging at a Jazz Band Carnival .. Boss was asked ... But he couldn't do it .. .Gave me the job ...First time I'd been at a Carnival ... I'll tell you what I was going to ask you ...
CAROL:	Listen to this, Ted ...
LES:	Do you need any help ... drilling the kids in your band ... I fancy doing something like that ... You see ... Since they stuck me in this office ... I miss that ... Bit of action ...

CAROL:	Train the Saints ...
LES:	That's it...
CAROL:	Would you like to *do* that ... Train a band ...
LES:	Watching some of the kids at that carnival .. You know, Mrs Dunn...? ...I could see ... With the nowse I have ... the experience ... You could really do something with these kids ...
CAROL:	I don't know *what* to say...
LES:	I mean ... If you don't think it's a good idea ...
CAROL:	..No .. I'm just .. What it is .. Sergeant Major ... I'll tell you .. It's just like you're the answer to our prayer... We're *desperate* for a good trainer ... We've an old man ... I think he was in the Crimean War ... We've to pay for a taxi to get him to the school ... to keep his strength for the practice..
	(TO TED) What are you looking at us like that for, pet? ..I know .. Apart from getting him to train the band .. I like him... I've never known any soldiers before.. Are you getting jealous... There's nowt to get jealous about .. He's married, Ted... ..I like him...
	...I'll tell you what it is.. He's dead straight.. and honest ..
TED:	You fancy him?
CAROL:	*You're* a nicer looking chap than he is.. So you don't need to worry on that score.. do you...?
TED:	Carol.. Listen.. It's good for you ... People fancying you... Gives you a lift.. No question about it .. Look at you... Given you a real lift... ...hasn't it...
CAROL:	It has... You're right...
	... Hasn't it...
TED:	Don't worry about *me*...
CAROL:	Alright... If you stop telling me *not* to... The main thing is... Getting him for the Saints, Teddy... Imagine... A *real* Sergeant Major ... Training the kids...
TED:	That's good... That's very good
	...That's a big thing.. I mean...
	...It's a total waste of time, as far as I'm concerned... Bunch of kids marching up and down in a field... I cannot imagine any more futile way of passing a Saturday... But that's alright.. People have got to do *something* to burn their days up...
CAROL:	It's harmless... isn't it..
TED:	It is... You're right... To the best of my knowledge there has been no record of Jazz Bands inflicting any serious damage on each other... despite their uniforms... Jazz Bands have no weapons... They might give you a bit of pain in the eardrums and in the arse at times... But Jazz Bands carry no weapons...
WENDY:	*(CALLING)* You there, Teddy...
TED:	*(TO WORLD)* In the kitchen, making a cup of tea for Les, sorting out all that in my mind, Wendy turns up. Looking for me. Bound to be, isn't she... I'm what they call one of them magnetic personalities.. The whole world's attracted to me...Wendy wants to talk to me...First thing she says...
WENDY:	I want to talk to you a minute, Teddy.

TED:	*(TO WORLD)* ... Beginning to feel like one of them Gurus in India...Maybe that's what I am... First Geordie Guru... Christ... I might *BE* Good lass, Wendy,... Christ knows how she comes to be drum major of the Saints... Sensible, intelligent lass like her... But that's people, isn't it... Never add up, looking at them from the outside... Always some kink in them, somewhere...
WENDY:	Ted... Your Peter gets on my wick at times... What's the matter with him...
TED:	*(TO WORLD)* ... And he comes in... In his armour... Ready for the fray... Look at him... Look at her... How does a lad like that get hold of a lovely lass like Wendy... Look at her... Now... *Her*... I fancy her ... I love that lass... I mean... I wouldn't do anything *about* it... But there's something about her...
PETER:	I'm blowing...
WENDY:	Blow... Blow...
PETER:	See you tomorrow night ... Right?
WENDY:	See you *tonight*...
PETER:	*Nuh*...
WENDY:	*Yeah* ... *(TO TED)* See what I mean...
LES:	*(DOORWAY)* You alright there ... want a hand...
TED:	Only making a *cup* of *tea* Les...
LES:	Listen... If you happen to bump into my wife... Wendy... I'd better tell you... I'm supposed to be in Aldershot... I'll explain to you... later... It's a bit complicated Wendy... Could I talk to Ted a minute...
WENDY:	*I'm* talking to him...
PETER:	I'm off...
WENDY:	No... You're not... *(BLOCKING DOORWAY)*
LES:	Could you not have your fight in the other room ...
TED:	What you doing in Aldershot...?
LES:	That's right... Aldershot...
TED:	What you doing there?
PETER:	*(LOOKING AT HIS CHAINS)* Them chains are not right.
WENDY:	Tell your *Dad*... Go *on*... See what *he* thinks..
LES:	*(TO TED)* I'm not going there...
PETER:	Aldershot's army headquarters... Isn't it ... Les...
WENDY:	*(TO PETER)* Don't dodge the question...
PETER:	I'm talking about *Aldershot* ...
TED:	You're off to Aldershot...
PETER:	*(TO LES)* Can't get them right, them chains. *(BEGINS TO ADJUST THEM)*
WENDY:	What about the Carnival, tomorrow.
LES:	I'm not *going* to Aldershot...
TED:	That's alright, then...

WENDY:	What did you say you were going for in the first place?
LES:	Could I talk to Ted a minute...
WENDY:	*I'm* talking to him...
PETER:	I'm off...
WENDY:	*(BLOCKING HIM)* Nuh... I'm *talking* to you...
PETER:	Thought you were talking to my *Dad*...
LES:	*(TO WENDY)* Just you bump into my wife... time to time... In the street... Wendy...
WENDY:	*(TO PETER) Tell* him... Go on...
PETER:	Nowt to tell... I'm *late*, Wendy, man...
WENDY:	Tell him you're finishing with me... Go on...
TED:	Is he?
PETER:	Is that how I had them chains before, Wendy?
TED:	Peter... Stand still and listen to me...
PETER:	I'm trying to get my *chains* right, man...
TED:	Listen to me. Are you listening to me... A simple question. I know it's very *difficult* answering people's questions. Just have a *try*, Peter... Right, Son?... I don't blame you... It's very *difficult speaking to people*... I *know* that... *I* find it very difficult speaking to people.
LES:	Ted... I'm in a bit of a jam,.. You see...
TED:	You're not going to Aldershot...
LES:	That's it...
WENDY:	Gives me a rotten kid...
TED:	*(TO WORLD)* She shouldn't have *said* that to Les in *his* delicate state... Les was not to *know* that... Only one, who knew it was me... as the Citizens' Advice Bureau... The poor soul had enough to handle without that... He was saying...
LES:	Wendy... God... Wait on... Oh, Jesus...
WENDY:	Gives me a rotten kid... then wants to finish with me...
LES:	...Jesus... Wendy... I'm *talking* to you...
WENDY:	Les... Let me talk to Ted... will you... You can't talk about things like that with *you*.
PETER:	I'm *not* finishing with you, man... That's a rotten, effin bloody lie...
TED:	That's what I want to know...
LES:	Wait on... One thing at a time... Wendy... You don't mean... Let's get this straight...
WENDY:	Les... Go on... Do me a favour... piss *off* a minute will you...
LES:	Wendy... I am not having language from any member of my band. ... Are you *pregnant*... that's all I want to know...
TED:	A *bit* pregnant... Nothing to worry about... Don't worry about it...
PETER:	How would I do that... Finish with you... I bastardin effin rotten bloody flaming love you... I rotten *love* you, you stupid rotten bitch!
WENDY:	Wouldn't rotten think so... would you...?

LES:	I don't understand that... I'm not with you, *How* a *bit* pregnant...?
TED:	It's alright... Don't worry about it... A *bit*...
PETER:	Wendy, man...I'll miss me mates...
LES:	How a *bit*?
PETER:	Three months gone... It's not *my* fault...
WENDY:	Like... I did it meself... How do you do that? ... Like the Virgin Mary...
PETER:	*(TO WENDY INDICATING CHAINS) That* how I had them before?
LES:	God... Wait a minute... three months gone... Wendy... I know these things happen...
WENDY:	*(TO PETER)* Sleeping here tonight... Right?
PETER:	Please yourself... Not sleeping in *my* room...
WENDY:	*(TO TED)* There you are... You see?
LES:	I don't understand what the whole argument is about... All I know is I am in a bad jam... I'm in trouble... and on top of everything else... Wendy gets pregnant on me... I make the Saints the top band in the north... and my drum major gets herself three months pregnant...
WENDY:	You *hear* him, Ted?
PETER:	Hear what? Not my rotten fault, you got yourself up the spout is it?
TED:	How is it not your fault, son?... I don't *get* that son...
LES:	We're talking about the *world championship! White City!*... This August... We're going to be *Junior World Champions*... And you're *three months gone*, Wendy...!
WENDY:	I know, Les, That's the one thing that makes me sick, having a kid... You not reckon I might get through...
LES:	Seven months gone... Leading the band... Wendy, man...
TED:	*(TO WORLD)* I still had to clear up this... *(TO PETER)* How is it not your *fault*, son?
LES:	I'm in trouble... I'm in big trouble... No question about it...
WENDY:	*(TO TED)* I mixed up me pills... That's all... I got me weeks mixed up...
PETER:	See what I mean... Marked on the rotten packet, isn't it? The days... Isn't it? So thick you can't rotten read the rotten days.
WENDY:	Piss off!
PETER:	You won't rotten *let* me.
LES:	Let him go out with his mates, Wendy... Have you got any aspirins...
TED:	In there... Take your pick... Everything in there... Aspirins... Valiums... Take a Valium – calm you down.
LES:	I *might* do... Are they any good...
PETER:	I don't rotten understand you, man... What's *wrong* with us getting rotten *married* ...?
WENDY:	I'll tell you tonight... In *bed*... *You know* what's wrong with it...
PETER:	Nuh...
WENDY:	I rotten flaming rotten love you... What you on about... That's just stupid rotten flaming blackmail. Isn't it, Ted?

TED:	If I knew what you were talking about...
PETER:	I don't feel like it anyway... not tonight
WENDY:	You getting it from some other lass... I'm rotten warning you... I'll *destroy* you... I'll *slaughter* you... You go with any other lass... Bloody had enough of that.
LES:	You see... What it is... Are you listening to me, Ted... I don't know where to turn... I am lost... You've no idea how lost I am ... It's like... Jesus... You've no idea what it's like,.. It's like... I'm caught in the middle of a storm... All round me... Not a rock... a bit of solid ground... round me... *(TAKES ANOTHER VALIUM)*...
TED:	They're not jelly babies... them... you know...
LES:	No...
PETER:	I haven't got another lass you know that... I bloody love you... you stupid *rotten cow*...
WENDY:	Why are you not sleeping with me tonight then ...
PETER:	You know rotten why...
WENDY:	That's blackmail...
PETER:	What's *wrong* with gettin rotten married...
LES:	Irene... my wife... *You* know my wife... Wendy...
WENDY:	I don't want to get married and tied to you, yet... I'm too *young* to get married...
PETER:	*Right*... Alright...
TED:	*(TO WORLD)* That was interesting... People interest me... Couldn't work that out... Like she was too young to get married... But it was alright having a kid...
WENDY:	So that's it... When we feel like it... We'll get married...
PETER:	*I* feel like it now...
WENDY:	Just because you want to grab me and get a hold of me. ...I don't want anybody to get a hold of me, yet... That's all...
PETER:	I rotten love you...
WENDY:	... You're a rotten flaming liar...
LES:	Wendy... You know my wife... I'm saying...
WENDY:	*(TO TED)* Isn't it? Rotten blackmail... Him saying... I'm not sleeping with you any more... till you marry us...
PETER:	Let me go to me mates, Wendy.
WENDY:	Are you sorry?
PETER:	Yeah...
WENDY:	Rotten aren't.
PETER:	I'm very sorry... What rotten *for*...
TED:	*(TO WORLD)* Linda started shouting from the stairs for me. It was getting too much for her... Waiting to talk to me... I left them all to work it out without me... She was wearing a new skirt she'd bought that week... and a sweater...

LINDA: Ted, love... What are you doing down there... I need to talk to you before I go to the practice... What do you think?

TED: Lovely...

LINDA: Not think it shows me boobs too much?

TED: Fine...

LINDA: Pet... What should I do about Jackie? He's got me all mixed up... I don't know *where* I am, now, love. I know Sheila's got her own boy friend. But that still doesn't mean it's right, taking a man away from his wife and kids, is it?

    (UP JAZZ BAND)

TED: I don't know, Linda, man... I've told you... It's a difficult question...

LINDA: I don't know *where* I am, love... What do you think I should do?

TED: You see... It's been going on for a long time, hasn't it...

LINDA: I shouldn't have got that flat, should I Teddy? Should never have started with him in the first place...

    (LIGHTS ON BENCH IN BYKER WALL...)

TED: *(GOING TO JACKIE...)*

    So the two of you are sitting on the bench... In Byker Wall... You and Linda...

    (LINDA GOES TO JOIN JACKIE...)

TED: Comes to me allotment to tell me all about it... Couple of months after we were finished at the yard... An entirely different world then... Another planet... Five year's back, for God's sake!... Shook you in them days, a lass having it off with another woman's bloke...

JACKIE: Lovely place, Byker Wall... Trees all over the place and gardens... She's sitting there... Her hair done... And that scent she puts on... I mean, she is... Isn't she? Jesus... She's a *lovely* woman.

    (UP JAZZ BAND)

    (LINDA IS SITTING ON THE BENCH ... IN THE COURT OF BYKER WALL..)

TED: Should get the prevention of Cruelty to Music society on to them... What they do to the Saints... I used to love that song.

JACKIE: They weren't playing the Saints... They were playing Puppet on a String...

TED: Any song... Certain death... Minute they touch it...

JACKIE: So I go up to her... Very politely... You know... But straight to the point, mind... Never know when Pam'll turn up... and interrupt...
    (TO LINDA) ... Linda... I hope you don't mind me asking you this... I know you've a week off at Race Week... I'll tell you what it is...

LINDA: Sit down beside me a minute... I don't like people talking to me standing over me...

LINDA: What I was thinking... I was thinking of going to Scotland.

LINDA: Be nice... Never been to Scotland... You know that...

JACKIE: That's what I mean... you know... If you don't mind me asking...

LINDA: Jackie... What do you keep saying that for...?

JACKIE: I'm saying... If you don't mind me asking...

LINDA:	Asking what?
JACKIE:	Talking about Scotland...
LINDA:	What's the *matter* with you, Jackie?
JACKIE:	*Me?*
LINDA:	It doesn't matter.
JACKIE:	You and *me*... Linda... Known each other for years... haven't we... *(TO TED)* Blew it! ... Because she twigs right away what I'm after and jumps on me...
LINDA:	Jackie... You're not trying to make a pass at me, are you, for God's sake...
JACKIE:	*Me?*
LINDA:	*Are* you?
JACKIE:	I'm talking about Scotland... Going to Scotland...
LINDA:	What's brought that out, all of a sudden, like... Jackie...
JACKIE:	I'm telling you... I'm getting my new car... next week... Race week... it'll be all run in... You know... red Cortina...
LINDA:	Jackie... Don't act the idiot... Like... You know... I might be a lass... But lasses have got it *up* as well as down... Now... Come on... What are you saying?... You want me to go to Scotland with you?
JACKIE:	*(TO TED)* See... had it all worked out... You know. And she comes out with this funny question...
LINDA:	What *for*, Jackie?
JACKIE:	Whole thing, man, was going haywire... Didn't know where I was... Made a big mistake... Jesus... It's not easy getting women... is it? What I did... I took her hand... Sitting there, in the middle of the wall... With like millions of old age pensioners round us... Looking down at us from the flats... I grabbed her hand... Bloody pulled it away from me...
LINDA:	What are you doing, Jackie? For God's sake... What's the *matter* with you...
JACKIE:	*(TO TED)* Dropped one brick after the other... Next brick... Listen to this... *(TO LINDA)* Listen, man... Tell you something. I've fallen for you... That's what it is... First time I started to help with the Saints... And you said to me... You liked the drumming routine I was doing... I *fell* for you...
LINDA:	Jackie... You haven't... Have you?
JACKIE:	I have, man...
LINDA:	How *could* you have, man...
JACKIE:	I have...
LINDA:	*How* have you
JACKIE:	I don't *know* how I have... People fall for people... Look at you... Lovely figure... Got a girl's figure... Figure like a young lass...
LINDA:	You're having me on...
JACKIE:	You have, man... You've a young lasses figure.
LINDA:	I know I've good figure... I'm talking about *you*... *Falling* for me...
LINDA:	That's it... Lovely face... Look at your face.

JACKIE:	Leave me alone, will you...
JACKIE:	Linda... If I've offended you... Listen to me... Honestly... The way I look up to you.
LINDA:	You listen to me... I'm not having it... I'm finished falling for men... and being sucked rotten dry by them... I've finished with that stupid game... Just leave me alone ...
JACKIE:	*(TO TED)* This is the funny thing that happens... you see... Teddy... I didn't think I had this in me... The funny thing is... How is that? ...Don't ask me. Been going around with her for years... and it never happened before... I *liked* her... Not only did I want to get her clothes off pronto you know... and have it off with her... I *liked* her. Christ... I says to myself... I like her... I tell you something... That's the first woman I've ever liked... I said to her *(TO LINDA)* Listen... Linda... You're right, man... I'll stop buggering about... You're right... I haven't fallen for you like I want you to run away with me for ever... Just for a week... Bit of a laugh... You know that... I fancy you, man... That's all... I fancy you...
LINDA:	Do you? *(EYES LIT NOW ... RELAXED)*... You *do*... don't you, Jackie.
JACKIE:	Telling you.
LINDA:	You're a lying rotten bastard aren't you... trying to get round me... like that...
JACKIE:	You know what I mean...
LINDA:	You want me to go to Scotland with you?
JACKIE:	What do you think?
LINDA:	What about Sheila?
JACKIE:	She's *had* her holidays, man... hasn't she... I mean... I've all the time in the world... This brand new Cortina ... Red... See it... Getting a car radio fitted... I'm loaded... just now... aren't I... And on my own... Nobody to go off with...
LINDA:	Aww...
JACKIE:	I haven't... We've been married eighteen years, Linda, man... and never looked at another lass... Have I? I'm entitled to a bit of a break... aren't I?
LINDA:	Is that all it is...
JACKIE:	Telling you... Bit of a laugh together...
LINDA:	Tell you this... This I will give you, Jackie... You're not a bad looking fellow for your age...
JACKIE:	I know...
LINDA:	I know you know...
JACKIE:	What do you say?
LINDA:	Eee... I don't know... I don't honestly know, Jackie... I've done all kinds of things in me time... But something like this...
JACKIE:	Just for a week... A laugh... Hotels... Go to Loch Lomond...
LINDA:	The whole thing's giving me a funny feeling... I don't know where I am... for the minute... Just leave me alone for a bit...
JACKIE:	What do you think?

TED:	I was thinking about my hothouse...
JACKIE:	What do you think... about *Sheila*... If Linda goes with us...
TED:	Your *wife*... I wouldn't think about your wife... Jackie.. That complicates the whole issue... You're right... You don't want to *think* about your wife...
JACKIE:	You're right...
TED:	I'm not thinking about your wife... You are going into dangerous territory when you think about wives, before committing adultery... Verboten... Wives... Husbands...
JACKIE:	You're right.
TED:	You see... *me* ... *You*... Paradise... Your idea of paradise... I can see that... and I can understand it... Is a hotel bedroom with Linda beside you with no clothes on...
JACKIE:	It is... You're right... Paradise... a week... man ...In my Cortina... Radio on... speeding up North... The two of us...
TED:	That's a lovely picture... I know... what I was thinking, was... Just now... I don't seem to have sex paradises... That's funny... isn't it... My idea of paradise... you know what it is... Me... In my glasshouse... Full of flowers and green plants. In a deckchair... sun shining... Reading a good book... with a bottle of booze... and ginger ale...
JACKIE:	I can see that... That's alright, too...
TED:	It's coming... you know... Next month... it'll be up and I'll have me deck chair... Plants... I'm not sure about... I mean... four thousand quid redundancy money, Jackie!
JACKIE:	Reckon she'll come... what do you think?... If she, doesn't... Teddy, an... What am I going to do.. For Christ's sake...
LINDA:	Are you there, pet?
TED:	*(TO PEOPLE)* Of course he's there. The Citizens' Advice Bureau stays open day and night...
LINDA:	I don't think he's after me... is he?... He's your mate... Teddy... Do *you* think he's after me... Him and Sheila are alright... aren't they... I mean ... This is just a bit of fun for him and me...
TED:	You know that... Linda, man... You can't guarantee anything about anything... Can you... What's going to happen... Where people are involved... A bloke and a lass. Very explosive mixture, that...
LINDA:	I've never *been* to Scotland...
TED:	Scotland is very good... You'd like Scotland... I mean... I was thinking the two of us would go to Whitley Bay for a day... maybe... and Gosforth Park... But Scotland's a better proposition entirely.
LINDA:	You not think I should go...? What do you think I should do... I'm sure he hasn't... you see... Teddy... He hasn't fallen for me... You can tell...
TED:	See... I've got this saying... please yourself and you're guaranteed one satisfied customer...
LINDA:	You're right, pet...
TED:	I doubt it... too straightforward that, nothing straightforward in this world... Most the time, I get so mixed up with what everybody *else* wants me to do, I can't be sure *what I* want.

LINDA:	Teddy... I feel like *going*...
TED:	There you are... That shows you, you can't say anything for sure about anything... doesn't it...
LINDA:	What do *you* think I should do? I mean... Sheila's working all that week... I'm not taking anything away from her... am I... I'm borrowing her man... that's all... For a week... and I'll tell you sometimes... Teddy, Pet, It's not the sex thing... I mean sometimes... it's alright...sometimes it's a waste of time and gets on me nerves... I don't think I'm all that sexy a character... I don't think so... I mean... I'd quite look forward to it... But I'm not expecting all that much... You know what it is... I'd love a few nights with a man's arms round me... Beside me in bed... That's what I want... Teddy, love... Go to sleep with a nice bloke beside me... and wake up with him... Just for a few days, even...
TED:	There you are then...
LINDA:	Times, the idea of him being with me all the time and not having to run back to Sheila... You know what I mean, Teddy... I've got to tell her... By next week... If I'm taking the flat or not, Teddy...
	I just don't seem to be able to make up my mind, pet... *What* I want to do... I don't *know*... Do you know what I mean... It's terrible...
TED:	*(TO WORLD)* She was just saying that when Carol shouted for me... From top of the stairs... Not a good voice... Panic voice...
CAROL:	Teddy... where are you... come up here a minute... where's Linda...?
TED:	*(TO WORLD)* Pair of us went up to her... Jackie was with her... In the bedroom... turned up for the practice... Les had just told him about Wendy... Got a problem... Jackie has... Got *dozens* of problems... One is... Never can keep owt to himself...
JACKIE:	You know what's Les's just told me... this is unbelievable... Teddy... why didn't you tell me... I thought the kids had that game all sussed out... Never had any of these problems... They get G.C.E's for them in school... don't they... sex...
TED:	*(TO WORLD)* I knew that... they didn't... *(TO JACKIE)* They *don't* get G.C.E's in sex, Jackie... Not yet... Maybe *next* year...
JACKIE:	They get it in school... *My* kids get it in school. I can't believe it... Sitting there... in the scullery... I say... I can't understand that... How it could happen... Les says, Don't *talk* about it... Les is not in good shape... have you seen him Carol... That man has aged ... Ten years... You should see him.. I said to him... Les... take it easy... He said something about Aldershot... Might've been called up... I said to him... What's it... A red Alert...
TED:	*(TO WORLD)* Carol was getting into a state... Listening to him... everybody was. *I knew* what it was about... and *I* was getting into a state... She said to him...
CAROL:	Jackie... What are you talking about...?
LINDA:	What's the matter with Les...?
LINDA:	You mean, *Wendy*...
CAROL:	Is it *Wendy*, now...
JACKIE:	How could it be, *Les*, like?

LINDA:	Why couldn't it be Les?
TED:	*(TO WORLD)* One of these stupid round and round conversations getting nowhere... In the end... They'd find out in another minute... So I told them... People will always surprise you ... Linda's face went all soft... and flushed a bit...
LINDA:	Ee... Is she... *Wendy*...
TED:	*(TO WORLD)* Carol said...
CAROL:	How many months?
TED:	Three ...
LINDA:	Ee... Isn't that lovely...
TED:	*(TO WORLD)* Everybody troops downstairs to see the happy mother-to-be... Carol and Linda rush to Wendy... Carol has her arms round her... Loves that lass... Les's eyes are looking very funny... Jackie's right... He's aged... looks ten years older than me... serves the rotten swine right... No it doesn't... Bloody *does*!
CAROL:	*(ARMS ROUND WENDY)* Wendy, pet... Eee... Wendy, darling...
LINDA:	Are you alright, love?
LES:	Carol... I told you I got this letter from training... For a week's course in Aldershot...
CAROL:	Wendy... what are we going to do, pet...
WENDY:	It's alright, Carol...
CAROL:	Ee... Wendy... I don't know *what* we should do...
LES:	I told Irene I had to go to Aldershot.
CAROL:	Les... She's having a baby... *(TO WENDY)* Was it an accident, pet...? It would be an accident... Three months, Jackie says...
WENDY:	Something like that... It's alright... Don't worry about it, Carol...
CAROL:	Ee... Will you have to marry him, now...
TED:	She's not marrying him...
JACKIE:	She's going to miss The White City... *(TO WENDY)* You're going to miss the world championship...
LES:	I'm going to miss it, too...
LINDA:	How are you going to miss it...
LES:	Don't ask, Linda... Don't *ask*... for Christ's sake... I'm in trouble, Carol...
CAROL:	Teddy, pet.... what are we going to do...?
LES:	What I was going to ask you... Carol... I got this letter for a course in Aldershot... Thank God... If I wouldn't have got it... Things have come to a head, Carol...
JACKIE:	That's what I'm talking about, Linda.. we've got to make a move.... One way or the other.. *(TO LES)* Linda's got this flat above the shop... She can move in tomorrow...
LINDA:	*(TO CAROL)* Will I make you a cup of tea, love...
TED:	She's had fourteen cups of tea... Go for her bladder if she has any more...

JACKIE:	I mean... we can't, can we, Carol...? Carry on like this, Linda and me, much longer... ...We should move into that flat together and settle ourselves down like a normal couple... Shouldn't we?
LES:	Wait a minute, Jackie... *(TO CAROL)* Irene's gone out of her mind, Carol... I mean... she hasn't gone out of her mind. But as far as you and me are concerned... She, can't stand it... She won't let me see you again... That's what I'm talking about...
TED:	What are you doing here, now, then?
JACKIE:	He's going to Aldershot... that's where you're going, isn't it, Les?
LES:	I'm not going to bastardin Aldershot!
JACKIE:	Where *are* you going, then?
LES:	I told you... I don't know where I'm going... I'm in trouble...
CAROL:	What's brought this about, all of a sudden, pet? She's never bothered up till now, has she?
LES:	Don't ask, Carol. I can't tell you. It's unbelievable. You'd never believe it. ... Ted... I'm in bad trouble.. Christ... This isn't happening to *me*? Jesus it isn't is it?..
JACKIE:	I'm telling you, Les... I'm in exactly the same boat... It's like you're at the crossroads, isn't it?
LES:	Is it?
WENDY:	I'm not bothered... One way or the other.. Having a baby... Be alright...
CAROL:	Are you taking plenty milk, pet?
WENDY:	I *hate* milk.
LINDA:	Les... You're not having jealousy problems with Irene are you?
CAROL:	He's not... is he? Les... You aren't... There's nowt for her to be jealous about...
LES:	that's it... That's what I'm telling you, man... That's the whole bloody point... Thank God I had this letter... For a training course in Aldershot...
JACKIE:	He *is* going to Aldershot.
TED:	I don't think he's *going* to Aldershot...
LINDA:	Les... I thought you and Irene had that all worked out years back... *You* went with who *you* fancied... *she* went her way... I really admired you for that.
LES:	I got this letter... From Aldershot... Right...
LINDA:	I looked up to you... In that respect... I did... I thought that was a very sensible arrangement for the way couples are nowadays...
LES:	Thank Christ I got this letter...
JACKIE:	From Aldershot...
CAROL:	I don't understand, Les, pet... What's she *jealous* About, for God's sake...
LES:	That's what I'm telling you, Carol, man... She's going off her rocker...
WENDY:	I love him...
CAROL:	I know you do, pet.
WENDY:	I can't help it.

JACKIE:	I mean... Irene's got another *bloke*, hasn't she?
LINDA:	I thought she'd two or three...
TED:	You not think you should let Les tell you what was in the letter?
LES:	*(GIVING UP)* Forget it.
WENDY:	I'm not getting *married*.
JACKIE:	That's up to you.
WENDY:	I might be *daft* but I'm not daft as *all* that
CAROL:	Ee... I know he's my own lad and I love him, pet... But you can't marry him... He's not good enough for you, love.
JACKIE:	We've got to do *something*, haven't we? Can't go on for ever like bloody this? Can we?
LINDA:	What do you want to do then, Jackie... *You* tell *me* ... What do *you* want to do...
WENDY:	Carol... I love him...
CAROL:	I know... I don't know what we're going to do...
TED:	*(TRYING AGAIN)* Right... You got this letter... from Aldershot Les?
CAROL:	What did it say, pet?
LINDA:	Isn't it time we were on our way?
LES:	It said "Report for a week's training"... came in the nick of time... she was driving me round the bend...
CAROL:	So you're *going* to Aldershot.
LES:	That's what I'm trying to tell you... I'm not going... I put them off... *She* thinks I've gone... Anything to get away from her for a few days... what I'm saying to you is... Christ knows why... But she's suddenly flipping on me... Barring me from seeing you again... that's what I'm talking about...
CAROL:	I don't understand that... Do *you* understand that?
TED:	*(TO WORLD)* Easy enough to understand, isn't it... Good news... I was getting shot of the bastard at last... I said to her *(TO CAROL)* He's having problems with his wife... that's all... He's got to give up the friendship... probably best thing, all round...
CAROL:	How is it the best thing all round?
LES:	She wants me to give up training the Saints, too... I've got to finish with them... for good...
JACKIE:	What I don't understand, Les, is why you've got to go to Aldershot because your wife's going round the bend.
LES:	I'm not *going* to bloody *Aldershot*, I keep *telling* you... I'm going *to* the bloody *Gosforth Park Hotel*... For the *weekend*... to straighten things out in my head...
CAROL:	Ee.. Les, pet... Is it as bad as that?
JACKIE:	*(TO LINDA)* I'm just saying, Linda... We've to do bloody *something*... Haven't we?
LINDA:	Alright, Jackie... What?
LES:	He's right... Something's got to be done.
LINDA:	I'm saying... *What*?

LES: You're *right*, Linda... Christ you are...

TED: *(TO WORLD)* They're all sitting there... lost, poor lost souls... all of them... I took a banana from the fruit bowl on the table... they were all black from lying there for days... *(TO EVERYBODY)* They're alright inside... *(TO WORLD)* They just sat there... all of them... staring at the bowl of black bananas when the doorbell rang...

          (TO WORLD) Jean next door had Dopey on the 'phone for me. I went to the 'phone... Carol went white.

CAROL: Something's happened to Peter. I know.

TED: *(TO WORLD)* She was right. Carol was sitting there when I got back.. Waiting for the worst... *(TO CAROL)* It's not *too* bad...

CAROL: What's happened, for God's sake?

TED: He hasn't been run over by a bus or anything... The Police have charged him with something... But he's not in the Police Station.

CAROL: Dear God in heaven... What's he done?

TED: You know what kids are like... Can never get owt off them... What's happened, I think, is Peter bashed in some old bloke in Ryehill.

CAROL: My God!

TED: It's alright. He's not too bad. He's just in hospital.

CAROL: Where's *Peter* I'm bloody asking you.

TED: I'm telling you. He's in hospital... The old bloke hit him over the head with a hammer.

ACT TWO

PETER AND JAGUAR ADVANCING ON EACH OTHER

JAGUAR: Right! Come on Shithead!... I'm gonna rotten *do* you!

PETER: Jag, man... What the shit you on about, for Christ's sake! What's this rotten for...

JAG: Don't give me that shit, you know what it's rotten for

PETER: *(TURNING TO TED)* I didn't know, Dad, man... Know what I mean? How the shit *would* I know?

TED: *(TO WORLD)* I picked up Peter at the General... All he had was a bit of plaster on the side of his head... That got on me nerves... I was looking forward all day to a quiet night in me allotment while they were at the Band Practice and I end up buggering about in the bloody General... But he had seven stitches, it turned out... He told me...

PETER: Seven stitches, Dad... And maybe concussion...

TED: *(TO WORLD)* So I swung round the other way... and started blaming myself for being a selfish bastard wrapped up in myself...
(TO PETER) You alright, then, son...
(TO WORLD) How *could* he be alright... He had seven stitches in his scalp... and concussion...

PETER: I've got seven stitches...

TED: We'll get a taxi...

PETER: I want to *talk* to you, Dad... Man... I don't want a taxi... Look man... I'm getting these heavy vibrations from you, Dad... Know what I mean... You're going *heavy* on us...

TED: Peter, that's not what's *happening*, son. I'm just getting a *taxi*...

PETER: Trying to *talk* to you, man... What do you keep going on about rotten bastardin taxis for!

TED: You're *white*, son. I'm just getting you a taxi, because you're white and I don't want you to collapse on me... going home.

PETER: I want a cup of coffee... That's what I want...

TED: *(TO WORLD)* So we went over to the Bowling Alley across the road... To the cafe there... I didn't like that bowling alley cafe... Bloody Les and Carol... go there odd times...
(TO PETER) You want a coffee or a tea...

PETER: I don't know...
...*Shit*! ... Bloody *shit*, Dad... Oh... *Jesus! Shit!*

TED: I'll get you a tea *and* a coffee...

PETER: Dad, man... I'm getting very heavy vibrations off you.

TED: What do you mean? *(TO WORLD)* Oh... God... He was my kid... I looked at him... White... in trouble... Lost... Christ... No question about it... I loved that kid... whatever that means... Christ knows why! Could be because he was my kid... What it was, too... Despite him being a shithead... as he said... he was a lovable kind of a character... I said to him again... Because you had to work very hard at getting to his meaning...
(TO PETER) Peter, man... I know... I know you think everybody's

getting at you and blaming you... *I don't blame you*... I don't blame anybody... I wish I bloody *could*... I can never find anybody to bloody blame anything on.. Nowadays...

(JAG HOLDS UP A DAGGER)

PETER: Brings out a slicer... You know? For *shit's sake*, Dad... Brings out this *Nazi* slicer...

JAGUAR: Right, Shithole! Come and rotten get it...

TED: Oh, *Jesus!*

PETER: *(TO TED)* You don't *know* Jaguar, man... An *evil* bloke! *Real evil*. Face... eyes... Whole bloke... *Evil* right through. There is, man... There's *real evil* people in the world... That's an evil rotten bastard. Should've seen his rotten slicer... I mean...What do you do, Dad... When an evil shit like that pulls a slicer on you... Right? *(PULLS HIS KNIFE OUT)*

JAG MOVES CLOSER TO PETER. AIMS A BOOT AT HIM. PETER DODGES IT.

PETER: Jag, man... what the shit's this about... I've done nowt to you. It's *Friday night*, man! I'm going out to enjoy myself... Alright... If you want a rotten fight... Right... But I've my good gear on... If it's just a *fight*, man

JAG: Don't rotten lie to me, arsehole. You shitting know what it's about.

PETER: *(TO TED)* I *didn't*, Dad... See what I mean... I rotten had... I'd forgotten all about what he had against me...

TED: What had he against you?
(TO WORLD) He sat there... Looking at his coffee... Feeling his head where the stitches were...

PETER: Oh... Oh... *shit!* One night you look forward to... and *look* at the *bastard!*

TED: I know, son... *(TO WORLD)* I was going to say to him... I believe in being sorry for yourself at times... sometimes what happens to you... You're entitled to it... but he started attacking me again.

PETER: You don't understand one single rotten thing I am saying to you... Do you?

TED: I *might* do... *Could* be not. I *think* I do...

PETER: You *don't*.

TED: Alright... Will we go home...

PETER: Friday night, You see... You don't know what Friday night is... *Friday* night... *I'm talking about Friday night*... A heavy, weird, *spaced out* night... See what I mean... *Friday*... You don't know what Fridays *mean*... man... Like... Oh... shit... You're not rotten interested... *Forget* it...

TED: *Tell* me... *don't* tell me... It's alright with me... Listen, son... tell you this. You hear me... Listen to me... are you receiving me... son... Bloody bastardin listen to me... I am your *friend*... You are with *a friend*... You bloody know that... Right SO... you can please yourself... Piss off... Jump in the Tyne,... if that's what you think you have to do... Dope yourself up to the eyeballs... Kick in the old man's teeth... I *know*... In this case, the old man kicked in *your* teeth...

PETER: Right... Right... Right... I've got the message, Dad... Alright. Lay off.. Right... I know man... It's just... You know... I mean...

TED: (*TO WORLD*) So I sat there... I didn't say a word... I didn't want to... I drank the tea... Not bad tea... Listened to the chat from the Bowling Alleys... Somebody had put a record on... "MESSAGE IN A BOTTLE"... Not bad... Like I could see their point of view... Putting out a cry for help... See that... Definitely... Peter was thinking... Suddenly started to talk...

PETER: You don't *know* me, Dad...
...See... My *week*, Dad... Since I finished at that Shitfreeze... You don't *know* my week... You're either at the allotment.. or out on your shitheaps.. ... Right...

TED: That's it...

PETER: For shit's sake... my shitting week... man... *Monday*... You know? ... You know what a shit day Monday is when you're *working*... When you're *not* working... Never think that... would you... You'd think... You do... When you're up to your eyeballs in work... You think... *Christ*... If I could go in *tomorrow*... Burn up *Mondays*... Dad.. man... I go out of my tiny rotten mind, Dad... Man... Lying around all shitting day... Playing records.. Listening to Radio One.. You go out of yer rotten mind...

TED: I *know*, son...

PETER: When I've got stuff... Alright... I trip... I try some of Mam's stuff... Or Auntie Linda's...
... when I get desperate...
... I get up... twelve o'clock.. One o'clock... Later you get up... better you burn the day... don't you...
That's what I am on about... *Monday*... *Tuesday*... *Wednesday*... *Jesus*... They're like a million-ton shitting rotten days... Every day.. man.. Gets *heavier* and *heavier*... See what I'm getting at... *Fridays*... *Friday night*... when you get togged up... You know... Weekend in front of you... right... ...It's like you're smoking away all week... and you start tripping on Friday...

TED: I can understand, son...

PETER: Do you?

TED: Bloody telling you...

PETER: You get this... Like... *lift*...
... Going out all together... Picking up your mates... Going on the bus together into the town... ...everybody in the air...
... First pint...

TED: I can... I understand, son... It is a *bastard*, the week... For you... I can see that... Yeah...

PETER: Can you understand what a beautiful, heavy kind of thing it is... Friday night... and Saturday's to come, man... *Saturday* night...

TED: (*TO WORLD*) ... Looking at him... I'm a soft bastard... no doubt about it... My heart went out to him... I could've cried for the kid... could've done... *He* was back with his fight with Jaguar...

 JAGUAR KICKS OUT AT PETER.. GETS IN A KICK AT HIS FACE... PETER RETURNS THE KICK... JAGUAR FALLS BUT QUICKLY GETS UP AGAIN...

JAGUAR: Saturday night... Right? Party at Snowhite's... right...

PETER: Jag, man... I haven't been to Snowhite's for months... tell you why... you know why... Snowhite's shipped back to London, hasn't he? Social Security pushed him back to London...

JAGUAR: Saturday night... Snowhite's... Rosie... you rotten knocking up Rosie...

PETER: *Shit! Jesus! (TO TED)* That was why I'd forgotten all about it... *months* ago... that happened... But as far as *he* was concerned, it was red hot... like it was two seconds ago, I'd knocked off his bird... You know what I mean... like... some mate of his had bumped into Snowhite in Birmingham...

JAGUAR: Gonna *do* you... Gonna cut it *off*! Gonna finish you with lasses for good... It's alright... That's what I'm gonna do... I'm gonna shittin cut it rotten OFF...

PETER: Yer off yer flamin rocker, Jag, man... How would I knock off yer lass... I've me own lass... I'm engaged... amn't I... I'm gonna be married... *(TO TED)* What else can you do, see... when he's got you in corner like that... you got to *lie*... Should've seen his eyes... Red... Evil... Telling you... I *know*... There is good and evil in this world... It's right... And that shithole was *total evil.* Got us, too...

JAGUAR: *(JUMPING ON HIM... PETER'S TOO SLOW)*
              Don't rotten shit lie to *me*... shithole!... Don't *try* it... I *know*... Don't... I *know*... right...

PETER: *(TO TED)* Had me on the ground... Out of his rotten mind... Eyes popping out his head... ROTTEN PULLING AT MY TROUSERS...

TED: *(TO WORLD)* Oh... Christ... I was saying to myself... God... For dear Jesus's bloody sake... What's going to *happen* to that kid...

PETER: *(TO TED)* So he's got me... for the minute... on the pavement... pinned down... sitting on me... slicer in one hand... pulling at me pants in the other... yelling at me...

JAGUAR: Bastardin lyin shithole... rotten lying *shit bastard*...

PETER: *(TO TED)* The whole lot... funny thing... what's worrying me... is my cords... them cords.. cost us nearly twenty quid... I'm shouting back at him *(TO JAG)* Lay off, you stupid shit... You're gonna tear my rotten cords...

PETER: *(TO TED)* He just keeps shouting... shit pouring out of him... out of his rotten mind... pulling at my belt screaming away...

JAGUAR: Shithole... Bastard... turd... Pigshitter..

PETER: *(TO TED)* Screaming away at the top of his stupid shithead... when this old idiot comes out one of the houses... In his vest and braces... stands over me and says...

OLD IDIOT: *Get!... Get!... Get!...*

PETER: And he gives Jag this kick with his old boots... knocks off Jag long enough for me to throw him.. and I'm up again.. Old Idiot's still standing there... shouting...

OLD IDIOT: Get... Get... Go on... Scum... Get...

PETER: *(TO TED)* Whole thing's turning into a rotten comedy. This old geezer here... Out of his mind...

JAGUAR: Piss off...

OLD IDIOT:	Get... You heard me...
PETER:	*(TO TED)* ... Jag turns to him...
JAGUAR:	You out of yer shittin mind, Granda... Blow... Go on... Get back to yer shithouse... Go on...
PETER:	*(TO TED)* ... But ... see.. this funny thing happens... I didn't know you could do that... could be Jag's sharpened his slicer too much.. who the shit knows... Jag's dropped his slicer... see... when the old Geezer boots him... Old Geezer's grabbed it... He's raving...
OLD IDIOT:	I am *sick*... I am *sick* up to the *eyeballs* with your *mindless, useless generation*... do you hear me?
JAGUAR:	Give me me shitting knife shitting back...
OLD IDIOT:	I am sick of you... vomiting on the pavement... your three or four pints you can't keep down... fornicating with yer mindless females with your transistors blasting away... Get ... Go on.. The two of you.. I'm not having dead bodies outside my house... this is my bloody bastardin home... You hear me... Get... now... I'm not taking sliced up bodies to hospitals... and 'phoning for ambulances... Kill each other some other bastardin place...
PETER:	*(TO TED)* Jag's turned to me... You know.. two of us... Mouths open... This old Geezer tripping in front of us... *One* of us could have flattened him to the ground... Jag... says...
JAGUAR:	Grandad... listen you old shitter... Before you get your rag up... Blow, man... I don't shitting care if you're eight or eighty... I'll shitting fill you in...
OLD IDIOT:	Are *you* Still here... *GET...GET...GET!*
PETER:	... Jesus... He's out of his rotten mind...
JAGUAR:	Shut your stupid old shit face, you old bastard...
OLD IDIOT:	You've been warned... You've been told... I'm telling you, slice each other up somewhere else... Screw each other... that's probably what it's about... That's what half of you are, anyway, these days... Load of nancy boys...
PETER:	*(TO TED)* that got both of us... pair of us were going for him... Oh... Christ... Dad... This was a *heavy* bloke... He kind of stabbed it into the pavement... Know what I mean... Bloody broke the blade... Like... It came to bits... steel blade... throws it to Jag...
OLD IDIOT:	Take it... Take it... scum...
PETER:	*(TO TED)* Jag... should've seen his face... knife in his hand... looking at the broken blade... like he was gonna cry...
JAGUAR:	That's a *shitting Nazi* dagger!
OLD IDIOT:	That's it!... that's what you are... A bastardin filthy Nazi... That's what I fought the war for... for you to go around the streets menacin everybody with Nazi Daggers...
JAGUAR:	I don't understand him... He's a raving maniac... look what he's done to my shitting dagger... *(TO OLD IDIOT)* That cost us nearly twenty quid, you stupid shitter...
OLD IDIOT:	right... You've been warned... Get.. Now... Go on...
PETER:	*(TO TED)* He had a whistle in his hand... Police whistle... Blows it... But something must've been wrong with it.. Because it didn't work... You

	see... He's standing there... you see... blowing his rotten lungs out for shit all...
OLD IDIOT:	Get... Now... Back to yer ratholes...
JAGUAR:	*(GRABBING HIM)* You give me twenty quid for that dagger ye've buggered up... Now... You old shitter... give...
PETER:	*(TO TED)* Minute Jag touched him... Old Idiot went rotten berserk... Flashed out at Jag... and knocked him to the ground... Jesus knows... I mean... I didn't know what was happening... I got my slicer ready... I mean... You know what I mean, Dad... when you get all worked up... All you can think of... is I'm going to do that bastard... But he's on me *(OLD MAN JUMPING ON HIM...)* And now see the old shits got a rotten hammer in his hand... Christ knows how I didn't see it before... Big dirty rotten hammer... And he's bringing it down on ye skull... Shit!... Trying to get my slicer into him... and the bastard brings it down right on top of my skull... flattens us to the ground... I hear him shouting to somebody...
OLD IDIOT:	Get the police... I've been attacked by two dangerous thugs...
PETER:	I must've knicked him... or Jag knicked him... Shit knows who knicked him... He had to get a couple of stitches in his hand.
TED:	*(TO WORLD)* I had to have a bit of time to work this out... Could've been worse... Everybody came out of it more or less alive... I said to Peter... The thing is not to get into a panic, Peter... Isn't it... *(TO WORLD)* We were walking home... Peter wanted to walk... He couldn't stand going on the bus... walking down Bentink Road... Me trying to keep myself out of a panic... You know... Jesus.. What kind of kid have I brought up... He hasn't killed anybody this time... But he's got... a lot of mileage in front of him... Is that *me*? I think it is me... I'm his father... I stopped myself doing that... I... you can... You can look at everything one way... and it's a desperate situation. *(TO PETER)* It's not a desperate situation...
PETER:	How did the old shit break Jag's knife...
TED:	Could be not tempered right... No... it's not at all a desperate situation... ...you see... It's not *too* bad... The old man's just got two stiches...
PETER:	Should've had seventy...
TED:	Nobody's dead *(TO WORLD)* then it hit me... *(TO PETER)* Are they?...
PETER:	*Dead*?
TED:	Jag's not dead...
PETER:	They took Jag to the West Road Police Station... Me to hospital... and the old geezer...
TED:	I'm with you... and your Mam's with you... *(TO WORLD)* He was frightened now...
PETER:	They won't put me away... will they? do you reckon? He just got two stiches... I mean... *he* nearly cracked my skull...
TED:	Don't worry about it... It's alright...
PETER:	What about my probation...
TED:	That's alright... You're finished that... Nine months ago...
PETER:	But I've got a record... haven't I?..What about Wendy Dad, man?...

TED:	*(TO WORLD)* Very difficult to grasp people... I can't grasp them... I never can get them... an hour or so ago .. he was knifing an old man... God... He could've killed the stupid old bastard... I looked at him... Who *was* he... for God's sake... Kniving somebody an hour before... Now... a kid... frightened he was going to be put away...
PETER:	Rotten annihilate you... in those places... I couldn't stand being put away, Dad, man...
TED:	Be alright, son... It's alright... everybody's behind you... Your mam... and me... Auntie Linda... Yer lass...
PETER:	Not rotten Wendy... That's for sure... Tell you that...
TED:	*(TO WORLD)* I didn't want to upset him any more that night... but it was getting... I had to say something...
	(TO PETER) It's a pity... when you have a nice lass like Wendy... You know what I mean... I know these things happen, son... But it's just a pity... you had to get involved with that other lass... *(TO WORLD)* He didn't understand that... I didn't understand that, either... He looks at me... Like I wasn't adding up one and one properly... Like it was one and one...
PETER:	Dad, man... I just knocked her off for a bit of a laugh... That's all there was to it.
LES:	Oh... Jesus!... *Listen... Christ...* Bloody hell... Listen to me... You see what I *mean*.... Jackie?
TED:	*(TO WORLD)* Just came back into the room, after settling down Peter. Les had this wild look in his eye... You couldn't blame him... He was desperate... Ready to jump at any straw... Peter getting hit on the head by an old geezer with a hammer was alright... If bloody Grey would've fallen off Eldon Monument that would've done just the same... looks at me and Carol... This funny look in his eye... Like he'd got the message at last... The light was flooding in...
JACKIE:	Telling you ...
LES:	Carol, man... *Look* at you... Look at *you*, Teddy...
LINDA:	What's wrong with them?
LES:	Oh... Jesus! These *two people*... Did you *see* it... For Christ's sake did you *see* it?
JACKIE:	Telling you...
CAROL:	Les... It's alright, pet... Calm down... It's alright...
LES:	*Look* at them... For Christ's sake...
TED:	*(TO WORLD)* I kind of looked at myself... I couldn't see anything...
LES:	I'm talking about *solid ground*... That's what I'm talking about... *Teddy* and *Carol*... that's what I'm talking about... Jackie knows what I'm talking about... Jackie, *you* know...
JACKIE:	I'm telling you... Same with me with Linda... That's it... You're right...
LES:	Did you *see* them... The two of them...
LINDA:	Saw what?
CAROL:	*(TO LES)* What are you talking about, love...

LES:	Peter comes into the house... *God*, Jackie... That was a revelation... wasn't it...
JACKIE:	Eye opener...
LINDA:	What the hell are they talking about...
LES:	...Listen... I *know* Teddy... I know this is a hell of a bloody cheek... I know that... Don't need to tell me... It's a bloody cheek... I need a bit of solid ground this weekend... *That's* what I need... I don't *need* the bloody Gosforth Park Hotel... and rooms with bastardin bathrooms...
TED:	You're not *going* to the Gosforth Park Hotel?
LES:	It's not what I *need*, man... Is it?
TED:	You see... I can't keep up with you, Les... The way you keep changing your plans... every minute. One minute you're going to Aldershot... Then you're not going to Aldershot...
JACKIE:	He's *not* going to Aldershot...?
CAROL:	For God's sake... Don't start all over again about Aldershot... What's the matter with you, Les... pet?
TED:	*(TO JACKIE)* He doesn't want to go to the Gosforth Park Hotel... That's for sure...
LES:	Teddy... If you have any friendship at all for me.. If you have any feelings for me... Don't make me go to the Gosforth Park Hotel... Do me a favour... I'm in trouble... You can see that... Be a pal... Look at me... I need a bit of *solid ground*
JACKIE:	I know what he means, Linda... I'm the same with you... I told you...
LINDA:	Jackie... stop *pushing* me, will you...
LES:	He comes in... That boy... Peter... In trouble up to his eyeballs... Nearly killed an old bloke...
TED:	Other way round, Les.
LES:	Totally irresponsible... got hold of a lovely lass... been looking forward for months to leading the band on to bloody Wembley... And he knocks her up... Not only that... Bloody nearly widows her before they're even *married*...
CAROL:	That's not decided, yet... We don't know if they *are* getting married, pet...
LES:	For Christ's sake... Look at him... What's he got left... The whole world's collapsed round him... he's bloody *drowning* look at him... And what happens... He comes in here... And his mother tucks him into bed... Takes him up a cup of cocoa.. His Dad takes him a hot water bottle... For God's sake... is that not a *wonderful* thing... In a desperate situation like that.. To have a bit of solid ground to come back to in the storm...
JACKIE:	Les... I'll tell you something... You're a better bloke than you let on... You know that.. telling you...
LES:	I'll sleep on the floor, Carol... I'm not worried.. On a chair... Just for the weekend.
CAROL:	Les, I can't let you sleep on the floor, pet...
LES:	I just need a few days, you see... On solid ground.. That's what this is for me... Good solid ground... Look at it... Feel that SOLID GROUND under your feet... What do you say, Teddy... Just a couple of days...

TED: *(TO WORLD)* I was trying to work that one out... Having him on top of me for a *whole weekend*... that was a bastard... I mean... I could off to sleep in my hut in the allotment... Could I *stand him for two days*... Tomorrow they'd be in Darlington all day, true... Sunday... I could go to the allotment... I mean... With Linda sleeping with Carol... they'd never get up to anything anyway... would they... And anyway... Carol's a straight lass... She'd do nowt before telling me, would she... *Would* she? Carol was just saying...

CAROL: We could put Les on the couch in the front room, couldn't we Teddy, pet...

TED: *(TO WORLD)* When Jackie makes this move... He's been working up to it for months... But this is it and we're right into the musical beds...

JACKIE: Know what I'm going to do.. Made up my mind.. I'm not going back to Heaton... That's it...

LINDA: Jackie... Go back to Heaton and have a good night's sleep... and get yourself settled... You're not yourself tonight... Nobody is...

JACKIE: I'm telling you I'm not going *back*, man... What do you think, Les?

LES: I'm happy to sleep anywhere... Front room... Hall... Bathroom...

JACKIE: Going to make a clean break... That's it... isn't it, Linda... That's what you've been *wanting* me to do for months... haven't you...

LINDA: I don't know *what* I've wanted you to do... Jackie...

JACKIE: Once I get back there... I get sucked in don't I... What do you think, Teddy?
            That alright, Carol... I stop here for a few nights. Till we get the flat organised...

LINDA: Jackie, man... we haven't decided anything yet...

CAROL: You see... with Wendy staying here... and now Les, Jackie, love...

JACKIE: Wendy's with Peter, Carol, man...

TED: *(TO WORLD)* For the time being...'

JACKIE: I'll be alright in Linda's room...

LINDA: You know you can't stand the two of us in a single bed, Jackie.

JACKIE: Just for a few nights.. That's what I've got to do, isn't it... Keep away from Heaton...

LINDA: Ee... I don't know, Jackie...

JACKIE: Got to make a clean break...

TED: *(TO WORLD)* So Carol starts working out the sleeping arrangements...

CAROL: Les can sleep on the couch in the front room... Wendy'll sleep with Peter... Jackie with Linda.. You're with...

TED: *(TO WORLD)* Linda was having problems... could see that, in her face...
            (TO JACKIE) You can't sleep, man... two in a single bed... you know that... you're tossing and turning all night...
            (TO WORLD) I had to get out of this.. away from everybody for a few minutes...
            (TO EVERYBODY) Just going to make myself some cocoa... Nobody wants any cocoa, do they?
            (TO WORLD) Bloody *everybody* wanted cocoa...

LES:	That's what I mean, Teddy... You see... Them kind of touches... Solid ground... Nice cup of cocoa before bedtime... *Jesus*... Jackie...
JACKIE:	Telling you...
TED:	*(TO WORLD)* That was a bad move ... Should never have done that... Just gave Linda a chance to get me on my own... Came into the kitchen and watched me watching the milk on the stove...
LINDA:	Tuesday night... Jackie was here... That night...
TED:	Linda I don't know, man...
LINDA:	We went up to the bedroom, that night... You remember? That's what started it... He'd come back from the practice... Said to me, upstairs...
TED:	*(TO LINDA)* It's a small room for *two* people... isn't it...
LINDA:	I like it... It's a lovely sunny room... It's too small... I know...
JACKIE:	I could do with one odd night a week... in peace with you...
LINDA:	I know...
JACKIE:	That bloody *bed*...
LINDA:	I know, pet... Listen... If you don't feel like it, tonight, love... I'm not bothered...
JACKIE:	I mean... It gets on yer nerves, doesn't it... Take off yer clothes... Into bed... Out of bed... Back with yer clothes on... Into the car... Back to Heaton... Off with yer clothes again... Like a bloody striptease artist!
LINDA:	I know, love...
JACKIE:	Anyway... You know that... That's not just all I want from you... You know that... I can't stand that... Getting up and pissing off back to Heaton... Just like that was all I was after... It *isn't*...
LINDA:	*(TO TED)* When he said that... I kind of squeezed his hand... You see what's *happening* to me, Teddy... *Before* if he'd said that... I'd run miles from him... Now... I squeezed his hand... and I said to him *(TO JACKIE)* I know, pet... *(TO TED)* I couldn't help it, Teddy... *(TO JACKIE)* Give us a cuddle... come on...
JACKIE:	I amn't, Linda, man... I'm not just after *that*...
LINDA:	*(TO TED)* I told you... I just couldn't help myself. Teddy... I said to him *(TO JACKIE)* I *know*, love... I know... I'm the same myself... Then he came out with what made me really feel for him... The way he said it, pet... My heart just went right out to him...
JACKIE:	Look at me... Bumming around all day... week in week out... I amount to *bugger all*...
LINDA:	Jackie, that's daft... What are you saying that for, love...
JACKIE:	*You* know that... I'm *nowt*, man... What I do all bloody day... You know that... I amount to bloody nowt...
LINDA:	You do for me, Jackie... Come on, man... Stop putting yourself down like that, love... You know that's not right... You amount to something for *me*, Jackie... Don't you?
JACKIE:	Do I? Might be something for you... Yeah... When I'm with you... that's right... yeah... You're right, Linda...

TED: (TO WORLD) Shook me, when she told me that... I knew what she meant... Her heart going out to him when he said that... Same thing happened to me, listening to her...

(TO LINDA) That *bloke*, Linda... *Jackie*... Him and *me*, Linda!

LINDA: I *know* love.

TED: He's *right*... Pair of us... What's happened to us... He's right... I know what he means...

LINDA: (TO TED) That's what pushed me into getting Mrs. Graham to give me the flat above the shop... She'd had students in it... and they'd messed it all up... I said we just needed two rooms... She could keep the one she was using to hold her stock... It was just like a place for us to have odd nights on our own together... That was all... Somewhere for us to go... I didn't have anything else at the back of my mind... As soon as he saw it... You see...

JACKIE: Cannie... Bit of paint... papering...

LINDA: Need to get some furniture...

(TO TED) He just came out with it... Standing in the middle of the empty room...

JACKIE: I want to marry you, Linda...

LINDA: Jackie, don't be a daft bugger, man...

JACKIE: I bloody want to marry you...

LINDA: You've a wife and four kids up the road, Jackie... Come on...

(TO TED) Came over to me, looked into my eyes... didn't touch me...

JACKIE: How about *you*? You not want to marry *me*?

LINDA: (TO TED) You know that... At first, when we started going with each other... If he'd asked me that... Getting tied again to another man... *Now*, Teddy...

JACKIE: We've got a place to go to, now... haven't we, man... I've fallen for you... I'm telling you... You know that... I've fallen for you... I want to be married to you, man... I'm sick of messing about... running from you back to her... I'm not married to *anybody*, way I am... Just now, am I... What do you say...

LINDA: I don't know, Jackie...

JACKIE: Christ... You know if you love me or not... don't you... You *do*... I know... Sheila bothers you and the kids... But you *know* that... I'm not a husband to her... or much of a father to my kids... am I... and 'm not much cop to *you*, either... Am I... This way?...

LINDA: Jackie... I don't know... Leave me alone... Just now... I don't know *where* I am...

JACKIE: Sheila'll get fixed up sharp again, man... Don't get in a state about Sheila... Got a bloke already, hasn't she?

LINDA: (TO TED) I looked at him... and I was saying to myself... Christ... I've bloody fallen for *him*... that's what's happened... I've landed myself really in the shit, now...

TED: (TO WORLD) No sooner is Linda out the kitchen with the cocoa, when Wendy comes in in her Dressing Gown... Totally mucks up all the sleeping arrangements... She'd just found out what Peter and Jag had been fighting about...

WENDY: I couldn't, Teddy... I couldn't sleep with that rotten pig in the same bed... Ever again... Could I? Did *you* know what him and Jag were bloody fighting over...

TED: It's alright... Wendy... It happened months ago...

WENDY: Fighting over that rotten slag... that got me pregnant... Do you know that... That rotten pig knocking her...

TED: *(TO WORLD)* I couldn't understand that... Peter knocks up this lass and gets *Wendy* pregnant... That was very difficult to grasp... I made the mistake of asking her how she worked that out...

WENDY: I was definitely going to finish with him that night he told me... We were baby sitting for Auntie Betty... I don't want my rotten baby, Teddy... I don't...

TED: Don't have it, then...

WENDY: It went so great... you see...

(MANIPULATING MACE)

I started to cry...

(CRYING... AS SHE MANIPULATES MACE)
I didn't know what to do, Teddy... Crying in front of all these people... Carol saw me... I don't think Les noticed... Les notices piss all...

TED: You're right... He can't help it...

WENDY: I wish he'd leave your Carol alone...

TED: He is... I think he is...

WENDY: Just stupid... I don't know what Carol's on about at times... Encouraging a wet slob like him...

TED: You're crying

WENDY: Crying my rotten eyes out...

TED: You alright now?

WENDY: I feel this weight... My stomach feels dead heavy... And it reminds me... what's happening... I'm finished with the band... and I'm lumbered with this kid... I want to stay with the Saints, Teddy... I don't want to be lumbered feeding kids, washing their nappies, putting them to bed... Tied down to them... No rotten freedom... I don't believe him... do you believe him... He said he knocked up his lass just to get at Jag... I don't know what it is... When everythings going right... and I'm manipulating my baton... The band's playing... Drums going... I'm leading the band... I really think I'm *somebody*, Teddy.

TED: You *are*, man...

WENDY: Yeah... I'm dead good at it, amn't I... he was funny you see... He was funny all that week... He was really funny... You know *me*... when I want to get something out of people... I just nag and nag and nag away...

(TO PETER) You alright, Peter?

PETER: Great...

WENDY: Watching the World about us... I like it... Peter just looks at the pictures... *(TO PETER)* Want some Pernod...

PETER:	Yeah... Give me some Pernod...
	I'm telling you, Wendy... Two of us were rotten stoned... Pissed out of our minds... Pernods... and pot and other stuff... Right... Just a laugh... Whole thing turned out a right load... She wanted to do it in the bath...
PETER:	*(TO ANNIE)* In the BATH
ANNIE:	For a change...
PETER:	Like with WATER in it?
ANNIE:	I don't want a *bath* with *you*... No water...
PETER:	Alright... If you want...
ANNIE:	They've a great bath upstairs...
PETER:	*(TO WENDY)* I saw nowt to it... It was cold... Didn't look all that clean...
WENDY:	I don't want to hear anything about it... The whole thing's horrible... Did you take your clothes off...
PETER:	It was too cold...
	(TO ANNIE) Bit cold, to strip... Isn't it?
ANNIE:	Please yourself... Take your jeans off...
PETER:	Do we need all that kind of music...
ANNIE:	Oh... *Jesus!* What's the matter with you...
PETER:	*(TO WENDY)* Like she'd got three transistors in the bathroom... Tuned into different stations...
	(TO ANNIE) Just... I get a bit mixed up... Trying to listen to what's happening...
ANNIE:	yeah...
PETER:	*(TO WENDY)* I think she took some weird stuff... Christ knows what it was... She went dumb on me... Flipped... I mean... she didn't go *dumb*... she *thought* she'd gone dumb...
ANNIE:	Oh... christ... I can't *speak*...
PETER:	Doesn't matter... Enough noise with all them blasting away...
ANNIE:	Rotten telling you... I can't rotten *speak*...
PETER:	It's alright...
ANNIE:	I've been struck dumb... Shitting hell!... Jesus...
PETER:	*(TO WENDY)* I'd have done nowt... Telling you... I didn't fancy her... for a start... She hadn't washed her neck for years... Dirty black neck... Like she lifted her hair... telling us to kiss her neck...
ANNIE:	Kiss my neck...
PETER:	In a minute...
ANNIE:	What's the matter with you, man... Kiss my neck... You not like my neck...
PETER:	You know what'd be a real turn on... I fancy washing your neck...
ANNIE:	*Do* you?
	Fancy that?... You could bath us...
PETER:	*(TO WENDY)* Started stripping off...
ANNIE:	Run the bath, man...

PETER:	*(TO WENDY)* I started to run the bath... there was a chance... you know... If she had a bath... she smelled... people kept knocking on the door...
ANNIE:	*(TO DOOR)* I'm having a bath... Piss off.
WENDY:	I can't understand that... How could you *do* that to me... Only *you* and *me* have a bath together...
PETER:	I wasn't *going* to have a bath... Just *her*...
WENDY:	I can't stand it... Don't talk any more to me about it...
PETER:	Right...
WENDY:	Did you bath her?
PETER:	I'm telling you... she flipped on me... and went dumb... while the bath was running.
WENDY:	*(TO TED)* I had this terrible feeling... like a panic... I was dead scared... While I was looking at him telling me about it... I got frightened... I could never sleep with him again... couldn't stand him *touching* me again...
ANNIE:	I'm rotten flaming bastardin *dumb*... I can't speak!
PETER:	What the hell are you doing, just now...
ANNIE:	I've lost my voice... for shit's sake... Do something about it...
PETER:	You're rotten *speaking*...
ANNIE:	Shitting stop pacifying me... Right...
PETER:	You're shitting *speaking*...
ANNIE:	Piss off...
PETER:	Right...
ANNIE:	Where you going...
PETER:	Going downstairs... For Christ's sake...
ANNIE:	What am I gonna do, for shit's sake...
PETER:	You're alright... You'll be alright... I'm telling you... you are speaking...
ANNIE:	I don't feel I'm speaking... Can you hear me... What I'm saying...
PETER:	I'm telling you...
ANNIE:	I don't believe you, lying bastard...
PETER:	Look, man... Show you... Right say something...
ANNIE:	How can I rotten say something... if I can't rotten speak...
PETER:	*Try*... man...
ANNIE:	Come into us... and stop shitting around...
PETER:	Right... In a minute... Hold on... wait till I get worked up a bit...
ANNIE:	You not fancy me...? What did you ask me to come up here with you, if you don't fancy us...
PETER:	I *do*, man... There you are... We're speaking together aren't we... That shows you you can speak...
ANNIE:	*Are* we?...
PETER:	*(TO WENDY)* See... she started shaking a bit... and crying... I said to her...

	(TO ANNIE) It's alright, man... You're just having a heavy trip... That's all... You shouldn't have taken that stuff before...
ANNIE:	Somebody gave me it...
PETER:	*(TO WENDY)* All it was... I was sorry for her... Just like that... It was a shame for her... we sat down on the bathroom carpet... I just kind of comforted her... because she was upset... *(TO ANNIE)* Be alright, man... telling you...
ANNIE:	Cuddle me, man... I'm cold...
PETER:	Put yer clothes on...
ANNIE:	I don't want to put any clothes on... cuddle me...
PETER:	I'm cuddling you... man!
ANNIE:	Are you?
PETER:	I *am*... look, man...
ANNIE:	Do you like me?
PETER:	You're great... yeah... *(TO WENDY)* Started crying... *(TO ANNIE)* It's alright... *(TO WENDY)* Brian Ferry was on one of the transistors... She got me to get him on the other two... so we had like three Brian Ferry's all singing at the one time in this bathroom... Her crying away with me arms around her... Fell asleep... Two of us... Don't know what people did about shitting or pissing... We were locked in the bathroom... Sleeping... Three Brian Ferry's singing away... I'm fast asleep... And I wake up... This is the truth, Wendy, man... She was crying her heart out...
WENDY:	What rotten for?
PETER:	I don't know... I just put me arms round her... and... did it to comfort her...
WENDY:	Bloody funny way of comforting somebody, isn't it?
TED:	Is it?
WENDY:	*(TURNING TO TED)* I don't know... I couldn't stand him touching me... for hours after, that night... Auntie Betty was at some night club... wasn't gonna come back till one o'clock or something. We watched the telly a bit... then I started crying again...
PETER:	Wendy... It's *nowt*, man... It isn't... Honest... I love you... You know that... You know I love you.
WENDY:	And then I went the other way... from not wanting him to touch us... I went really weird... I knew I'd mucked up me pill and everything... But I went mad... I don't know what happened to me... I kind of started attacking him... Do you understand that... How is that... That was the best sex we ever had all the time we'd been together... It was great... How could *that* be Teddy? I rotten *hated* him... and we were having that great sex together...
TED:	Made you a cup of cocoa...
WENDY:	I wish he was like you... Teddy... The way I can speak to you... I wouldn't think twice... I'd marry him in the morning... You're a great bloke... You know that...
LINDA:	Wait on, Carol... How about the three men downstairs in the front room you and me in your room... Wendy in mine.

TED:	I know that... Yeah... I am... You're right... *(TO WORLD)* Going into the living room, we had to start all over again with the sleeping arrangement.
WENDY:	I *couldn't* Linda, man... Could I?
CAROL:	I know, love...
LES:	This is not *happening* to me, Carol. Is this happening to me?.. I don't believe it's happening to me.. Jesus...
JACKIE:	Look if I'm in the front room with the lads... I might as well go home...
LES:	You're right, Jackie. I know about *nothing*. Look at me... Forty three years on this earth... Through some of the roughest campaigns in the history of the British Army... Married twenty odd years... Friendships with Christ knows how many women...
CAROL:	I didn't know it was all that many, pet...
LES:	And I know *nothing*... *I do not know a thing*, Teddy. Teddy... *You tell* me something... Do me a favour... Tell me something...
TED:	You're not drinking your cocoa, Les...
WENDY:	Nearly getting himself killed... Over that rotten filthy slag... I couldn't *look* at him, now... Could I...?
CAROL:	I *know*, love... I'm just trying to work out the sleeping arrangements, pet...
LES:	Carol... I know... It's a hell of a cheek putting you out like this... She's never been jealous like this before... You think it could be the change of life...
CAROL:	Might be pet... Has she hot flushes? Just calm down... It'll be alright... You're just getting yourself upset, love...
LES:	Will it be alright? Tell that again, Carol. It'll be alright... My wife has flipped and turned on me... But it will be alright. Will it?
TED:	Your cocoa's getting cold, man... You asked me to make it for you...
LES:	I should just go off to the Gosforth Park Hotel... *That's* what I should do.
JACKIE:	*(TO LINDA)* Listen... We'll go to the Gosforth Park Hotel... Take Les's room...
LINDA:	It's a *single* room...
LES:	... You're very welcome, Jackie... I'll foot the bill... It's a *double* room...
JACKIE:	Right... We'll go to the hotel... Problem's solved...
CAROL:	A double room, Les?
LINDA:	Jackie... I don't want to go to an hotel, tonight... It gives me a funny feeling... Going there... You and me...
LES:	*(TO CAROL)* That's all I could get
JACKIE:	Right... I'll piss off back to Heaton... if that's what you want...
CAROL:	Oh...
LINDA:	I don't *want*... Don't be like that... Jackie... you know that... I don't know *what we should do*...
TED:	*(TO WORLD)* Looking at him... Jackie... My mate... God... Bloke like that... Mates like we were... And Linda telling me how down he was... having nowt to do all bloody day... Mates like we were... I'd only the one mate... That was me... My days... If I didn't have Jackie for Christ's sake...

	(TO JACKIE) Monday, Jackie... Eh?... You and me... Take the day off from the tips...
LES:	Linda... You're very welcome to my room in the Gosforth Park Hotel... On *me*... I'm telling you...
TED:	*(TO JACKIE)* Take a day off from working the tips... Go over to Durham... Fancy that?
CAROL:	Wait a minute, pet... We're trying to settle the sleeping arrangements...
JACKIE:	*DURHAM?*
LES:	You see... If I could hold on here till Tuesday...
TED:	*(TO WORLD)* Jesus... *Tuesday*
LES:	I'm going to Aldershot on Tuesday...
JACKIE:	I thought you weren't going to Aldershot...
LES:	I'm going on Tuesday.
TED:	Look... Best thing is, I go and sleep in me hut in the allotment... Easiest thing all round...
CAROL:	Teddy... I want you to stay here... Where are you going...
TED:	Just going to get Peter's sleeping bag... It's warm there, man... I *like* sleeping in the allotment...
CAROL:	You're stopping *here*, Teddy... You're not sleeping out of the house... Do you *hear* me...
TED:	*(TO WORLD)* And she kind of grabbed my hand and held on to me... like to keep with her...
CAROL:	Come on... Give me a hand to get the air bed fixed in the front room, will you...
TED:	*(TO WORLD)* Pulled me into the front room...
CAROL:	Teddy... I want you in with me, tonight... Do you hear me...
TED:	That's what I want, too, man... *(TO WORLD)* I did... problem was with Linda and Jackie in the front room... and Wendy in the spare bedroom on a mattress... Where did you put bloody Les... In the bath... people might want to use the toilet... I said to her... serious... *(TO CAROL)* We should get a bigger house... If we're going to have all these people staying with us. *(TO WORLD)* And here's the bad bit... Took my hand... and kind of stroked it... You know... then said...
CAROL:	Love... I've got to tell you this... I can't keep it in any longer...
TED:	*(TO WORLD)* Jesus... What's coming now...
CAROL:	You know how we were talking about it not being physical... between me and Les...
TED:	*(TO WORLD)* Oh bloody hell! It was coming... been expecting this, minute she started bloody coffeeing with him... Why do people get so bloody buried in other people, for... I can see they have to have kids and bring them up... But somebody could've worked out a better arrangement than this... couldn't they?... No... They couldn't... Because there's nobody to work it out... is there... That's it... That's how it works... Carol kept stroking my hand...
CAROL:	Ee... I don't think I can tell you...

TED: Come on, man... What is it...

CAROL: I *can't*... Teddy...

TED: Come on, Carol... What is it... Come on... It's alright...
           (TO WORLD) Was it bloody hell...

CAROL: I can't help it, Teddy... It doesn't mean I don't love you pet... I still fancy
           you too... I do... I don't know what it is... Times I wish I'd never have
           smiled back at him... That time I first saw him outside the home...

TED: *(TO WORLD)* Could say that again... Came out with it... Been there all
           the time... she'd kept it to herself... For months... This bloody pull
           between them...

CAROL: I can't help it, pet... I just fancy him... He does something to me... I seem to
           do something to him... I fancy *you*, too, pet... It's not I don't fancy you,
           too... He just gets me excited I don't know what it is... The idea of
           sleeping... with him...

TED: *(TO WORLD)* All came pouring out... Her lying in bed at nights, making
           up stories about her and Les together... Times her and me were having a
           session... Having pictures of doing it with him... I'd noticed... that...
           Times I'd never known her so bloody sexy in her life... that bothered me...
           Never happened before to us, that... Her going for me... All over me... I
           wasn't used to it...

CAROL: I'm sorry, pet,... I can't help it...

TED: *(TO WORLD)* The amazing thing is... she hadn't *done* anything about
           it... *SO* far... That's what she *said*... No... She's a straight lass... I believe
           her... *Do* I?... I *do*... Look at her face...

CAROL: You can't... can you... You can't help your feelings... I don't know what it
           is...

TED: *(TO WORLD)* Still kept stroking my hand... But like she was soothing
           herself... not me... I said my usual thing...
           (TO CAROL) Yeah... I know, Carol...
           (TO WORLD) She began to make up the air bed... Looking at her... The
           kind of sad look on her face... Jesus... I don't know where the bloody hell I
           am at times... I felt bloody *sorry* for *her*... Not me... Definitely something
           seriously bloody wrong with me... Stood there, watching her... Feeling for
           her... Jesus... She hasn't had all that much cop of a life, has she? I mean...
           For Christ's sake... A bloke and a lass having a bit of sex together... What
           is it, for God's sake... Why's it got to be such a big bloody deal... I know...
           Bloody *is* to me... But what the hell for God's sake... If she really is pulled
           to do it with the bastard... she's miserable *not* doing it... I'm a right sod,
           amn't I? Blocking her... I know that she loves me... I know that...

CAROL: It's not anything to do with you, love... I do... I still fancy you... and love
           you...

TED: I know... man...
           (TO WORLD) Bloody *felt* for her... But I could, couldn't I... I could
           afford to... He was finishing with her... Not much chance of anything
           happening, now... was there? She must've been thinking the same... she
           said...

CAROL: Anyway... It's finished, now... She won't even let him train the band any
           more, will she?

TED:	He'll still train the band, man... *(TO WORLD)* But she was back on the sleeping arrangements.
CAROL:	How about if Linda slept in her room with Wendy... We brought in the double mattress... and Jackie and Les were the in front room...
TED:	Jackie wants to be with Linda, tonight, Carol, man...
CAROL:	I know, pet... we could see what they think, anyway...
TED:	*(TO WORLD)* We went into the living room to announce the latest sleeping arrangements... like in the Central Station where they put up the latest times of the trains... Les was not in good shape... Sitting there with his bottle of Southern Comfort... Drinking it like lemonade...
LES:	Don't worry about me... I'll sleep anywhere...
JACKIE:	*(TO LINDA)* That what you want? Sleep upstairs with Wendy...
TED:	*(TO WORLD)* They were all arguing this out when Wendy comes down again, and throws the sleeping arrangements again...
CAROL:	You're *sleeping* with *Peter*, now pet?
WENDY:	I can't let him sleep on his own, tonight, Carol... He's dead upset...
CAROL:	Should I go to him...
WENDY:	I'm just making him a hot cup of cocoa... ... He's alright... I just went in... You know... To say 'goodnight' to him... See he was alright... He was sleeping... To tell you the truth... What it is... I don't know what it is...
CAROL:	I know, pet...
WENDY:	I got into bed... You see... It was dead funny... *(WENDY INTO BED)* I'm lying there... you know... And I know Peter's next door... in bed... I can't settle down...
CAROL:	I know how you feel, love...
WENDY:	It's like he's pulling me... you know... So I get up... and look into his room... He's sleeping. *(LOOKS AT SLEEPING PETER)* It's funny looking at somebody sleeping you have a thing about isn't it...
LES:	You're right... Yeah... it is...
WENDY:	I'm standing by his bed... looking at his face... I know... It's stupid being tied to him... He's not right for me... You're right, Teddy.
TED:	You could do *better*...
WENDY:	I'm looking at him... And thinking about that bitch he knocked up at that party... trying to understand what it was about... You know... Like trying to get into him... You know... What it was like for him...
TED:	It's a shame for him...
WENDY:	That's it...
TED:	He's a poor soul... I'm a poor soul... Les is a poor soul...
LES:	Am I?
TED:	You're a poor soul... Whole world's poor souls...
LES:	Not at all. I refuse to lie down like that... I'm *not* I'm a *fighter*...

WENDY: I can't help it... There's something between us... I love him... He opens his eyes... looks at me...
(PETER DOES THIS)

WENDY: Did I wake you up...

PETER: Nuh...

WENDY: How you feeling...

PETER: Diabolical...

WENDY: I know...

PETER: Come and give me a cuddle, Wendy...

WENDY: *(STROKING HIS BROW)*... I will, Yeah... You're a bit hot...

PETER: Look... Wendy, man... Listen to me... It was nowt... That lass...

WENDY: It doesn't matter... Forget it... I'll get you some Aspros... and a drink...

PETER: Cup of cocoa...

WENDY: Alright...

PETER: You coming in with me...

WENDY: I *told* you

PETER: If you finished with me...

WENDY: I'm not going to finish with you, Peter, man... I'll get yer cocoa...
(TO OTHERS) I'm still not going to get *married*... That's definite... I'm not getting tied up to him... If I go daft and change me mind... Hit me over the head or something, Teddy... will you... Tie me up... until I get sensible again...

TED: *(TO WORLD)* That's what finished Les... Wendy goes into the kitchen to make the cocoa... I go upstairs a minute to have a quiet pee... leave them to work it out on their own...
Locked myself in the toilet for ten minutes... When I came out... They were all settling in their rooms... Carol was in bed in her nightie... she was just saying to me... she should not have said... but she did... things like that should not be *said*...

CAROL: God! Peace at last...

TED: *(TO WORLD)* Knock at the door...
(TO CAROL) Probably haven't got the sleeping arrangements right, yet... Try again...

LES: It's me... Les...

TED: Hullo, Les... Come in, man...

LES: I'm sorry to trouble you... Listen... I've been thinking about it... What am I doing *here*?... I'm going home...

CAROL: *Tonight*... It's after one o'clock in the morning...

LES: I don't feel *right* here, Carol... You see what I mean... Lying there on my jack...

TED: I know what you mean...

LES: Got it worked out... I'll 'phone her up... you know... tell her I've had a break down on the road to Aldershot... and it's fixed... and I'm coming back to Newcastle... Too late to go to Aldershot...

TED: (TO WORLD) Sounded a bit complicated to me... but I suppose he knew what he was talking about... Carol was worried... He'd been at the Southern Comfort again... No doubt about it... He was not in good shape...

CAROL: Pet... are you fit to go *back* to Fenham, tonight...

LES: Only ten minutes... I'll 'phone her, first...

TED: (TO WORLD) Carol... of course... has to open her big mouth and volunteer me to go to the 'phone with him...

CAROL: Les doesn't know where the 'phones are, Teddy...

TED: Might as well... make a night of it...
(TO WORLD) Les kept saying he didn't want to bother anybody...

Alright... you're bothering people... I can stand another half an hour of you... (TO WORLD) So he gets his coat on... Carol comes downstairs... for the last goodbye... She's got no doubt in her mind... This is the end... finished... I do not count my chickens till they're laying eggs... Les says... Tear in his eye... Southern Comfort

LES: (TO CAROL) See you, then...

CAROL: Yes

TED: (TO WORLD) Waiting for a kiss... I think... Say to myself... It's only decency to let them have a farewell kiss in peace together... So I go in front of him... Leaving them on their jack for a bit... That gets a bit too long... You see what I mean... Give an inch... It's right... I go in again... It's a cold, wet night... and I say...

TED: (TO LES) Are you coming?

LES: Yeah... Let's go...

TED: (TO WORLD) Then we go into the wet, misty summer night... I notice Les has brought his Southern Comfort with him...

TED: What did you bring that with you for, Les, man?

LES: That's right...

You see... You and Jackie... Great lads... God in heaven... You and Jackie... *Magic* hands... *Magic*... Look at these hands... Magic bloody hands...

TED: (LOOKING AT THEM) You reckon?

LES: Magic bloody hands, Teddy... Can turn a piece of steel... Right... You take a sheet of steel... Turn it into a ocean going ship... God... Is that not a wonderful thing... Take a bit of a steel... Build something like a *ship*... A ship, for sweet God's sake... Holding hundreds of people... Ploughing through the oceans...

TED: (TO WORLD) I'd never thought about it that way before... He was right... Had a look at my hands... Came to the first 'phone box...

(TO LES) 'Phone Box...

LES: What I'll say... You see... How does this sound to you... I've had a breakdown on the road to Aldershot...

TED: You *could've* had...

LES: I *could*... couldn't I?... *Where*?

TED: That's a point...
                      Darlington

LES: That's it... Darlington...
                      (DIALING)

TED: *(TO WORLD)* He was dialing the number... holding up the 'phone... I noticed some shithead kids had cut the cord...

LES: I thought it was a very quiet 'phone...

TED: Try the next one down the road...

LES: A bloke like you, Teddy... Look at you... You have a bad lousy break... I've had a lousy break... *Jackie* has... You see what I'm getting at... Me... Fought through the war... Malaya... Korea... India... Ireland... look at me... All the ships you've made... All the places I've fought... and they've thrown them away... It's all thrown away... like a empty chip bag on a Saturday night...

TED: That's it...

LES: We've ended up with nowt... I mean... They're right... It's *their* bastard countries... India... and Africa... The wogs... Isn't it... the wogs country... entitled to it...

TED: Les... It's alright... Don't worry about it...

LES: Just saying... What a *futile bloody life*... isn't it... All that magic in yer hands... gone for shit all... Me fighting my guts out to keep Britain Great and ordered to lay down yer arms... and give it all up... Listen... Teddy... Don't *do* that to me... You hear me? *Don't* man...

TED: Nuh...
                      (TO WORLD) What?

LES: I know... You're right... Friendship is the most important thing in the world... I know you do not like me... You can't be my pal... Do you know something... I've no pals... You know that...

TED: It's not as bad as that, Les, man...

LES: It is very bad, Teddy... You have no *idea* how bad it is...
Listen... Teddy... *Forgive* me... *Forgive* me... give me yer hand... Give me yer hand...

TED: *(TO WORLD)* Forgive him for *what*? What's coming *now*, for Christ's sake!

LES: Give me your hand, Teddy...
Forgive me... for upsetting you with my friendship with Carol... I gave you a bad time... I'm sorry... You're a great bloke... It's upset me... It's shaken me... If you know how much I value your feelings for me... Teddy... Do not *do* that to me... Will you not...

TED: Nuh...

LES: Scrappin around the rubbish tips for bits of junk... Carrion crows... the shits have turned you into... Magic hands like yours and Jackie's... And what we have done with them...

TED: Les... Don't let it upset you... It's alright, man...

LES: Do you want to know what it is... I'll tell you what it is... I do... I will be straight with you... I fancied your wife... she is a lovely woman... Jesus...

she is... I respect her... and enjoy her company... But I will tell you something... If I have to choose between her and you...

TED: *(TO WORLD)* See what I mean...

LES: It'd be *you*, every time... because you are a great bloke... On top of yer magic hands...

TED: *(TO WORLD)* Then he comes out with a really weird thing...

LES: I wouldn't care... But I've got a glass eye... Did you know I had a glass eye...

TED: You wouldn't know...

LES: *I* would know... It's robbed me of stereoscopic vision... and it frightens us... I'll be honest with you... It's like you have two endorsements on your licence... One more and you're finished driving... Me good eye goes... I'm finished... Malaya... Got it... what was I fighting for in Malaya... Do *you* know? Fucked if *I* know... So they stick us behind a desk... The One-eyed-Sergeant Major... They sit there... listen... what is... Isn't it... They don't give a *shit*... Jesus... They don't... They don't give a shit... Nobody gives a shit... The games up... The country's knackered... And nobody gives a monkey's shit... Do *you* give a shit... *I* don't give a shit... *Nobody* gives a shit...

TED: Why *should* they?

LES: Why the shit should they *give* a shit... You're right.

TED: See... Getting worked up about the state of the country like *you* do... Doesn't feel to me I *have* a country...

I mean... I can see how *you've* got a country... You've got a uniform, haven't you?

(TO WORLD) If the next 'phone box would've been working, it've been alright... Or the next one... Nothing would've happened... Got into the third 'phone box...

LES: Third time lucky, eh, Teddy?

TED: *(TO WORLD)* I'm wet, cold, miserable and dying to get back to bed for a bit of peace with Carol. And sick up to my *eyeballs* of this drunken bastard. I can't stand *looking* at him. Carol *fancying him*. Bloody greed of him! One wife and Christ knows how many on the side's not enough for him, he has to have *my* wife, too...

LES: *(LIFTING 'PHONE)* I think this 'phone's going to work, Teddy... Got a feeling...

TED: *(TO WORLD)* Bloody *praying* it would... Desperate for him to get his bloody wife and piss off out of my life back home to her. *(TO 'PHONE)* Work... Work... Work! you *bastard*!

LES: It's alright. Got a dialing tone.

TED: Hallelujah! Never learn, will I?
Should *never* have said that.

LES: Hullo... Hullo...
...Hullo... Fucking *shit*!
...Gone dead...

TED: Let me try it...
(TAKING 'PHONE) What's the number?

LES: 324745

TED: No bloody *dialing* tone, now.
(TO WORLD) I'm banging the rest up and down... Desperate to get some life out of it... And something goes in me... I bloody explode... Turn on the 'phone...

(ATTACKING 'PHONE... KICKING IT... VENTING ALL HIS BLOCKED RESENTMENT ON IT)

... Come on, you bastard, Come on... Come *on*!

LES: Teddy... What you *doing*, man.
You're going to smash it...

TED: *(STILL ATTACKING IT)*
Bloody *annihilate* the bastard. Come on you *swine*!

LES: Take it easy, Teddy. Take it easy...

TED: Keep out of this... I'm trying to get this bastard 'phone to bastardin work, for Christ's sake...

LES: Teddy... You're going to smash that 'phone... Give it to me, for Christ's sake, man...
(TRYING TO PULL 'PHONE OUT OF TED'S HAND)
(TED LASHES OUT AT HIM... KNOCKING HIM DOWN...)

TED: I'm trying to get the 'phone to work... I'm warning you... keep off till I get it working... Just don't provoke me. I have had it up to *here* with you... I am *sick* up to the bastardin *eyeballs*. Thick, greedy, bloody shithead! Lay off... I'm warning you!
(LES IS SITTING ON THE CONCRETE, MOANING...)

TED: *(TO WORLD)* I mean I'd never have stood up to him if he'd been sober... Standing there shouting at him... Hits me... He's not moving... Just sitting there... Moaning... His hands over his eyes...

LES: Jesus... Fucking hell. I can't *see!*... You've fucking *blinded* me, for fuck's sake.

TED: *(TO WORLD)* Jesus! I hadn't...
(TO LES) I just pushed you, Les, man...

LES: Got me good fucking eye... I can't *see*... Oh. *Fuck... Jesus...*

TED: Take it easy... Calm down, Les...
Let's see it...

LES: Oh.. Jesus... For Christ's sake... God...

TED: Take a drink... Be alright.
Where's the bottle? *(SEARCHING FOR THE BOTTLE)*

LES: *(LIFTING HIS HANDS FROM HIS EYES)* Wait a minute... *(FINDS BOTTLE)*

TED: Just... that bloody 'phone... Les,... Got on my wick...

LES: I think it's coming back... God... I think it is... Got a drink there.

TED: *(PLACING BOTTLE IN LES'S HAND)* There it is... Got it?...

LES: I can *see* it, man.. Bit blurred..But I can see it..I can see you...Getting better... Must've been the way you caught it...

TED: *(TO WORLD)* Standing there.. The sight of the poor sod, sitting on the concrete floor... I completely turned round..
(TO LES) Les.. Listen.. It's alright.. It's not your fault... I don't *blame* you... It's alright...

LES: You've no idea what it's like, Teddy... Living in daily fear for your sight...

TED: If Carol fancies you... That's how it is... Isn't it?

LES: What's it look like?... Is it alright?

TED: *(LOOKING AT LES'S EYE..)* It's alright. No marks..

LES: Christ. I thought that was *it*, there, Teddy.. Jesus...

TED: If she fancies you, she fancies you. That's how she *feels*, isn't it?

LES: She's a great lass, Teddy. True as a die. You've no idea.

TED: Right. I can't *stand* it. Her fancying you – or any other bloke... That's how she *feels*.. I know... It gets me... Gets me.. when it *rains*... Getting *old*.. Not having sunshine all the time... But that's how it is, isn't it, Les?

LES: *Feelings*... Very difficult people's *feelings*, Teddy... you're right...

TED: I don't blame you.. That's what *happens*.. You maybe slipped into it a bit too easy.. But it's not the old Ten Commandments days any longer, is it? Adultery is forbidden..

LES: Teddy... Listen... You've got something there. You're right... We need something to *believe* in.. Like the old Ten Commandments...

TED: That's what I'm *saying*, Les, man... Them days are finished... Never have it off with anybody except your wife or your husband... Making it the *end* of *the world*, isn't it? *Biggest deal under the sun* – What *is* it? What are we *talking* about, Les? A bloke having it off with a lass... *You* having it off with Carol...

LES: Teddy. Believe me. I swear to God. I'd never do anything like that to you. I respect you and Carol far too much to even *think* about it... You hear me? The way I look up to you and Carol, Teddy.

TED: I'm talking about how it's *nothing*, now, Les. If you *had* it off with Carol. It's *nowt*. I bloody *know*... She's *my* lass... and I'm her bloke.. I *know* that... Bloody twenty odd years we've been together. She's not going to run off with *you* or any other bloke she has it off with... It's *nowt*. I *know* it's nowt. The trouble is.. like... I don't *feel* it's nowt... *That's* the trouble.

LES: Want to try the 'phone again, Teddy? I could do with getting hold of my wife... I need that badly, just now...

TED: I'll have another try... Les... Alright...

     (TO WORLD) Lifted the 'phone off the rest... It was bloody working again...

LES: *(INTO 'PHONE)* ... Hullo... Hullo... Who's that... That 32475... Yeah... *(TO TED)*... SHIT!

TED: What's the matter...

LES: That Maitland?... Maitland's house... Yeah... looking for Les Maitland... Is he in... Nuh... Oh... Gone off... To Aldershot... Yeah... Right... Phone back... Nuh.. Doesn't matter... 'phone him back...

TED: *(TO WORLD)* Puts the phone down... beaten man... finished... Light gone right out of his eye...

LES: A bloke answered... She's got a bloke with her... that's alright... That's the way we work...

TED: Yeah...

LES: That's the way we work, you see... You know? If she feels like a bit of a change... It's up to her... Same with me... Fair enough...

TED: That's it... Everybody works out their own way of working, don't they?

        (TO WORLD) Didn't know *what* to say to comfort him... When we got back to the house... Stood at the bottom of the stairs for a minute, with his bottle of Southern Comfort, looking at me...

LES: Teddy. Listen to me... I don't hold it against you... You turning on me, like that, in the phone box before... It's understandable... I don't blame you, Teddy... You hear me...

TED: Just... I didn't hurt you, did, I...

LES: It's O.K.... Don't worry about... Old eye is back one hundred percent again...

        Teddy... I would like you to give me your hand... I understand... If you don't feel like.. It's alright... But it would help me to go to bed with an easier mind...

TED: (TO WORLD) What can you do...When a poor sod like that says that to you... (HOLDS OUT HAND TO HIM)...

LES: (SHAKING HIS HAND) I wish you liked me enough to be my mate. You know that?

TED: (TO WORLD) Trying to think of something to say to him... to cheer him up... But he stopped me...

LES: No... That's it... Wish the world was full of sunshine and smiles...

TED: Yeah... That's it, Les... You're right... Goodnight, Les... Have a good sleep.

LES: Yeah... I will... Pissed up to the eyeballs

TED: (TO WORLD) I went into our bedroom... Carol was sleeping... Looked at her sleeping... Wendy was right... something about somebody you loved... seeing them sleeping... I was too knackered to get me pyjamas on, just slipped off me trousers and went into bed alongside her... she kind of turned in her sleep... and put her arm round us... It was a nice ending to Friday...